*Though Der. is "man of other import pomo figure of letters for RK, Heid (an M), of ome Heid & Hus, for Marion.*

*The book as a whole seems to pick up on Caputo's sense of Derrida as an Augustinian (P & T)*

# God, the Gift, and Postmodernism

*For all theory, either pomo or a negative theology*

*brings together questions - as Marion does in his opening; also Aug & self - certainty (83, etc)*

*Some take up Marion - Westphal, Tracy*

THE INDIANA SERIES IN THE PHILOSOPHY OF RELIGION
MEROLD WESTPHAL, GENERAL EDITOR

# God, the Gift, and Postmodernism

Edited by John D. Caputo and Michael J. Scanlon

INDIANA UNIVERSITY PRESS
BLOOMINGTON AND INDIANAPOLIS

This book is a publication of

Indiana University Press

601 North Morton Street

Bloomington, IN 47404-3797 USA

http://www.indiana.edu/~iupress

*Telephone orders*   800-842-6796

*Fax orders*   812-855-7931

*Orders by e-mail*   iuporder@indiana.edu

© 1999 by Indiana University Press

The paper used in this publication meets the minimum requirements of American National Standard for Information Sciences—
Permanence of Paper for Printed Library Materials, ANSI Z39.48-
1984.

Manufactured in the United States of America

**Library of Congress Cataloging-in-Publication Data**

God, the gift, and postmodernism / edited by John D. Capto and
    Michael J. Scanlon.
            p.      cm.—(The Indiana series in the philosophy of
    religion)
    Includes bibliographical references and index.
    ISBN 0-253-33572-8  (cl: alk. paper).—ISBN 0-253-21328-2
    (pb: alk. paper)
        1. Christianity—Philosophy Congresses.  2. Postmodernism—
    Religious aspects—Christianity Congresses.    I. Caputo, John D.
    II. Scanlon, Michael J.    III. Series.
    BR100.G63      1999
    200—dc21                                        99-32397

    1    2    3    4    5    04    03    02    01    00    99

To **Edmund J. Dobbin**, O. S. A.
*For his leadership and inspiration*
*For his interest and support*

# Contents

# ACKNOWLEDGMENTS

The editors wish to acknowledge the support of Villanova University in making possible the conference "Religion and Postmodernism," on September 25–27, 1997, upon which this volume is based. We thank in particular John R. Johannes, Vice-President for Academic Affairs, without whose generous financial assistance we would not have been able to bring together such a distinguished group of philosophers and theologians, and Barbara Romano, the secretary to the David R. Cook and Josephine C. Connelly Chairs, who managed a multitude of matters for us, both large and small, with efficiency, grace, and aplomb.

# God, the Gift, and Postmodernism

# Introduction

## Apology for the Impossible: Religion and Postmodernism

### John D. Caputo and Michael J. Scanlon

I

This volume is based upon a conference held at Villanova University on September 25–27, 1997, entitled "Religion and Postmodernism," which brought together a distinguished international body of philosophers and theologians in dialogue with Jacques Derrida in order to discuss the question of religion at the end of the millennium. In particular, the conference provided a forum for a face-to-face dialogue between Derrida and French theologian Jean-Luc Marion, their first public exchange—in Pennsylvania, not Paris; in English, not French—on the questions of mystical theology and the gift. The conference was an attempt to seize a particular moment in recent work in philosophy and theology, a moment in which the "overcoming of metaphysics" characteristic of continental philosophy since Heidegger and questions of a profoundly religious character have become increasingly and surprisingly convergent.

The man of the hour at this conference was Jacques Derrida. That seems an unlikely choice for a conference on religion and postmodernism, given that Derrida says of himself, "I quite rightly pass for an atheist" and given also that he steadfastly avoids the word "postmodernism."[1] In fact, while everyone we invited to this conference was deferential toward the word "religion," most of them were abusive toward the word "postmodernism." Derrida would describe himself not as a postmodern, but as a man of the Enlightenment, albeit of a *new* Enlightenment, one that is enlightened about the Enlightenment and resists letting the spirit of the Enlightenment freeze over into dogma. Derrida seeks an Enlightenment "of our time," here and now, in the sprawling wealth and bottomless poverty, in the uncontainable plurality and virtual reality of this very late-modern, high-tech, televangelist, free-market, multi-media, millennial fin de siècle, this time of need and greed, in which the "certainties and axioms" of the *old* Enlightenment require reconsideration, translation, and transformation.[2]

That, if we may say so, is pretty much all we meant by "postmodernism."

Our interest, in particular, was to examine the evasive maneuvers and outright overcomings that have been undertaken with regard to the axioms and certainties of the Enlightenment in the last quarter of this century, precisely insofar as that work has resulted in a discourse which is more congenial to religion. Let us suppose that the inaugural and constituting act of modernity in the seventeenth century was an act of exclusion or bracketing; that the modern epoch turns on an *epoche*, a methodological imperative, in which modernity made up its mind to abide by human reason alone. In the *via moderna*, the rule will be that we are to make our way along a way (*meta-odos*) illuminated by the light of reason alone, of what *was called* reason in the seventeenth and eighteenth century. If that is so, then one way to think of the effect we were trying to provoke in this conference is to imagine its participants as engaged in the common pursuit of pushing past the constraints of this old, methodologically constricted, less enlightened, strait and narrow Enlightenment, which found it necessary to cast "reason" and "religion" in mortal opposition. We sought to seize the contemporary moment which has loosened the grip of the old Enlightenment, questioned its intimidating authority, complained about the exclusionary force of its certainties and axioms (among which *secularism* has enjoyed pride of place), and thereby made some room for a religious discourse and restored the voice of a religious imagination, the Enlightenment, as Derrida said of Marx, having chased away one ghost too many.[3] Our wager was, the more enlightened we get about Enlightenment, the more likely religion is to get a word in edgewise.

Let us say, further, for the sake of discussion and as a kind of heuristic device, that for the thinkers gathered here, modernity and *its* Enlightenment imposed certain restraints upon our thinking, certain "conditions of possibility," to use Kant's expression, which, like border police, mark off the boundaries and patrol the limits of possible experience. The modern *Aufklärer*, Kant said in a famous prize-winning essay, is a grown-up who behaves maturely by confining himself to what is possible. Like any sensible, law-abiding adult, he disciplines himself to abide by the conditions that make things possible, to drive within the yellow lines, to keep the rules that are programmed in advance to produce what is possible. On this telling, the *new* Enlightenment would constitute a second childhood which is given over to dreaming of the *impossible*, arising from a deep desire for what, given the constraints and conditions imposed by modernity, is precisely not possible, which for that reason is precisely what we most deeply desire. Let us say that what brought the participants in this conference together is a desire to *experience the impossible*, to go where we cannot go, as Angelus Silesius said, where the "method" prescribed by modernity prohibits; to cross these limits, to defy the border patrol, to think the unthinkable. Let us say that this august assembly of philosophers and . theologians was gathered together for the express purpose of restoring the good name of the impossible, of what the old Enlightenment declared impossible; to make it respectable, to give it its day in court, to defend it, to produce in short an apology for the impossible.

Producing an apology for the impossible is a particularly apt way to describe the debate between Derrida and Marion. For Derrida, the experience of the impossible represents the least bad definition of deconstruction. Deconstruction is a dream and a desire of something *tout autre*, of something that utterly shatters the present horizons of possibility, that confounds our expectations, that leaves us gasping for air, trying to catch our breath, the first words out of our mouth being, "How did that happen? How was that possible?" That is what Derrida calls *l'invention de l'autre*, the incoming of the other, the coming of something we did not see coming, that takes us by surprise and tears up our horizon of expectation. Faced with the (unforeseeable) prospect of this "incoming," deconstruction does not timidly shout "heads up" and then head for cover; rather, it boldly and brazenly calls "come" (*viens*), "yes, yes" (*oui, oui*), and offers it its hospitality. The incoming of the "same," on the other hand, would simply further confirm the present, already familiar horizon, would be more of the dreary, pedestrian, humdrum sameness of the possible —a mediocre fellow, Climacus said—and what Lyotard would call merely a new move in an old and familiar game. But everything *interesting* for Derrida is impossible, not simply, logically or absolutely, impossible, but what he calls *the* impossible. "Let us begin *by* (*par*) the impossible; let us be set in motion, let us get underway *by* "the" impossible. For *the* impossible is indeed an "aporia"—which means "no way to go"—but in deconstruction aporias are made to be broken, not to drive us off the road. They are broken not by a bit of academic cleverness and theoretical adroitness but by a dream, a desire, and a deed. "Go where you cannot go!" To the aporia of the impossible, where the way of knowledge has been blocked, there corresponds the imperative of *doing* the truth, *facere veritatem*, which is what deconstruction is all about. To put it all in a very condensed formulation, in deconstruction, the very conditions under which something is impossible, is declared impossible by what calls itself "the light of reason" or "philosophy," are likewise and especially the conditions of its possibility. Being impossible is what ignites our passion, gets us off dead center, and drives our desire to make it happen.

Take the gift—for the give-and-take about the gift is one of the principal points of interaction between Derrida and Marion. As soon as we think about it, Derrida thinks, we realize that the gift is impossible. As soon as a donor gives someone a gift, that puts the recipient in debt and makes the donor look good, thereby taking from the recipient and adding to the donor, which is the opposite of what the gift was supposed to do. As soon as we appreciate that we are cornered by that aporia, as soon as we submit to that insuperable difficulty, then, at that moment, we can *begin*. In order to give a gift, we must give in to that aporia but without giving up. With the madness of father Abraham himself atop Mount Moriah, we must, dagger in hand, tear up the circle of time and the debt and plunge into the impossible, *doing* what is impossible, going where we cannot go. That moment of madness is the time of the gift. That is why Derrida can say he has spent his whole life "inviting calling promising, hoping sighing dreaming." Of the gift, of justice, of hospitality, of the incoming of the wholly other, of *the* impossible.

All of which is a way of saying that *deconstruction is structured like a religion*. Like a *prayer* and tear for the coming of the wholly other (*tout autre*), for something impossible, like a messianic prayer in a messianic religion, *viens*, like a vast and sweeping *amen, viens, oui, oui*. Like a *faith* in the coming of something we cannot quite make out, a blind faith where knowledge fails and faith is what we have to go on, which even believes in ghosts or specters. *Il faut croire.*[4] Deconstruction thus turns out to be not the final nail in the coffin of the old God, but rather the affirmation of the religious, not the *leveling* but the *repetition* of the religious, and this while Derrida can "quite rightly pass for an atheist." To be sure, in deconstruction the repetition of religion is developed "*without* reference to religion as institutional dogma," *without* getting involved in some "article of faith," *without* "theologems," while "proposing a non-dogmatic doublet of dogma . . . a *thinking* that 'repeats' the possibility of religion *without* religion."[5] Deconstruction is structured like a religion *without religion*, which is its way of being enlightened about Enlightenment, of passing through the critique of religion set forth in modernity. Deconstruction delimits the dogmatism, authoritarianism, fundamentalism, and violence of what Derrida calls the concrete "messianisms," the religions of the Book, in order to make its way to a *new* Enlightenment, which undertakes the repetition of the *structure* of the religious, the structure of hope and hospitality, of a "messianic" faith in the coming of a justice to come, which is the stuff on which deconstruction dreams. Deconstruction is structured like a religion (which makes it suspect to secularists) without religion (which makes it suspect to the faithful of the religions of the Book, the religion with religion). It is a religion, let us say, within the limits of what the old Enlightenment declared off limits.

That is not the way it was supposed to turn out. For on this point of religion in particular, deconstruction's more secularizing, Nietzscheanizing admirers expected not the loosening up of the Enlightenment but the *fulfillment and completion, the tightening up and nailing down of Enlightenment secularism.* They expected Derrida's stylus to deliver a coup de grace to the old God, to administer the truly lethal dose (*dosis*, gift/dose/poison) to a still gasping deity. Deconstruction was to finish up the work started by the nineteenth-century critics of religion who, by their faith in science and objectivism, still subscribed to the ascetic ideal, to the transcendental signified, which simply allowed the place of "God," the center, to be filled by another occupant, to be re-centered around "man" or "science." But today Derrida speaks of "my religion about which no one knows anything," the failure to appreciate which means that he has been read "less and less well for twenty years."[6] Much to the horror of the secularizing deconstructors, the notorious "free play of signifiers," which frees us from the shackles of the transcendental signified, and the famous saying, "there is nothing outside the text," which set off a Dionysian dance on the grave of the old God, has taken the form of the *kenotics of faith.* The deferral of presence turns out to imply messianic waiting and expectation, and the deconstruction of presence turns out to be not a denial of the presence of God but a critique of the idols of presence, which has at least as much to do with Moses' complaint with Aaron as with Nietzsche. It is idolatry to think that anything *present* can embody the *tout autre* or claim to be its visible form in history, the instantiation and actualization of *the* impossible, for whose coming, like teary-eyed old Augustine, deconstruction always prays and weeps.

Jean-Luc Marion, who numbers Derrida among his sources,[7] is no less an advocate and apologist of the impossible, no less in love with that impossible something, or non-thing, which shatters the limits of what modernity calls "possible." But Marion's move beyond the old Enlightenment and modernity is cast in very different terms. For Marion, modernity means the tradition of the "subject," stretching from Descartes through Kant and Husserl and even extending as far as the Heidegger of *Being and Time*, which places prior constraints upon the *self-giving of phenomena.* The transcendental subject holds court over the phenomenal field and sets out conditions in advance for the emergence of phenomena. But according to the very idea of phenomenology, and the famous "principle of all principles" announced by Husserl, phenomena are to be accepted just as they give themselves,[8] allowed to show themselves from themselves, as Heidegger said (*Being and Time*, §7), left alone to arise on their own (*à partir de soi*), without being subjected to prior restraints. It is thus Marion's purpose to be more loyal to phenomenology than Husserl or Heidegger themselves, to propose a more radical phenomenology which stretches phenomenology to the limits of its possibility, to that limit where a radical "reduction" of the subject releases a seemingly impossible "givenness" (French: *donation*, German: *Gegebenheit*). "So much reduction, so much givenness."[9] The more radical the reduction of modernity's subject, the more fully givenness is released, culminating in an event of bedazzling overflow beyond the objectivity of objects (Descartes, Kant, Husserl) and even beyond or "without" the Being of beings (Heidegger), which opens up a field or horizon where being and objectivity have no sway. For Marion, to push beyond, to "reduce" the restraints imposed by modernity upon experience, to experience what these prior constraints declare impossible, is to experience what does not have to be, to experience something whose givenness neither objectivity nor being can contain.

Consider the different directions in which Derrida and Marion wish to extend or radicalize Husserl, the different ways in which they wish to push phenomenology to or beyond its limits. They both go back to a basic distinction made in Husserl's *Logical Investigations*, between "intention" (meaning, signification) and "fulfillment" (givenness), according to which the ego "intends" or "means" an object which can only in varying degrees be "fulfilled" or "given" to intuition, whose total givenness remains always a regulative ideal for further experience. In *Speech and Phenomena* Derrida maintains that in this analysis Husserl discovered but then repressed "the emancipation of speech as nonknowing," the *structural capacity* of the signifier to function in the *absence* of the fulfilling intuition.[10] For Derrida, speech is good speech whether it is fulfilled ("this leaf is green") or not and, more important, it is still good speech even if it is false, or without any possible fulfillment in intuition, and even if it is not well formed ("green is or"). That liberation of the signifier from the demands of intuitive redemption—where *intuitive fulfillment or givenness is impossible*—is what *makes possible* everything from non-Euclidean geometry to the highest reaches of the unintuitable structures of theoretical physics (*pace* Alan Sokal), everything from the poetry of Mallarmé or James Joyce, in whose sheer phonic resonance we all rejoice, to—this is what we have recently been hearing—the *essential structure of faith*, which has to do with what eye cannot see or foresee. But that structural emptiness and unintuitability is a scandal and a stumbling to Husserl himself, an outcome too impossible to contemplate, from which Husserl shrinks. For Husserl is still obedient to the metaphysical imperative of intuition, the desire of the subject to see that remains steadily in place from Plato and Aristotle, through *les lumières*, all the way to phenomenology.[11]

But Marion pursues the possibility of a completely opposite impossibility. Husserl confined himself, Marion says, to poor or commonplace phenomena in which the intention always overreaches the measure of givenness—"The Library of Congress is a place I have always wanted to see, whose intuitability I will not exhaust even after visiting the place and seeing it for myself." But Marion analyzes the possibility of a phenomenon of such unmanageable givenness that the intention cannot contain the intuition, so that the intention is not fulfilled but *saturated* by an overflow of givenness, leaving the intention, meaning, or signification to rub its eyes in wonder, stunned and amazed by the visitation. So if Derrida pursues the case of empty signifiers where intuitive fulfillment or givenness is impossible, what interests Marion is those phenomena of such givenness that any containing intention is impossible.

Thus for Marion questioning the certainties and axioms of the old Enlightenment takes the form of releasing the phenomena from Cartesian demands for mathematical clarity, from Kantian demands for a priori categorial synthesis, and from Husserlian demands to be measured by the reach of the intention or signification. The challenge of this *new* phenomenology, which would let that which gives itself be given from itself, not merely within the limits of reason alone (Kant), not merely "within the limits in which it is given," which is the limit that Husserl put upon the principle of all principles, but to go to the limit of what gives itself without limits, to prepare oneself for the possibility of the impossible. Marion gives various examples of the "saturated phenomenon"—including intensely packed and vivid historical events; events of great personal moment, like birth or death, love or betrayal; the experience of the "gift"—culminating in the experience of experiences, the experience of the impossible par excellence, *id quo major nequit cogitari*, the thought we cannot think, conceive or contain, the givenness beyond concept, category, or intention, the infinite givenness of what cannot be an object and does not have to be, God without being, which is testified to in mystical theology.

Marion's new phenomenology would be enlightened about Enlightenment by admitting upon the scene the light that modernity banished, indeed whose very exclusion is the inaugural and constituting act of modernity, viz., the light of lights, the light beyond human lights, the divine light. The divine light shines in the world, in the icon, not as something we see but as something in which we are seen, and it shines in the heart or soul, which is the constant testimony of mystical theology. Phenomenology sketches the possibility of a givenness which leaves the phenomenologist as such confused, visited, as Marion puts it, by a *donné* which leaves phenomenology as such *aban-donné*. The un-nameability of this phenomenon provides an entree for a theological turn and the light of revelation, a point which has sparked a considerable debate about what Dominique Janicaud regards as Marion's theological hijacking of phenomenology, a move beyond the limits of phenomenology which goes back to Levinas himself and the phenomenology of the invisible.

The debate between Derrida and Marion, already pre-delineated by their competing radicalizatons of Husserl, focuses on two points of contention: (1) the interpretation of the *hyperousios* in mystical theology, which is the topic of Marion's paper, "In the Name," to which Derrida afterwards briefly responded, and (2) the interpretation of the "gift," the topic of the roundtable entitled "On the Gift." But the issue of "givenness" monitors everything in this debate. Is the impossibility lodged in a givenness that can never be intended or in an intention that can never be given? Depending on the answer, the transgression of the old Enlightenment, the movement beyond the constraints imposed by modernity's conditions of possibility, the apology for the impossible, will take either of two very different forms which bear the proper names Marion and Derrida.

For Marion, it is a matter of releasing an excess of givenness beyond the limits of any concept to conceive of or of any word to name it, a givenness that saturates any subjective condition or precondition that would contain its overflow or pre-delineate its possibility. For Derrida, the impossible is the stuff of a faith or a desire with which we *begin*, which sets us in motion. We have always to do with what is *always yet to be given*, a givenness to come, a givenness which is *never given*, whose givenness is structurally impossible of "being given" (*étant donné*). The impossible is like a Messiah whose very structure is never to appear in the present and who, by thus deferring his appearance, keeps the future open, a Messiah whose condition of possibility is the very impossibility of his ever showing up, who does not have to be because he must not be. In Marion we have to do with a dazzling glow, a glory which leaves the faculties of subjectivity stunned and silenced, but in Derrida we encounter the kenotics of faith, of a groping blindness, like a blind man feeling his way with a stick or a stylus, "writing in the dark." The mistake would be to treat this blindness, as do deconstruction's critics, as so much nihilism and despair, instead of seeing there exactly the opposite, a work of faith, of hope, and desire for a future to come. The non-appearing of the Messiah, the non-givenness of any saturating givenness, is for Derrida a way to protect us against idols, to protect us from the Hegelian *aigle*, from divinizing something that presents itself here and now, in the present, as God's form on earth. For Marion it is a question of admitting an impossible givenness (*donation*), an impossible event, for which we lack both the name and the thought. For Derrida, it is a matter of the advent (*ad-veniens*) of the impossible, the coming of something *tout autre*, whose coming (*venue*) or incoming (*in-veniens*) we cannot see or foresee or conceive.

This difference shows up clearly in their differing interpretations of the gift, which for Marion is an event of saturating givenness, an event of donatative excess or of gifting which so catches up both giver and recipient in its dazzling dynamics that they are not to be regarded as the causal agents of the gift but rather as the scene of its impossible gifting or self-giving. But for Derrida, the movement of the gift is instantly destroyed by exposure to the light of givenness: From the very moment that the gift is given as a gift, it begins to annul itself and undo itself as a gift by weaving a chain of debt and gratitude and congratulation around donor and recipient. But that is not the *end* of the gift—and this is an important point to follow in the exchange between Marion and Derrida—but its *beginning*, for we begin *by the impossible*. This very aporia or impossibility is the condition under which the gift is possible. The gift is this impossible thing, or no thing, which we love and desire, in which we hope, for which we maintain a daily faith. The gift, yes yes. To put the difference between these thoughts of the gift in a nutshell then: Is the gift a gift only *in* (*dans*) its dazzling gifting? Or is the gift a gift only *without* (*sans*) gifting, givenness, and donation? *Le don dans la donation? Le don sans la donation?* In a word: *Dans* or *sans?*

The same sort of difference between Marion and Derrida shows up in the debate about the status of the *hyperousios* in mystical theology. Early on, Derrida had occasion to say that, however much he admires the discursive resourcefulness of negative theology, deconstruction is not to be mistaken as itself a negative theology, because negative theology is always committed to a "hyperessentialism," viz., the higher affirmation of a God or Godhead beyond God, and *différance* (however highly Derrida esteems it!) is not God. In his conference presentation, "In the Name," Marion takes issue with Derrida and argues that mystical theology is not a hyperessentialism, because in mystical theology the *hyperousios* is not the object of either affirmation or negation—which is why he prefers to speak of "mystical," not negative, theology—indeed not an object at all, or even a being, but an event of givenness that gives itself in a "third way" that Derrida simply misses. Affirmation and denial alike belong to a constative or apophantic order, while the event of givenness belongs to an entirely different and *pragmatic* order of pure "reference" without meaning, of pure praise and prayer without apophansis. It takes the form of a naming which un-names or de-names that Marion calls "de-nomination." This pragmatic order is the order of the inundating givenness of the saturated phenomenon, which overflows the limit of the intention or "concept" of "presence," and thereby safeguards mystical theology from the "attack" which Derrida launches upon it as a form of the "metaphysics of presence." In his abbreviated response, Derrida rejoins that the "third way" lying beyond affirmation and negation is carefully accounted for in his works, that in *Sauf le nom* he stresses the multiplicity of voices in negative theology, in addition to its hyperousiological one, and that his concern in this text is to not attack mystical theology but to save the name of God from attack. At least two questions are raised by Marion's provocative paper. (1) How much is really changed from Derrida's point of view if, instead of characterizing the *hyperousios* in terms of an excess of presence, we speak of an excess of givenness beyond the "concept" or intention of presence (since it is not clear that Derrida is married to the idea that presence is always conceivable and determinable by a concept and assertable in a proposition)? From Derrida's point of view, has Marion simply offered a more refined definition of hyperessentialism in terms of givenness? (2) Does Derrida "attack" mystical theology or does he, as he claims in *Sauf le nom*, seek to "save its name" and this by way of "translating" it into a form that everyone can share, not just Christian Neoplatonists?

## II

From the point of view of work being done in contemporary theology, the discussions that took place at the conference touch on several important issues centered on the question of God. Tertullian's famous rhetorical question,

"What has Athens to do with Jerusalem?" has returned with new energy to the theological scene, not only in terms of recent criticism of onto-theology but as a pervasive perception that Athens has been for too long the tutor of Jerusalem as regards proper speech about God.

The claim of Descartes was that it is the proper task of philosophy, not theology, to investigate the questions of God and the soul.[12] It seems that this claim went unchallenged at the time, since theology itself was content with a basically philosophical approach to its *praeambula fidei*. Philosophical or "natural" theology even became a required course in the curricula of Roman Catholic seminaries both as a philosophy course and as the first theology course, *De Deo Uno*. Pascal's was a rather lonely voice in preference for the "God of Abraham, Isaac, and Jacob" over the "god of the philosophers." Theologians came to prefer what seemed to them to be the far more rigorously rational (and, therefore, true) philosophical God than the homiletically more attractive (but not quite true) anthropomorphic portrayals of the biblical God.

Christian theology has been concerned with the issue of "dehellenization" ever since the famous historian of early Christian thought, Adolf von Harnack, described Catholic dogma as "in its conception and development a work of the Greek spirit on the soil of the gospel."[13] Despite the grain of truth in this claim most theologians have deemed it a misleading exaggeration. Indeed, some have registered the counterclaim that dogma itself is a dehellenization that throws up "a wall against an alien metaphysic"[14] — hellenization is found not in dogma but in the speculations and heresies against which the dogma was directed. Against von Harnack and Albrecht Ritschl the Lutheran theologian Wolfhart Pannenberg insists that the patristic reception of the philosophical theology of antiquity was "the most important historical presupposition of the acceptance by non-Jews of the God of Israel as the one God of all peoples. For how were non-Jews to believe in the God of Israel as the one God without themselves becoming Jews?"[15]

And yet the grain of truth in the project of dehellenization remains. Contemporary Christian theology finds its focus in the God of Jesus, the biblical God, "fleshed out" in the words, deeds, and destiny of Jesus. The fundamental question of Christology is not the divinity of Jesus but what kind of God is disclosed in him. Jesus, of course, is not the only revelation of God for Christians (who have as scripture the story of God with Israel and Judaism), but for Christians he is the definitive Word of God — "Long ago God spoke to our ancestors in many and various ways by the prophets, but in these last days he has spoken to us by a Son, whom he appointed heir of all things, through whom he also created the worlds" (Hebrews 1:1–2). The God of Israel, the God of *pathos*, is the God of Jesus through whom this divine *pathos* descends to the extremity of vulnerability in the Passion of Christ. In the suffering and death of Jesus, God *for us* becomes God *with us*, "the fellow sufferer who understands."[16]

In terms of the history of official theological dogma the grain of truth in the project of dehellenization seems apparent. When the bishops gathered at Nicea to proclaim the divinity of Christ the Greek philosophical notion of a divinity with the attributes of eternity, necessity, and immutability was taken for granted. All changes in Christ were to be attributed to his human nature only. As the doctrine of the Trinity developed, the classical distinction between the immanent Trinity (the inner Trinitarian life of God) and the economic Trinity (the triune salvific activity of God as portrayed in the New Testament) emerged. It seems that this distinction reflects the dualist worldview the Fathers of the Church shared with the Platonic religious philosophies they used. Corresponding to the ideal/empirical divisions of that time is the immanent/economic Trinity.[17] The Fathers avoided tritheism, but their relational formulae for the immanent "threes" were so abstract and obscure that they failed to provide clarification of the inner life of God. Another example of hellenist presuppositions would be the neo-Chalcedonianism of the Second Council of Constantinople in 553, where the "one person" of the Chalcedonian Definition is "clarified" as a divine person, the second person of the Trinity—the "ideal" Son before (behind?) the "empirical" Jesus.

Aware of these hellenistic presuppositions in the history of dogma, contemporary theology is performing what might be called a Hegelianism in reverse. Recognizing Christianity as "the absolute religion," Hegel offered absolute knowledge by sublating the symbolic language of this religion into the full clarity of the concept. Theology rejects this move by maintaining the perduring primacy of the symbolic and metaphorical language of faith (first-level religious language) and by employing conceptual language as a second-level, always partial and transitory clarification of the density of the symbolic.

Even though many scholars at this conference were uneasy with the word postmodernism, it may perform a useful heuristic function. It certainly points to the difference between our time and that era of confidence in reason's mighty progress in history that we name modernity. The title of our conference illustrates a major difference. In the modern period religion was ignored, tolerated, repressed, and (sometimes, not without reason) persecuted. But today we witness a massive return of religion, with all of its ambiguity, together with a "return of God to the center of theology" and to certain streams of postmodern thought in general.[18] And this conference bears witness to the return of the biblical God, explicitly or implicitly in the various essays presented—a return which resonates with contemporary theological efforts to reclaim the God of Abraham, of Isaac, of Jacob, of Jesus.

At the end of his discussion of St. Augustine's *Confessions* in *Sauf le nom*, Derrida leaves Augustine but reminds us that "he always haunts certain landscapes of apophatic mysticism."[19] Even though Villanova University is no landscape of apophatic mysticism, it is a landscape always haunted by Augustine. Perhaps more than any other theologian Augustine viewed authentic Christianity as "an aporia of the impossible." The *Doctor Gratiae* attributed the actual possibility of passing through the impossible path to the Gift, his favorite name for the Spirit as God's Self-donation. Through the Gift he did what he knew he could not do—he did the truth which is the only path to God.

The postmodern return of God continues in two very recently published collections.[20] Essays by or about Marion and Derrida appear in both volumes; in one of them "postmodern" gives way to "post-secular"! This divine return occasioned the planning of a second Postmodernism and Religion Conference at Villanova University in the fall of 1999 which will focus on God.

## III

In the contributions that follow Marion's essay and "On the Gift,"[21] an international body of philosophers and theologians addresses the constellation of problems that we have tried at least to characterize, however imperfectly, as constituting a certain "apology for the impossible."

We begin with noted Augustinian scholar Robert Dodaro's careful study of the Augustinianism of Derrida. Derrida refers often to his "fellow countryman" Augustine of Hippo with affection and admiration. In this essay Dodaro explores the relationship between Derrida's and Augustine's thought on the basis of Derrida's *Circumfession*. "For what have you that you have not received? (I Corinthians. 4:7)" is the Pauline "canon," the "yardstick" with which Augustine is beaten in his pride and with which he beats those who oppose him. Meaning literally a thin reed stalk or cane, "canon" can refer to an instrument of correction and to a writing instrument such as the stylus used by Augustine to correct heresy and to fix the limits of orthodoxy. Thus, this highly suggestive field—orthodoxy, writing, and violence—provides the backdrop for much of Dodaro's paper. In *Derridabase*, Derrida's friend Geoffrey Bennington essayed a systematic circumscription of Derrida's thought that would even anticipate whatever he would write in the future. Bennington challenged his friend to write something that would surprise his systematization. Derrida responded with *Circumfession* in which the surprise is his story of his relationship to Judaism, his "broken covenant," his "religion without religion and without religion's God." This circumfession, "confession around," refers to Derrida's own circumcision. He refers to Bennington as "G," which also refers to his mother, Georgette, (compared to Monica), and, of course (in English), to "God." Dodaro then explores Augustine's path to self-discovery by way of confession to God. Just as Derrida's text moves in deconstructive harmony with "G's" superimposed text, Augustine interpenetrates his text with God's discourse, the text of Scripture. Dodaro shows that Augustine's sense of self is less assured than a surface reading of his *Confessions* might suggest. Again, Augustine's use of the Scriptural canon enforced his own brand of orthodoxy which at some point deconstructs in the face of self-doubt. Dodaro provides us with a fascinating comparison/contrast between these fellow countrymen as he shows that Augustine's model of truth, *ueritatem facere*, in his self-discovery reveals itself to be closer to Derrida's immanent, unknowing "truth" than one might at first believe.

Then we turn to "Desire of God," in which Dublin philosopher Richard Kearney, who also moderated "On the Gift," proposes two different ways of desiring God—namely, onto-theological and eschatological. Onto-theological desire is desire as lack, expressing itself as a drive to be and to know absolutely. This desire is the source of evil in the Bible, censured as vain curiosity by Augustine, and condemned as "the fornication of the Spirit" by Luther. Eschatological desire is another kind of desire, a desire for something that eye has never seen nor ear heard—Augustine's restless heart, a desire for the God who first desires us (a "hot God"). In the hyperbolic excess of his ethics of alterity Levinas gradually identifies the desire for an absolutely other with the biblical God as he moves beyond the Platonic "good" to a "good" that gives itself from "beyond" history, inscribed, as vigilance and summons, in each instance of our existence. Derrida links the desire of God with atheism. Derrida, however, does not dismiss God per se, but he insists on a general openness to an alterity without name, without identity, which he calls the "Messianic" in contradistinction to any particular "messianism" of positive revelation. Like Levinas's eschatological desire, Derrida's desire of God goes beyond the desire to have, to know, etc. It is foreign to every "anthropo-theomorphic form of desire." But beyond Levinas deconstruction is a desire of the wholly other as *every* other, regardless of its theistic pedigree—*tout autre est tout autre.* So Derrida's desire of God is an impossible God of such indeterminate and undefined alterity that it always remains to be invented. But Kearney is worried that God needs to be recognized, identified, to protect us from false gods, demons, evil spirits. Can we desire God without *some* recourse to narrative imagination, without some appeal to criteria and tradition(s)? Kearney notes some modification in Derrida "desertification" of God in his reintroducing a certain complementarity of the messianic and messianism. Derrida responds to several of these issues in the discussion that follows and in "On the Gift."

In "Overcoming Onto-theology," Merold Westphal argues that theology does not become onto-theology simply by employing philosophical concepts like omniscience or foreknowledge to elucidate the biblical understanding of God or even by speaking of God as the Highest Being. Theology only becomes onto-theology when philosophers or theologians sell their soul to philosophy's project of rendering the whole of reality intelligible to human understanding by using God to do so. Thus, onto-theology consists of the pride that refuses to accept the limits of human knowledge. The critique of onto-theology is directed not at *what* we say about God but at *how* we say it, to what purpose, in the service of what project. Much of Westphal's paper is a conversation with Heidegger on God, theology, and the atheistic character of philosophy. His project is to appropriate Heidegger's critique of onto-theology for theistic theology, which is authentic to the extent that it is in service to the praxis of the believer. St. Augustine would love Westphal's paper; he always insisted that God is to be enjoyed, never used. Furthermore, Westphal's invocation of singing as a non-onto-theological model, is quite close to Marion's notion of the pragmatics of "praise." The name of God is not a nominating name, but a de-nominating one, which transmutes into prayer and praise. At the name of God, we ought to sing and praise God, "Hallelujah!"

David Tracy wants to destabilize the distinction between modern and postmodern by showing the extent to which the postmodern "fragment" is already an important figure for early modern thinkers like Bruno and Nicholas of Cusa. In the interesting exchange with Derrida that follows the paper, Derrida voices his concerns about the suitability of either the fragment or postmodernism as categories of thought. Both postmodernity and modernity must yield to the fact that there are only postmodernities and modernities in our new global sense of polycentrism. Modernity, for example, cannot be identified with rationalism and the Enlightenment. It includes the more fragmented culture of the fifteenth, sixteenth, and early seventeenth centuries, that creative period of early modernity. Postmodernity in its many forms is an explosion of forgotten, marginalized, and repressed realities of Enlightenment modernity—the other, the different, and above all the fragments which disrupt all totality systems. The key phenomenon provoking new study is religion, the non-reductive saturated phenomenon par excellence, which could never be assimilated by the narrow rationalism of modernity. The "isms" of modernity —deism, pantheism, modern atheism, modern theism, even panentheism— could never domesticate God as a religious saturated sacred phenomenon. Kierkegaard and Nietzsche stand as the two greatest unveilers of modernity's secret dream to be the logos of its own onto-theology. Religion was not a possibility for the horizon of classical modernity. Today religion becomes the possibility of impossibility. With the two great unveilers Tracy rejects all systems of totality with the claim that fragments are our spiritual tradition, fragments seen theologically as saturated and auratic bearers of infinity and hope for redemption. Tracy distinguishes three kinds of contemporary thinkers for whom the category of fragments is crucial. First are the radical conservatives who see fragments with regret and nostalgia as all that is left of what was once a unified culture. Among them the most curious is T. S. Eliot, whose prose should be forgotten but whose poetry endures as one of the great testaments to the fragmented character of our times. Second are the postmoderns who see fragments as part of their love of extremes and thereby emancipatory because transformative of the deadening hand of the reigning totality system, the rationality of modern onto-theology. Among them are those postmoderns who have surprised us by turning to the mystics and to the tradition of radical apophatic negative theologies, to that possibility of impossibility wherein religion and philosophy have found each other again as fragments, keeping them from a return to modern totality. The third group are the most suggestive in the early twentieth century—thinkers like Walter Benjamin and Simone Weil who see fragments as alive with the memory of suffering and hope, with whom Tracy allies himself. Nicholas of Cusa deserves retrieval here, and then there is Pascal who left us fragments which could give rise to salutary thought today.

Conference coordinators John D. Caputo and Michael J. Scanlon, unable to hold their tongues any longer, have also contributed to this volume. John D. Caputo's "Apostles of the Impossible" has been added to the present volume by way of commentary on the exchange that took place between Marion and Derrida at the conference. Caputo maintains that while "On the Gift" has brought the views of Marion and Derrida closer together on the "impossible"—they are both "apostles of the impossible"—it shows that they are most divided on the issue of givenness, a point Caputo develops in reference to their respective views of the gift and debt. Arguing for a more generous reading of Derrida than Marion allows, Caputo holds that Derrida does not "attack" mystical theology but tries to save it by translating it, and that Derrida does not pose "objections" to the gift from which Marion needs to rescue it, but takes the aporia of the gift as a point of departure for the madness of the leap of the gift. In the end, Caputo proposes, although their work overlaps in the most interesting ways, that perhaps what divides Marion and Derrida is "denominational" after all, having to do with differing ideas of a Messiah who has already pitched his tent among us in the flesh and a Messiah who is structurally *to come*.

In "A Deconstruction of Religion: On Derrida and Rahner," Michael J. Scanlon offers a suggestive sketch of the communication between Derrida's "religion without religion" and the work of Catholic theologian Karl Rahner. Scanlon's paper pursues the point of what Derrida might call the "undecidability" of the distinction between theism and atheism. He argues for a provocative similarity between Karl Rahner, the Catholic theologian who took seriously the ethical earnestness of atheism, and the passionate faith in prophetic justice of Jacques Derrida, who rightly passes for an atheist. Scanlon studies in particular the relationship between Rahner's distinction between an a priori or universal-transcendental revelation, which is the presence of the Spirit in the world, and the world religions, which are the a posteriori historical realizations of this a priori, on the one hand, and Derrida's distinction between the messianic and the concrete messianisms. Scanlon concludes, fittingly, on an Augustinian note. When Augustine converted the Johannine formula "God is love" into "Love is God," he pointed to the inner communication—Derrida would again say "undecidability" or the "translatability"—between the love of God and the love of neighbor, which underlies the destabilization of the distinction between the atheism and theism in deconstruction and Rahner.

It was in Mark Taylor's landmark *Erring: An A/theology* (1984) that the question of religion and deconstruction was first established as an important issue in English-speaking philosophy and theology. In "Betting on Las Vegas," Taylor, a thinker who loves to push against the limits, wants to push past deconstruction, which has become "distressingly familiar," where signifiers signify other signifiers, toward the problems posed by what he called in a recent book "imagology," where images are images of other images, where the virtual becomes the real and the real becomes virtual. While most of the contributors to this volume tend to take "postmodernism" primarily to mean overcoming the metaphysics of presence, or the end of onto-theo-logic, Taylor understands it in the wider and more current sense of the culture of images, of surfaces without depth, the age of virtual reality, of the unprecedented, unconstrained rule of what the French call the "simulacrum." Baudrillard is the high priest of this notion of postmodernism and Derrida—who is himself quite insistent on the sea change brought about by the advanced communication systems—part of ancient hagiography.

To understand America, Taylor contends, we need to understand Las Vegas, where the death of God—a constant in Taylor's thought—is "staged as the spectacle of the Kingdom of God on earth." Turning to the architecture— the field in which the word postmodern was coined—of Las Vegas he shows how Vegas has outstripped the postmodernism Venturi first described in *Learning from Las Vegas* (1972). The Vegas hotels of the 1990s are organized around a theme, like a Disney theme park, the most instructive of which is the MGM Grand Hotel, which by replicating Disney World itself puts the constitutive act of these hotels on display, miming an imitation for which there is no original. Vegas is not nostalgia but the free play of imitation itself. The Vegas train terminal has become a computer terminal, with a 1500-foot computerized canopy of lights and lasers. The Luxor Hotel is a massive black glass pyramid, miming an ancient Egyptian tomb in the desert sands, whose tip is made of translucent glass, so that in the daylight it is pointless and when illuminated at night it is without foundation. But if the tip of the pyramid—a funeral pyre, a figure also studied by Derrida, Poe, and especially, for Taylor, Bataille—is for the ancient Egyptian the point where time touches eternity, in the Luxor the sacrifice is a sacrifice without point, the sacrifice of sacrifice, housing the death of God as a theology of a glorious laser show. The prodigal son goes off and sows his seed in an expenditure without reserve only to die and never return—quite a different version of that parable than the one offered by Marion—leaving behind only an empty tomb. "Virtual reality" is the trope of our times, which lack *both* reality *and* mere appearance. Vegas is about absolutely nothing, the errant play of signs. The pointlessness is the point, which is the point on which Taylor concludes: God is dead, there is no transcendental signified, nothing outside the image.

The issue of icon and idol runs throughout this conference and the work of Marion and Derrida can be seen as deeply anti-idolatrous, as different strategies for resisting the idolatrous calf erected by Aaron which Moses came upon. So it is fitting that Edith Wyschogrod would explore the interaction between Moses—who represents the writing of God, the ideality of the written law, the invisible and unimaginable God—and Aaron—who embodies the idol, the golden calf, the power of the image, of the phenomenal manifestation of the divine—as it is played out in Schoenberg's opera *Moses and Aaron*.

Wyschogrod is interested in the way in which Aaron, and perhaps even Moses, "talk back" (Adorno) to God. She explores the unorthodox idea—contradicting the Moses of both Augustine and Maimonides—that the calf is not an idol but a bearer of the divine, a way of "conjuring" the divine (Derrida), a form of the very thaumaturgy practiced by Moses himself. How, after all, are we to distinguish the calf from the "disseminative" flow of images issuing from Moses himself—the pillar of fire, the burning bush, the rod that turns into a serpent, the division of the Red Sea, the bronze serpent? In the standard commentaries on Exodus Moses smashes the tables on which God himself had written the commandments because he is enraged by an idolatrous, unworthy people. But in Schoenberg, almost as if the composer subscribed to a theory of *archi-écriture*, it is when Aaron objects to Moses that the tablets too are images that Moses smashes them—forcing Moses later to make a copy in his own hand, which raises the question of the original or exemplar. Like Mark Taylor's study, Wyschogrod's analysis is framed by Derrida's disturbance of the distinction between the original—the Absolute, the pure Word—and the copy and Derrida's insistence on the "specter" which hovers between the two.

Françoise Meltzer's argument in "Re-embodying: Virginity Secularized" helps us understand the considerable interest recently shown by feminists in religious virginity, and would be nicely complemented by a reading of Edith Wyschogrod's *Saints and Postmodernism* (1991). Meltzer addresses the question of religion and postmodernism by examining the ways in which postmodernism reflects a nostalgia for pre-modern religion. In particular, she argues, on this point following the analysis by Jean-Luc Marion, postmodernity wants to twist free from the Cartesian dualism of mind and body and from the notion of a self-constituted transcendental consciousness, to displace, in Althusser's words, the speculative-theological, "seeing" Thomas (Aquinas) with the doubting Thomas who would touch with his hands. The model for this radical embodiment is found in early Christianity, which explains in no small part the great interest of postmoderns like Foucault and Kristeva in early Christian texts. What attracts postmodern interest is what Meltzer calls the "thinking body," the incarnated body subject, which reaches its most intense form in the virgin martyr. This extraordinary sacrificial phenomenon, which threatened and finally overturned the order of pagan antiquity, made of the body a radical gift of love, an expenditure without reserve. The virgin martyr does not rise above or transcend her body but rather is immersed in her corporeality as a vehicle of grace and gift, expressing a unity of body and self for which postmodernity longs.

This theology of the body is also explored in John Dominic Crossan's paper, "Our Own Faces in Deep Wells: A Future for Historical Jesus Research." Crossan makes an effective apologia for current scholarship on the "historical Jesus" against criticisms of this project and he does so in the name of what he calls "Catholic" Christianity. In answer to the question "Is historical Jesus research necessary for Christian faith?" Crossan insists "for Catholic

Christianity yes, for Gnostic Christianity no." Catholic Christianity is identified, not with the Roman Catholic "denomination," but with a radical belief in the incarnation and bodily life, a notion to be compared with Meltzer's "thinking body," while Gnostic Christianity dilutes this belief in favor of its spirit/matter dualism in which spirit conquers matter. History is not the same as story, even if all history is presented as story. Crossan's "postmodern" working definition of history is the past reconstructed interactively by the present through argued evidence in public discourse. Instead of settling for the gospel as story while ignoring the gospel as history Crossan gives three reasons for historical reconstruction of knowledge about Jesus: the historical reason (the fact that Jesus lived in history is the first historical question to be asked about him), the ethical reason (where do *you* find the divine especially, particularly, or even uniquely present?), and the theological reason (do you really accept incarnation [*sarcophilia*] with Catholic Christianity, or are you a Gnostic Christian [*sarcophobia*]?). The theological reason is the most important, for Catholic Christianity is a dialectic between history and faith. The Gospels show "how Jesus-then becomes Jesus-now," how the historical Jesus became the risen Jesus, and how, while you can have history without faith—although Derrida would likely question that—you certainly cannot have faith without history.

## NOTES

1. Jacques Derrida, "Circumfession," in Geoffrey Bennington and Jacques Derrida, *Jacques Derrida* (Chicago: University of Chicago Press, 1991), 155. Derrida recently commented on his experience at this conference in an entry dated "Villanova, Prés de Philadephia, le 26 Septembre, 1997," in Jacques Derrida and Catherine Mallabou, *La Contra-Allée* (Paris: La Quinzaine Littéraire, 1999), 99 (our translation): "Depart tomorrow for New York, after a conference on 'Postmodernism and Religion' (two things that are strange to me, you know, but they situate me everywhere among the two, you also know this, . . . My atheism gets on in the churches, all the churches, do you understand that?)."

2. *Points . . . : Interviews, 1974–94*, ed. Elisabeth Weber, trans. Peggy Kamuf and others (Stanford: Stanford University Press, 1995), 428.

3. Jacques Derrida, *Specters of Marx: The State of the Debt, the Work of Mourning, and the New International*, trans. Peggy Kamuf (New York: Routledge, 1994), 174.

4. This is the first and last line of Jacques Derrida, *Memoirs of the Blind: The Self-Portrait and Other Ruins*, trans. Pascale-Anne Brault and Michael Naas (Chicago: University of Chicago Press, 1993).

5. Derrida, *The Gift of Death*, trans. David Wills (Chicago: University of Chicago Press, 1995), 49, emphasis mine. Derrida is speaking in this text of Levinas, Marion, Kierkegaard and others, but we think that he describes here a law of his own thought, a law that his own distinction between the messianic and the concrete messianisms obeys to the letter. Understanding the logic of the *sans* is central to both Derrida and Marion.

6. See Derrida, "Circumfession," 154–55.

7. See Jean-Luc Marion, *L'idole et la distance* (Paris: Grasset, 1977), 13.

8. See Ideas I, §24; Jean-Luc Marion, *Reduction and Givenness: Investigations of Husserl, Heidegger, and Phenomenology*, trans. Thomas Carlson (Evanston, Ill.: Northwestern University Press, 1998), 18.

9. Marion, *Reduction and Givenness*, 203. Marion's argument in this book is itself nicely summarized in his "Conclusion: The Figures of Givenness," 203–205.

10. Jacques Derrida, *Speech and Phenomena and Other Essays on Husserl's Theory of Signs*, trans. David Allison (Evanston, Ill.: Northwestern University Press, 1973), 97.

11. See Marion, *Reduction and Givenness*, 20–22. On Derrida's reading of Husserl, see John D. Caputo, *Radical Hermeneutics: Repetition, Deconstruction, and the Hermeneutic Project* (Bloomington: Indiana University Press, 1987), 120–52.

12. René Descartes, *Meditations on First Philosophy* (Indianapolis: Hackett Publishing Company, 1979), 1.

13. Cf. Jaroslav Pelikan, *The Emergence of the Catholic Tradition*, vol. 1 of *The Christian Tradition: A History of the Development of Doctrine* (Chicago: The University of Chicago Press, 1971), 55.

14. Ibid.

15. Wolfhart Pannenberg, *Systematic Theology* (Grand Rapids: Eerdmans, 1991), 100.

16. Alfred North Whitehead, *Process and Reality* (Toronto: Macmillan, 1929; New York: Free Press, 1969), 413.

17. Cf. James Mackey, "Are There Christian Alternatives?" in *The Christian Understanding of God Today*, ed. James Byrne (Dublin: Columba Press, 1993), 68.

18. Cf. David Tracy, *On Naming the Present: God, Hermeneutics, and Church* (Maryknoll, New York: Orbis Books, 1994), 45.

19. Jacques Derrida, *On The Name*, trans. David Wood, John Leavey, Jr., and Ian McLeod (Stanford: Stanford University Press, 1995), 40.

20. Graham Ward, ed., *The Postmodern God: A Theological Reader* (Boston: Blackwell, 1997) and Phillip Blond, ed., *Post-Secular Philosophy: Between Philosophy and Theology* (New York: Routledge, 1998).

21. In the conference, the papers were framed by Derrida and Marion. Marion opened the conference with "In the Name," while "On the Gift" was the final session.

# In the Name

## How to Avoid Speaking of "Negative Theology"

by Jean-Luc Marion

*Because for us it is a*
*fearful task to name with our*
*proper names Him "to whom God*
*has bestowed the gift of the name above*
*all names."*

—*Philippians* 2:9 [1]

### "Metaphysics of Presence" and "Negative Theology"

That the two questions of the "metaphysics of presence" and of "negative theology"—questions which to all appearances come from such dissimilar provenances—should today end up encountering one another, indeed end up being by and large superimposed, could be surprising.

No doubt they have a paradoxical characteristic in common—that of having neither precise definition nor clear-cut historical legitimacy. For instance, Heidegger never (to our knowledge) used the phrase "metaphysics of presence," a point which is all the more remarkable as he was forever radically questioning the constitution of metaphysics as well as the essence of presence (the οὐσία of the παρουσία). Likewise never, it seems to us, does Derrida himself explain exactly what can and should be understood by this phrase.[2] It follows that certain basic questions are left open: Is "metaphysics" always

Translation by Jeffrey L. Kosky

identified as and by presence, or can it also include absence? Is presence exactly equal to onto-theo-logy, does it extend beyond, and does it even admit of being defined? Surely the indeterminacy of the "metaphysics of presence" characterizes it essentially (as essentially without essence), indeed provides support for it. This does not mean, however, that it is any more accessible, especially in the popular and polemic uses of deconstruction; and this indeterminacy perhaps also implies a fundamental imprecision, one that would inevitably be harmful to its hermeneutic efficacy.

Now it also happens to be the case that the formula "negative theology" suffers from a similar indeterminacy. First because, as A. Solignac testifies, "To speak more accurately, Dionysius employs the formula 'negative theology' only once, in the title to the third chapter of the *Mystical Theology.*" Even more could have been said: first because this single occurrence appears only in a chapter heading and therefore is likely to have come from the redactor; next and most important because it is precisely not a matter of defining *a* or *the* negative theology, but of knowing "which are the affirmative theologies [the words spoken about God] and which [are] the negative—τίνες αἱ καταφατικαὶ θεολογίαι, τίνες αἱ ἀποφατικαί." Quite clearly, the plural and also the ancient meaning of the substantive must be re-established in the rendering of this text, in order not to break the parallel with "affirmative theologies;"[3] but above all it must be understood that for Dionysius the term θεολογία always designates the expressions Scripture uses to say (or to not say) God, at a great distance from the concepts of metaphysics.[4] Thus, since even a great scholar, Solignac, prefers to continue with an approximation rather than break entirely with the supposedly established theme of a single "negative theology," it will not be surprising that the run-of-the-mill commentators insist on invoking this formula in authors who, to our knowledge, are ignorant of it. For neither the Alexandrian nor Cappadocian Fathers, nor Irenaeus nor Augustine, nor Bernard, Bonaventure, nor Thomas Aquinas—all of whom resort to negations when naming God and build a theory of this apophasis—none of them use the formula "negative theology." As a result, it can reasonably be supposed that this formula is nothing but modern.[5]—Consequently, we will from now on no longer consider the phrases "metaphysics of presence" and "negative theology," if by chance we have had to use them, as anything but conceptual imprecisions to be overcome or as questions awaiting answers—never as secure bases.

However, beyond such parallel aporiae, these two questions maintain a much more intimate relationship. Derrida himself recognized that they were intertwined at the center of his own work during the seminal lecture of 1968 on "Différance": "And yet what is thus denoted as *différance* is not theological, not even in the most negative order of negative theology. The latter, as we know, is always occupied with letting a superessential reality go beyond finite categories of essence and existence, that is, of presence, and always hastens to remind us that, if we deny the predicate of existence to God, it is in order to recognize him as a superior, inconceivable and ineffable mode of Being."[6] This, it may be said, is an example of a denegation. This Parisian denegation precedes by twenty years another one, made in Jerusalem, in the lecture "How to Avoid Speaking: Denegations."[7] This persistent denegation can be presented in three inseparable, but not unhierarchical, moments: (i) first, an explicit denegation—that by which, according to Derrida, "negative theology" says it is saying nothing positive about God; (ii) next, an implicit denegation—by which, according to Derrida, "negative theology" claims not to do what it nevertheless does all the time: namely, again say something, predicate τὶ κατὰ τίνος of God, and thereby re-inscribe him in the "metaphysics of presence;" (iii) finally and most important, an explicit denegation made by Derrida—in which he denies that he himself repeats, with différance, the project and the failures of "negative theology." This last denegation—différance does not repeat "negative theology" because it alone deconstructs the "metaphysics of presence" without compromise—obviously governs the other two. For différance to differ from "negative theology," it must be shown that the latter always remains in submission to the privilege of presence. Derrida's criticism of so-called "negative theology" therefore concerns not just this particular method of conducting discourse, but first of all the dominance of différance in the deconstruction of presence. Here, for Derrida, it is not, as it is in his other readings of decisive moments in the history of metaphysics, a matter of deconstructing figures of presence that confess or lay claim to being as such; rather, it is a matter of deconstructing a project which is already an explicit denegation of presence, thus of deconstructing a quasi-deconstruction. What is more —and this is the burning question—this quasi-deconstruction cannot be said simply to anticipate, unknowingly, the authentic deconstruction since it claims to reach *in fine* what it deconstructs: It claims to put us in the presence of God in the very degree to which it denies all presence. Negative theology does not furnish deconstruction with new material or an unconscious forerunner, but with its first serious rival, perhaps the only one possible. In short, for deconstruction what is at issue in "negative theology" is not first of all "negative theology," but deconstruction itself, its originality and its final pre-eminence. Thus it is strategically important to deconstruction that it deconstruct as radically as possible the twofold claim of the so-called negative theology: that is, its claim to deconstruct God and nevertheless to reach him. If this were missing, the deconstruction which proceeds by means of différance would suffer first a rivalry (presence can be deconstructed without it), then a marginalization (deconstruction would not forbid access to God, outside presence and without Being) When deconstruction sets out to attack what it, along with the entire tradition, still designates with the imprecise title "negative theology," it is not making an attack so much as it is defending itself.

The argument made by Derrida therefore has nothing in common with the reproach most often made against "negative theology"—namely, that on the pretext of "honoring in silence," it in fact leads to the most radical form of atheism.[8] For Derrida, quite to the contrary, the task is to stigmatize "negative theology's" persistence in making affirmations about God—while denying that it does so—in particular the affirmation of existence—and thereby to point out its failure to think God outside of presence and to free itself from the "metaphysics of presence." This fundamental and unified argument can be orchestrated in several objections, which we will distinguish for the sake of the clarity of the debate: Neither Jewish, Muslim, nor Buddhist but only Christian, and only belatedly assigned to the conceptual hermeneutic of the New Testament alone,[9] "negative theology" could be assimilated to a Christian philosophy, indeed to what is most "Greek" about onto-theo-logy (Objection 1).[10] It could even be inscribed within the horizon of Being (Objection 2). In effect—and this is the sole objection which seems capable of justifying the crudeness of the first two—it would always end up as a quasi-affirmation: It "often calls to mind the sentence, verdict or decision, the statement." For "the apophatic has always represented a sort of paradoxical hyperbole" and negation "[which is] everywhere, but never by itself," just like the adverb "without" "transmutes into affirmation its . . . negativity."[11] In short, "negative theology" does not annul [ne nie pas] the essence, Being, or truth of God, but denies [les dénier] them so as to better re-establish them, in something like a hyperbole (Objection 3). As it could be answered that mystical theology obviously does not intend to re-establish in fine what it denied, but to pass, through the way of eminence, from predication (affirmative and/or negative) to a decidedly non-predicative form of speech, namely the prayer which praises (ὑμνείν), the remaining task, for Derrida, is to disqualify the latter (ὑμνείν) as a disguised form of predication (one always praises with the title . . . or insofar as . . . , thus by naming). This is done by opposing the prayer which praises to prayer pure and simple (εὐχή)[12] (Objection 4).

The crudeness of these objections—which we will have to discuss at greater length—could lead one to underestimate them and set them aside. We will not give in to this temptation, for two main reasons. First, because at least one of them (Objection 3) obliges Christian theology to undertake a serious line of questioning: To what extent does its negation not just re-establish in the *via eminentiae* what the apophasis seemed to have disqualified? In particular, wouldn't the divine eminence serve to protect, validate, and maintain the real attribution to God of Being, essence, thought, etc.—in short, of all the founding concepts of metaphysics—simply at the ever-so-low price of a hyperbolic passage (by means of ὑπέρ and its substitutes)? Next, and more generally, we will take these objections seriously because all of them put into question the possibility, for theology, of making an exception to the metaphysical conditions of discourse. In short, can Christian theology as a theology evoked by a Revelation remove itself in principle, if not in actual accomplishment, from the "metaphysics of presence"—or is it, in the final analysis, reducible to this metaphysics? Which amounts to asking: Is Christian theology subject to deconstruction, or not?

## The Third Way: De-nomination

The answer to such a question, or even the barest outline of one, poses such a great difficulty that we will have to proceed one step at a time. We will begin by confronting those objections to the corpus, no doubt exemplary for this debate, traditionally attributed to Dionysius the Areopagite—namely, that comprising *The Divine Names* and *The Mystical Theology*.[13]

At the outset, one fact presents itself to us: Not only does Dionysius not isolate "negative theology" as such (a point which we have already observed), but he uses apophasis only by including it in a process that includes not two but three elements. It therefore does not contend face-to-face with the affirmative way, as in a duel where the last to enter the fray would be at once the victor over and the heir to the first; for both must in the end yield to a third way. Thus it is "by the arrangement of beings insofar as they come from Him and contain certain icons and semblances of the divine paradigms [affirmative way] that we approach, as far as our capacities allow, the beyond of all [beings] through its way and its position and in the negation and overcoming of all [negative way], and in the cause of all [third way]—ἐν τῇ πάντων ἀφαιρέσει καὶ ὑπεροχῇ, καὶ ἐν τῇ πάντων αἰτίᾳ." More clearly, "It is necessary at first [καὶ] to impose and affirm [καταφάσκειν] all theses of beings insofar as it is the cause of all [ὡς πάντων αἰτία], then [καὶ] deny them even more radically [κυριώτερον ἀποφάσκειν], as it surpasses all, finally [καὶ] let us not believe that the affirmations are the contrary of the negations, since [the cause] which is above every negation as well as every position—τὴν ὑπὲρ πᾶσαν καὶ ἀφαίρεσιν καὶ θέσιν—is still more above all privation." Also relevant here are the final lines of the final Dionysian treatise, the most formal and the most abstract, the *Mystical Theology*: "for the perfect and unique cause of all things is above every assertion [ὑπὲρ πᾶσαν θέσιν] in the same way that what surpasses the total suppression of all things and is found beyond their totality [ἐπέκεινα τῶν ὅλων] is also above every negation [ὑπὲρ πᾶσαν ἀφαίρεσιν]."[14] The game is therefore not played out between two terms, affirmation and negation, but between three, different from and irreducible to each other: ἢ πάντων θέσις, ἢ πάντων ἀφαίρεσις, τὸ ὑπὲρ πᾶσαν καί ἀφαίρεσιν καί θέσιν.[15] It is possible to not understand, indeed to not take seriously, this three-fold division, but it cannot be denied that Dionysius spoke and thought in this way.

On this threefold division, even the authors who set themselves at a noticeable distance from Dionysius display indisputable agreement. Thomas Aquinas begins with the names attributed negatively and then acknowledges a pre-eminence to the names spoken of God absolutely and affirmatively— contrary to the Dionysian way of proceeding. But even affirmation finally yields to eminence because God can be named as the cause of the perfections stated by the names—though with a causality surpassing their significations "in a more excellent and higher way [secundum modum altiorem]" or "in a more eminent way [secundum eminentiorem modum]" so much that it re-establishes (or rather deepens) the unknowing.[16] Still more revealing is the final position of Nicholas of Cusa. To be sure, Nicholas provides one of the rare, ancient examples of the explicit use of *theologia negativa*—he even devotes the title of the final chapter of *De docta ignorantia* to it. However, he does not end up with apophasis pure and simple, but with infinity: "According to negative theology, infinity is all we discover in God [Et non reperitur in Deo secundum theologiam negationis aliud quam infinitas]." This infinity does not revert to affirmation after passing through negation, but lays bare and circumscribes the divine truth as the experience of incomprehension: "prae-cisionem veritatis in tenebris nostrae ignorantiae incomprehensibiliter lucere —in the shadows of our ignorance shines incomprehensibly the truth defined more precisely." This is not a description of an hypostasized apophasis, but of a third position, the sole target ever since the beginning: "That, then, is the learned ignorance for which we have been searching [Et haec est illa docta ignorantia, quam inquisivimus]."[17] The path is thus cleared for thought of the incomprehensible as such (Book II), opening onto a complete dogmatic the-ology (Book III). The Christian place of the negative way is not in doubt; it is found in the threefold character of the ways, which the eminence, cause, and incomprehensibility of God each dominate.—Henceforth, the task will be to assess how the establishment of a triplicity instead of and in the place of a duality modifies the status of each of the terms, and in particular, the scope of the negative way. Put otherwise, what advantage does the deconstruction of so-called negative theology draw from its ignorance (or refusal) of the three-fold character of the ways? In short, what end is served, for Derrida, in denying the third way and in sticking with a straightforward opposition between affir-mation and negation?

The answer can be divined by simply re-reading Objection 3 itself. In effect, this objection consists wholly in suspecting the supposedly ultimate and freestanding negation of implicitly and surreptitiously smuggling in and re-establishing an affirmation—"the apophatic has always represented a sort of paradoxical hyperbole," "transmutes into affirmation its . . . negativity," "of-ten calls to mind the sentence, the decision or verdict, the *statement*."[18] The hermeneutics of suspicion always runs the risk of arbitrariness and therefore should intervene only in the last instance, when no other interpretation ap-pears possible any longer. Now this is not the case here where the third way, however difficult to thematize it might at first seem to be, clearly indicates Dionysius's intention. It appears neither possible nor even useful to push the characteristics of the affirmations, by denying them, onto the negative mo-ment because the triumphs and the failings of the first two ways are in principle overcome by a third. Put otherwise, Dionysius (and the theologians who fol-lowed or preceded him on this path) has no need to overdetermine or falsify the negative moment because he opened (or at least claimed to be open to) a final, more radical, and also more direct way, which alone leads to the end.

Before going farther, let us observe that this shift to the lexicon of the mountain climber, as strange as it might be, indicates at the very least that one is attempting to free oneself from the binary terms of the metaphysical (in fact Aristotelian) doctrine of judgment and truth: The third way is played out beyond the oppositions between affirmation and negation, synthesis and separation, in short between the true and the false. Strictly speaking, if thesis and negation have in common that they speak the truth (and spurn the false), the way which transcends them should also transcend the true and the false. The third way would transgress nothing less than the two truth values, between which the entire logic of metaphysics is carried out. If the third way is no longer about saying the true or the false, if it is precisely a matter of its not saying them, one can no longer claim that it means to affirm a predicate of a subject, not even beneath the absurd dissimulation of a negation, nor that it has the least bit of interest in doing so. The third way does not hide an affirmation beneath a negation, because it means to overcome their duel, just as it means to overcome that between the two truth values wherein metaphysics plays itself out. Moreover, Dionysius thought of the relation between affirmation and negation explicitly—in terms of an unambiguous hierarchy. On the one hand, negation prevails over affirmation: "The negations are true in what concerns divine things; the affirmations are unfitting."[19] That is, affirmation can give one the feeling of attaining the unattainable essence of God, while negation not only never claims as much, but remains valid by denying the most remote determinations of the divine. On the other hand, negation itself submits its very own operation, and above all its duel with affirmation, to the final transgression. For as we have already seen, at the very moment of recognizing the superiority of the negations over the affirmations—"and still more radically should we deny all affirmations [κυριώτερον ἀποφάσκειν]" —, Dionysius still and always aims at what remains "above every negation and affirmation [ὑπὲρ πᾶσαν καὶ ἀφαίρεσιν καὶ θέσιν]" and therefore "considerably above every privation [ὑπὲρ τὰς στερήσεις]."[20]

The most elevated names (and the ones that are most theological, most directly concerned with the formulation of the Trinity itself) are in this way disqualified without looking back, without remorse: "Neither one nor oneness, neither divinity nor goodness, nor spirit in the sense we understand it; neither sonship nor fatherhood, nor anything else that is known by us or by any of the other beings."[21] Let it not be suggested that these negations restore, more or less subtly, disguised affirmations. Dionysius in fact insists explicitly that "we cannot even speak of [God]" as goodness, "the most revered of names [τὸ τῶν ὀνομάτων σεπτότατον]."[22] Thus, a negation by itself is never enough to make a theology, no more than an affirmation is. There is never a proper or appropriate name to speak of God. The proliferation of names here amounts to anonymity: "He who is praised manifoldly with a manifold of names [τὸν πολύυμνον καὶ πολυώνυμον], is called by the Scriptures ineffable and anonymous [ἄρρητον καὶ ἀνώνυμον]."[23] It is no longer a question of naming Him, nor by contrast of not naming Him, or of de-nominating him—in the twofold sense that this term can have: to name (to name in view of . . . , to nominate), but with something close to a negation, and consequently also to undo Him from all nomination. In its ambiguity, de-nomination bears the twofold function of saying (affirming negatively) and undoing this saying of the name. It concerns a form of speech which no longer says something about something (or a name of someone), but which denies all relevance to predication, rejects the nominative function of names, and suspends the rule of truth's two values. Dionysius indicates this new pragmatic function of language, aiming at He who surpasses all nomination by giving him the title αἰτία—not the metaphysical "cause," but what all those who demand [αἰτιατά] demand [αἰτέω] when they aim at Him from whom they come and to whom they return. The αἰτία has no other function but to pass beyond every affirmation and negation: "[As] the αἴτιον of all things, it itself is not one of them, insofar as it superessentially transcends all things;" "the ungraspable αἰτία which comes from the total love beyond all things."[24] Here it is important to note that αἰτία does not by any means claim to name or to deny a name of God; it breaks with every predicative or designative function and is limited to what each creature, as it is what it is, aims at—which is indicated by a passage to the infinite: "[E]verything may be predicated [κατηγορεῖται] of Him and yet [He is] none of that."[25] αἰτία in no way names God; it de-nominates him by suggesting the strictly pragmatic function of language—namely, to refer names and their speaker to the unattainable yet inescapable interlocutor beyond every name and every denegation of names. With αἰτία, speech does not say any more than it denies—it acts by transporting itself in the direction of Him whom it denominates.

At this point, it is necessary that we be sure of the exact scope of the adverb or suffix ὑπέρ. First of all, is it equal to the ambiguity of "without," an adverb suspected of re-establishing an affirmation? This can be doubted: "The prefix—ὑπέρ has a negative rather than a positive form. To say that God is ὑπερούσιος is to deny that God is a being of any kind, even the highest or original being."[26] When the New Testament has recourse to the suffix—ὑπέρ—it can hardly be doubted that it is understood negatively. For instance, when Paul speaks of "knowing the charity of Christ who surpasses all knowledge [ὑπερβάλλουσαν τῆς γνώσεως]," it is not a matter of once again knowing charity in the guise of a formal negation, but of "taking root and establishing oneself in charity" and nothing other than this (Ephesians 3:18–19). The relation of knowledge to ἀγάπη must yield to its integration in it. Assuming that this ὑπέρ comes up quite frequently in the Dionysian corpus and plays a decisive role in it, it would still remain to be proven that it contradicts Paul's usage.[27] This is not all that evident, given that the letter of the text claims the contrary: "[T]he proposed goal of discourse is not to expose the superessential essence as superessential [οὐ τὴν ὑπερούσιον οὐσίαν ἢ ὑπερούσιον ἐκφαίνειν] (for it is unknown and totally unsayable, surpassing union [with the mind]); rather it is to praise the essentializing procession of the thearchy into the principle of all essence and thence to all beings."[28]—ὑπέρ re-establishes neither essence nor knowledge, but transgresses them both in view of praising what precedes and makes possible all essence.

There is at least one theologian of the divine names who saw the objection of deconstruction and responded to it explicitly, John Scotus Eriugena: "For when I consider the aforesaid designations lack the particle 'not,' I fear to relegate them to the negative part of theology. If I put them with the affirmative part, however, I recognize this does not agree with what I know of them. For one who asserts [God] to be superessential clearly denies that he is essential. And consequently, although the negation does not appear in the words, it is evident to one who considers the matter carefully that it is not lacking in the understanding. For that reason, I think, I am forced to admit the aforesaid designations which seem to lack any negation are more in harmony with negative than affirmative theology. . . . Let us conclude with this brief example: '[God] is essence'—affirmation! 'He is not essence'—negation [abdicatio]! 'He is superessential [superessentialis]'—both affirmation and negation! For what superficially seems to lack negation is strongly negative in meaning. One who asserts God to be superessential [superessentialis] does not say what he is, but what he is not, for he declares he is not essence, but more than essence."[29]

It must therefore be concluded that Dionysius (followed by the best of his interpreters) denies first that negation by itself suffices to define a theology, next that negation opposes affirmation in a simple duel, and finally that negation re-establishes affirmation while pretending to invert it. In short, Dionysius always thinks negation exactly as he thinks affirmation—as one of the two values truths can have, one of the two forms of predication which it is precisely a matter of transgressing completely, as the discourse of metaphysics. With the third way, not only is it no longer a matter of saying (or denying) something about something, it is also no longer a matter of saying or unsaying, but of referring to Him who is no longer touched by nomination. It is solely a matter of de-nominating. We can therefore, at least from Dionysius's point of view, deny Objection 3.

## Praise and Prayer

Before moving on, it becomes possible to discuss in passing Objection 4—which claims the prayer that praises (ὑμνεῖν) should be disqualified as a disguised predication because it always praises with the title . . . , therefore by naming, while a prayer pure and simple (εὐχή) would have no need of naming, nor even denying a name. In fact, at least two objections can be raised against this objection.

First, it presupposes that it is unquestionable that praising, that is attributing a name to an interlocutor, indeed dedicating to him one name in particular, necessarily implies identifying him in and with his essence and thereby submits him to the "metaphysics of presence." Now what is proper to the proper name consists precisely in the fact that it never belongs properly—by and as his essence—to the one who receives it. *Never* is the proper name a name for the essence. This rule is even more applicable in the case of a possible God than in that of the finite recipients of names (men, animals). Here is not the place to develop this paradox with all its implications;[30] but we can call to mind its principal components. First of all, the name for the essence—the secondary essences, the universal—never completely succeeds in designating the individual as such because an individual cannot be individualized completely except through the indefinite nomination of accidents. Second, it is precisely this denomination by accidents that one tries to accomplish with the list of names, surnames, forenames, place names, or gentile names, etc., that make up what is accepted as *the* proper name—but is in fact the summary of a supposedly convergent, but in any case indefinite, series of improper names. The supposedly proper name has in fact always already been used for and by another—the family name by the whole family, the forename (*Christian name*) by not only all those who share it in space and time but above all by the saint (or something similar) who inaugurated it. Therefore, the proper name properly has only a certain use of certain common names. Third, this use appropriates the common proper name only in a factual, not necessarily legitimate, reference which makes it function more as a deictic than as a definition. Consequently, the common/proper name implies that others besides me use it to intend me and designate me, in short call me by it. The name that I bear (that by which I call myself, name myself, and identify myself) simply reproduces after the fact the name with which others first called me (that to which I answer, by which I am known and mistaken, and which has been imposed upon me). Therefore, the experience of the proper name—received or given—never ends up fixing the essence of the individual in presence, but always marks that, as a principle, the individual does not coincide with its essence or its presence exceeds its essence. In short, the proper name marks the fact that an individual's presence remains anonymous in direct proportion to the degree to which its name becomes more present. Thus, supposing that praise attributes a name to a possible God, one should conclude that it does not name him properly or essentially, nor that it names him in presence, but that it marks his absence, anonymity, and withdrawal—exactly as every name dissimulates every individual, whom it merely indicates without ever manifesting. In this sense, praise in mystical theology would in the case of divine proper names only reproduce an aporia that is already unavoidable in the proper names of the finite world.

Next, the objection presupposes that praise, since it names, cannot be suitable to prayer which is supposed not to name. But can prayer pure and simple (εὐχή) be accomplished without naming—giving a name, however improper? No doubt we can contest this, given that no prayer can pray without giving a name, without acknowledging an identity even and especially an improper one. Not only does naming not contradict the invocation of the prayer, but without the invocation the prayer would be impossible—what would it mean to praise without praising anyone, to demand without demanding from anyone, to offer a sacrifice without offering it to anyone? An anonymous prayer would make no more sense than does the claim to attain the proper by an (im)proper name. This is why Dionysius not only always carries out his praise but his prayer as well (εὐχή) by an invocation as:[31] "[I]t is fitting for us to raise ourselves towards it [the Trinity] first by our prayer to it *as* the principle of goodness."[32] At issue is not so much a strict denomination since, according to the same text, prayer does not consist in causing the invoked one to descend into the realm of our language (he exceeds it, but also he is found always already among us), but elevating ourselves toward him by sustained attention. The approach of prayer consists simply in de-nominating—not naming properly, but setting out with the intention to approach in all impropriety. Thus, prayer and praise are carried out in the very same operation of an indirect aim for the αἰτία, which they never claim to name properly, but always to de-nominate as . . . and inasmuch as . . . what this intention can glimpse and interpret of it. To a large extent, these operators—*as* . . . and *inasmuch as* . . .—anticipate in theology what Heidegger will designate the phenomenological as—the interpretive comprehension of what is aimed at on the basis of and to the measure of the intonation of the one who intends.[33]

As such, the de-nomination operated by prayer (and praise) according to the necessary impropriety of names should not be surprising. In effect, it confirms the function of the third way, no longer predicative (whether this means predicating an affirmation or a negation) but purely pragmatic. It is no longer a matter of naming or attributing something to something, but of aiming in the direction of . . . , of relating to . . . , of comporting oneself towards . . . , of reckoning with . . .—in short of dealing with. . . . By invoking the unattainable as . . . and inasmuch as . . . , prayer definitively marks the transgression of the predicative, nominative, and therefore metaphysical sense of language. One therefore has several reasons to oppose Objection 4.

### Without Being—Otherwise Than Being

It now becomes possible to approach Objection 2 and ask if mystical theology is really inscribed within the horizon of Being, and as a result is inscribed in the onto-theo-logical figure that metaphysics imposed on it.

A preliminary remark is in order here. Even if Dionysius (or some other) understood the question of God on the basis of Being, this simple fact would not be enough to establish that he is inscribed within onto-theo-logy. That is, as we have tried to show in the privileged case of Thomas Aquinas, if an onto-theo-logy wants to attain conceptual rigor and not remain at the level of a polemical caricature, it requires first a concept of being, next a univocal application of this concept to God and creatures, and finally the submission of both to foundation by principle and/or cause. If these conditions are not met, if in contrast Being remains an inconceivable esse, without analogy, indeed *penitus incognitum*, then the mere fact that Being comes up is not enough to establish an onto-theo-logy.[34] If this caution implies great difficulty bringing a thought as discursive and formalized as that of Thomas's into the onto-theo-logical constitution of metaphysics (and Heidegger himself shied away from the task), how much more so are our efforts to be marked with prudence when it is a question of theology—and especially mystical theology!

But in the case of Dionysius, prudence is not even necessary when interpreting the possibility that he determines God by Being. For, in fact, such a de-nomination is clearly and precisely rejected—at least as the first, principal, and most powerful de-nomination. Once again, since this ever-so-important fact seems to have been passed over in silence, we will re-iterate: For Dionysius, neither Being nor being offer a proper, or even an improper, name of God. The major argument gives no cause for doubt: το ον is always preceded by ἀγαθόν because even non-beings not only "desire" the ἀγαθόν but participate in it. "If one may speak this way, even non-being desires the good which resides above all beings [τἀγαθοῦ τοῦ ὑπὲρ πάντα τὰ ὄντα, καὶ αὐτὸ τὸ μὴ ὄν ἐφίεται]." Better, "Even non-being participates in the beautiful and the good"; or more explicitly, "in short all beings [come from?] the beautiful and the good, and also all the non-beings [οὐκ ὄντα] [are found] in the beautiful and the good in a mode which exceeds essence [ὑπερουσίως]."[35] Positively, it has to be said that "the divine de-nomination of goodness manifests, in their totality, all the emanations coming from the αἰτία of all things and which it extends to beings as well as to non-beings [τὰ οὐκ ὄντα], surpassing [ὑπέρ] beings and non-beings."[36] This surpassing should not be understood simply, in the classically metaphysical meaning, in the sense that God "is not a being who is in a certain way, but who is absolutely," nor even in the more radical sense that He "is not, but is himself the Being of beings; not that beings alone come from the being before all time, but also the very Being of beings [αὐτὸ τὸ εἶναι]." Rather, this surpassing of beings must be understood otherwise, in the decisive sense according to which God, as goodness and αἰτία, designates "the principle of beings, on the basis of which all beings whatsoever as well as Being itself [καὶ αὐτὸ τὸ εἶναι] and every principle are characterized."[37] The theses supported by these texts thus are not tainted by any ambiguity. (i) The horizon of Being remains regional, because by definition it leaves out all non-beings. (ii) It always remains possible to take them into consideration, because they refer to the good, even when not being, in the mode of "desire." (iii) Therefore the first (or the last) of the de-nominations of God will have to be drawn from the horizon of the good, rather than that of Being—it being understood that even this de-nomination attains neither what is proper to God nor God properly.

What remains is to measure the import of these theses. It is not enough simply to declare the horizon of Being to be overstepped by goodness if one wants to think this transgression. What must be understood by goodness? In contrast to the Neo-platonists who would overcome Being only for the sake of coming unto the One and would pass beyond the One only in order to retrieve it, Dionysius not only does not privilege the one which he paradoxically places in the last position of the divine names; he also does not accord any essential privilege to goodness—while nevertheless still granting it the title "most revered of names."[38] Goodness transcends Being on principle, but it itself does not attain the essence and hovers, so to speak, between the derived names and the un-namable. Thinking God without Being and only without Being does not, however, end up thinking goodness otherwise than Being—goodness remains undetermined and, in any case, without essential impact. In light of this, how are we not to suspect the elision of Being to be insignificant? How are we not to suspect the denegation of Being of re-establishing Being without saying it has done so, indeed without owning up to it? Since it does not succeed in thinking beyond, shouldn't it end up turning back toward Being? But it is here that the objection is turned against itself. For if it is exact to say that we cannot think beyond Being—with the de-nomination goodness (or the one) — must this be held as a reproach against mystical theology and its third way? Should mystical theology be reproached for not knowing how to say, for not knowing or not wanting to say to us what this otherwise than Being *is* all about—but doesn't this reproach at once seem a bit absurd? For if it is a question of not naming, of not re-affirming any more than denying, why be surprised that the third way cannot say anything about "without Being?" If it were to predicate of it anything and everything that might *be*, wouldn't it legitimately deserve to be reproached precisely as contradictory? And more important, if it committed itself to saying what "otherwise than Being" *is* all about, wouldn't it have to be denounced as inconsistent? On the contrary, shouldn't we take it to be perfectly coherent, indeed something to be wished for, that the transgression of Being and the overcoming of predication that it authorizes, and by which it is characterized, be marked by the impossibility of *saying* (of affirming or denying) anything more about what the goodness "without Being" is or would be? For as soon as it is a question of the "otherwise than Being" it is no longer a matter of saying something about something, but of a pragmatics of speech, more subtle, risky, and complex. It's a matter of being exposed in one's intending a non-object, exposed to the point of receiving from this non-object determinations that are so radical and new that they speak to me and shape me far more than they teach and inform me. Henceforth, the words spoken no longer say or explain anything about some thing kept for and by my gaze. They expose me to what lets itself be said only for the sake of no longer permitting me to say it, but to acknowledge it as goodness, thus to love it. About this inversion in the gravity and orientation of speech— which we have been thematizing as de-nomination, just as Dionysius fixed it beneath the titles ὑμνείν and εὐχή—, it is therefore fitting that one no longer be capable of saying or denying anything whatsoever. The suspension of all predication does not betray the failure of the transgression toward "otherwise than Being," it attests to it and registers its symptoms.

The decisive and paradoxical importance of the objection raised by Derrida now appears fully evident: In stigmatizing the fact that mystical theology no longer says anything more after its passage to negation, and thus runs the risk that this negation might revert to an affirmation, Derrida's objection observes that in fact, but also rightfully, the third way cannot open onto any (newly) predicated said—or non-said or pre-said. With praise, it is no doubt no longer a matter of saying but of hearing, since according to the conventional etymology that Dionysius takes from Plato, bountiful beauty bids [la bonté belle appelle]—καλλὸς καλεί.[39]

## The Privilege of the Unknowable

It goes without saying that here, as is often the case, it is not simply a matter of disputing or refuting the objections raised by Derrida; rather they are to be taken as the bases from which we can construct, or at least outline, the scope of the question. At this point, we can begin to make out the basic thesis implicitly advanced by Derrida. It amounts to the following: (i) theology knows, according to an undiscussed hypothesis, only the two figures of metaphysical predication (affirmation and negation) and does not broach any third way; (ii) so as not to drift into atheism, the negative way inevitably compels the theologian to fall back into positivity, more or less scandalously, more or less honestly; (iii) the simply rhetorical recourse to "super-essential" eminence re-enforces, far from weakening, the claim that the question of God is inscribed within the horizon of essence, thus of Being; (iv) and therefore, the so-called negative theology falls beneath the sword of deconstruction just like any obviously metaphysical discourse—and perhaps more so since its claim to be removed from it must also be unmasked. This argument, however, presupposes a major assumption: Across all its claims to de-negation, theology, and first of all Jewish and Christian theology, in the end intends only the positivity of presence, envisages nothing higher, nothing more suitable, nothing more divine than the most intense presence possible. In short, theology succumbs in full to the obsession with presence. But is it so self-evident that theology suffers this fascination to such a degree? Is it self-evident that it has always thought to defend the "cause of God" so desperately that it would lash it to "metaphysical presence"? Finally, is it self-evident that the theologians did not really try to accomplish what they said they were undertaking—the third way—and that in the final analysis they again insisted on a kataphatic nomination of God? In short, must it be held as evident that, from the point of view of Revelation, what is at issue in the question of God has something to gain by being integrated in presence in its most clearly metaphysical sense? Put otherwise: Doesn't theology have the means, the intention, and also every reason not to yield to the "metaphysics of presence"? The advantage that it would draw from such a tactic is in no way clear, but the danger—that goes without saying.

In the case of Dionysius, the answer to these questions leaves no room for doubt—it is the theologian himself who insists that de-nomination maintain

God outside of all proper names, without sinking into presence: "God is known through all things and also apart from all things. God is known by knowledge and also by unknowing. . . . And it is the most divine knowledge of God that one knows through unknowing [ἢ δι' ἀγνωσίας γινωσκομένη]."[40] It must be insisted here that positing this absolute principle has nothing particularly Neo-platonic about it, nor anything of the hyperbolic excess of the so-called negative theology. It is first and above all a direct and inescapable consequence of the Biblical thesis "No one has seen God" (John 1:18), "nobody can see my face" (Exodus 33:23). God cannot be seen, not only because nothing finite can bear his glory without perishing, but above all because a God that could be conceptually comprehended would no longer bear the title "God." It is not much to say that God remains God even if one is ignorant of his essence, his concept, and his presence—he remains God only on condition that this ignorance be established and admitted definitively. Every thing in the world gains by being known—but God, who is not of the world, gains by not being known conceptually. The idolatry of the concept is the same as that of the gaze: imagining oneself to have attained God and to be capable of maintaining him under our gaze, like a thing of the world. And the Revelation of God consists first of all in cleaning the slate of this illusion and its blasphemy.

Consequently the requirement to neither know nor name God in terms of presence traverses the entirety of Christian theology. (a) It appears in the Apologists of the second century—first Justin Martyr: "No one can utter a name for the ineffable God [ὄνομα τῷ ἀρρήτῳ θεῷ];"[41] then Athenagoras: "Hear this, oh man: the form of God cannot be uttered [τὸ εἶδος τοῦ θεοῦ ἄρρητον], nor expressed and eyes of flesh do not have the power to see it."[42] (b) Likewise, it shows up in the first of the Alexandrians—take the Christians, first Clement "the First Cause is not in space, but above space and time and name and conception. . . . For our interrogation bears on the formless and invisible [ἀόρατος]"; "invisible and incapable of being circumscribed [ἀόρατος καὶ ἀπερίγραφος]"; "the invisible and ineffable God [ἀόρατος καὶ ἄρρητος]."[43] Then Origen: "God is incomprehensible and incapable of being measured"[44] Consider also Philo, the Jew: "It is a great good to comprehend that God is incomprehensible [ἀκατάληπτος] in terms of his Being and to see that he is invisible [ἀόρατος]."[45] (c) And also Athanasius: "God is good and the friend of men. . . . By his nature, he is invisible and incomprehensible, residing beyond all begotten essence."[46] (d) Basil clearly indicates the paradox with this remark: "[K]nowledge of the divine essence involves sensing His incomprehensibility [αἴσθησις αὐτοῦ τῆς ἀκαταληψίας]."[47] (e) And there is nothing surprising in the fact that Gregory of Nyssa should have repeated it almost word for word: "This is the true knowledge of what is sought [sc., seeing the invisible and incomprehensible God]—[ἀκατάληπτον]; this is the seeing that consists in not seeing [τὸ ἰδεῖν ἐν τῷ μὴ ἰδεῖν], because that which is sought transcends all knowledge, being separated on all sides by incomprehensibility as by a kind of darkness."[48] (f) John Chrysostam parses it in a slightly different form: "All the while knowing that God is, he [Saint Paul] does not know what his essence is," for "the essence of God is incomprehensible [ἀκατάληπτον]."[49] (g) Of course John of Damascus comes next: "No one has seen God. The only-begotten Son who is in the bosom of the Father has himself taught this. The divine is ineffable and incomprehensible [ἄρρητον καὶ ἀκατάληπτον]"[50] (h) Nothing different from Augustine: "God the highest, who is known better than knowing [de summo isto Deo, qui scitur melius sciendo]."[51] (i) Nor from Bernard: "Non ea disputatio comprehendit, sed sanctitas: si quo modo tamen comprehendi potest quod incomprehensibile est."[52] (k) Nor even from Thomas Aquinas, for whom seeing as "what God himself is remains hidden and unknown [hoc ipsum quod Deus est remanet occultum et ignotum]," it is necessary that man know how to unknow. Thomas therefore comments on the principle advanced by Dionysius in perfectly appropriate terms: "[W]hat the substance of God is remains in excess of our intellect and therefore is unknown to us; on account of this, the highest human knowledge of God is to know that one does not know God [hoc ipsum quod est Dei substantia remanet nostrum intellectum excedens, et ita a nobis ignoratur: et propter hoc illud est ultimum cognitionis humanae de Deo quod sciat se Deum nescire]."[53] Without continuing ad infinitum with this anthology of citations, it seems legitimate to admit as a fact still to be explained that at least for the Church Fathers theology does not consist in naming God properly, but in knowing him precisely as what cannot be known properly—what must not be known, if one wants to know it as such.

There is a powerful argument confirming that it is indeed the theologians themselves who have the most extreme speculative interest in freeing God from any and all inclusion in presence. In fact, it is the heretics who pretend to include God within presence by assigning him a proper name and offering a definition for his essence. That is, the development of speculative theology in the fourth century, and first of all in the Cappadocian Fathers, happens in response to the no less impressive assault of the Arians who wanted to refute the conclusions of the Nicean Council (A.D. 325). To demonstrate the inequality not only of Christ but of the Son to the Father, therefore to prove their non-divinity, the Arians argued for defining the divine essence as strictly un-begotten, ἀγέννητος—being God requires being not begotten, ἀγέννητος. From this equality, it obviously followed that the Son, begotten by definition, could not be God, of the same essence as the Father. Thus Acacius, first in line in the second generation of Arians, made unreserved use of the lexicon of the "metaphysics of presence," if such a thing can be said: "We believe that non-generation is the essence [ἀγεννησίαν εἶναι οὐσίαν] of the God of all things."[54] Similarly, his pupil and the most celebrated theoretician of Arianism uncritically submitted God to a metaphysical conceptuality: "When we say 'Unbegotten [ἀγέννητος]', we do not imagine that we ought to honour God only in name, in conformity with human invention; rather, in conformity with reality, we ought to repay him the debt which above all others is most due God: the acknowledgment that he is what he is [τὸ εἶναι ὅ ἐστιν]. . . . But God . . . was and is unbegotten." Or, "he is unbegotten essence." And "it is not by way of privation" that these affirmations nail God to the wall of presence, but with all metaphysical violence; for "his substance is the very same as that which is signified by his name [ὑπόστασιν σημαίνει τοὔνομα]."[55] In effect, Eunomius, like all the Arians, held that the metaphysical ideal of the equality between a word and/or a name and the concept of the essence is accomplished even (and paradoxically above all) in the case of God. It is by contrast Basil who, as a quasi-deconstructionist, interrupts this violence: "He is a liar who affirms with his sophisms that an essential distinction follows from a nominal one. For it is not the nature of things which follows that of names, but the names which are found after the things."[56] Consequently, if one of them plays the role of a metaphysician of presence, it can only be the Arian, Acacius, or Eunomius. Confronted with him, the Christian theologian who practices de-nomination and is opposed to this supposed drawing of God into presence is outraged that "the man dares to say that he knows God as God himself knows himself."[57] For the demand (and still more the pretension) to know God in an essence must be stigmatized not only as impossible but above all as indecent—it is simply not appropriate to what is at issue because it relates to mere curiosity. Here deconstruction and theology can be in agreement, for the sake of contesting the same adversary—not the orthodox theologian, but the Arian, the sole metaphysician of presence.

God therefore can be known only as not being known. In contrast, to know him as he is known appears to be the presupposition on which rests not only Arianism but also all conceptual—and above all metaphysical—grasps of the question of God. Just think for a moment of Spinoza's extravagant claim: "The human mind has adequate knowledge of the eternal and infinite essence of God [Mens humana adequatam habet cognitionem aeternae et infinitae essentiae Dei]" (Ethica II, §47). To know him by not knowing is obviously not the same thing as not knowing, nor is it the same as not knowing with the intention of knowing more (and not confessing as much). It is not a matter of a kataphasis ill-disguised in an apophasis, but of a radical apophasis which, precisely as radical, opens—by means of a paradox that is to be taken into consideration—onto knowledge of another type. To know in and through ignorance itself, to know that one does not know, to know incomprehensibility as such—the third way would consist, at least at first glance, in nothing else. But how to conceive this? On what conditions would the renunciation of comprehension remain an authentic form of knowledge and not just a failure of knowing? Perhaps if we reason in this way: Even if we were to comprehend God as such (by naming him in terms of his essence), we would at once be knowing not God as such, but less than God, because we could easily conceive an other still greater than the one we comprehend. For the one we comprehend would always remain less than and below the one we do not comprehend. Incomprehensibility therefore belongs to the formal definition of God, since comprehending him would put him on the same level as a finite mind—ours—, would submit him to a finite conception, and would at the same time clear the way for the higher possibility of an infinite conception, beyond the comprehensible.[58] Comprehension suggests adequate knowledge as long as one is dealing with things of the world. As soon as one tries to catch sight of God, the relation must be inverted—knowledge holds only if comprehension ceases. Except for incomprehensibility, it is no longer a matter of what one intends when one says "God": "Of God, we say: what wonder is it if we do not comprehend him? For if you comprehend it, it is not God. . . . To touch some part of God through one's mind is a great blessing. To comprehend him is entirely impossible [De Deo loquimur, quid mirum si non comprehenderis? Si enim comprehendis, non est Deus . . . . Attingere aliquantum mente Deum, magna beatitudo; comprehendere autem, omnia impossibile]."[59] In the case of God, knowledge cannot rise up to itself except by transgressing itself until it becomes an unknowing, or rather until it becomes a knowledge that is capable of acknowledging the incomprehensible, and thereby respects the operative, pragmatic, and endlessly repeatable de-nomination of God as *that than which nothing greater [better] can be thought [id quo majus (sive melius) cogitari nequit]*.[60]

De-nomination therefore does not end up in a "metaphysics of presence" that does not call itself as such. Rather, it ends up as a *theology of absence*—where the name is given as having no name, as not giving the essence, and having nothing but this absence to make manifest; a theology where hearing happens, as Paul remarks, "not only in my presence but also in my absence [μὴ ἐν τῇ παρουσίᾳ μοῦ μόνον, ἀλλὰ πολλῷ μᾶλλον ἐν τῇ ἀπουσίᾳ μοῦ]" (Philippians 2:12). But if essence and presence, and therefore a fortiori ground and the concept of Being, are missing from this name, one can no longer speak of onto-theo-logy or metaphysics or a "Greek" horizon. And, besides, can one ignore the fact that the work of the Greek Fathers consisted precisely in freeing the Christian theological concepts from the Greek (and perhaps metaphysical) horizon where they first arose?[61] No ground, no essence, no presence. We thus have stood up to Objection 2.

By theology of absence, therefore, we mean not the non-presence of God, but the fact that the name that God is given, the name which gives God, which is given as God (each of these going hand in hand, without being confused) serves *to shield God from presence*—weakness designating God at least as well as strength—and offers him precisely as an exception to presence. Gregory of Nyssa saw and described this perfectly:

> What is the significance of the unnamable name [ἀκατονόμαστον ὄνομα] of which the Father speaks [when he says] "Baptize them in my name," without adding the signification uttered by this name? On this matter, here is our opinion: we grasp all the beings in creation through the signification of their names. Thus, he who says "sky" conveys to the mind of the one who is listening the creature shown by this name; and if one mentions "man" or

one of the living things by his name, his form is at once impressed upon the one who is listening. And likewise all the other things are, by the names that they are given, inscribed on the heart of him who receives, through listening to them, the denomination imposed on the thing in question [τὴν προσηγορίαν τὴν ἐπικειμένην τῷ πράγματι]. In contrast, only the uncreated nature, which we believe [to be] the Father, the Son, and the Holy Spirit, surpasses all signification that a name can convey. [κρείττων πάσης ἐστὶν ὀνοματικῆς σημασίας].This is why the Word, in saying this name, did not add to the tradition of faith what it is (how could he have found a name for a thing above all names?). But he gave our understanding the power to set about piously to find, according to its capacity, a name which indicates [ὄνομα ἐνδεικτικόν] the supereminent nature and which is equally fitting to the Father, the Son and the Holy Spirit. . . . And this, it seems to me, is what the Word decreed by this form-ula [sc., say "the name" without saying which one] — in order to convince us that the name of the divine essence is unsayable and incomprehensible.[62]

The Name does not name God as an essence; it designates what passes beyond every name. The Name designates what is not named and says what is not named. There is nothing surprising then in the fact that in Judaism the term "Name" replaces the Tetragrammaton which should not and can never be pronounced as a proper name, nor that, amounting to the same thing, in Christianity it names the fortunate and necessary "absence of divine names" (Hölderlin). For the Name no longer functions by inscribing God within the theoretical horizon of our predication, but by inscribing us, according to a radically new praxis, in the very horizon of God. This is exactly what baptism accomplishes when, far from our attributing to God a name that is intelligible to us, we enter into his unpronounceable Name, with the additional result that we receive our own. The Name above all names therefore de-nominates God perfectly, by excepting him from predication, so as to include us in it and allow us to name it on the basis of its essential anonymity. The Name does not serve knowledge by naming, but by including us in the place de-nomination clears out. The basket never overflows except with bread which first was lacking. Thus mystical theology no longer has as its goal to find a name for God, but to make us receive our own from the unsayable Name. Concerning God, this shift from the theoretical use of language to its pragmatic use is achieved in the finally liturgical function of all *theo*-logical discourse.

Hence this absolute rule in the theology of absence, by which it is opposed to the "metaphysics of presence" at least as much as deconstruction is: "[O]ur best theologian is not he who has discovered the whole, for our present chain does not allow of our seeing the whole, but he who has better pictured or represented in himself the image of the Truth, or its shadow or whatever we may call it."[63] Or: "God as such cannot be spoken. The perfect knowledge of God is so to know him that we are sure we must not be ignorant of Him, yet cannot describe Him [Deum ut est, quantusque est, non eloquetur. Perfecta scientia est, sic Deum scire, ut, licet non ignorabilem, tamen inaerrabilem scias]."[64] The theologian's job is to silence the Name and in this way let it give us one—while the metaphysician is obsessed with reducing the Name to presence, and so defeating the Name. The dividing line has been established by an inescapable formulation: "[B]etween creator and creature no likeness can be recognized which would be greater than the unlikeness that is to be recognized between them [inter creatorem et creaturam non potest tanta similitudo notari, quin inter eos major sit dissimilitudo notanda]."[65]

## The Third Way as Saturated Phenomenon

We have thus wound up with a complete reversal of the initial problematic. But to observe this by examining the theological tradition of mystical theology and reconstructing its logic is one thing. It is quite a different matter to describe the phenomenon to which it is trying to do justice. The remaining task then is to conceive the formal possibility of the phenomenon which seems to demand an "absence of divine names" and our entering into the Name. Let this be noted: We have said "to conceive its formal possibility" and nothing more than this possibility, since phenomenology cannot, and therefore must not, venture to make any decisions about the actuality of such a phenomenon—this is a question entirely beyond its scope. Phenomenology is to make decisions only about the type of phenomenality which would render this phenomenon thinkable.[66] The question is to be formulated in this way: If that with which the third way of mystical theology deals in fact is revealed, how should the phenomenon be described, such that we do justice to its possibility?

Let us suggest a response. If one admits, with Husserl, that the phenomenon is defined by the inescapable duality of appearing and what appears [l'apparaître et l'apparaissant] and that this duality is deployed in terms of the pairs signification/fulfillment, intention/intuition or noesis/noema, one can imagine three possible relationships between the terms at issue: (i) The intention finds itself confirmed, at least partially, by the intuition, and this tangential equality defines adequation, therefore the evidence of truth. (ii) In contrast, the intention can exceed all intuitive fulfillment, and in this case the phenomenon does not deliver objective knowledge on account of a lack. The first case would correspond to the first way, kataphasis, which proceeds through a conceptual affirmation that justifies an intuition. The second would correspond to the second way, apophasis, which proceeds by negating the concept because of an insufficiency in intuition. Husserl (in this following Kant) admits only these two hypotheses and thus remains stuck within the horizon of predication, and therefore of a possible "metaphysics of presence." But, a third possibility still remains. (iii) The intention (the concept or the signification) can never reach adequation with the intuition (fulfillment), not because the latter is lacking but because it exceeds what the concept can receive, expose, and comprehend. This is what we have elsewhere called the saturated phenomenon.[67] According to this hypothesis, the impossibility of attaining knowledge of an object, comprehension in the strict sense, does not come from a deficiency in the giving intuition, but from its surplus, which neither concept, signification, nor intention can foresee, organize, or contain. This third relation between the two inseparable facets of the phenomenon—the saturated phenomenon—can perhaps allow us to determine the third way, where mystical theology is accomplished. In this third way, no predication or naming any longer appears possible, as in the second way, but now this is so for the opposite reason: not because the giving intuition would be lacking (in which case one could certainly make a favorable comparison between "negative theology" and atheism or establish a rivalry between it and deconstruction), but because the excess of intuition overcomes, submerges, exceeds, in short saturates, the measure of each and every concept. What is given disqualifies every concept. Dionysius states this to the letter: "It is stronger than all discourse and all knowledge—κρείττων ἐστὶ πάντος λόγου καὶ πάσης γνώσεως—and therefore surpasses comprehension in general and therefore [is also excepted from] essence [ὑπὲρ οὐσίαν]."[68] Indeed it is precisely by means of this undoing of the concept and intentionality that the theologians reach de-nomination. For example Athenagoras: "On account of his glory, he cannot be received [ἀχώρητός]; on account of his greatness, he cannot be comprehended [ἀκατάληπτος]; on account of his sublimity, he cannot be conceived [ἀπένοντος]; on account of his strength, he cannot be compared; on account of his wisdom, he can be referred to nothing at all; on account of his goodness, he cannot be imitated; on account of his goodwill, he cannot be described."[69] The undoing of knowledge here arises explicitly from an excess, not from a lack. Likewise John Chrysostom: "We therefore call him the unutterable, the inconceivable, the invisible, and the incomprehensible, he who conquers the power of human language [τὸν νικῶντα γλώττης δύναμιν ἀνθρώπινης]."[70] Excess conquers comprehension and what language can say. We have already heard from Gregory of Nyssa: "[T]he uncreated nature . . . surpasses all signification that a name could express [κρείττων πάσης ἐστὶν ὀνοματικῆς σημασίας]."[71] This text describes a shortcoming, one that results from a lack of utterable signification, not of intuition. In short, God remains incomprehensible, not imperceptible—without adequate concept, not without giving intuition. The infinite proliferation of names does indeed suggest that they are still there, but it also flags as insufficient the concepts that they put in play and thereby does justice to what constantly subverts them. Consequently, the third way cannot be confused with the sufficiency of the concept in the first way nor with the insufficiency of intuition in the second; rather, it registers the ineradicable insufficiency of the concept in general. The de-nomination which puts us in the Name has nothing in common with one or the other possibility opened by predication and nomination.

No doubt a final objection will be advanced: How, without resorting to a meaningless and even mad paradox, can the excess of giving intuition in the case of God be considered plausible, when the evidence attests that precisely and par excellence he is never given intuitively? Rigorously considered, this objection does not deserve a response since it no longer concerns the formal possibility of a phenomenon corresponding to the third way but is already concerned with its actuality. Nevertheless, we will address it, since it reflects a quite common point of view. It will be noted first of all that there is nothing mad about having recourse to paradox in this matter since this is precisely a case of a phenomenon that arises from the particular phenomenality of the paradox. It is by no means self-evident that every phenomenon must be submitted to the conditions for the possibility of experiencing objects and cannot sometimes contradict them. It could even be the case that this is a requirement proper to the phenomenality of God—supposing one admits its formal possibility, and what right does one have to exclude it? Next, one should keep in mind that even in the case when the positive form of the giving intuition would be missing, apparently or factually, this intuition is not wholly submerged beneath two of its undeniable figures, even if we can describe them only negatively. First, the excess of intuition is accomplished in the form of stupor, indeed of the terror which the incomprehensibility resulting from excess imposes on us. "God is incomprehensible not only to the Cherubim and Seraphim but also to the Principalities and the Powers and to any other created power. This is what I wished to prove now, but my mind has grown weary. It is not so much the great number of arguments which tires me, but a holy terror at what I had to say [ἡ φρίκη τῶν εἰρημένων]. My soul shudders and becomes frightened [τρέπει γὰρ καὶ ἐκπέπληκται] since it has dwelt too long on speculations about heavenly matters."[72] Access to the divine phenomenality is not forbidden to man; in contrast, it is precisely when he becomes entirely open to it that man finds himself forbidden from it—frozen, submerged, he is by himself forbidden from advancing and likewise from resting. In the mode of interdiction, terror attests to the insistent and unbearable excess in the intuition of God. Next, it could also be that the excess of intuition is marked—strangely enough—by our obsession with evoking, discussing, and even denying that of which we all admit that we have no concept. For how could the question of God dwell within us so deeply—as much in our endeavoring to close it as in our daring to open it—if, having no concept that could help us reach it, an intuition did not fascinate us?

## The Vocative Name

The question of the names of God is never about fixing a name to God nor opposing a "non" to him. "Name" and "non," when heard (in French), sound the same sound and nothing responds to the one any more than to the other. The "non" of the so-called negative theology does not say the Name any more than do the "names" of the affirmative way.

For if no one must say the Name, it is not simply because it surpasses all names, passes beyond all essence and all presence. In fact, not even not saying the Name would suffice to honor it since a simple denegation would still belong to predication, would again inscribe the Name within the horizon of presence—and would even do so in the mode of blasphemy since it treats it parsimoniously. The Name must not be said not because it is not given for the sake of our saying it, even negatively, but so that we might de-nominate all names of it and dwell in it.

The Name—it has to be dwelt in without saying it, but by letting it say, name, and call us. The Name is not said, it calls.

And because nothing terrifies us more than this call, we hold it be a "fearful task to name with our proper names Him ' . . . to whom God has bestowed the gift of the name above all names.'"[73]

## DERRIDA'S RESPONSE TO JEAN-LUC MARION

*Jacques Derrida.* I would like first to express my deep gratitude to our hosts: to this University, to Father President, Edmund Dobbin, and to my friend Jack Caputo. I am very pleased and honored to be back here on the occasion of this discussion with so many friends and distinguished colleagues, philosophers, and theologians. I am all the more grateful to Villanova University and to my friend Jean-Luc Marion after this illuminating, rich, and generous lecture. This is one of the very first opportunities we have had to discuss these difficult issues publicly, and certainly the first in a foreign language. The English language will be the third party to our discussion. I am not sure it will help. No doubt the discussion will be uneasy for many reasons and not only because of the language. I am afraid we might suffer from the lack of time and from the impossibility of returning to a number of texts, of quoting and re-reading them as closely as possible, as I think it would be urgent and indispensable to do.

I would now like to restrict my brief remarks to my own limited and preliminary steps into these intimidating problems, which were referred to in Jean-Luc Marion's wonderful lecture, steps which are at the same time both shy and terribly risky. But since Jean-Luc's argument often took the form of responses to my alleged objections (three or four of them), and since his responses were friendly and generous, no one would understand, and it would sound surprisingly unfriendly on my part, if I should not try at least to come back to some of the places he has chosen himself for this discussion. But again this discussion will be difficult without the possibility of re-reading closely, micrologically, a number of texts, even within my little corpus, some texts that he honored and quoted and some others that he did not mention. The discussion will be all the more difficult and even paradoxical insofar as I very often agree with Marion and share some of his views, and insofar as the arguments that he opposed to me, notably around what he calls the third way and denomination, can be found in my own texts, in the ones he quotes and in some others that he did not quote. They even play a decisive role in these texts.

So I do not think that he has not been generous enough or that he did not give me enough credit. Perhaps he gave me too much or he gave me what I did not want to receive. We know the well-known transformation by Lacan of Plotinus's and Heidegger's statements about giving what one does not have. Lacan, without quoting Plotinus or Heidegger, spoke of "giving what one does not have to someone who does not want it." I love this definition. Perhaps Jean-Luc gave me too much, as to the alleged objections, to the so-called negative theology and the "metaphysics of presence." I was telling Jack just a moment ago that I do not remember having ever used the expression "metaphysics of presence" in the context of negative theology. Perhaps I have, but I do not remember having done so. In the same way, when I read Pseudo-Dionysius, I paid a lot of attention, precisely to the liturgical, to prayer, to the non-predicative form of discourse. So I would perhaps say that he gave me too much as to the alleged objections to the so-called negative theology, and by giving me too much, I am afraid that he did not find enough in my texts on the subject.

Now from lack of time for a close reading and for the required quotations, let me mention very schematically a few points. First, Marion constantly refers to what I said about negative theology as if I had a thesis, one thesis, phrased in one form through a single voice — concerning the metaphysics of presence, the distinction between position and negation, and so on. Now I think that if time permitted I could show that my texts on the subject are written texts, by which I mean that they are not a thesis on a theme. They have a pragmatic aspect, a performative aspect that would require another kind of analysis. There is a long displacement of a number of voices, not only in myself, on my side, but on the other side, so to speak, on the side of what I always refer to as "what one calls negative theologies." Each time I address the question of negative theology, I very cautiously put these words in quotation marks, in the plural. Especially in *Sauf le nom*,[1] I transform the expression "what one calls negative theology" or "negative theologies" into a problematic entity. It is this expression that is for me a problem and not simply a reference. I could give a number of such examples, going back to my first texts.

Take, for instance, in "How to Avoid Speaking: Denials,"[2] the expression "negative theologies," appears in the plural and in quotation marks. Jean-Luc Marion refers to this precaution. Admittedly, after having mentioned, rather than used, this expression, I situate what he called the third way, which he opposed to me, to my alleged objection. I quote Pseudo-Dionysius when he goes beyond position and negation or privation. Allow me to quote myself at this point, because this third way is a decisive point in his argument, and I insist on this in this text. Let me try to translate myself into English:[3]

> The paragraph I'm going to read has, in addition, the interest of defining a beyond that exceeds the opposition between affirmation and negation. In truth, as Dionysius expressly says, it exceeds the very position (thesis), and not merely curtailment, subtraction ($\dot{\alpha}\varphi\alpha\acute{\iota}\rho\varepsilon\sigma\iota\varsigma$). By the same token, it exceeds privation. The without (*sans*) we mentioned a moment ago marks

> neither a privation nor lack nor absence. As for the beyond (*hyper*) of the superessential (*hyperousios*), it has the double and ambiguous value of what is beyond or above in the hierarchy, thus at the same time beyond (in English in my text) and more (*au-delà et plus*). God (is) "beyond being" but because of that more being than being. No more being and being more than being: being more. The French syntagm "*plus d'etre*" phrases this equivocality in rather economic fashion. (*Psyché*, 552/HAS, 90)

There follows a long quote from Pseudo-Dionysus. I will not read it all, just the last lines of this quote which goes perfectly with the third way argument that Marion opposes to me and which I take into account very precisely here. Pseudo-Dionysius says:[4]

> It is even more fitting to deny all these attributes, because it transcends every being, without believing that these negations contradict the affirmations, but rather that, in itself, it remains perfectly transcendent to every privation (*steresis*), because it is located beyond every position, either negative or affirmative (*hyper pasan kai aphairesin kai thesin*).

So you see that the argument of the third way has been taken into account as far as possible in this context.

    *Sauf le nom*, with its multiplicity of voices and ways, *multiplicité des voix/voies* (*Sauf*, 15–16/ON, 35) on the side of what I sign and the side of what I designate, is clearly different from a thesis about the metaphysics of presence and negative theology. Allow me to quote something. I apologize for this, but since my texts are part of the topic, I must do this. I cite the very beginning of *Sauf le nom*, a title which is untranslatable, the way *dénomination* is untranslatable. In English, "denomination" is a monetary term. *Dénomination* works wonderfully in French, meaning at the same time to name and to unname. The same is true of *Sauf le nom*. So, at the beginning of *Sauf le nom*, which remains untranslatable as a title, the starting point is one voice saying (I cite the English translation):

> —Sorry, but more than one, it is always necessary to be more than one in order to speak, several voices are necessary for that . . .
>     —Yes, granted, and par excellence, let us say exemplarily, when it's a matter of God . . .
>     —Still more, if this is possible, when one claims to speak about God according to what they call apophasis, in other words, according to the voiceless voice (la voix blanche), the way of theology called or so-called negative. This voice multiplies itself, dividing within itself: it says one thing and its contrary . . . (*Sauf le nom*, 15/On the Name, 35)

I could quote a number of passages in which the expression the "so-called" negative theology, the "expression" negative theology becomes a problem. Just one more quote about the identity of the metaphysics of presence, indeed, the identity of anything:

—But for a while now I have the impression that it is the idea itself of an identity or a self-interiority of every tradition (the one metaphysics, the one onto-theology, the one phenomenology, the one Christian revelation, the one history itself, the one history of being, the one epoch, the one tradition, self-identity in general, the one, etc.) that finds itself contested at its root. (*Sauf le nom*, 85/*On the Name*, 71)

Now, the denegation which came back again and again in Jean-Luc Marion's lecture—denegation as denial, as disavowal—the logic of denegation I use or thematize or problematize is much more complex, if I may say so, than the one Marion uses or attributes to me at the beginning, as if it were mine. Somewhere in "How to Avoid Speaking" I suggest that the way I use this logic of denegation is again as negation and the negation of a negation, but also that it is more complex than in a psychoanalytic sense (*Psyché*, 550/HAS, 87). This multiplicity of negations is at work everywhere in my text and in the texts I analyze, so this would require a long discussion with texts in hand. We would have to sit down and re-read the texts. As for pragmatics, I agree with Marion. That's one of the points on which I feel very close to him. At some point I spoke of what I called the performative aspect of prayer, of liturgy. We should have a discussion about praise and prayer; it would be a difficult discussion. But this pragmatic aspect is granted a real privilege in the way I address this question.

A last point about denomination. This is a point of agreement. What I tried to do, especially in "How to Avoid Speaking" and in *Sauf le nom*, is precisely to inscribe all these questions within the very question of the name and of the name of God, as the proper name which is never proper. As a sign of my agreement with Marion I would quote again, if you allow me to do so:

I understand by that a reflection on self, an autobiographical reflection, for example, as well as a reflection on the idea or on the name of God. (*Sauf le nom*, 20/*On the Name*, 37)

This is very close to what I think Marion says about *der Ort* and *das Wort*, the place and the word, in Angelus Silesius (cf. *Sauf le nom*, 94/*On the Name*, 75):

—The event remains at once in and on language, then within and at the surface. . . . The event remains in and on the mouth, on the tip of the tongue, as is said in English and in French, or on the edge of the lips passed over by words that carry themselves toward God. They are carried (*portés*), both *exported* and *deported*, by a movement of ference (transference, reference, difference) toward God. They name God, speak of him, speak *him*, speak *to* him, *let him speak in them*, let themselves be carried by Him, make (themselves) a reference to just what the name supposes to name beyond itself, the nameable beyond the name, the unnameable nameable.

(I think this is in agreement with what Marion says.)

As if it was necessary both to save the name and to save everything except the name, *save the name* (*sauf le nom*), as if it was necessary to lose the

45

> name in order to save what bears the name, or that toward which one goes through the name. But to lose the name is not to attack it, to destroy it, or to wound it. On the contrary, to lose the name is quite simply to respect it: as name. (*Sauf le nom*, 60–61/*On the Name*, 58)

I come now to a conclusion, in this large space of agreement, in which I share, paradoxically enough, the conclusions on the basis of which Jean-Luc Marion objects to me. I would say that one of the difficulties, one of the discussions we should have, beyond the difficult discussion on praise and prayer, which is a very complicated one that I cannot address now, one other point or place of discussion would have to do with baptism. Because, if I agree with him about the formal structure of what he said about the name, about the non-propriety, the inappropriateness, of the proper name of God or of anyone, if I agree in principle on a very general and structural level with him, I would not so easily take Christian baptism as the paradigm for this structure. I think this structure is more universal, or more formal. So I would have a question about the reference Marion made more than once to baptism, to the act of giving the name in this situation. But perhaps we could address this question on Saturday. I apologize for my English first and for taking so long.

*Jean-Luc Marion.* I will answer in a few words. I thank Jacques Derrida for his general agreement. I think that we are dealing with the same issues. May I add that perhaps we disagree on some of the issues. I just want briefly to emphasize the points where I think I am trying to add something new, perhaps not completely different, to his work, to his several texts on these topics, thereby improving my first attempts. For me, some new, very important points have emerged here. We agree that there are three ways of speaking about God, but the difficulty is to understand how it is possible to say that there is a third way. According to a metaphysical theory of discourse, there are only two possible ways. So what exactly is the meaning, the status, the legitimacy of the third way? The point is not whether there is a third one, but how to understand that the third one remains rational, although it does not remain confined within the possibilities opened by metaphysics. My answer would be that the only way to understand the third way, beyond affirmation and negation, without coming back implicitly or explicitly to affirmation is to take seriously the pragmatic use of language. What exactly is the pragmatic use of language? There are different possible answers. One, which I have bracketed today because of the lack of time, has to do with the question of prayer and praise. That is one point.

The new thing for me now is exactly this question of baptism. I speak of baptism not because I am absolutely certain that baptism is the most prominent way to explain the pragmatic use of language, but because in my discussion I was using a text by Gregory of Nyssa. At the end of a discussion with the Arians about the divinity of Christ, one of Gregory's main arguments was the end of the Gospel of Matthew: "[Y]ou will baptize them in the name of the Father, the Son, and the Holy Spirit." For Gregory, this is an argument for the divinity of Christ and also for baptism. For him, the name here is the name of God precisely because the name is only the name, the word "name," without any name which is given in the place of the name. So he says that for every other name we have a representation, a definition of the essence, which is immediately imposed upon our mind. But with that name, we have only "name" as a name, with no essence, no representation, no intellectual image or definition. So the name implies that there is no name. For him, it is in the situation of baptism, in theology, that we have the obvious task of thinking about a name which has no name, the name of nobody. This is the name. In that case, it is close to baptism.

Of course, I think, as Jacques Derrida says, and this is true, perhaps this is a structure that operates in many other cases. Perhaps, with any kind of proper name, the name in fact is the name without essence. The fact is that each of us bears a proper or Christian name, and the property of that name is precisely that it is not proper to us. There are a lot of different people who have the same first name, the same Christian name, as we have. So those alleged proper names are not proper and that is their property. I think the general function of the name, this pragmatic function of the name, which is opposed to a meta-physical interpretation of the name, is true of course in the case of God. For Christians and Jews, where man is made in the image of God, if God is un-knowable, then man is unknowable too. So that structure can be applied per-haps to the case of every man. This is the reason I referred to baptism, because of that text of Gregory of Nyssa, and not as a presupposition of anticipating a final position. In fact, in my next book, *Etant donné*, I expressly say that every proper name has as a property not to be proper. So I think we agree.

The other new point for me, which was very illuminating, concerns Derrida's objection that perhaps the third way is, from time to time, used by some theologians to re-establish a new affirmation and that the *super* or *hyper* is a way to disguise an affirmation. This of course is a very serious objection and I have tried to ponder it. Two things are now very clear to me. First, John Scotus Erigena and others were all aware that we have to find another interpretation of the super or hyper than that of a new affirmation. This is very clear and this problem is faced exactly by Erigena. Secondly, the history of this so-called negative theology is very striking. Of course, God was always said to be un-known. But it is to reply to the Arians that the Capodocian fathers invented or formalized negative theology, because the Arians claimed that the essence of God was within our grasp, and that the essence of God was to be unbegotten. I think that orthodox theology was in fact a powerful endeavor to deconstruct the naïve metaphysics of presence used by Arianism. In that situation, I would say, the part of deconstruction was played by the orthodox theologians.

*Jacques Derrida.* That is not surprising.

*Jean-Luc Marion.* I was surprised. In any case, I am very glad that we agree to a large extent on many issues and nevertheless the questions remain open.

## NOTES

1. Saint Basil of Caesarea, *Against Eunomius*, II, 8, Patrologia Graeca (hereafter PG), 585b.

2. For that matter, the first occurrence (at least to our knowledge) of this phrase refers, strangely enough, to Husserl, as the thinker of "phenomenology, the metaphysics of presence in the form of ideality." *La voix et le phénomène* (Paris, 1967), 9. (*Speech and Phenomena*, trans. David Allison [Evanston, Ill.: Northwestern University Press, 1973], 10). It could be that it was Derrida's critical reading of Husserl during the years 1953–54 that led to this question being formulated ("Phenomenology would no longer be master of its own house. Ontology would *already* be within it." *Le problème de la genèse dans la philosophie de Husserl* [Paris: Presses universitaires de France, 1990], 117). But is it self-evident that one can legitimately count on such a "metaphysical speech of phenomenology"? "La différance," in *Marges de la philosophie* (Paris: Editions de Minuit, 1972), 21 (*Speech and Phenomena*, 152).

3. A. Solignac, *Dictionnaire de Spiritualité*, vol. 15, (Paris, 1990–91), col. 513. Under discussion is *Mystical Theology* (MT) III, PG 1032d. Derrida seems aware of this difficulty when he evokes "what one calls, sometimes erroneously, 'negative theology'." *Psyché* (Paris: Galilée, 1987), 535 (*Derrida and Negative Theology*, ed. Harold Coward and Toby Foshay [Albany: SUNY Press, 1992], 73).

4. R. Roques, *L'univers dionysien: Structure hiérarchique du monde selon le Pseudo-Denys* (Paris, 1954), 210f.

5. It will be observed that when F. Bourguoin offers the modern definition of theology—"we must remark that there are three sorts of theology—the positive, the scholastic, and the mystical. The positive has as its object the interpretation of the Holy Scriptures. . . . The scholastic illuminates the truths of faith methodically, mixing with it some of human reasoning. And the mystical applies these truths and serves to elevate the soul to God" ("Préface" [of 1644] to *Oeuvres Complètes du Cardinal de Bérulle*, ed. J.-P. Migne [Paris, 1856], 83)—he completely ignores "negative theology," or else includes it with the two other "ways" in mystical theology. On the complicated fate of this term, see M. deCerteau, "'Mystique' au XVIIe siècle: Le problème du langage 'mystique,'" in *L'homme devant Dieu: Mélanges offerts au Père Henri de Lubac*, vol. 2 (Paris, 1964), 267f. (where it is emphasized that Dionysius was at this time the mystic par excellence). We also want to make ours the prudent reservations of M. Sales, "La théologie négative: méthode ou métaphysique," *Axes* 3, no.2 (1970): 11–22.

6. Delivered before the Société Française de Philosophie in 1968 and reprinted in *Marges de la philosophie* (*Speech and Phenomena*, 134). We have discussed this denegation in *L'idole et la distance* (Paris: B. Grasset, 1977), 318.

7. "Comment ne pas parler: Dénégations," reprinted in *Psyché: Inventions de l'autre* (Paris, 1987) ("How to Avoid Speaking: Denials," trans. Ken Friedan, in *Derrida and Negative Theology*). See also *Sauf le nom* (Paris: Galilée, 1993) ("Post-Scriptum: Aporias, Ways, and Voices," trans. John Leavey, in *Derrida and Negative Theology*). (Note that the English translation of the former essay is entitled "How to Avoid Speaking Denials." I have chosen to render the French "Dénégations" as "Denegations" rather than "Denials" because this seems to better capture the sense intended by the author of the present study: namely, it is not simply a matter of denying that one, be it deconstruction or "negative theology," does something, be it predicate of God or

"negative theology"; rather, at issue is whether or not in claiming not to speak about X, or in denying that they do Y, negative theology and/or deconstruction are in fact speaking about X, doing Y—Trans.) As *Psyché* made generous reference to our works (in particular *L'idole et la distance*, then *Dieu sans l'être* [Paris: Fayard, 1982] [*God Without Being*, trans. Thomas A. Carlson (Chicago: The University of Chicago Press), 1991]), the pages which follow could be read as a response, or rather as a complementary moment in an already old, and for us at least, quite fruitful discussion. Concerning the remarks that *Donner le temps I: la fausse monnaie* (Paris: Galilée, 1991) (*Given Time I: Counterfeit Money*, trans. Peggy Kamuf [Chicago: The University of Chicago Press, 1992]) addresses to our study *Réduction et donation: Recherches sur Husserl, Heidegger et la phénoménologie* (Paris: Presses universitaires de France, 1989), consult *Etant donné: Essai d'une phénoménologie de la donation* (Paris: Presses universitaires de France, 1997), L. II.

8. Recently, C. Bruaire: "It is therefore necessary to assign negative theology its official place, to give it its exact status, apart from the pious sentiments which cover with a sensible outer layer, with religious scraps, the unalterable absolute, sign of the Nothing: negative theology is the negation of all theology. Its truth is atheism." *Le droit d Dieu* (Paris, 1974), 21. This finds a surprising echo in Derrida: "If the apophatic inclines almost towards atheism" *Sauf le nom*, 18 ("Post-Scriptum," 284). In contrast to this crude assimilation, see H. de Lubac, *De la connaissance de Dieu* (Paris, 1945), chapter 5.

9. *Sauf le nom*, 69–70 ("Post-Scriptum," 305) (which here, as elsewhere, depends on R. Mortley, *From Word to Silence*, vol. 2 [Bonn, 1986], 57—a work which is at once knowledgeable and profoundly foreign to what it claims to be treating, as much by its prejudices as by its omissions).

10. *Sauf le nom*, 39, 41, 69–70, 79, 84 ("Post-Scriptum," 293, 294, 305, 309, 310–311); and *Psyché*, 564, and 573 ("How to Avoid Speaking: Denials," 102–103, 136–37 n.16).

11. *Sauf le nom*, 16, 70, 81 respectively ("Post-Scriptum," 283 [modified], 305, 310). See, in particular, on "being" and "truth," 72, 80, 82 ("Post-Scriptum," 306, 308–309, 310) and *Psyché*, 542 nn.2 and 3 (see 540–41) ("How to Avoid Speaking: Denials," 79 [see 77–78]). This assertion too rests on R. Mortley, who strangely praises it in Proclus (supposedly the only true theoretician of the *via negativa*) and then reproaches Gregory of Nyssa and Dionysius with it: "This manoeuvre resembles [?] the positive *via negativa* [?] of Proclus [?], in that negation is implied only [?] to allow for a positive statement of transcendence" (*From Word to Silence*, vol. 2, 229). This argument is repeated by the same author with even less caution in "What Is Negative Theology?" in *Prudentia*, ed. R. Mortley and D. Dockerill. Supplementary, 1991. It is also assumed as evident by H. Coward and M. C. Taylor in their respective contributions to *Derrida and Negative Theology*, ed. H. Coward and T. Foshay (Albany: SUNY Press, 1992), 176f., 188, 200, etc. Similarly, F. Kermode, "Endings, Continued," in *Languages of the Unsayable: The Play of Negativity in Literature and Literary Theory*, ed. S. Budick and W. Iser (New York: Columbia University Press), 89, and in particular, 75f.

12. *Psyché*, 572f., n.1 ("How to Avoid Speaking: Denials," 111f., especially 136 n.16).

13. We will spare Dionysius of the useless title "Pseudo-" which modern criticism insists on inflicting upon him, as if it were necessary to denounce a fraud in the title "the Areopagite" (for a classic example, see M. de Gandillac strenuously denouncing

"the Dionysian myth" in the introduction to his translation of *Oeuvres complètes du pseudo-Denys l'Aréopagite* [Paris, 1980 (1948)]). This is obviously a religious name: Dionysius does not pretend to be the convert of Saint Paul (Acts 17:4), but assumes the name as that of a role model and patron saint. Otherwise, why would he confess his spiritual father to be not Saint Paul but "the divine Hierotheus" (*Divine Names*, IV, 15–17, PG 3, 714a f. and the paraphrase of Pachymère, 778b f.)? It takes some naïveté to imagine Dionysius and his ancient readers more naïve and ignorant of monastic practices than we have become.

14. Respectively, *Divine Names*, VII, 3, 869d–872a; MT, I, 2, 1000b; and MT V, 1048b (Note that all English translations of Dionysius have been modified in order to capture the rendering of the Greek by the author of this essay. For this reason, I have omitted citing the English page reference.—Trans.).

15. *Divine Names*, II, 4, 641a.

16. *Summa theologiae*, Ia, q. 13, a. 2c and 3c (*The Summa Theologica of Thomas Aquinas*, vol. 1 [New York: Benziger Brothers, 1947], 61, 62).

17. *De docta ignorantia*, I, c. XXVI, in 292–97 (*On Learned Ignorance*, trans. Fr. Germain Heron [New Haven: Yale University Press, 1954], 61).

18. See note 11 above.

19. *Celestial Hierarchy*, II, 3, 141a. See *Divine Names*, VII, 3, 872b and XIII, 3, 981b and *Mystical Theology*, I, 2, 1000b.

20. *Mystical Theology*, I, 2, 1000b (What the English translators render as "beyond," the Greek υπερ, the author has rendered as "au-dessus," which we translate as "above"—Trans.)

21. *Mystical Theology*, V, 1048a.

22. *Divine Names*, XIII, 3, 981a.

23. *Divine Names*, VII, 1, 865c. See also *Divine Names*, I, 6, 596ab in its entirety.

24. *Divine Names*, respectively I, 5, 593c–d and IV, 16, 713c. See also, recapitulating with αιτια alone the overcoming of the two values of truth and predication, I, 6, 596b; I, 7, 596c; I, 8, 597c; II, 3, 640bc; II, 5, 644a; IV, 3, 697a; IV, 7, 704a; IV, 12, 709b; IV, 16, 713c; V, 1, 816b; V, 2, 816c; V, 4, 817d; XIII, 3, 970c. See also our analysis in *L'idole et la distance*, xxx (we will not go back over this translation nor the interpretation of this concept, which have not been contested).

25. *Divine Names*, V, 8, 824b.

26. K. Hart, *The Trespass of the Sign: Deconstruction, Theology and Philosophy* (Cambridge: Cambridge University Press, 1989), 200, cited by T. Foshay, as confirmation of our position opposite that of J. Derrida, "Introduction: Denegation and Resentment," in *Derrida and Negative Theology*, 12.

27. See for example, among other echoes of Paul, "the good above [υπερ] all logos, unsayable by all logos" (*Divine Names*, I, 1, 588b); or "to know how to discover the unknown hidden (?) by all the knowledge which is found in all beings" (*Mystical Theology*, II, 1025b).

28. *Divine Names*, V, 1, 816b. See also II, 4, 641a (cited above in note 15).

29. *De Divisionae Naturae*, I, 14, Patrologia Latina (hereafter PL) 122, 426a–d (English trans. in *Medieval Philosophy from St. Augustine to Nicholas of Cusa*, ed. John Wippel and Allan Wolter, O.F.M. [New York: The Free Press, 1969], 130–31). As the Greek terms in columns 459–60 indicate, this is quite obviously a discussion of the Dionysian superlatives. F. Bertin, the French translator of Eriugena's work, offers a perfect commentary: "[T]he prefixes *suoer* or *more than* in no way imply a way of

eminence which surreptitiously re-introduces affirmations at the heart of the negations. When one says that God is Superessence, one does not at all suggest that God is
an Essence situated at the apex of the hierarchy of essences, but rather that God is
essentially void" (*De Divisionae Naturae*, French translation, vol. 1 [Paris, 1995], 97).

30. As we have recently done in *Etant donné*, V, §28–29.

31. *Divine Names*, I, 6, 596a–b, 2, 596c; II, 5 644a; V, 4, 817c; XIII, 3, 980b:
"Consequently theology [Scripture] praises the thearchy, as αιτια of all things, with
the name unity."

32. *Divine Names*, III, 1, 680b. John Chrysostam takes up this theme by confounding prayer and praise in δοξα alone. *On the Incomprehensible Nature of God*,
trans. Paul W. Harkins (Washington, D.C.: Catholic University of America Press,
1984); III, 37f. [P.G. 48, 719]).

33. *Sein und Zeit*, §32.

34. See our study "Saint Thomas d'Aquin et l'onto-théo-logie," *Revue Thomiste*
(janvier-mars 1995), 33–66.

35. *Divine Names*, IV, 3, 697a (see IV, 18, 713f.); IV, 7, 704b; IV, 10, 705d (see IV,
19, 716c).

36. *Divine Names*, V, 1, 816b.

37. *Divine Names*, respectively V, 4, 818d; V, 7, 822b. See John of Damascus: "To
say what God is in his essence is impossible. It is more fitting to construct a discourse
through the suppression of all. For he is not among beings, not as not being, but as
being above all beings and being above Being itself [υπερ αυτο το ειναι]." *De fide
orthodoxa*, I, 1, 4 (modified) (PG 94, 800b).

38. *Divine Names*, XIII, 2, 3, 977c–981b.

39. *Divine Names*, IV, 7, 701c–d. See Plato, *Cratylus*, 416c–d.

40. *Divine Names*, VII, 3, 872a.

41. *Apology I*, 61, PG 6, 421b (*Ante-Nicene Fathers*, vol. 1 [Grand Rapids: Wm.
B. Eerdmans Publishing Co., 1981], 183 [modified]). See *Apology II*, 10, 461b and
*Dialogue with Trypho*, 127, 2, 4.

42. *To Autolycos*, I, 3 PG, 1028c.

43. *Stromates*, respectively V, 11, 71, 5, then V, 11, 74, 4 and V, 12, 78, 3 (*Ante-
Nicene Fathers*, vol. 2 [Grand Rapids: Wm. B. Eerdmans Publishing Co., 1983], 461,
then 462 and 463).

44. *On First Principles*, I, 1, 5 (*Ante-Nicene Fathers*, vol. 4 [Wm. B. Eerdmans
Publishing Co., 1982], 243): "dicimus secundum veritatem quidem Deum incompre-
hensibilem esse atque inestimabilem. . . . Quid autem in omnibus intellectualibus, id
est incorporeis, tam praesens omnibus, tam ineffabiliter atque inaestimabiliter praecel-
lens quam Deus? Cujus utique natura acie humanae mentis intuendi atque intueri,
quamvis ea sit purissima ac limpidissima, non potest" (PG 11, 124a/b–c).

45. Philo, "On the Posterity of Cain and His Exile," in *Philo*, vol. 2., trans. F. H.
Colson and G. H. Whitaker. (Cambridge, Mass.: Harvard University Press, 1958), 337.

46. *Against the Pagans*, 36, PG 25, 69. Likewise, Irenaeus, *Against Heresies*, IV,
20, 5: "incapabilis et incomprehensibilis et invisibilis" (SC 100).

47. *Letter 234*, 1, PG 32, 869 (*The Nicene and Post-Nicene Fathers*, vol. 8 [Grand
Rapids: Wm. B. Eerdmans Press, 1983], 274 [modified]).

48. *Life of Moses*, II, 163, PG 44, 377 (*The Life of Moses* [New York: Paulist Press,
1978], 75).

49. *On the Incomprehensible Nature of God*, respectively I, 1g. 293 and IV, 1g.733

(PG 48, 706, 733 [See also *On the Incomprehensible Nature of God*, 126, 253]). See V, 1g.385, p. 304 (PG 743), which should be compared with Gregory of Nyssa "That God is, everyone knows; but to know what and how he is, that is beyond the reach of all natural beings" (*De Trinitate*, III, 16, [PG 39, 873]).

50. *De Fide Orthodoxa*, I, 4 (modified) (PG 94, 789b [see 1, 4, 800b]).

51. *De ordine*, II, 16, 44, PL 32, 1015.

52. *De consideratione*, V, 14, 30, PL 182, 805d.

53. Respectively, "Prologue" to the *Commentary on the Divine Names* (in Opuscula omnia, vol. 2, ed. P. Mandonnet [Paris, 1927], 221), and *De potentia*, q. 7, a. 5, ad 14.

54. Formulation reported by Epiphanius of Salamine, *Panarion*, III, vol. 1, 76 (PG 42, 536, cited by Basil of Cesarea, *Against Eunomius*, I, 4, PG 29, 512b).

55. Eunomius, *Apology*, respectively 8, 7, 8, 12 (PG 30, 841c, 841d–844a and 848b) (*Eunomius: The Extant Works*, trans. Richard Paul Vaggione [Oxford: The Clarendon Press, 1987], 41–43, 41, 43 [modified], 49).

56. Basil, *Against Eunomius*, II, 4, PG 29, 580b. B. Sesboüe, in the introduction to his edition of the *Apology*, gives some good references supporting the inscription of Eunomius within Greek metaphysics.

57. *On the Incomprehensible Nature of God*, II, 1g. 158–59, PG 48, 712.

58. Descartes, *Responsiones V*, AT VII, 368, 1–3.

59. Augustine, *Sermo* 117, 3, 5, PL 38, 663. See *Sermo* 52, 6, 16: "Si enim quod vis dicere, si capisti, non est Deus; si comprehendere potuisti, cogitatione tua decepisti. Hoc ergo non est si comprehendisti: si autem hoc est, non comprehendisti" (PL 38, 663).

60. *Proslogion*, XIV, vol. 1, ed. F. S. Schmitt (Edimbourg, 1938), 111. This formulation, which comes from Augustine (*De Trinitate*, V, 2, 3, etc.) and Boethius (*De Trinitate*, IV), will be taken up by Bernard: "Quid est Deus? Quo nihil melius cogitari potest" (*De Consideratione*, V, 7, 15, PL 182, 797a). On the theoretical validity of Anselm's formulation, see our study "L'argument relève-t-il de l'ontologie?" *Questions cartésiennes I* (Paris: Presses universitaires de France, 1991).

61. See, among other works, E. von Ivanka, *Plato christianus* (Einsiedeln: Johannes Verlag, 1964).

62. *Against Eunomius*, II, §14–15, ed. W. Jaeger, vol. 2, pp. 301–302 (PG 45, 471d–3c). "The use of the uniformative term 'name' is deliberate," acknowledges R. Mortley (*From Word to Silence*, 181). This can be compared to the argument for the comprehensibility of εστι in the predications concerning God in *Against Eunomius*, III, 5, n.60, vol. 2, p. 172 (PG 45, 764).

63. Gregory of Nazianzus, *Fourth Theological Oration* 30, 17, PG 36, 125c (*Nicene and Post-Nicene Fathers*, vol. 7 [Grand Rapids: Wm. B. Eerdmans Publishing Co., 1983], 316 [modified]).

64. Hilary of Poitiers, *De Trinitate*, II, 7, PL 10, 36 (*Nicene and Post-Nicene Fathers*, vol. 9 [Grand Rapids: Wm. B. Eerdmans Publishing Co., 1981]).

65. Fourth Lateran Council (1215) in H. Denziger, *Enchiridion Symbolorum*, §432. Despite its title, the work of E. Przywara, *Analogia entis* (Einsiedeln: Johannes Verlag, 1962), has indicated this in an exceptionally strong fashion.

66. Concerning this distinction, see "Métaphysique et phénoménologie. Une relève pour la théologie," *Bulletin de littérature écclésiastique* 94, no. 3 (1993): 189–

205 and "L'autre philosophie première et la question de la donation," *Philosophie* 49 (mars 1996): 29–50.

67. See *Etant donné*, §24–25.

68. *Divine Names*, I, 5, 593a.

69. *To Autolycos*, I, 3, PG 6, 1028c.

70. *On the Incomprehensible Nature of God*, III, PG 48, 720 (see also, among other examples, III, p. 713 and 723). Likewise, "The invisible, the incomprehensible . . . he who surpasses all understanding and conquers every concept [νικων παντα λογισμον]" (*Sermon "Father, if it is possible,"* 3, PG 51, 37).

71. *Against Eunomius*, II, §15, ed. W. Jaeger, vol. 2, p. 302 (PG 45, 473b).

72. *On the Incomprehensible Nature of God*, III, loc. cit. 214 (PG 48, 725) (English trans., 108 [modified]). We refer to the wise and well-argued suggestion made by J. Daniélou, who interprets the theme of the "holy terror" (and all the conjoint terms) as attesting the excess of divine intuition, which subverts all man's expectations and his capacity ("Introduction," III, 30–39).

73. See note 1.

## DISCUSSION

1. *Sauf le nom* (Paris: Galilée, 1993), Eng. trans. John Leavey in *On the Name*, ed. Thomas Dutoit (Stanford: Stanford University Press, 1995). Hereafter *Sauf le nom*/*On the Name*.

2. "Comment ne pas parler: Dénégations," in *Psyché: Inventions de l'autre* (Paris: Galilée, 1987), 535–96 ("How to Avoid Speaking: Denials," trans. Ken Frieden, in *Derrida and Negative Theology*, ed. Howard Coward and Toby Foshay [Albany: SUNY Press, 1992], 73–142. Hereafter *Psyché*/HAS).

3. Derrida is doing a sight translation. We supply a reference to the published translation.

4. Again, we have transcribed the sight translation that Derrida was making of the French translation of *Mystical Theology*. For the standard English translation of this passage in Pseudo-Dionysius (1:1000ab) by John Jones, *The Divine Names and Mystical Theology* (Milwaukee: Marquette University Press, 1980), occasionally modified, see HAS, 90–91.

*[handwritten marginal note: "Aporia or receiving theme / Note Marion divining"]*

## two

# On the Gift

### A Discussion between Jacques Derrida and Jean-Luc Marion

Moderated by Richard Kearney

### Introductory Remarks

*Michael Scanlon.* Villanova University is an Augustinian University, and I know the affection that Jacques Derrida has for Augustine. So, by way of introducing this afternoon's roundtable, I want to say just a word on Augustine and the gift. One of Augustine's favorite words for the Spirit, the Holy Spirit, the Spirit of God, the Spirit of Christ, is God's Gift, the *donum Dei*. Augustine puts it very nicely, "God gives us many gifts, but *Deus est qui Deum dat*" ("God is He Who gives God"). The highest gift of God, the gift of God that we call our salvation, is nothing less than God. I leave this to the profundity of Jacques Derrida. I thank all of you, participants and audience alike, for being here.

*Richard Kearney.* It is a great honor to be here among you all and in particular between Jacques Derrida and Jean-Luc Marion. It is somewhat of a daunting and intimidating task to be asked to moderate this dialogue, but I will do my best. I see my own role as a very secondary one, to be — to use one of Jack Caputo's favorite phrases from Kierkegaard — a "supplementary clerk," serving in the background to supplement or intervene or translate or mediate, where

54

necessary, between our two interlocutors. Another metaphor I might use, to pick up on one of the signifiers that has been floating around here for the last two days, is that of a ghost (no doubt of an *un*holy one), between father and son, in a dialogue that has been going on for some fifteen to twenty years. Jacques Derrida, as most of you probably know, was a former teacher of Jean-Luc Marion's at Ecole Normale Supérieur in Paris. They have exchanged views on several occasions and in several very important texts since, principally on the theme of negative theology. I think on foot of the inaugural steps of a renewed debate on the subject, after Jean-Luc Marion's paper two nights ago, it is timely that we try to pursue that today.

In the last year in Ulster we have witnessed attempts to mediate between Unionists and Nationalists where the two parties would not even sit in the same room. So we had what were called "proximity talks," where the mediators would sit down with one group and they would tell them what they think, and then they would go into the next room and talk to the other group, and so on, back and forth. The whole purpose of such dialogues, which were extremely laborious, was to bridge gaps. If I can play a constructive role here today, it will be in trying to move in the opposite direction, that is, to acknowledge gaps between the two interlocutors, who are, as I am sure they would be the first to agree, largely in agreement on many philosophical issues. Time is too short to agree this afternoon, at least initially, although I hope we will end up with some sort of fusion of horizons. Lest they be too premature and too polite and too consensual, I suggest we begin by disqualifying the term "I agree" for the first hour and then work towards convergence.

So, I propose we cut to the chase and corner our quarry, which today is called the "gift," and without doing undue violence to the quarry, lay it out, cut it at the joints, then try to put it together again. Hermeneutic incision is required here. Jean-Luc Marion ended his talk the other night with the term "denomination," and Jacques Derrida took him up on this term. One of the senses of denomination that did not come out in that discussion is that of declension, division, differentiation, distinction; as when we speak of denominational schools, Catholic, Protestant, Jewish, and so on. Since two major themes of this conference are "gift" and "religion," I think it might be wise to start by asking the two interlocutors to identify the denominational nature of their discourses on the gift. As I see it, Jacques Derrida comes to this debate as a *quasi-atheistic*, quasi-Jewish deconstructor. Jean-Luc Marion comes to the debate as a *hyper-Christian*, hyper-Catholic phenomenologist. I use the term "*hyper*" in Jean-Luc's sense, as it was enunciated the other evening. Most of you are aware of Jacques Derrida's work on the gift over the last decade; since most of the texts are available in English — *Given Time, The Gift of Death*, and, of course, his recent writings on hospitality. Jean-Luc Marion has made two very important contributions to this debate: *Reduction et donation* and *Etant donné*; *Reduction et donation* has recently become available in English under the title *Reduction and Givenness*.[1]

I would like to begin by asking Jean-Luc Marion to put his cards on the table with regard to the specifically religious and theological nature of gift, giving, and given-ness, particularly under the rubric of "donating intuition" and the "saturated phenomenon." I would ask Jean-Luc to bring us through some of the steps of the argument on these notions of giving, gift, and givenness before asking Jacques Derrida to respond.

*Jean-Luc Marion.* Thank you. Well, I shall disappoint you by saying that right now, at this stage of my work, I have to emphasize that I am not interested in the gift and I am not interested in the religious meaning of the gift.

*Kearney.* A great start! Right. And now, Prof. Jacques Derrida. (laughter)

*Jacques Derrida.* I told you it would be unpredictable.

*Marion.* In fact, I was interested in the gift when writing theology, some ten years ago or even more. But, with *Reduction and Givenness*, the question of the gift turned out to be profoundly modified for me by the discovery of the issue of givenness, *Gegebenheit*, in phenomenology, and by phenomenology I mean Husserl, and by Husserl I mean the early Husserl, the Husserl of the *Logical Investigations*. In Husserl, we discover that the most efficient and profound definition of the phenomenon was expressed in the language of "being given," in German, *Gegebensein*. Briefly, and this was occasioned by a discussion of a book by Jacques Derrida, *Speech and Phenomena*, for Husserl, who took up the traditional definition of the phenomenon by Kant, the phenomenon arises from the synthesis or conjunction of two different components: intuition, on one side, and, on the other side, intention—intentionality, concept, signification. I realized at that moment that Husserl did not simply assume the decision taken by Kant on intuition—that it has the philosophical role to give and deserves to be called the "giving intuition"—but he claimed boldly enough that even the signification has to be given, too, as such, and more: that the essences, the *logical* essences, truth and so forth had to be given, too. Everything, not only the intuition, is *gegeben*, or can be *gegeben*, or at least you can ask about every signification whether it is *gegeben* or not.

So then I tried to re-open some of the greatest issues in the history of phenomenology, mainly between Husserl and Heidegger, wondering whether it would be possible to re-read phenomenology as such as the science of the given. I found it possible to proceed in that direction. I do not have the opportunity here to explain this in detail, but many of you, for instance, are well aware of the fascinating doctrine that I endeavor to use as a concept, the *es gibt*, the *cela donne*, I would translate, in Heidegger. Other phenomenologists, Levinas, for instance, and Jacques Derrida, and Michel Henry, are interested in the fact that a phenomenon cannot be seen as only and always either an object (which was roughly the position of Kant and to some extent of Husserl) or a being (which was in the main the position of Heidegger). Rather something more genuine, or poorer and lower, perhaps more essential (if essence here is a good word, which I doubt) can appear as *gegeben*, as given. Let me emphasize this point. Starting with the achievement of the path of thought, the *Denkweg*, of Heidegger, what has phenomenology achieved, when you consider the greatest phenomenologists, including Gadamer, Ricoeur, Levinas, Michel Henry, and others? They are interested in some very strange phenomena, insofar as you cannot say that they "are"—for instance, for Levinas, quite expressly and obviously, you cannot say that the other "is." To describe the other means not to refer to being, which would on the contrary forbid an access to its phenomenon. So, in fact, they are describing new phenomena, like the self-affection of the flesh, the ethics of the other, the historical event, narrative, *différance*, and so forth, which, of course, cannot be said to be in any way objects and should not be said to "be" at all. Of course you can say that the other is, but simply saying "is" does not describe it. To describe these phenomena concretely and precisely, we need another way of seeing them. My guess amounts to saying that the ultimate determination of the phenomenon implies not to be, but to appear as—*given.*

And if everything which appears has come unto us as given, one of the most decisive characters of any phenomenon establishes it as an event, which definitely happens. To happen makes us see in a most striking way that the happening phenomenon happens as given—given only to consciousness if you want, given to me, but in the end always given. So givenness achieves—it took me some time to realize this—first of all, a phenomenological determination. Starting from that phenomenological determination, of course, it becomes possible to go back to some types of phenomena expressed, explained, used, produced—if not produced, put into play—by what we used to name religious experience. Those phenomena seem given par excellence. The Eucharist, for instance, the Word which is given, forgiveness, life in the Spirit by the sacraments, and so forth, all this has to be described as given. Theological items could appear as phenomena, too, because they have at least something in common with all the other phenomena, at different degrees, viz., to appear as given. Now my real work will endeavor to explain what it implies that phenomena cannot appear, without appearing as given *to me*. In other words, does every given thing appear as a phenomenon? This point should not be confused with another one: Everything that appears has to appear as given. So, I want to focus my interest on the phenomenological dimension of givenness, first of all and in general. In that case, and perhaps we shall see this later, we could ask why and how far some phenomena appear as more given, or given to a larger and higher degree than others, and we may call them paradoxical or saturated phenomena.

**Kearney.** Thank you, Jean-Luc. Given that initial enunciation of the position, Jacques, do you think that there is such a thing as a *theological* donation? Do you think that there is a "saturated phenomenon" that is in fact divine and that is greater than language?

**Derrida.** Contrary to Jean-Luc, I am interested in Christianity and in the gift in the Christian sense, and I would be interested in drawing conclusions in this respect. I will start, of course, by saying how happy and proud I am to have this discussion with Jean-Luc Marion. You recall, as a given, that he was my student long ago. I do not know how to interpret this. If I say, fortunately he was not my student, or unfortunately he was not my student, the given, the givenness, the fact that he was enrolled at the Ecole Normale Supérieure when I was teaching there becomes a problem. Unfortunately, he was not my student, although he was at the Ecole Normale Supérieure. That is the reason that he wrote such an important work, an original one, and fortunately he was not my student, because we do not agree on some essential issues. So was this givenness of Jean-Luc Marion as a student a gift? That is a problem. I would start with this distinction.

Before we go on to other points, I will try to speak as if there were no supposed knowledge of texts behind the discussion, in order to make things as clear as possible. I refer to what you just recalled. I am not convinced that between the use of *Gegebenheit* in phenomenology and the problem we're about to discuss, that is, the gift, there is a semantic continuity. I am not sure that when, of course, Husserl refers, extensively and constantly, to what is given to intuition, this given-ness, this *Gegebenheit* has an obvious and intelligible relationship to the gift, to being given as a gift. What we are going to discuss, that is the gift, perhaps is not homogenous with *Gegebenheit*. That is one of the problems with the connection to phenomenology. I will come back to this later on. Now, the way, the mediation or the transition, you made between *Gegebenheit* in phenomenology and the *es gibt* in Heidegger is also problematic to me. The way Heidegger refers to the *Gabe* in the *es gibt* is distinct from intuitive *Gegebenheit*. When Husserl says *Gegebenheit*, and when phenomenologists in the broad sense say *Gegebenheit*, something is given, they refer simply to the passivity of intuition. Something is there. We have, we meet something. It is there, but it is not a gift. So, one of my first questions would be, Are we authorized to go directly from the phenomenological concept of *Gegebenheit*, given-ness, to the problem of the gift that we are about to discuss? Now, what will make the discussion interesting and difficult at the same time, and I hope endless, has to do, not with this disagreement between us, but with a sort of chiasmus. *Etant donné* is a powerful book with a beautiful title. Jean-Luc Marion has a genius for titles. *Dieu sans l'être* was a tour de force as a title. I am not sure that the English translation *God without Being* does justice to what I find very interesting in the title, that is, not only God "without Being" but also God "without being God." Here we address the question of the name, of the name God. We will come upon this question again along our way. *Donum dei*. I will come back to this question. I am interested in Christian theology, of course, although I am totally incompetent. But I know that is the point that we are going to discuss. What is in a name? We are going to discuss the name gift and the name God. And we started to do this last night. What is the chiasmus, if I try to summarize it after having read this powerful book, within the title, which is more easily translated into English, *Being Given*? Is that correct? *Etant donné*: I want to praise what is beautiful in this title: Being as Being Given. I came here to praise Jean-Luc Marion's genius. But then he wants to free the gift and givenness from being, in a way. We will come back to this. The chiasmus that I found in this book would be this, schematically summarized: Jean-Luc summarized in a very fair way what I said about the gift in *Given Time*, about all the aporias, the impossibilities. As soon as a gift—not a *Gegebenheit*, but a gift—as soon as a gift is identified as a gift, with the meaning of a gift, then it is canceled as a gift. It is reintroduced into the circle of an exchange and destroyed as a gift. As soon as the donee knows it is a gift, he already thanks the donator, and cancels the gift. As soon as the donator is conscious of giving, he himself thanks himself and again cancels the gift by re-inscribing it into a circle, an economic circle. So I want to reconstitute my text here and insist on what looks like an impossibility: for the gift to appear as such while remaining a gift, to appear as such on the side of the donator and on the side of the donee, the receiver, and the impossibility for a gift to be present, to be a being as being present. So I dissociate the gift from the present. Jean-Luc in a very fair way reconstituted this demonstration, but then he says that all these alleged objections or obstacles that I am supposed to have built against the gift, far from blocking the way, so to speak, far from preventing us from having access to the gift or a phenomenology of the gift, in fact, are a sort of springboard for what you try to do as a phenomenologist.

So, up to that point, we agree. Where we disagree, if we do disagree, is that after this stage, Jean-Luc says that I have problematized the gift in the horizon of economy, of ontology and economy, in the circle of exchange, the way Marcel Mauss has done, and we have to free the gift from this horizon of exchange and economy. Here, of course, I would disagree. I did exactly the opposite. I tried to precisely displace the problematic of the gift, to take it out of the circle of economy, of exchange, but *not* to conclude, from the impossibility for the gift to appear as such and to be determined as such, to its absolute impossibility. I said, to be very schematic and brief, that it is impossible for the gift to appear as such. So the gift does not exist as such, if by existence we understand being present and intuitively identified as such. So the gift does not exist and appear as such; it is impossible for the gift to exist and appear as such. But I never concluded that there is no gift. I went on to say that if there is a gift, through this impossibility, it must be the experience of this impossibility, and it should appear as impossible. The event called gift is totally heterogeneous to theoretical identification, to phenomenological identification. That is a point of disagreement. The gift is totally foreign to the horizon of economy, ontology, knowledge, constantive statements, and theoretical determination and judgment. But in doing so, I did not intend to simply give up the task of accounting for the gift, for what one calls gift, not only in economy but even in Christian discourse. In *The Gift of Death*, I try to show the economy at work, the economic axiomatic at work, in some Christian texts. So I try to account for this and to say that this so-called circle, this economic circle, in order to circulate, in order to be put in motion, must correspond to a move-ment, a motion, a desire—whatever the name—a thought of the gift, which would not be exhausted by a phenomenological determination, by a theoreti-cal determination, by a scientific determination, by an economy. I would like this discussion not to be disagreement, and not to be too easily consensual, of course, but not to be polemical. I would like us to try to find some new opening. I would suggest that what this question of the gift compels us to do, perhaps, is to re-activate, while displacing, the famous distinction that Kant made between knowing and thinking, for instance. The gift, I would claim, I would argue, as such cannot be known; as soon as you know it, you destroy it. So the gift as such is impossible. I insist on the "as such." I will explain why in a moment. The gift as such cannot be known, but it can be thought of. We can think what we cannot know. Perhaps thinking is not the right word. But there is something in excess of knowledge. We have a relation to the gift beyond the circle, the economic circle, and beyond the theoretical and phenomenologi-cal determination. It is this thinking, this excess, which interests me. It is this excess which puts the circle into motion. Why is there economy? Why is there exchange, in Marcel Mauss's sense? Why are there return gifts with delay? Where does this circle come from? I never said—that is a misunderstanding which happens all the time in France—I never said that there is no gift. No. I said exactly the opposite. What are the conditions for us to say there is a gift, if we cannot determine it theoretically, phenomenologically? It is through the experience of the impossibility; that its possibility is possible as impossible. I will come back to that.

A second distinction, and I will stop here, is available now through this question of the gift as a living thread. It is not only the distinction between knowing and thinking, but the distinction between knowing and doing, or the distinction between knowing and an event. An event as such, as well as the gift, cannot be known as an event, as a present event, and for the very same reason. So here is another place for the distinction between knowing and doing. A gift is something you do without knowing what you do, without knowing who gives the gift, who receives the gift, and so on.

Now, just a last statement, about phenomenology, of course. The virtual disagreement between us has to do with the fact that Jean-Luc Marion, after having left me on the curbstone, after having summarized me, says "he thinks the gift in the horizon of economy." That, I would say, is wrong. So Marion would try to account phenomenologically for the gift (which, again, I distin-guish from *Gegebenheit*). But I doubt that there is a possibility of a phenom-enology of the gift. That is exactly my thesis. Perhaps I am wrong, but if what I say is not totally meaningless, what is precisely challenged is the possibility of a phenomenology of the gift. I understand that Jean-Luc Marion, of course, has his own concept of phenomenology. But he cannot practice any phenom-enology without at least keeping some axioms of what is called phenomenol-ogy—the phenomenon, the phenomenality, the appearance, the meaning, intuition, if not intuition, at least the promise of the intuition, and so on. I do not say this against phenomenology. I do not say this even against religion or even against *donum Dei*. I try to think the possibility of this impossibility and also to think the possibility of *donum Dei*, or the possibility of phenomenology, but from a place which is not inside what I try to account for. I will stop here now.

**Kearney.** Thank you. Could I just try to put what Jacques has just said to you, Jean-Luc, in terms of two quick points? First, Jacques has pointed to a virtual disagreement between you on the interpretation of the phenomenology of the gift, and perhaps you might like to say something—but not too much, I hope—about that. Second, I suggest we push this virtual disagreement on the *phenomenology* of the gift towards a greater potential disagreement between you on the *theology* of the gift. Is there a Christian philosophy of the gift?

**Marion.** First, quickly, on the technical questions, I disagree with you on the point that givenness, *Gegebenheit*, would be restricted for Husserl to intuition. I would quote some texts and I stick to that. For him, even significations are given, without intuition. He assumes openly a "logical givenness."[2]

**Derrida.** You know, I would agree with you. The point was, what is the gift?

**Marion.** This is a good point, and I emphasize it, because Paul Ricoeur asked me the same question and raised the same objection which I myself would sum up as such: Between the givenness, if any, in the phenomenological meaning of the word, and the gift, there is nothing but pure equivocity. I tried to demonstrate the contrary, because to assume this so-called equivocity as a starting point proves to impoverish both the question of the gift and that of givenness. Let me explain. I think of the gift as a kind of issue reaching to the most extreme limits, that should be described and be thought and neither explained nor comprehended, but simply thought—in a very radical way. I suggest that, in order to achieve description, if any is possible, of the gift, we can be led to open for the first time a new horizon, much wider than those of objectivity and being, the horizon of givenness. Through the issue of the gift, and we shall go back precisely to that issue, we may perhaps establish that a lot of phenomena immediately can be explained according to the pattern of the gift—the problem otherwise raised by Mauss and others. In fact, this is by no means a particular problem on the border of the mainstream, for through this problem a large number of other phenomena suddenly appear as gifts or as given themselves, even though previously we had no idea that they could turn out as given. So givenness perhaps opens the secret, the final result and the potentially lost analysis of the gift. I would disagree on that point with Paul Ricoeur and with Jacques Derrida, too.

But, now back to the issue of the gift itself. I said that the failure to explain the gift was due to the fact that the analysis remained in the horizon of the economy, and I concluded that the horizon of the economy makes the gift impossible, but in that case I was not referring to you. I think I never said that *you* thought that the gift was impossible. As you are suggesting right now, I too think that if we want to go on with the issue of the gift, we have to give up the hope of any explanation, that is, of any comprehension of it as an object. But you would add further—to give up any description, too. For myself, I assume that we can describe the gift, notwithstanding all its obvious and prima facie inescapable aporias according to economy. I disagree with you on some other points, but we share a common conviction: We cannot explain, and we have no access to the gift, so long as we keep it within the horizon of economy. This has been demonstrated for me and is taken for granted. Nevertheless, another question has to be asked: Is it possible to describe the gift, taking seriously the aporias on which we agree? If it proves to be possible, this is simply phenomenology, because phenomenology first of all means to see and to describe the phenomena. So, as long as such a description is possible, I think that we have to say that we remain in the field of phenomenology. So, how is it possible to describe the gift as a phenomenon? My demonstration—and I sum it up because it looks after all, very simple—amounts to saying that, even though the most abstract and common pattern of the gift implies a giver, an object to be given, and a receiver, you can nevertheless describe the gift, I would say the enacted phenomenon, the performative of the gift, by bracketing and putting aside, at least one and even from time to time two of those three features of the gift. And this is new: It makes clear that the gift is governed by rules that are completely different from those that are applied to the object or to the being.

First, for instance, you can perfectly well describe a fully achieved or given gift without implying any receiver. For example, if you give something to your enemy; this is given up and you will get nobody to receive it. So you have achieved an anonymous gift. And, as we give money to a humanitarian association, we do make a gift, a real gift, that is money, but that gift will go to nobody, at least nobody personally known by us. Nevertheless we have achieved a gift. We can even imagine—and here a religious description of the gift may take place—for instance, that one does not know now to whom one gives the gift. An example of such a situation can be found by Christ in the eschatological parables; when some have given something to poor people, in fact they have given it to Christ; but, until the end of the world, they have not been able ever to imagine that this was given directly to Christ. So, they gave their gift to an anonymous receiver, or even the really absent receiver. In my case, the eschatological status of the receiver makes it that we never meet him in this world. This absence of the receiver does not forbid describing the gift, but to some extent this absence allows the gift to appear as such. A gracious gift appears precisely because there is no response, no answer, no gratitude back, all of which is obvious because we can give without any receiver. You can imagine also a gift without any giver, which would nevertheless be absolutely achieved. Take the example of an inheritance, where the giver is by hypothesis no longer here, and perhaps has never met, never known the receiver. And more: Why not imagine the case where we do not know if there is any giver at all? This is very well described in *Robinson Crusoe*, where he finds something on the sand, on the beach, a tool, for instance, something like that. He asked himself, is that given or not? Is there any giver at all—or mere good luck? And to that question, there is no plain answer. But the question has first to be raised and this is the important point. It is within the horizon of such absences that the possible phenomenon of the gift may appear, if it appears. So, of course, the absence of the giver does not simply imply that there is a giver. But it implies that we may *ask* that question, Is there a giver? which already opens us into the horizon of givenness. We could easily find other examples.

Let us now go quickly to the last point, the most striking in my opinion: We can describe a gift in a situation where nothing, no-thing, is given. Because we do know cases where no *thing* is given: When we give time, when we give our life, when we give death, properly and strictly speaking, we give no *thing*. Just consider this: When somebody is given power, for instance, when President Clinton was inaugurated as President of the United States of America, has he received anything? No, nothing, except perhaps for a sheet of paper, a hand-shake, or the secret number for some military advice.

*Kearney.* Could I intervene for just a moment on this, because we've only got about an hour left. You've given a number of examples, and very useful ones, President Clinton, *Robinson Crusoe*, the Scriptures. But I would like to suggest that in your analysis of the phenomenology of the gift as donation, there is a privileged example, a "highest" example, of the saturated phenomenon, and that is revelation.

*Marion.* I shall try to answer you. Indeed, I think that it is possible to describe, in the horizon of the phenomenology of givenness, what I would call the empty and just possible figure of revelation, which makes sense as a possibility within phenomenology. I suggest that revelation—of course, for me, the revelation of Christ, but also any kind of revelation, if there are other claims to revelation—can acquire phenomenological status and match other kinds of phenomena. In that precise sense, the distinction between the field of philosophy and the field of theology, the "limits" between them in the meanings of Kant and Fichte, could be bridged to some extent. Let us go on, using my former example. The gift does not always imply that something is given. Now this remains true, not only in daily life, but in the most important and meaningful experiences of human life. We know that, to some extent, if the gift is really unique, makes a real difference, cannot be repeated, then in such a case, the gift does *not* appear as something that could shift from one owner to another owner. Each genuine gift happens without any objective counterpart. When we give ourselves, our life, our time, when we give our word, not only do we give no *thing*, but we give much more. Here is my point: We can describe the gift outside of the horizon of economy in such a way that new phenomenological rules appear. For instance, the gift or the given phenomenon has no cause and does not need any. It would sound absurd to ask what is the cause of the gift, precisely because givenness implies the unexpected, the unforeseeable and the pure surge of novelty. And also the gift cannot be repeated as *the* same gift. So we discover with the gift, and to let it display its visibility according to its own logic, we have an experience of a kind of phenomenon that cannot be described anymore as an object or as a being. Here is the reason why, if I agree with Derrida to go beyond economy, I disagree with him on another point: This description of the gift can be made, but only in a very particular way. For we cannot make this description, which brackets one or perhaps two of the elements of the so-called economical gift, if we have not previously, in pragmatic experience, enacted by ourselves a gift without a receiver, or a gift without a giver, or a gift without anything given. And indeed this is not a neutral description: We have to commit ourselves by achieving the gift by ourselves, in such a way that we become able to describe it. But, nevertheless, I think that this description goes far beyond that of the gift by Marcel Mauss. The gift, that is, the phenomenon as given, is also, I would say, a dimension of the experience of the world including the possibility of revelation too.

*Kearney.* If we could pick up on the last sentence, where Jean-Luc finally touches on the connection between the phenomenology of the gift and the revealed word. I appreciate that one has to come at these things tangentially, obliquely and piecemeal, but given the limits of time and given that this is not, strictly speaking, a phenomenology seminar on givenness but a conference on religion and postmodernity, do you think, Jacques, that it *is* possible to conduct a phenomenology of *religious* donation? Is it possible, to quote Jean-Luc Marion in "Metaphysics and Theology," "to have a rational thought of God which philosophy cannot forget without losing its dignity or its mere possibility"?

*Derrida.* But by asking me this question, you are recontextualizing and authorizing me to go backwards, not to start from the last sentence, his last sentence or your last sentence. I will try not to avoid your question, but I would like to come back to something.

*Kearney.* I give up!

*Derrida.* No, no. But we do not want to be too framed. The reference to the gift which gives nothing is exactly something I thematized. Now, as to phenomenology, I will try to answer the question. Since you agree that the gift, according to the logic which is virtually at work in the name gift (I will come back to the name), does not imply necessarily the presence of a receiver, the presence of a giver, or of a given thing, then my question is this: What would be the theme of such a phenomenology? What would phenomenological analysis describe if not the experience of the giver, the experience of the receiver, the thing which is presently given, or the intention? As you know, phenomenological analysis has as its main theme intentional experience. Now if, as one says in English, you "economize on" the intentional experience of giving, what is left for phenomenology? If you do not have the receiver, the donator, or the thing given, what remains for the "as such"? Allow me to quote something you have said at some point after having summarized my problematic. You say that what is left is to give up the economic horizon of exchange in order to interpret the gift *à partir*, starting from, the horizon of donation itself. What remains to be described, you say, is donation, not anymore after what it rejects, but as such, *en tant que telle*. Then you add, with a scruple that I would like you to comment upon—*si une telle en tant que telle convient encore*, if such an as such still fits. That is my question. I think that phenomenology, as well as ontology, as well as philosophy, implies the *als Sturktur*, the as such. Now, if the event of the gift, for me, excludes the presence of the as such—of the giver, of the receiver, of the given thing, of the present thing, and of the intention—then what is left for the "as such?" That is my problem.

*Kearney.* Could I interrupt for just a moment and then we will go on? Could I ask Jean-Luc to comment on that "as such"?

*Marion.* The answer is that of course you cannot describe the gift without all three elements of the gift at the same moment. In that case nothing remains at all and there is neither an *as such* nor any possibility even to question givenness. What I have emphasized is something quite different—that we can at least describe a phenomenon with two of the elements, not with the three. Thus a gift could still achieve itself with a gift, a receiver, but without any giver; or, in another solution, with a giver, a gift, but no receiver; or, in a third figure, with a giver, a receiver but no *thing* which is given. And if we know all three terms, there is no question. So what raises my interest is that we can always give up at least one of them and perhaps two, and nevertheless keep a genuine and thorough phenomenon. Even in the most abstract cases, the interest of such a description lies in our getting something which can still be described although it does not amount to an object and not a being either. Previously you asked me the question why I have added the "as such": I can tell you that I have added the as such because I was thinking exactly of you and your terrible critics. But, it was why I have added, "if such an 'as such' still fits givenness."

*Derrida.* Thank you. It is a gift.

*Marion.* The final answer could be that as the "gift" remains equivocal, that is, has two different structures, so it is possible that there could be no "as such" in that case, and it is perhaps necessary. Because in a situation which is precisely a shift within the definition of the phenomenon, when something is given or received without any cause, in that case, the exigencies for a phenomenological sense of the as such, in Heidegger's *Sein und Zeit*, cannot be satisfied anymore. So I think that there is no "as such" in our case. But it is not so easy to reach a place which you can describe as free of any "as such."

*Derrida.* Of course. That is exactly my problem. I think what you describe . . .

*Marion.* There is no "as such" in a structure which is by definition open, not closed, which admits no cause, no repetition, and so on, which cannot appear but as an event. As the late François Furet said,[3] *en passant*, where he described the starting moment of the World War I, by this absolutely magnificent statement, *"Plus un événement est lourd de conséquences, moin il est possbile de le penser à partir de causes."* I would add that even any sort of historical event never has any exclusive sufficient cause. I think that when we reach the territory, I would say, of the given phenomenon, described not according to the method of economy, but according to the essential lack of one or perhaps two of the three terms, at that moment we have already gone within the horizon where the event without cause, where something, appears insofar as it is given, as it gives itself.

**Derrida.** The question is whether you can describe the event itself as such phenomenologically. You say it is not easy to reach. That is what I am saying. It is not easy to think the gift and to describe the gift. But what you describe phenomenologically, when, even if there is a giver without a receiver at the same time and so on, what you are describing under the authority of the phenomenological as such, is precisely the process of the destruction of the gift.

**Marion.** I do not recognize the "as such" as mine. What I have said, precisely in that horizon, is that the question of the claim to the "as such" has no right to be made.

**Derrida.** Then would you dissociate what you call phenomenology from the authority of the as such? If you do that, it would be the first heresy in phenomenology. Phenomenology without as such!

**Marion.** Not my first, no! I said to Levinas some years ago that in fact the last step for a real phenomenology would be to give up the concept of horizon. Levinas answered me immediately: "Without horizon there is no phenomenology." And I boldly assume he was wrong.

**Derrida.** I am also for the suspension of the horizon, but, for that very reason, by saying so, I am not a phenomenologist anymore. I am very true to phenomenology, but when I agree on the necessity of suspending the horizon, then I am no longer a phenomenologist. So the problem remains if you give up the as such, what is the use that you can make of the word phenomenology? That is the problem for me. I would like not to forget Richard's question about revelation. I want to speak not about what I am doing but about what you are doing. My hypothesis concerns the fact that you use or credit the word *Gegebenheit* with gift, with the meaning of gift, and this has to do with—I will not call this theological or religious—the deepest ambition of your thought. For you, everything that is given in the phenomenological sense, *gegeben, donné, Gegebenheit,* everything that is given to us in perception, in memory, in a phenomenological perception, is finally a gift to a finite creature, and it is finally a gift of God. That is the condition for you to redefine *Gegebenheit* as a gift. This is, at least, a hypothesis and a question to you. The logic of *Etant donné,* finally, to me, is to reinterpret as a gift everything that a phenomenologist—or anyone, a scientist—says is given, is a given, a fact, something that we meet in perception, given to my intuition. I perceive this; it is a given. I did not produce this. I did not create this, which is what Kant would call *intuitus derivativus*. The finite subject does not create its object, it receives it, receptively. Receptivity is interpreted as precisely the situation of the created being, the creature, which receives everything in the world as something created. So it is a gift. Everything is a gift. Is that not the condition for the extraordinary extension that you propose of *Gegebenheit* and of the category of the gift? Just one more thing. I would like to come back at some point to the question of the event, and the reason why I am interested in the gift.

Finally, we have the word gift in our culture. We received it; it functions in the Western lexicon, Western culture, in religion, in economics, and so on. I try to struggle with the aporias which are located in this heritage. I try to account for this difference between knowing and thinking that I was referring to a moment ago. But at some point I am ready to give up the word. Since this word finally is self-contradictory, I am ready to give up this word at some point. I would simply like to understand what the event of the gift and the event in general is. I try in *Given Time* and in other texts to account for, to interpret, the anthropo-theological reappropriation of the meaning of the gift as the meaning of the event on the groundless ground of what I call *khora*, the groundless ground of a "there is," "it takes place," the place of the taking place, which is prior to and totally indifferent to this anthropo-theologization, this history of religions and of revelations. I do not say this against revelation, against religion. I say that without the indifferent, non-giving structure of the space of the *khora*, of what makes place for taking place, without this totally indifferent space which does not *give* place to what *takes* place, there would not be this extraordinary movement or desire for giving, for receiving, for appropriating, for *Ereignis* as event and appropriation. That is why religion is interesting to me. I do not say anything against it, but I try to go back to a place or a taking place where the event as a process of reappropriation of an impossible gift becomes possible. One last word on this point, because it is a question of the event, no doubt. It is a question of the name, the noun, God, gift, and a question of what happens. I would say in French, *arrive*, comes, arrives, happens. I agree with what you said about the happening, the event, but at some point, although I agree with the fact that the event must be unique, singular, as well as that the comer, the newcomer must be unique, singular, and so on, I am not sure that I would subscribe to what you said about what should not be repeated. I would associate the singularity of the gift as an event with the necessity for it or the promise for it to be repeated. When I give something to someone, in the classical semantic of the gift—be it money, a book, or be it simply a promise or a word—I already promise to confirm it, to repeat it, even if I do not repeat it. The repetition is part of the singularity. That is what makes the event, the structure of the event, so difficult to describe, because it is at the same time absolutely singular and unique while carrying in itself the promise of repetition. It is in this promise that all the questions we are discussing get complicated.

*Kearney.* Would you not say, Jean-Luc, that you part company with Jacques Derrida on the route to the *khora*?

*Marion.* On the last part, no.

*Kearney.* Not on the point of the event per se, but on the relationship between the event and revelation. Jacques seems to go towards the *khora* and you seem to go towards *revelation*.

*Marion.* Not necessarily. I disagree with his interpretation of what I am supposed to say about the relation of gift and givenness. This is a point where we really disagree. As Derrida said, he is not interested in the gift as such but in the profound structure of something which from time to time may be named the gift and appears as possible. On the contrary, I say that we have to go back from the gift to givenness, and there is such a way to reach it. But, to be brief, the event is unique and cannot be repeated, and for Derrida it is unique, but has to be repeated. I agree. It has to be repeated, of course. For instance, I give my word, I have to repeat it and go on; but I cannot repeat it as an identical act; the repetition is never identical (just refer to Kierkegaard, Heidegger, or even Deleuze). As to the question of whether what I am doing, or what Derrida is doing, is within phenomenology or beyond, it does not seem to me very important. Let me just quote here a famous sentence of Heidegger, "We are not interested in phenomenology, but in the things phenomenology is interested in." Whether *Etant donné* is still phenomenology we shall see ten years later. But now it is not very important. I claim that I am still faithful to phenomenology and I guess that you are more inside the field of phenomenology than you admit. But this will be an issue, if any, for our successors.

*Kearney.* It is easier to get Unionists and Nationalists in Ulster to talk about peace than it is to get you two to talk about God! We have less than half an hour left. I want to put a straight question to you both. I think that these issues of the phenomenology of givenness and of the event are absolutely crucial and indispensable, and it is a great privilege for us to hear you address them. I know that they are basic work for getting on to higher things. But I want to rush you a little now towards those "higher things" and pursue the relationship between gift and grace, which you touched on, Jean-Luc, in the conclusion to your talk the other night on negative theology. In the last paragraphs of that talk, you spoke about (1) a difference between deconstruction and your view of negative theology and (2) a "third way" that it opens up. One of the phrases that you used was, "if there is not an intuition of grace, or of revelation, of some kind, if there is not an intuition of this exemplary hyper-essential saturated phenomenon, then there is no difference between negative theology and deconstruction." You seemed be holding out for some kind of distance between the two positions. What is it and how do you defend it?

*Marion.* I think that the difference between negative theology in my way of thinking and deconstruction, at least as it is currently accepted, which is not necessarily the view of Derrida, is this: In negative theology the difficulty is not that we lack intuitions concerning God (we are overwhelmed by them), but that we lack concepts fitting God. What we share in common, Derrida and myself, is that the concepts have to be criticized even in theology, as they are deconstructed in deconstruction. But it is for opposite reasons. In theology — and I am *not* referring now to my work on givenness — we receive an amount of experiences through prayer, liturgy, life in the community, fraternity, etc. The difficulty lies in that we have an utmost experience without the words, the significations, and the concepts able to utter it, to explain it, and to articulate it. One of the best examples, for instance, and I do refer here to theology, may be found in the transfiguration of Christ. The disciples witness the transfiguration and they say nothing but "Let us make three tabernacles. For he [Peter] knew not what to say" (Mark 9:5–6). The gospel emphasizes that they say that because they have nothing more to say; that is, no concept matching their intuitions. Or let us add the example of the disciples on the road to Emmaus, listening to Christ explaining, in what should have been an outstanding lesson of exegesis, all the Scriptures referring to him, but making no mention of his name, all the while remaining anonymous. After they have recognized Christ, they say, we remember that "our hearts burn[ed] within us, while he talked with us" (Luke 24:32). That is to say, the experience was so intense that they were overwhelmed and that no concept could grasp anything of that experience. In philosophical language, there was an excess of intuition over the concept or the signification. So, we have deconstruction in that sense, that the most fundamental concepts of theology before Christ — Son of God, Messiah, Isaiah, Elijah, the prophet, and so on — all these concepts which nevertheless remain meaningful for us in theology now, were rejected as meaningless, not because they were criticized as such, but because they were devaluated by the excess of intuition. This is the very special situation in the so-called negative theology. This is also the reason why it is not a good choice of words to describe it as "negative theology" — as it seems much more an excessively positive theology. Concepts are negative and, by the way, put out of play only because they do not match the excess of intuition. This is the reason why in theology, in fact, pluralism is implied in the very notion of revelation. If there is a real revelation, no concept could achieve to say and to make intelligible in its own way the excess of intuition. Pluralism is implied at the inner core of revelation. There are four gospels and an infinite number of spiritualities within the same experience of the Church. I conclude that deconstruction and the so-called negative theology have something very much in common; that is, the fact that no concept is able to give us the presence of what is at stake, and that presence not only is impossible but cannot be claimed. If there could be any revelation, I would say that no heart, no mind, and no word would be wide enough to host that revelation. The presence of any self-revealed event remains impossible in our world. That is the reason why Christ has to come again — because now we could not receive him yet, nor have enough room for him (John 1:10–11).

So let us sum it up: Deconstruction and mystical theology — I definitely prefer to speak of mystical theology rather than of negative theology—share the same conviction, that we have no concept, therefore that we never reach such a thing as the presence of meaning, of signification, of science. But in mystical theology, this fails always by an excess. I do not want to claim that deconstruction is opposed to all this, but I assume that deconstruction cannot say it deconstructs because of an excess of the gift. But clearly mystical theology has to claim that it is because of an excess of intuition that there could never be such a thing as a final and unified theology.

May I make a last point in answer to a question of Jacques Derrida: I am not trying to reduce every phenomenon to a gift and then to say that, after that, since this is a gift, and given to a finite mind, then there is perhaps a giver behind it all. This was said by many critics, unable or unwilling to understand my project. My project attempts, on the contrary, to reduce the gift to givenness, and to establish the phenomenon as given.

**Derrida.** Now, if you . . .

**Marion.** No, please, let me go on. I really think that this point has to be emphasized and its misunderstanding worries me more than I dare say. In *Reduction and Givenness*, but more at length in *Etant donné*, I made it my goal to establish that givenness remains an immanent structure of any kind of phenomenality, whether immanent or transcendent. We can imagine and say that something is given and appears as given without referring it to another thing or being or object that would be the cause of its givenness. It is very important to understand that you can describe a phenomenon as given without asking any question about the giver. And in most of the cases, there is absolutely no giver at all. I am not interested in assigning a giver to a given phenomenon. I am interested in saying that our deepest and most genuine experience of the phenomenon does not deal with any object that we could master, produce, or constitute, no more than with any being which belongs to the horizon of Being, where onto-theology is possible, and where God can for the first time and in the first place play the role of the first cause. Rather, there are many situations where phenomena appear as given, that is, without any cause or giver. When they appear to us as given, of course, we have to receive them, but this does not imply that we should claim God as the cause of what we receive. Notice that in philosophy and phenomenology we have already the experience that subjectivity is not the actor, but the receiver, so that such an original passivity of subjectivity is a way, I think a radical way, to deconstruct the transcendental ambition of the ego. So, I suggest that my proposal remains merely philosophical and without any theological presupposition or bias here. On the contrary, any theological bias and second thought would ruin my project and it is perhaps that some do their best to put by force such bias into my work. I think the difficulty for phenomenology now is to become more fair to some phenomena which cannot be described either as object or as being. We all try to make sense out of those phenomena—the gift, the *khora*, the other, the flesh and others that we cannot describe either as an object or as being. So, my hypothesis as a phenomenologist is that we should not try to constitute them, but accept them—in any sense of accept—as given and that is all.

*Kearney.* Jacques, do you think that brings Jean-Luc Marion closer to your position or further away?

*Derrida.* It is difficult for me to understand how to describe something not as an object; as something other than an object, and to claim that we are still doing phenomenology. What I was interested in with this problem of the gift, among other things, was precisely to check the limits and possibility of phenomenology. It is difficult for me to understand how an excess of intuition can be described phenomenologically. If deconstruction—I do not want to use this word and to speak as if I were speaking deconstruction—is interested in the excess I was mentioning a moment ago, in some excess, it is not an excess of intuition, of phenomenality, of fullness, of more than fullness. The excess, the structure, in which I am interested, is not an excess of intuition. When you say, for instance, protesting against my prior hypothesis about the reason why you interpret everything, every *Gegebenheit* as gift . . .

*Marion.* Every gift as *Gegebenheit*.

*Derrida.* You said the immanent structure of phenomenality is *Gegebenheit*. There are two hypotheses. Either you equate *Gegebenheit* with gift and then that is my hypothesis: Everything is a gift, a gift from God, from whomever. Or you dissociate or mark a gap between a *Gegebenheit* and a gift; then you cannot transfer your point on *Gegebenheit* to the problem of a gift. But if you say the immanent structure of phenomenality is *Gegebenheit*, and if by *Gegebenheit* you refer to something given, to some common root, then every phenomenon is a gift. Even if you do not determine the giver as God, it is a gift. I am not sure that this is reconcilable or congruent with what I know under the name of phenomenology.

*Marion.* But why?

*Derrida.* Because what I understand as phenomenology, the principle of all principles, which you have recalled here, implies finally intuition, that is, the fullness of the intuition, the presence of something. When there is a gap between intuition and intention, there is a crisis, there is a symbolic structure. But the principle of all principles is intuition. If you agree, as I think you agree, about the impossibility of equating the gift to a present, then you cannot define every phenomenon as a gift. That is what puzzles me.

I wanted to make another point referring to your book. At some point you refer to something I say, in translation, "Let us go to the limit." I am smiling at some of the typos in your book, in which my book *Donner le temps* is transformed a number of times into *Penser le temps*.[4] That is interesting. Allow me to quote myself, "Let us go to the limit. The truth of the gift . . . suffices to annul the gift. The truth of the gift is equivalent to the non-gift or the non-truth of the gift" (*Given Time*, 27). That is what I say, then you comment, in a long footnote:

> Formally, one could distinguish two meanings in this formula. a) If "or" has conjunctive value, one obtains "non-gift" = "non-truth," then, by canceling the double negation, "gift = truth." b) If "or" has disjunctive value, one will have "non-truth" or "non-gift," hence, "either gift or truth." Thus the formula is able to be understood either as an equivalence between gift and truth, or as their mutual exclusion. If one had to choose, Jacques Derrida would probably hold for the second interpretation; and we would do the same, while the first remains conceivable. But the strange thing is elsewhere, that, in both cases, the gift keeps a privileged relation to the truth."
> (*Etant donné*, 117 n.1)

I would say that, in fact, if I had to choose, it would not be so simple. When I say, "the truth of the gift is equivalent to the non-gift or the non-truth of the gift," I am referring to a traditional concept of truth, that is, an ontological-phenomenological concept of truth, as revelation or unveiling or adequation. From that point of view, I would say that there is no truth of the gift, but I do not give up truth in general. I am looking for another possible experience of truth, through the event of the gift, with all these conditions of impossibility. What I am interested in—and I often repeat that the deconstruction I try to practice is impossible, is *the* impossible—is precisely this experience of *the* impossible. This is not simply an impossible experience. The experience of *the* impossible. What happens in the experience of *the* impossible, which would not be simply a non-experience. That is what I try to do. What does the word "possible" mean? At some point, when I said that the conditions of possibility are conditions of impossibility, you replied that this is not enough and you criticized my use of the word "condition." But I am interested in precisely in thinking otherwise about the concept of condition and the concept of possibility or impossibility. I will refer here to what Richard Kearney has said about "possibility" in theology, where *Möglichkeit* does not simply mean possible or real as opposed to impossible. But in German, in A *Letter on Humanism*, Heidegger uses *mögen* as desire. What I am interested in is the experience of the desire for the impossible. That is, the impossible as the condition of desire. Desire is not perhaps the best word. I mean this quest in which we want to give, even when we realize, when we agree, if we agree, that the gift, that giving, is impossible, that it is a process of reappropriation and self-destruction. Nevertheless, we do not give up the dream of the pure gift, in the same way that we do not give up the idea of pure hospitality. Even if we know it is impossible and that it can be perverse, which is what we said the other night. If we try to draw a politics of hospitality from the dream of unconditional hospitality, not only will that be impossible but it will have perverse consequences. So despite this perversion, despite this impossibility, we go on dreaming or thinking of pure hospitality, of pure gift, having given up the idea of the subject, of a subject-giver and a subject-receiver, and of thing given, object given. We continue to desire, to dream, *through* the impossible. The impossible for me is not a negative concept. That is why I would like, in order not simply to give up the idea of truth, to measure it or to proportion it to this problematic of the impossible.

Now let us go back to the problem of revelation, since Richard Kearney wants us to speak about religion.

**Richard Kearney.** *Enfin!*

**Jacques Derrida.** What I really do not know, and I confess I do not know, is whether what I am analyzing or trying to think is prior to my own culture, our own culture, that is, to the Judeo-Christian, Greek heritage of the gift. If I am interested in the *khora*, I am trying to reach a structure which is not the *khora* as interpreted by Plato, but by myself against Plato. I do not know if this structure is really prior to what comes under the name of revealed religion or even of philosophy, or whether it is through philosophy or the revealed religions, the religions of the book, or any other experience of revelation, that retrospectively we think what I try to think. I must confess, I cannot make the choice between these two hypotheses. Translated into Heidegger's discourse, which is addressing the same difficulty, this is the distinction between *Offenbarung* and *Offenbarkeit*, revelation and revealability. Heidegger said, this is his position, that there would be no revelation or *Offenbarung* without the prior structure of *Offenbarkeit*, without the possibility of revelation and the possibility of manifestation. That is Heidegger's position. I am not sure. Perhaps it is through *Offenbarung* that *Offenbarkeit* becomes thinkable, historically. That is why I am constantly really hesitating. That is part of—what can I call this here?—let us say, my cross. Since it is impossible for me to choose between these two hypotheses, my last hypothesis is that the question is not well posed, that we should displace the question, not to have an answer, but to think otherwise the possibility of these two possibilities.

**Kearney.** This will be our last question because the time is short. I would like to pick up on what Jacques said earlier and put a question to you, Jean-Luc. On the whole issue of *thinking religion*, Jacques invoked the Kantian distinction between *thinking* and *knowing* in relation to the gift and by implication to the desire of God, which we spoke of two days ago, which opens on to the "impossible." He implied that even if we cannot *know* these things, because we reach a limit, we still should *think* them. Arguably, that is what his thought about the messianic is and what he has just said about revelation. Even though it is an apocalypse without apocalypse, a messianicity without messianism, a religion without religion, without vision, without truth, without revelation, it is still a *mode of thinking*. Now what I would like to ask you, finally, Jean-Luc, is this: Surely you go some way along the same path, you share that same crux. In the conclusion to your negative theology paper the other night, you talked about an encounter with revelation which fills us with incomprehensibility, which infuses us with terror and stupor. There seems to be there, too, an encounter with what we might call the "monstrous," the utterly other, that fills us with fear and trembling, the *mysterium fascinans*. What, for you, is the religious thinking that is appropriate to that particular limit? You speak, as I mentioned earlier, about "a rational thought of God which philosophy cannot forget without losing its dignity or even its possibility." What would you say, in conclusion, that might help us get more of a fix on the religious nature of such thinking?

*Marion.* As Jacques Derrida just said, the question now is to think impossibility, *the* impossible as such. That was exactly my point in *Etant donné* and I shall try to make it right here. One may sum up modern philosophy by saying it was, and perhaps it still is, a transcendental enterprise by which something is taken for granted a priori, which is the I, ego, subjectivity, in order, starting from it, to establish the limits of the possible, of any kind of possibility. To think amounts to foreseeing the possible, and to construct objects within the horizon of the possible. The result, as is well known, is that some effective experiences cannot be reconstructed within the limits of the possible. In a transcendental philosophy, the question of revelation is always looked on as a question of its impossibility, or at least partial impossibility, within the limits of reason alone — according to the title of books by Kant and Fichte, which inquire into the "limits of any possible revelation." As pointed out, Heidegger, and also Hegel, make a distinction between *Offenbarung* (revelation) and what is supposed to be understood and revealed within the revelation, within *Offenbarkeit*. In the end, only within the limits of the concept does it become possible for the impossible to come to thought. I think that what we can glimpse here and aim at may still be called phenomenology, and implies a complete reverse of the former situation. That is to say, we now admit that we do have an experience of the impossible. The definition of such an impossible can no more arise within metaphysics. In metaphysics, the impossible simply contradicts the possible, which already known and has, afterwards, to be fulfilled or not. But the impossible now is no longer what cannot be thought, but whose fact has to be thought. So the question is, how is it possible to remain rational and to have a discourse dealing with the impossible? There are different strategies. We may first distinguish between a strong intelligibility and a weak intelligibility. We may also say that we should face what I call the excess of intuition or, more exactly, the excess of the given, which achieves a kind of impossibility. More generally, we have to ask ourselves, how it is that we say that something may seem impossible (that is, contradict the a priori conditions of experience) and nevertheless could happen as an event, which takes place within our experience? To think it, we have to deconstruct, first, all the concepts according to which the effective experience is supposed to appear from time to time impossible and irrational. That is the first step. We have to deconstruct or criticize our concepts, even in philosophy, perhaps more than ever in philosophy. At that point, mystical theology and philosophy agree with deconstruction. We all were at least once led to describe a real situation in which we were confronted with excess, what was both impossible and nevertheless effective. To achieve this, we have to take seriously the fact that we cannot have an experience of the impossible in the same way that we have an experience of the possible. To have an experience of the impossible means to have an experience of impossibility prima facie, which I call the "counter-experience" of be-dazzlement, of astonishment or *Bewunderung*. This counter-experience has to do with the fact that we can see, but cannot designate as an object or a being, an event that we cannot comprehend but nevertheless we have to see. This counter-experience is, in fact, the correct and consistent kind of experience appropriate to every decisive evidence in our life—death, birth, love, poverty, illness, joy, pleasure, and so on. We see them but we know our inability to see them in a clear manner; and nevertheless, these impossible and unintelligible evidences play the most important role for us. So, if we cannot, at the moment, reach a conceptual definition of those evidences, of those phenomena, then we have to take the counter-experience seriously, which exemplifies our not being able to reduce them to objectivity, which result, I think, is from time to time the only one we can hope to achieve. Such a counter-experience of the impossible is not nothing, but a new kind of modality. As Jacques Derrida explains it very well, if the possible, in this moment of philosophy, that is, after the end of metaphysics, is precisely the experience of the impossible, then the only rationality able to match the impossible as such will be the experience of the counter-experience. We take seriously the fact that our experience, the more that it is decisive and unquestionable, de facto, nevertheless cannot be an experience of objectivation. To know without knowing in the mode of objec-tivation, it is *incomprehensibiliter comprehendere incomprehensibile*, as Augus-tine said. But this comprehension of and by the incomprehensible is not nothing. In fact, we already have this kind of counter-experience when we deal with an historical event, a painting, the self-affection of the flesh, and the experience of the other. All those are experiences of the impossible which I call paradoxes and we cannot make sense of them in an objective way. Never-theless, we have those experiences. The incomprehensible, the excess, the impossible, are part and parcel of our experience. We have to learn how to get a concept of experience which should not and will not be univocal again.

*Kearney.* Thank you, Jean-Luc. A final word from Jacques Derrida.

*Derrida.* Just one more word about phenomenology, because this is the point. When Levinas refers to the excess of the infinitely other, he says that the other, the face, precisely does not appear as such. He says many times that he wants to find within phenomenology the injunction to go beyond phenom-enology. There are many places where he says that we have to go phenomeno-logically beyond phenomenology. That is what I am trying to do, also. I remain and I want to remain a rationalist, a phenomenologist.

*Marion.* You are!

*Derrida.* A man of the Enlightenment, and so on and so forth. I would like to remain phenomenological in what I say against phenomenology. Finally, what leads me in this matter about the non-phenomenality of the gift is also the non-phenomenality of the "other" as such, which is something I learned from Husserl's *Cartesian Meditations*. Husserl says that in the case of the alter

Richard Kearney

ego we cannot have pure intuition, an originary perception of the other; we have to go through appresentation. That is a limit of phenomenology that appears within phenomenology. That is the place where I work also.

One last word. When I referred a moment ago to *Offenbarkeit* and *Offenbarung*, I was sincere but at the same time I am also perplexed. I am also perplexed without a guide in this respect. The discourse of *Offenbarung* and *Offenbarkeit*, in Heidegger or anywhere else in this context, implies the historicity of *Dasein*, of man and God, the historicity of revelation, historicity in the Christian or European sense. My problem is that when I refer to *khora*, I refer to some event, the possibility of taking place, which is not historical, to something non-historical that resists historicity. In other words, there might be something that is excluded by this problematic, however complex it may be, of revelation, of *Offenbarung* and *Offenbarkeit*, whether in Heidegger or out of Heidegger. That is why I refer to what I call the "desert in the desert." There is a biblical desert, there is an historical desert. But what I call a "desert in the desert" is this place which resists historicization, which is, I will not say "before," because that is chronological, but which remains irreducible to historicization, humanization, anthropo-theologization of revelation. This resists even *Offenbarkeit*, which is not revealed and cannot be revealed, not because it is obscure, but because it has nothing to do with the gift, with revelation or with anything we are discussing here. That is what I point to when I refer to *khora*. But this place of resistance, this absolute heterogeneity to philosophy and the Judeo-Christian history of revelation, even to the concept of history, which is a Christian concept, is not simply at war with what it resists. It is also, if I may use this terrible word, a condition of possibility which makes history possible by resisting it. It is also a place of non-gift which makes the gift possible by resisting it. It is the place of non-desire. The *khora* does not desire anything, does not give anything. It is what makes taking place or an event possible. But the *khora* does not happen, does not give, does not desire. It is a spacing and absolutely indifferent. Why do I insist on this, on this perplexity? Why, for instance, in *Sauf le nom*, do I try to articulate this with the problem of negative theology and phenomenology? If you read this small essay, you will see that I try to point to a strange affinity between negative theology and phenomenology. I think that this reference to what I call *khora*, the absolutely universal place, so to speak, is what is irreducible to what we call revelation, revealability, history, religion, philosophy, Bible, Europe, and so forth. I think the reference to this place of resistance is also the condition for a universal politics, for the possibility of crossing the borders of our common context—European, Jewish, Christian, Muslim, and philosophical. I think this reference to this non-history and non-revelation, this negativity has heavy and serious political implications. I use the problematic of deconstruction and negative theology as a threshold to the definition of a new politics. I am not saying this against Europe, against Judaism, Christianity, or Islam. I am trying to find a place where a new discourse and a new politics could be possible. This place is the place of resistance—perhaps resistance is not the best word—but this non-something within something, this non-revelation within revelation, this non-history within history, this non-desire within desire, this impossibility. I would like to translate the experience of this impossibility into what we could call ethics or politics. Perhaps, and this is my hypothesis, if not a hope, what I am saying here can be retranslated after the fact into Jewish discourse or Christian discourse or Muslim discourse, if they can integrate the terrible things I am suggesting now. Just to underline, it is not a war machine that I am locating here but another type, another place for questions, in fact, the question of the place.

*Kearney.* I would like to say a few words of thanks. One of the nice things about the gift is that it gives you the opportunity to express gratitude for the gift, even if you betray the gift in doing so.

*Derrida.* No one knows who is thanking whom for what.

*Kearney.* I am going to put a few names on it, nonetheless. I would like to thank Jacques Derrida and Jean-Luc Marion for giving us their thoughts on the phenomenology of the gift, and all of you for coming here. I would also like to thank Mike Scanlon and Jack Caputo for coming up with the idea of this conference and, even at this eleventh hour, I would like to invite Jack Caputo to offer us some concluding thoughts on this conference.

*John D. Caputo.* This has been a marvelous moment for us all and we are all very grateful to Richard Kearney for leading this exciting conversation so genially and so deftly. I would like to make three brief points.

I have the sense that Marion and Derrida are answering the question of the gift differently because they have different problems. I think that Marion's problematic of the gift is very Heideggerian and that he wants to move the question of the gift out of the economy of causality, out of the horizon of onto-theologic, and to take up the "gifting of gift," the emerging of a gift as what has been released from onto-theological and causal constraints, so that it becomes excess. I do not think that this is exactly Derrida's concern. My sense is that the question of the gift for Derrida has to do primarily with the economy of credit and debt, and that Derrida wants the recipient not to contract a debt and the giver not to acquire acclaim for such generosity. I think that in *Etant donné* Marion removes the gift from the sphere of causality but my question is whether it is removed from debt. Do we not come into a universal indebtedness to God the giver, even though the gift has been released from a causal economy? Economy for Marion means causality. Economy for Derrida means credit and debt. I worry whether we do not end up in debt in Marion. But is not for-giving the highest moment of the gift? Should anyone end up in debt from a gift? Should we be in debt to God for the gift of creation? If creation is a gift, then it is not a debt but something we affirm and celebrate.

The second thing I would say is that I now appreciate Marion's position better. I took Marion to be criticizing Derrida more than he now says he is criticizing him. When Derrida says that the gift is impossible, I thought

Marion took him to be saying that it is *simply* impossible and that for Derrida the gift remains forever stuck within economy, and that Marion was going to show how this very impossibility is what makes it possible—which is of course Derrida's position in the first place. But Marion said today that he did not mean Derrida when he made this criticism, although I did not know who else he could have meant. So now it seems to me that they are both saying very much the same thing on this question of the impossible and that the round-table today has very much clarified this point.

The last point concerns the saturated phenomenon. I find this analysis very beautiful, but if, as Marion says, the saturated phenomenon falls into confusion or bedazzlement, I do not know how to distinguish the confusion of bedazzlement or of excess from the confusion of defect. How do we know that we have been visited by a supereminent excess and not just simply invaded by *khora*? How do we know that the source of the confusion is God, not *khora*?

*Marion.* I shall answer you at the next conference.

*Caputo.* Jacques Derrida, Richard Kearney, Jean-Luc Marion, thank you all so much.

## NOTES

1. Jean-Luc Marion, *Reduction and Givenness: Investigations of Husserl, Heidegger, and Phenomenology*, trans. Thomas Carlson (Evanston, Ill.: Northwestern University Press, 1998). *Etant donné* is currently being translated by Jeff Kosky.

2. Edmund Husserl, *The Idea of Phenomenology*, trans. William P. Alston and George Nakhnikian (The Hague: Martinus Nijhoff, 1964), 59.

3. François Furet, *Le passé d'une illusion* (Paris: Calman-Lévy, 1995), 49.

4. Jean-Luc Marion, *Etant donné: Essai d'úne phénoménologie de la donation* (Paris: Presses universitaires de France, 1997), 14, n.1–2, 116 n.1, 117 n.2.

# Loose Canons

## Augustine and Derrida on Their Selves

Robert Dodaro

It is fitting and just that I, too, excuse myself in advance of daring to speak about a man and his work which I can never completely understand, but for whom I confess an enormous respect, if for no other reason than because of the courage with which he now dares to expose the most private parts of himself, and for such a serious purpose.[1] So I confess the inadequate preparation of my reading, of my thoughts and of my words in this moment;[2] and in grateful recognition of your patience with my abuse of your generosity, I ask that you place no importance on what I say, but that you allow my words to suggest to you what one Augustinian has received from another.[3]

Jacques Derrida's *Circumfession* will now change the way we shall read Augustine's *Confessions*, and, thus, the way we shall read Augustine. To make this claim is no mere *captatio benevolentiae*, though it is also and obviously that, too. For Professor Derrida has shown us that we need not fear Augustine as we otherwise might have done, as do those who read in him the arrogance of the "hammer of heretics,"[4] who consider his certainty about himself, assured through confession, as the canon, the cane, with which he beats down the unwarranted certainty of his adversaries—those too proud to acknowledge their sinfulness, to acknowledge that he, the humble penitent kneeling in the confessional, Augustine the sinner, is nevertheless always already justified.[5]

Our Algerians love to recall their beatings: Augustine at school learning grammar,[6] then at Milan, where his African-accented Latin, the not-quite-Roman *elocutio* beaten into him at Madaura, left him standing outside even while within the Italianate, imperial Establishment into which he was eager to insinuate himself.[7] Jacques the Jew, the *pied-noir* whose transmarine adventure into the Paris academic Establishment was made the more difficult, not the least on account of his own philosophical heresies, derived in part as a result of humiliations received first as a schoolboy in Vichy Algiers,[8] then later at Paris, while still standing in the corner, on the margins, in the shadow of his Algerian compatriot,[9] the ontotheologian par excellence—today is fêted among us, the center of a tension at a university conference.

*Quid enim habes quod non accepisti:* for what have you that you did not receive (I Corinthians 4:7)? Herein lies the Pauline canon, the yardstick which in Augustine's hands becomes the cane with which to be beaten and with which to beat. The Latin words *canon/canna* are derived from the Greek *kanon/kanna*, which are also related to each other. Both *kanna* and *canna* refer to a thin reed stalk or cane which, because it was used as a measuring rod much like a ruler, led to the coining of the word *kanon* and of the loan-word *canon*. But *kanna* was also used to refer to a writing instrument such as a stylus.[10] Both the English and French words for cannon (*canon*) are linked with *canna*, and are etymologically related both to cane (*canne*) and to canon, and thus with instruments of correction, violence, and repression. So in considering Augustine and Derrida, I am also struck by the semantic relationships between canon, pen, and cane wherein boundaries (drawn with yardsticks) of various orthodoxies can be seen in relationship with the act of writing, insofar as writing has to do with circumscribing, with fixing limits which dare not be transgressed,[11] and therefore with creating canons.[12] This highly suggestive field—orthodoxy, writing, and violence—provides the backdrop for much of this paper.

### Circumfession

*Circumfession: Fifty-nine Periods and Periphrases* was written on a dare. "I dare you," Geoffrey Bennington told his friend Jacques Derrida, "to let me write an essay in which I shall circumscribe your thought, offering thereby an account so systematic that it will even anticipate whatever you might write in the future." Bennington's effort was to be modeled upon an interactive software program "which, in spite of its difficulty, would in principle be accessible to any user." There were other conditions to the contract, but they need not detain us. Let it suffice to say that the wager called for Derrida to read what Bennington had written, and then to write "something escaping the proposed systematization, surprising it."[13]

Bennington produced *Derridabase* (named after the software dBase), a masterful exposition of Derrida's thought, one which strove to situate its subject "with time" (*contemporaneus, cum + tempus*),[14] that is, within the canonical modern and contemporary histories of philosophy. In this sense, Bennington's project chafes not a little at the bit of Derrida's own thinking, since the latter eschews fixed categories and comparisons and holds with regard to a systematization of his own thought that "any such system must remain essentially open."[15] In the end, Derrida offered the surprise that Bennington says he intended all along to "provoke and welcome."[16]

The surprise is shown to us by Derrida in the narration of his relationship to Judaism:

> [T]hat's what my readers won't have known about me, the comma of my breathing henceforward, without continuity but without a break, the changed time of my writing, graphic writing, through having lost its interrupted verticality, almost with every letter, to be bound better and better but be read less and less well over almost twenty years, like my religion about which nobody understands anything any more than does my mother who asked other people a while ago, not daring to talk to me about it, if I still believed in God. . . .
>
> But she must have known that the constancy of God in my life is called by other names, so that I quite rightly pass for an atheist, the omnipresence to me of what I call God in my absolved, absolutely private language being neither that of an eyewitness nor that of a voice doing anything other than talking to me without saying anything, nor a transcendent law or an immanent *schechina*, that feminine figure of a Yahweh who remains so strange and so familiar to me.[17]

So Derrida's readers, including Bennington, have not known about the history of his religious struggle, of his coming to terms with his broken covenant, of his "religion without religion and without religion's God."[18] And because they have not known this side of him and of his thought, they have read him "less and less well over almost twenty years."[19] By confessing his "faith" in this way, Derrida surprised Bennington by writing a text which demonstrated the inadequacy of attempts to circumscribe that thought, to imprison it within the confines of a closed, predictable system or method.

*Circumfession*, derived from *circum + fateor*, describes the act of confessing "around" something. As Derrida employs it, the prefix *circum* refers at once to "around" and to "circumcision," which along with confession provides the work with its central metaphor. For he intends to circumvent the circumference "the one that has always been running after me, turning in circles around me,"[20] by which he refers to his own circumcision, to his Jewishness which, since childhood, both his parents and then he himself had tried to hide as a secret. Now Derrida proposes to "fess up," to tell the family secrets about that circumcision, to display his circumcision to us, but at the same time to "talk around" it.

The metaphoric field is rendered even more dense by Derrida's awareness that Bennington has also performed a "circumcision" of sorts on him, by tracing a circle around his thought.[21] In so doing, Bennington also claims Derrida for a tradition "with time." He opens *Derridabase* with the statement,

> We ought, then, to show how Derrida is a "contemporary." In doing this, we would be setting ourselves two distinct but complementary tasks: on the one hand, that of justifying, as it were, Derrida's contemporaneity by describing this impact in order to show its topicality without reducing it to a phenomenon of fashion; and on the other, that of placing this thought in a tradition or a filtration in order to say how Derrida is new, to define an originality with respect to predecessors from whom Derrida would stand out in some way.[22]

So the question of received traditions intrudes early into Bennington's appreciation of Derrida. *Quid enim habes quod non accepisti*: But what have *you* that you have not received, Professor? Augustine, too, would remind us that gift (*donum*, but also *gratia, traditio*) implies debt, responsibility. For Derrida, gift and indebtedness cancel each other out in an exchange in which gift becomes poison (playing on the German word for poison, *Gift*) because it binds us too tightly to a determined interpretation or course of action.[23] In *Circumfession*, Derrida reveals himself to be cognizant not only of the weight on his shoulders of Western philosophical traditions, but of "a certain" Jewish tradition as well.[24] For what *does* he have that he has not received? Does Derrida's "originality" of which Bennington speaks "stand out" in a way that negates the existence of a debt? By adopting this confessional or circumfessional approach to his relationship to Judaism and to religion, Derrida shows how his thought depends upon, while it also pokes fun at, the contemporary canon of philosophical concerns in which Bennington is eager to locate him.

Throughout *Circumfession*, Derrida remains in constant dialogue with Bennington's text, *Derridabase*. Derrida's text is printed on the same page as Bennington's, but beneath it in smaller typeface (in a manner befitting the humble, kneeling position of prayer, of confession). The juxtaposition of the two discourses mimics the *Confessions* insofar as Augustine remains in dialogue with God throughout his discourse (which is after all a prayer, a confession of praise and of sinfulness), and only comes to know himself insofar as God reveals him to himself through memory. In *Circumfession* Derrida indicates his relationship to Bennington by reference to the capital letter "G," which stands for Geoff, but also for Georgette, Derrida's mother (whom he compares to Augustine's mother Monica).[25] Yet one can also detect a relationship in Derrida's text between the roles assigned to "G" and God (the capital "G" in the English translation alludes as well to "God," just as the capital "D" in Djef, the phoneme of Geoff, recalls *Dieu, Deus*).[26]

Nor are these relationships accidental. Derrida intends that his acknowledgment in *Circumfession* of the friendship and love that binds him to Geoff[27] should recall the love that binds Augustine to God along with the perichoresis of knowledge and love at the heart of Augustinian interiority. For Augustine can only know God inasmuch as—and in the manner that—he can love God, and he can only know himself insofar as he knows God's knowledge and love for him. In the end, this is why Augustine must confess to a God who already knows everything about him. The pretense of the *Confessions* is that God does not need to know Augustine; Augustine needs to know himself. And he can only know himself only by coming to know concretely how, in what manner, God knows him and loves him. Confession is thus Augustine's tried-and-true mode of self-discovery because it involves a minute and attentive recollection of his history, a recollection in which he is revealed to himself within the providential love of God which he gratefully and painfully recalls to have been present at each significant juncture of his past and present life.

Augustine's predicament of confessing to a God who already knows everything about him is signified in the wager that obliges Derrida to try to surprise Geoff, to say something that falls outside of the circumference of Derrida's thought which *Derridabase* purports to offer. By reading both texts together, moving from one to the other and back again, one observes that Derrida's discourse moves in deconstructive harmony with Bennington's superimposed text.[28] This structure, too, is purposefully allowed to signify the intercourse of the *Confessions* in which God's discourse, the text of Scripture, interpenetrates Augustine's own text, just as Derrida intersperses his *Circumfession* with quotes from the *Confessions*. These intertextualities draw Derrida's reader into the structure of self-knowledge for Augustine.

### *Savoir Absolu:* Augustinian Interiority

But one wonders whether Derrida does not also have in mind the fear on the part of many about the absolute foundation of self-knowledge in Augustine, of a "self" whose epistemic integrity is authorized by an ontological foundation beyond appeal. The form or style of Derrida's response to the prescient, programmatic, predestinatory *Derridabase* pokes fun at the pose of certainty on the part of SA, of *savoir absolu*, of *Saint Augustin*. After all, Derrida ends up surprising his friend Geoff (capital "G") by revealing something that the program (the theo-logic or geo-logic, the Geoff-logic) had not foreseen. Reading *Circumfession*, we are prompted to ask ourselves whether Augustine's sense of self is less absolute, less assured than the surface of his text might suggest. And in tandem with that question, we inquire further whether the self-assurance, the canon, with which Augustine the bishop enforces the brand of orthodoxy to which he sub-scribes (and which is often his own *brand* of orthodoxy) does not at some point deconstruct in the face of self-doubt.[29]

For Augustine, self-knowledge is also always provisional and contingent.[30] In his own terms, then, he realizes that the "poison" of the gift lies in the risk that he will be drugged by an illusory simulacrum of himself, one which passes away just as he abstracts or distills it, just at the precise instant in which he "knows himself" through God's revelation of himself to himself within his memory. Thus, as he also sees, even the experience of pardon, of divine acceptance and presence, which is enclosed in each grasp of himself painfully and gratefully attained through confession, becomes also an occasion of sin, of pride.

At the opening of Book 10 of the *Confessions* Augustine prays to God, "Truth is what I want to do, in my heart by confession in your presence, and with my pen before many witnesses."[31] His wish "to do truth"[32] when he confesses is granted to him by the God who reveals him to himself. He inquires as to what advantage there is in confessing in this way, and answers his own question by pointing out that he is able to rejoice in the forgiveness of his sins, to rejoice in God who transforms his soul by faith and by sacrament (10.3.4).

Yet this confidence masks an equally weighty lack of confidence about himself. He introduces the doubt immediately following this optimistic self-portrait, when he begins to talk about himself as he knows himself contemporarily with writing his *Confessions*. What follows from 10.28.39 until just about the end of the book (10.41.66) is the confession of Augustine, the bishop of Hippo Regius. The most telling admission of all seems to be placed at the beginning, where he admits categorically that his joys are at odds with his sorrows, his sins, and that he does not know which of the two states of being will be victorious in him (10.28.39).

He begins his confession by admitting that he remains troubled by sexually suggestive dreams and that his reason, which enables him to resist them during waking hours, is powerless over them during sleep, on account of which he also suffers nocturnal emissions (10.30.41–42). Furthermore, he admits that he occasionally overeats (10.31.43–47). When it comes to sins related to the sense of smell, he tells us at first that he is not aware of any, but quickly adds that he may be "deceived" in saying this. He allows himself to digress on the difficulties of discernment, and warns himself that he should not be complacent. He claims that when his mind questions itself about itself "it can scarcely trust any reply it receives." Moreover, he would not know whether the progress he had perhaps made in the Christian life had subsequently been undone to the point that he has actually regressed (10.32.48).

Thus, while discussing sins against the sense of smell, Augustine has already established the pattern of contradiction that characterizes the remainder of his confession. His admission that he could be self-deceived in his examination of conscience parallels his earlier assertion that his griefs (his sins) are at battle with his joys and that he does not know to which the victory will fall (10.28.39). Both of these statements contrast with the certainty expressed at the outset of the book, where he assures his readers that what he confesses about himself is truthful, because he hears it first from God. If Augustine can be deceived about himself when it comes to sins related to the sense of smell (10.32.48), by what logic does he insist that even those who love him, those who are in his church, may discern whether he confesses truth-fully?

This same pattern of contradiction is present in his discussion of con-cupiscence of the eyes. On the one hand, he assures us that he is now free of attraction to theatrical shows and astrology, and that, although both these activities had captivated him earlier on in life, he is no longer drawn to any practice aimed at discerning occult knowledge through sacrilegious practices. But then he admits that there is after all in him a hankering for some kind of "signs" from God, a condition which constitutes vain *curiositas*. He asks that God drive far from him these traces of his former ways. This prayer functions in this text much like a photographic negative, by highlighting his concern that such suggestions may not always lie far away. The text (10.35.56) thus reveals itself as a composite of claims in conflict. Each attempt to recognize progress in his moral life is matched by a more cautious retraction. Even his assertion that God's grace enables him to maintain his *intentio* fixed upon its object (*finis*) when he prays for someone's health or safety is chaperoned by negation in which he admits that his attention is distracted each day by many trivial and insignificant matters (10.35.57).

Even leaving aside Robert O'Connell's important thesis suggesting ech-oes of the Plotinian "fall of the soul" in these sections of Book 10,[33] the bishop's confession, when read in the light of these lapses, must begin to raise doubts about the stability of Augustinian self-knowledge.

By the time he examines himself on the sin of pride (toward the close of Book 10), he has provided himself with sufficient enough a case for his own moral self-doubt that he is well armed against complacency. So while he con-fesses that God has "crushed his pride" (10.36.58), he acknowledges that "the temptation to want veneration and affection from others" may have some hold upon him (10.36.59).

Gentle confessors that we all are, who among us would refuse compassion for the penitent's plight in this situation? His laudable humility enables him to avoid the pitfall of those whom he mentions at 10.38.63, who are tempted to vainglory through performances of humility: Yet we ought not to allow our understandable enchantment with Augustine's rhetoric to distract us from observing the extent to which his self-knowledge has once again come loose from its moorings. For he finds that he has no self-knowledge in any situation in which he can be flattered by the praise of others.

> I am sorely afraid about my hidden sins, which are plain to your eyes but not to mine. In other areas of temptation I have some shrewdness in self-examination (*facultas explorandi me*), but in this matter almost none (10.36.60).

The problem is magnified when he asks himself why he is less concerned when someone else is unjustly criticized than when he is himself. The extent to which he acknowledges that this is the case indicates to him the depth of his own self-delusion. The question he asks himself, "Is there nothing left to say, but that I am deluding myself and not acting truthfully with heart and tongue in your sight?" (10.37.62) recalls the opening of Book 10 where he announces his intentions for the book: "Truth is what I want to do, in my heart by confession in your presence, and with my pen before many witnesses" (10.1.1).[34] How successful does he believe himself to have been? His observation that he is deluding himself and therefore not acting truthfully with heart and tongue in God's sight is not a rhetorical flourish. The *ueritatem facere* of his self-discovery reveals itself to be closer to Derrida's immanent, unknowing "truth" than one might at first believe.[35] The prayer which follows these tears and with which Augustine summarizes his self-discovery through Book 10 reveals the extent of the project's demise:

> From time to time you lead me into an inward experience (*affectum*) quite unlike any other, a sweetness beyond understanding. If ever it is brought to fullness in me my life will not be what it is now, though what it will be I cannot tell. But I am dragged down again by my heavy burden of distress, sucked back into everyday things and held fast in them; grievously I lament, but just as grievously I am held.
>
> . . . I have taken stock of the sickly state to which my sins have reduced me, and I have called upon your right hand for saving help. I have seen your blazing splendor, but with a wounded heart; I was beaten back, and I asked, "Can anyone reach that?" I was flung far out of your sight. You are the Truth, sovereign over all. I did not want to lose you, but in my greed I thought to possess falsehood along with you, just as no one wants to tell lies in such a way that he loses his own sense of what is true. That was why I lost you, for you did not consent to be possessed in consort with a lie (10.40.65–41.66).

The experience of true insight into himself and of the true peace (10.38.63) which is the product of divine pardon, of reconciliation with his past deeds, is fleeting and elusive. Augustine gained certain insights into himself, and these he shared with his readers as a *gratiarum actio* to God. But he was "beaten back" because he could not maintain the gaze on the truth of himself while in possession of lies. This is not an account of an Ostia-like vision,[36] but of a failed attempt at self-knowledge, one which was ultimately sabotaged by Augustine himself, as indeed it had to be. "You did not consent to be possessed in consort with a lie," he finally admits to God, thereby acknowledging a self-delusion that he could really ever be free from the sway of pride in its many, insidious varieties. Thus, to the degree that self-knowledge is destabilized by its own structure, i.e., by the ongoing nature of conversion that this self-knowledge requires of necessity, the "self" that Augustine can posit, situate, is both there and is not there.

And therein lies the surprise of Augustine's circumfession. He claims to know himself to the extent that God who is Truth reveals himself to himself, and yet he comes to the awareness that he knows no "self" because the truth of himself, a truth which he constructs (*ueritatem facere*), is necessarily a tissue of illusions. No more than Augustine can Derrida escape living this irony:

> From the invisible inside, where I could neither see nor want the very thing that I have always been scared to have revealed on the scanner, by *analysis* . . . a crural vein expelled my blood outside that I thought beautiful once stored in that bottle under a label that I doubted could avoid confusion or misappropriation of the vintage, leaving me nothing more to do, the inside of my life exhibiting itself outside, *expressing* it before my eyes, absolved without a gesture, dare I say of writing if I compare the pen to a syringe, and I always dream of a pen that would be a syringe, a suction point rather than that very hard weapon with which one must inscribe, incise, choose, calculate, take ink before filtering the inscribable, playing the keyboard on the screen, whereas here, once the right vein has been found, no more toil, no responsibility, no risk of bad taste nor of violence, the blood delivers it all alone, the inside gives itself up and you can do as you like with it, it's me but I'm no longer there.[37]

In these opening pages of *Circumfession*, Derrida associates two distinct but related images with the pen, the syringe, and the stylus. The blood (*cruor*)[38] drawn from his vein with the pen/syringe and carefully stored in a bottle symbolizes his self-externalization, a process which he views as both necessary and yet hateful. His attraction to this "bleeding," in which he remains passive ("no more toil, no responsibility"), suggests his desire to be known both to himself and to others, without the need to write.[39] Here, his attitude recalls Augustine's longing for peace, *quietus*. Would that he could rest in Geoff's knowledge/love for him, in the *Derridabase* which has been extracted from him, or even in his Jewishness. Yet he cannot abide the closure signified by the labeled bottle of his blood, the *cruor* or "crude word" in which his blood is "exposed outward, and thus to its death."[40] He signals this *cor inquietum* already in the opening words of *Circumfession*.

> as though I were attached to him so as to look for a fight over what talking crude means, as though I were trying relentlessly, to the point of bloodshed, to remind him, for he knows it, *cur confitemur Deo scienti*, of what is demanded of us by what's crude, doing so thus in my tongue, the other one, the one that has always been running after me, turning in circles around me, a circumference licking me with a flame and that I try in turn to circumvent, having never loved anything but the impossible.[41]

Derrida's tongue, "the other one, which has always been running me," the tongue in which he makes his confession, can be taken as the Hebrew tongue, and thus as a metaphor for his Judaism. It is for him the "other" tongue/*langue* insofar as Christian French is his assumed language. Hebrew, on the other hand, is the language that he always ran away from through his many efforts to hide his Jewishness (only at first in an ethnic, but always in a religious sense). Derrida's attempt to "circumvent" the Judaism that has pursued him is ex-

Robert Dodaro

pressed in his never having loved anything but the impossible (the character of his "religion").

So he cannot live without the pen as stylus, as tool for circumcision, "that very hard weapon[42] with which one must inscribe, incise, calculate, take ink before filtering the inscribable."[43] The pen/stylus is represented on Geoff's side as circumcision, as the cut that Geoff makes around Derrida's thought, by which he encircles it in a computer program. On Derrida's side, the pen/stylus is circumfession in which he must reveal his real circumcision, his secret Judaism, and at the same time reveal his circumventing of it. His writing here, which, as in the case of Geoff's, is a cutting out, a cutting around, has the character of a compulsion.

> I have been seeking myself in a sentence, yes, I, and since a circumbygone period at the end of which I would say I and which would, finally, have the form, my language, another, of what I have turned around, from one peri-phrasis to the next.[44]

Hence, his affirmation regarding his bottled blood, "it's me but I'm no longer there," echoes while it also mocks Augustine's confession that whereas he is able to know *that* he is, he cannot really know *how* he is. Augustine's con-fidence, *"Tu es ueritas super omnia praesidens"* (You are the Truth, presiding over all) is signified in Geoff's text *super omnia praesidens*, the theo-logic or Geoff-logic (which is not after all the truth above all, but the "cruelty above all"[45]) in which Derrida is supposed to recognize himself, the *ueritas* in which he is supposed to see himself. By circumfessing this and all the truths encom-passing his life with *ueritatem facere*, the immanent truth that he "makes" or "does" himself, Derrida remains consistent with his avowed atheism,[46] and suggests that the Truth in which Augustine recognizes the successive illusions masquerading as a self has not, in the end, assured him of anything: "[I]t's me but I'm no longer there."

### *Regula Fidei:* **Augustinian Exteriority**

We come now to the second aspect of *savoir absolu:* the relationship between Augustine's self-assurance and the assumed arrogance with which he derides the pride of his theological adversaries. Must Augustinian interiority continue to exclude other forms of theological reason?

In *Theology and Social Theory*, John Milbank seems to challenge the assumptions implicit in this question:

> [T]he suspicion in Augustine of drawing over-tight boundaries around orthodoxy (or perhaps "orthopraxis") implies not at all that true belief is inscrutably locked within interiority, but something more like the very opposite.[47]

Milbank offers this position in the course of contrasting Augustine's theory of church with that of the Donatists. He holds that Augustine's view of the church is that of "a historical community bound together by a historical transmission of signs, whose dissemination will necessarily be muddled, imperfectly coordinated with 'true belief,' and not fully subject to prediction or control."[48] In Augustine's view, according to Milbank, the Catholic church differs from the Donatist church inasmuch as the latter intends "to base a community entirely on an 'inward' purity of intention" which "cuts them off from the main body of Christians who share the same basic beliefs and practices." For Milbank's Augustine, the Donatists fail to see that "the unity and inter-communion of Christians is not just a desirable appendage of Christian practice, but it is itself at the heart of the actuality of redemption."[49]

So for Milbank, Augustine's cri de coeur for unity stands over against Donatist interiority, an interiority which is both heresy and privatization. Augustine, on the other hand, allows for the dissemination of signs, "imperfectly coordinated with 'true belief'" when, for example, he opposes the re-baptism of returning Donatists, or when he admits that certain Catholics whose baptisms were valid stand outside the city of God. In this sense, he "attaches greater weight than the Donatists to the public, symbolic aspect of Catholic truth."[50]

One may doubt, however, whether Milbank pays sufficient attention to the violence at the heart of what he terms Augustine's quest for "the unity and inter-communion of Christians." Milbank's treatment of "Christianity and coercion" is limited to the religious coercion of the Donatists (Augustine's involvement in the coercion of Pelagius and his allies would, I suspect, have given Milbank even greater problems),[51] and he examines even this case restrictively, under the rubrics of church-state relations and the ontology of punishment. As a result, his discussion never arrives at the question of the legitimacy of pluralism for Augustine.[52] Milbank's account of Donatist ecclesiology is largely dismissive and prejudicial; his account of the "peace" at the center of Augustine's church is apologetic and optimistic.[53]

Answers to the question of how Augustine's opposition to theologies other than his own brand of Catholic orthodoxy relates to his interiority depend, in part, upon the clarity that can be achieved in explaining the dynamics of self-knowledge in Augustine. The problem is already posed for us at the end of Book 10 of the Confessions, immediately following what I have referred to as the close of the bishop's confession (10.41.66). There, Augustine criticizes practitioners of Neoplatonist theurgy. He accuses them of being "deservedly deluded" because they seek God in an arrogant manner through the acquisition of "haughty knowledge."[54]

Note, however, just how closely his condemnation of the theurgists parallels his own self-criticism just a few passages earlier in the same book. Augustine locates the "haughty knowledge" sought by practitioners of theurgy with the curiositas of the magicians and astrologers, a specific form of concupiscence of the eyes which he believes he has largely warded off, but which he also admits lingers in himself. At 10.35.56, he prays, "[W]hen dare I claim that

Robert Dodaro

by no such sight am I ever drawn to gaze, ever trapped into frivolous fascination?" But it is in his own attachment to flattery, his desire to be held in esteem by the members of his church and to be praised for the quality of his thought, that he most closely approaches the arrogance of the theurgists whom he condemns shortly thereafter. So, for example, he admits that "the affection and honor we receive come to be something we enjoy not for your sake but in your stead" (10.36.59). Given all he has to say at the conclusion of his confession concerning the moral blindness that plagues him generally, the reader of his confession is permitted (indeed prompted) to ask him how far he would want to push the differences in purity of *intentio* (attention) between himself and his Neoplatonist rivals.[55]

The period of the composition of the *Confessions* is contemporary with another set of interior struggles in the bishop of Hippo. At the turn of the fourth century, north African bishops witnessed the advance of new imperial legislation banning pagan religious practices and stripping their temples of replicas of divinities.[56] The action prompted polemics between pagan and Christian intellectuals and led to violent clashes between pagans and Christians in north African towns and cities.[57] At roughly the same time, north African Catholic bishops began to change their strategies in dealing with their Donatist rivals. In *Letter* 185 (written almost 20 years later in A.D. 417), Augustine explains the reluctance he experienced at the time to endorse a policy of civil intervention against the Donatists. He and a minority group of bishops within the Council of Carthage had succeeded in persuading the majority (and more senior) of the bishops to endorse a less coercive policy.[58] But this frame of mind was not to endure, and within a couple of years Augustine had convinced himself of the need for imperial intervention.[59]

The tension between these two attitudes in Augustine toward coercion of the Donatists may already be felt in his confession of the sin of pride at the close of Book 10 of the *Confessions*. He acknowledges that human flattery represents a pitfall for "those of us who by reason of our official positions (*officia*) in human society must of necessity be loved and feared (*timere*) by our fellows."[60] Looking more closely at his own attitude toward his popularity, he admits the pull on his soul exercised by occasions of flattery and criticism.

His description of himself at this point is reminiscent of his criticism of the emperor Valentinian II in Book 6 of the *Confessions*. Augustine recalls there how, just over ten years earlier when he served as the public orator at Milan, he declaimed two panegyrics in A.D. 385 and 386, one in honor of the emperor, the other in praise of his military commander in chief, Flavius Bauto.[61] Augustine describes the personal dilemma he experienced while "intending that the speech in praise of the Emperor should include a great many flatteries which would certainly be applauded by an audience who knew how far from the truth they were" (6.6.9).

Now, in Book 10, Augustine the bishop remembers the eulogistic strate-

gies of imperial propaganda skillfully deployed by Augustine the master rheto-
rician, and wonders whether the bishop has not changed places with the
emperor. The bishop of Hippo Regius acknowledges his power, the fact that he
is *loved and feared* by his people, that he must take decisions which can be
unpopular. He who has an admitted weakness for flattery finds himself more
and more on the theological defensive while composing the *Confessions*.
Recall that at the opening of Book 10, he declares his intention to confess his
sins "to a brotherly mind, not the mind of a stranger, not the minds of alien foes
who mouth falsehoods and whose power wreaks wickedness" (10.4.5). The
idea of a sitting bishop confessing faults which would render his ministry
invalid in the eyes of his Donatist adversaries cannot have been far from his
mind as he penned these words.[62]

Recall, too, the earlier discussion of unjust criticism and Augustine's
expressed remorse that he does not feel as great a pain when an other is misjudged as when he is misjudged himself (10.37.62). This is the point at which
his self-delusion comes most into focus for him, the point at which he has to
write "Is there nothing left to say, but that I am deluding myself and not acting
truthfully with heart and tongue in your sight?" His reflection on the power of
self-esteem over himself and the extent to which he can fail in this way, as he
tells us, to practice justice toward others whom he is obliged to love, calls to
mind his numerous meditations elsewhere in his writings on the text of John
8:3–11, the pericope of the woman caught in adultery.

It is this text which, in my view, best expresses Augustine's understanding
of the interplay between self and other in the determination of justice. Augustine treats of the pericope most often in conjunction with his expression of
opposition to capital punishment.[63] In *Sermon 13*, he challenges magistrates
and provincial administrators empowered to impose the death penalty to
"enter themselves, observe themselves, debate with themselves, listen to themselves," and before imposing that penalty to "judge first themselves within."
There, they should judge what their consciences tell them of themselves, what
they have done, what they have received, what sins they have committed and
what sentence they have pronounced on themselves. If they have been lenient,
merciful toward themselves, punishing their sin by their repentance, then that
is how they should punish their neighbor. "See how you interrogated yourself
and listened to yourself and punished yourself, and yet you spared yourself.
Listen to your neighbor in the same way."[64]

Christ's words to the pharisees and scribes, "Who among you is without
sin? Let him be the first to cast a stone against her" (John 8:7) create for
Augustine the interior conditions whereby one is drawn to acknowledge a
moral symmetry with the "other" present as criminal or enemy. This introspec-
tion, which always involves a perlocutionary activity, creates the possibility of
conversion and repentance from *libido uindictae*, the lust for vengeance.
Augustine is frequently engaged in bringing out such moral symmetries in his

treatments of violence. In Book 1 of the *Confessions* where he speaks of his beatings from the schoolmaster, he asks, "Is the teacher who beat me himself very different from me?"[65] Augustine was beaten for playing games instead of doing his schoolwork. He analyzes his punishment and the cause behind it, and concludes that it was unjust because he was being punished for playing games instead of preparing himself for a career in which he would only play more sophisticated games. "Grown-up games are called 'business' (*negotia*)," he observes (1.9.15). In Book 4 of the *City of God*, while discussing the injustice of the militaristic expansion of the Roman Empire, he tells the tale of Alexander the Great and the captured pirate. The emperor asked the pirate, "[H]ow come you infest the sea with piracy?" The pirate replied, "I do the same thing you do. But because I have a tiny craft, I'm called a pirate. Because you have a mighty navy, you're called an emperor."[66]

The structure of these recounted ironies conforms to the pattern exhibited by Christ in his confrontation of the pharisees and scribes. Self-knowledge is prompted by a verbal retort which draws its object inward into consciousness of its own injustice, an injustice which normally outweighs that of which the enemy is accused. Moreover, the experience of self-confrontation in this mode subverts a conventional notion of justice which, while not discarded entirely, gives way to a deeper sense of justice, one which defies codification. Augustine is being a good Platonist here; progress in human understanding of justice is prompted by such experiences but is always asymptotic with respect to the form of justice.[67]

But what of interiority and justice in the case of heretics or heathens? Is there any evidence that Augustine's sense of self-knowledge as provisional and contingent with respect to its full realization ever leads him to question the absolute character of his grasp of religious truth? Does Augustine ever view the heretic or the theurgist *in interiore modo*, in a symmetry to himself, and therefore as an "other" for whom his invitation to dialogue ever amounts to anything more than a rhetorical pose?[68] Finally, can Augustine the bishop reach back into the *Confessions* and recognize in the unnamed, cane-wielding schoolteacher of his youth one who, as he once pointed out, was not very different from himself?[69]

For many reasons, some of them cultural, some personal to Augustine, we would not expect affirmative answers to these questions, and we are not disappointed. Never once do we catch Augustine, who was arguably more capable than most Church Fathers of both subtlety in judgment and of relentless self-accusation, in the act of second-guessing his condemnations of those whose theological positions either he or his church had judged heterodox.[70] Many today would argue that the expectation that he should do so belongs to modernity and not to antiquity. Yet Augustine's contemporaries—Catholic adversaries in the Pelagian controversy, and even neutral parties to the dispute such as Pope Zosimus—tried to persuade the African bishops that, in the matter of this particular controversy, they were acting unjustly.[71]

Augustine's consistent retort, *"quid enim habes quod non accepisti"* (for what have you that you did not receive?) represents for him the essential insight, the starting point for any orthodox theological reflection, viz., that each human being is a sinner and is thus incapable of practicing the justice which is owed to God and to others. What justice human beings are capable of realizing in their own conduct comes from divine grace and not from unaided human intentions and efforts. Augustine makes this point in a long letter to Boniface, which he later refers to as *The Correction of the Donatists*,[72] and in which he justifies the imperial repression of the Donatist church.

> Far be it from any of us, then, to call himself just. Then he would want to establish his own justice, that is one granted to himself by himself; for the words, *What do you have that you did not receive?* are addressed to him. Or else, he would dare to boast of being sinless in this life, just as during our own conference[73] [the Donatists] said that they were in a church that already has *no spot or wrinkle or anything of that kind* (Ephesians 5:37). They do not realize that at present this word is fulfilled in individuals who leave their bodies either immediately after baptism, or after the forgiveness of their trespasses, for which forgiveness we plead in prayer.[74] However, for the whole church, it will not be the case that it is completely without *spot or wrinkle or anything of that kind* before it is the time to say, *Where is your victory, O Death? Where, O Death, is your sting? For the sting of death is sin* (I Corinthians 15:55–56).[75]

In his own way, Augustine also understands that gift implies debt. Whatever in ourselves there is of justice has been received as gift. The debt of this freely given justice is confession. And this confessional stance of Augustine the penitent, the full and frank admission that neither he nor his Catholic church is spotless or wrinkle free, further compels him to condemn the arrogance of the Donatists, who "dare to boast" of their presumed justice while Catholics "plead in prayer" for pardon.

Speaking in the *Confessions* of his conversion to the Scriptures after having read the books of Platonists, Augustine acknowledges there, too, that in returning to God by this path he had been led "to recognize the difference between presumption and confession."[76]

> It was therefore with intense eagerness that I seized on the hallowed calligraphy of your Spirit, and most especially the writings of the apostle Paul. . . . So I began to read, and discovered that every truth I had read in those other books was taught here also, but now inseparably from your gift of grace, so that no one who sees can boast as though what he sees and the very power to see it were not from you—for who has anything that he has not received?[77]

Augustine feels the same obligation to confess his sinfulness and to condemn the Pelagians as he has felt all along toward Neoplatonist theurgists and Donatists, and always for the same reason, the refusal to acknowledge a gift. He cites the text of I Corinthians 4:7 so frequently in his arguments against

Pelagius, Celestius, and Julian of Eclanum that it becomes a virtual slogan in his campaign against them.[78] But it is to *Sermon 13* that we must turn once again in order to understand the force of the linkage between interiority, confession, and the enforcement of orthodoxy.

The sermon was preached in A.D. 418, a year or so later than *The Correction of the Donatists*, and is therefore also contemporary with the Pelagian controversy. It opens with the image of the apostle Paul chastising himself, and closes with that of a father beating his son. Paul is heard speaking at I Corinthians 9:27: "I pound my body and reduce it to servitude, in case in preaching to others I myself fail to win approval."[79] Augustine is preaching on the verse of Psalms 2:10, "Be instructed, all you who judge the earth," and he interprets "to judge the earth" to mean "to tame the body."[80] So the sermon concerns divine instruction about *disciplina* in its various contexts. It is an important theme in Augustine's opus.

The following verse of the Psalm, "[S]erve the Lord in fear and rejoice in him with trembling" (Psalms 2:11), establishes the pattern of the instruction which Augustine believes ought to inform self-discipline. He invites his listener to rejoice in God and not in himself.[81]

> [I]f you think that the source of your being is him, but the source of your being just is yourself, then you are not serving the Lord with fear, nor *rejoicing in him with trembling*, but in yourself with arrogance (*praesumptio*).[82]

Being by this time in his life an experienced penitent and confessor, Augustine knows how easy it is for people to be deluded into thinking themselves just.

> You will be thinking yourself just already because you *do not steal* other people's possessions or *commit adultery* or *murder*, or *bear false witness by speaking against your neighbour*, and you *honour your father and mother*, and *worship the one God*, and serve neither idols nor demons.[83]

Faithful observation of the Decalogue is not, however, sufficient guarantee that the mind and will are strong enough to maintain one's justice. Continuing his sermon by commenting upon Psalms 2:12, "Blessed are all who trust in him," Augustine warns his listeners that trust in oneself rather than in God is presumption. Paul's advice to "work out your salvation in fear and trembling" (Philippians 2:12) denotes the proper attitude of distrust and suspicion which ought to be maintained toward one's self.

> Then you might find yourself in him, as you have lost yourself in yourself. For in yourself, you had no power except to lose yourself; and you don't know how to find yourself unless God who made you also looks for you.[84]

At this point, roughly the conclusion of the first third of the sermon, Augustine returns to the expression "judge the earth" which he had initially interpreted as self-discipline, and re-interprets it to mean "judging the people who are on the earth." He says that he is speaking to political leaders, "kings, leaders, rulers, judges."[85] He now introduces the account of the woman caught in adultery (John 8:3–11), and warns judges to enter into themselves and to judge themselves before condemning any accused person who stands before them. While Augustine insists that the death penalty is to be avoided in the administration of justice, he reiterates the importance of instilling fear in the hearts of convicted criminals through punishments adapted to this purpose. But here, too, his attention is focused on the attitudes, the intentions, of judges as they apply punishment.

> You are a man judging others; foster love of them in your heart, and judge the earth. Love to instill fear in them, but do so out of love.... Punishments should be imposed; I don't deny it; I don't forbid it. But this must be done in the spirit of love, in the spirit of concern, in the spirit of reform.[86]

It is important to Augustine's point in this sermon to understand that the love with which the judge or ruler is to apply punishments for serious crimes is born in that interior self-examination whereby he is able to see himself etched in the moral profile of the accused. This is the fuller sense of his admonition, "[Y]ou are a man judging others; foster love of them in your heart." The heart referred to here was introduced just a few paragraphs earlier as the site at which the judge was to have tortured himself while in the course of judging the other.

> Judge yourself first, then you'll be able to leave the inner cell of your conscience in safety and go out to someone else.... Return to yourself, observe yourself, debate with yourself, listen to yourself.... If you listened well, if you heard aright, if you were being just as you listened, if you climbed up to the judgment seat of your mind, if you stretched yourself out in front of yourself on the rack of your heart, if you applied to yourself the heavy torture of fear—if that is how you listened, you listened well.... Listen to your neighbour in the same way.[87]

Hence the love with which the judge punishes is the love born in the interior recognition of a moral symmetry between himself and the other. His judgment of the other occurs at the intersection of love of self, neighbor, and God.[88] This is a significant element in Augustine's conception of just punishment. The justice by which the judge punishes is a justice born in love, but love understood as a concern to reform the other, a concern reflexively founded upon the desire for one's own ongoing conversion.

> Vent your rage on the failing, which you dislike as much in yourself....
> Punishments should be imposed; I don't deny it; I don't forbid it. But this must be done in the spirit of love, in the spirit of concern, in the spirit of reform.

> After all, you do not refrain from instructing your own son. In the first place you try, as far as possible, to instruct him by using shame and generosity, wanting him to be ashamed of offending his father rather than afraid of a harsh judge. You're delighted to have such a son. However, if he happens

> to take no notice of this, you would also apply the cane. You punish him and inflict pain on him, but your aim would be his security. Many people have been reformed through love, and many through fear; the latter, though, have progressed through the horror of fear to reach love. *Be instructed, all you who judge the earth.* Love, and then judge (*Diligite et iudicate*).[89]

*Dilige, et quod vis fac* is, consequently, a dangerous principle, a license to love one's neighbor enough to beat the daylights out of him. It is instructive to remember that Augustine's best-known aphorism derives from an ethic of reform. It is found once in Augustine's writings,[90] in a sermon on the *First Epistle of John* preached in April 407 in the wake of yet another imperial repression of the Donatists.[91] Augustine utters these words with this repression in mind.[92]

Clearly, in his writings against the Donatists, as elsewhere, Augustine locates himself within a broad tradition of ecclesiastical authority where the determination of heresy and orthodoxy is concerned.[93] He accepts the church's condemnation of heretics as he also accepts the standard patristic rejection of the truth claims of other religions. However, by examining exponents of heterodox teaching and of other religions according to the criteria for just judgment, criteria which depend upon the structures of confession and conversion, Augustine is able not only to sustain the church's boundaries of orthodoxy, but even to tighten them, as the Pelagian controversy demonstrates. More important, he grounds his condemnation of members of other religious movements not only upon the authority of the Catholic church, but in tandem with the self-knowledge upon which his own *intellectus fidei* depends. By failing to understand the nature of salvation according to the structures of confession and conversion implied in the Pauline canon *quid enim habes quod non accepisti*, adherents of religious movements as diverse as Neoplatonists, Donatists, Pelagians, Manicheans, Arians, and Jews obstinately refuse to acknowledge the divine gift of justice through which pride gives way to humility, presumption to confession.[94] Augustine admits that there may be ways in which Christ has been revealed and has brought salvation to human beings other than through the Christian religion, but he holds that in order for this to have happened, it would still require on the part of the believer the acknowledgment of a gift, one which negates the pride and presumption on account of which those blind to the Truth understand justice to be their own accomplishment.[95]

However, if, as Book 10 of the *Confessions* indicates, Augustine is also able to doubt the certainty of the justice by which he judges himself through confession (a justice given to him as divine gift), how certain can he be of the justice by which he condemns the heterodoxy of others?

The prayer with which Augustine closes *De trinitate* adds further weight to this doubt:

Directing my attention toward this rule of faith (*regula fidei*) as best as I could, as far as you enabled me to, I have sought you and desired to see intellectually what I have believed, and I have argued much and toiled much. O Lord my God, my one hope, listen to me lest out of weariness I should stop wanting to seek you, but let me seek your face always, and with ardor. Do you yourself give me the strength to seek, having caused yourself to be found and having given me the hope of finding you more and more. Before you lies my strength and my weakness; preserve the one, heal the other. Before you lies my knowledge and my ignorance; where you have opened to me, receive me as I come in; where you have shut to me, open to me as I knock. Let me remember you, let me understand you, let me love you. Increase these things in me until you refashion me entirely.[96]

Though it is only directly referred to eight times in the course of *De trinitate*,[97] *regula fidei* exercises a fundamental role in the theological method through which Augustine conducts his trinitarian speculation in this work. His injunction that if "we keep to the rule that just because a thing is not yet clear to our understanding, we must not therefore dismiss it from the firm assent of our faith,"[98] coupled with that Augustinian topos, "we must believe before we can understand,"[99] does not suggest a clear distinction between the acts of believing and understanding (*credere* and *intellegere*), but rather their unity conceived as mutual dependence.

Yet when Augustine relates that he directed his attention to that rule of faith as much as he was able, as much as God enabled him, he indicates that although the rule of faith is an object of *intentio*, the intellectual activity which *intendere* implies is insufficient for him to perceive clearly the rule of faith. In essence, he admits that he does not understand (*intellegere*) fully what he believes (*credere*). By implication, Augustine suggests that the *regula fidei* is understood to differing degrees depending upon the extent to which divine grace has healed the intellect and the will of the consequences of sin.

Thus, Augustine concludes this theological speculation on the nature of God by pleading that God enable him to remember, understand, and love him more. "Increase these things in me until you refashion me entirely" is also a plea that the *regula fidei*, the object of his *intentio*, would come into clearer intellectual focus. The reader of *De trinitate* is rightly surprised at the personal tone with which he concludes this work,[100] and with the frank admission, unique within Augustine's discussions of *regula fidei*, that the bishop's comprehension of the norm of Catholic faith is obscured by his own sin. *Ignorantia* and *infirmitas* in this particular text, as elsewhere in Augustine's writings, refer to the consequences of original sin.[101] Augustine does not ascribe his lack of adequate comprehension of the *regula fidei* to a lack of study, to an inadequate application of dialectic to the scriptures or to the theological conclusions of his orthodox predecessors. Here, we need no further "development of dogma" in order to achieve a fuller understanding of the rule of faith. No, instead,

Augustine confesses that his deepening understanding of the rule of faith depends upon the extent to which God refashions his self.

And so, for Augustine, conversion must be ongoing, the work of confession is never complete, there will always be need for further writing (even his *Retractationes* will not suffice here). It is perhaps emblematic of his entire theological enterprise that his last work, a polemical treatise against the Pelagian sympathizer and bishop Julian of Eclanum, was an *opus imperfectum*. The essential difference between Augustine and the schoolmaster who beat him ("not very different from me") reveals itself only to the extent that the bishop is able to recognize the complete character of the symmetry between them. There are but glimpses of this capacity to be seized upon in Augustine's writings, but they are sufficient to alert us to the multiple, interrelated senses of *ueritatem facere* at work in his thought.

## DERRIDA'S RESPONSE TO ROBERT DODARO

*Jacques Derrida.* I had decided not to say anything because I was so impressed with your lecture, and so grateful, and so unable to address Augustinian questions in competent terms. I had made a decision not to speak. But now you surprise me with an invitation to speak. I want to thank you very warmly. I was very impressed by what you said, by your lucidity and generosity. I learned a lot from what you said about Augustine, especially on the level of his politics. I look forward to reading your work on that subject. There is a hidden thread in *Circumfession* about politics, but I cannot improvise on the topic here. Speaking about surprise, and the surprised subject, I had a surprise this morning when you translated the "G" of Geoff as "God." I had not thought about that. But of course you are right, because I often identify Geoff's position with God's position, but also with my mother's position, whose first name is Georgette. So "G" was my mother. Perhaps it makes no difference. So today, for the first time, I realize that "G" might mean God. Speaking of surprise, or of surprising Geoff, or of not being able to surprise him, I am not sure I surprised him. Insofar as he wanted to provoke a surprise, he was anticipating a surprise, so he was not surprised at all. In that case, he was no doubt in the position of God.

What I wanted to do in *Circumfession* was just to analyze in my own modest way the *structure* of this situation in which the confession is addressed to someone who is supposed to know, which means that the confession has nothing to do with knowledge. You do not discover, reveal, or inform the other; you just do something else than learning, teaching, informing, or even knowing. I tried practically, pragmatically, as Marion would say, to experience this situation analytically in order to read Augustine in my own way and to read what I was doing at the same time, to analyze the structure of the confession in which the act of confessing has nothing to do with knowledge, not intrinsically. Of course, it conveys a lot of knowledge, of self-analysis and so on, but in its structure it is totally foreign and heterogeneous to knowledge. It is from that point of view that I would read or re-read what you said in the last part of your lecture about faith and knowledge and the radical heterogeneity between faith and knowledge. That does not mean they have nothing to do with each other, or, as you have so wonderfully demonstrated, that the truth is not beyond faith. But even if truth is not beyond faith, it is heterogenous to the experience of faith, and there would be no faith otherwise. I tried at the same time to experience and analyze this structure. Taking my own experience as a modest and small example, I tried to play with Augustine's immense text in this way.

By the way, I would say that if I am so grateful for what you said, it was not only because I learned a lot and you said so many generous things about my text, but because, as you can imagine, when I wrote this text, I was not only scared by the possibility of my being violent or blasphemous, but scared by the possibility of being simply naively incompetent, of naively missing something. So I easily accept the charge of having been violent, or having missed something in Augustine through incompetence. But I suffer when I have the feeling that I could be simply complacent about my own incompetence. What you said about complacency touched me very deeply.

The only question I can articulate now — I will have a number of questions when I re-read your paper and your books — is the question about the relationship between Augustine's actual politics, which you refer to as finally a conservative politics, as you would say, and what you analyze as deconstructive. How can you associate this conservative side with this subversive side from a political and theological point of view? That would be the perspective of a possible question. I thank you for your paper.

*Robert Dodaro.* Yes, I think, that Augustine's politics were conservative and yet subversive at the same time. Repressive with respect to pluralism, intolerant, but then, as Peter Brown has reminded us, brilliantly, in an essay entitled "The Limits of Intolerance" in his book *Authority and the Sacred,* there was no option in late antiquity, no religious toleration, not Christian, not Jewish, not pagan. The claim may be exaggerated but I think Brown and others make a strong case. That is not to excuse Augustine either, nor is it a way of placing him in an historical context in such a way as to deny that there is any theory other than historical context. But the important thing is this notion of ongoing conversion, ongoing repentance. We never exhaust the need to examine ourselves, to see the emperor in ourselves when we judge the pirate, to see the pharisees and scribes in ourselves when we are judging the adulteress, to see all of that in ourselves even while we are judging, repressing, controlling, administering the city or the church. It is not as if — and here is where I do not feel entirely at ease with John Milbank's position — the church will ever really *not* practice some form of ontological or institutional violence. It will repress heretics. This will go on. I guarantee it. But if it were Augustinian, then it would be self-flagellating at the same time. It would be . . .

Robert Dodaro

> *Jacques Derrida.* . . . invisible.
> *Robert Dodaro.* Invisible? Well, I would say it would be visible, but not with any consequence.

## NOTES

1. "Serious play" is a key concept for Derrida, and his oeuvre ought to be approached in its light. During a roundtable conversation held in October 1994 at Villanova University, Derrida broached the topic with regard to his treatment of Augustine in *Circumfessions:* "If I had to summarize what I am doing with St. Augustine in *Circumfession*, I would say this. On the one hand, I play with some analogies, that he came from Algeria, that his mother died in Europe, the way my mother was dying in Nice when I was writing this, and so on. I am constantly playing, seriously playing, with this, and quoting sentences from the *Confessions* in Latin, all the while trying, through my love and admiration for St. Augustine—I have enormous and immense admiration for him—to ask questions about a number of axioms, not only in his *Confessions* but in his politics, too. So there is a love story and a deconstruction between us." Cf. *Deconstruction in a Nutshell: A Conversation with Jacques Derrida,* edited and with a commentary by J. D. Caputo (New York: Fordham University Press, 1997), 20–21, along with Caputo's remarks about Derrida's "seriousness" in reading Plato (71–105).

2. So also J. D. Caputo, *The Prayers and Tears of Jacques Derrida: Religion without Religion* (Bloomington: Indiana University Press, 1997), 285, writing about *Circumfession:* "The text disseminates in so many directions—autobiographical, psychoanalytic, literary, political, pedagogical, theological and philosophical—as to make nonsense of the idea of a definitive commentary. . . . Thus do I excuse myself from getting this text right, let alone getting all of it right; thus do I confess and ask pardon, right at the start."

3. I was invited by the Villanova University conference organizers to examine the relationship between Derrida's and Augustine's thought on the basis of "Circumfession: Fifty-nine Periods and Periphrases Written in a Sort of Internal Margin, between Geoffrey Bennington's Book and Work in Preparation (January 1989–April 1990)," in G. Bennington and J. Derrida, *Jacques Derrida,* trans. by G. Bennington (Chicago: University of Chicago Press, 1993). In attempting to honor this invitation (for which I wish to express my gratitude), I have been less interested in producing an exposition of Derrida's interpretation of Augustine than in returning to some of the issues present in the *Confessions* in the light of a sympathetic reading of *Circumfession.* I ask the reader's indulgence for having allowed the revision to retain much of the character of a *pièce d'occasion.* I want to acknowledge gratefully Professor Wayne Hankey of Dalhousie University and of the University of King's College, Halifax, Nova Scotia, for many crucial conversations with me over an extended period of time on both Augustine and Derrida.

4. "*validissimus malleus haereticorum.*" Cf. Bernard of Clairvaux, *Homiliae super Canticum Canticorum* 80.7, in *Opera omnia,* ed. J. Leclercq, G. H. Talbot, and H. M. Rochais, vol. 2 (Rome: Editiones Cistercienses, 1958), 282, who applied the term to Augustine with reference to his arguments against the Arians at *De trinitate* 6.11. Cf. R. Arbesmann, "The *Malleus* Metaphor in Medieval Characterization," *Traditio* 3

(1945): 389–92; J. Courcelle-Ladmirant and P. Courcelle, *Iconographie de Saint Augustin. Les cycles du XIV^e siècle* (Paris: Etudes augustiniennes, 1965), 78–79.

5. This criticism of Augustine is commonplace, but cf. J. O'Leary, *Questioning Back: The Overcoming of Metaphysics in Christian Tradition* (Minneapolis: Winston Press, 1985), 165–202: "Overcoming Augustine." W. E. Connolly, *The Augustinian Imperative: A Reflection on the Politics of Morality* (Newbury Park, Calif.: Sage Publications, 1993), offers a critique of Augustinian authoritarianism rooted in an analysis of the role of confession in his theology.

6. Cf. Augustine, *Confessiones* 1.9.14–15; 1.10.16; 1.14.23; 1.16.26; 1.17.27.

7. On Augustine's pronunciation of Latin, cf. his *De ordine* 2.45; P. Brown, *Augustine: A Biography* (London: Faber & Faber, 1967), 88. On his political ambitions at the time, cf. Augustine, *Confessiones* 6.6.9; 8.1.2; 8.7.18; 8.12.30; 9.1.1. He tells us that, on the basis of his service as *orator urbis Mediolanensis*, and with the aid of additional influential patrons, he was hoping at least to win a provincial governorship (cf. ibid., 6.11.18–19). Cf. C. Lepelley, "*Spes Saecvli:* Le milieu social d'Augustin et ses ambitions séculières avant sa conversion," in *Atti del congresso internazionale su s. Agostino nel XVI centenario della conversione,* vol. 1 (Rome: Institutum Patristicum Augustinianum, 1987), 99–117. Cf. also Brown, *Augustine* 65–72.

8. Cf., for example, Derrida, *Circumfession* 210–11. References to Derrida's discussion of his Jewishness in relation to the other as outsider, and on the childhood humiliations which he suffered as a Jew are conveniently listed in Caputo, *Prayers,* 230–34; 303–305. Cf. also G. Bennington, "Acts (the Law of Genre)," in Bennington and Derrida, *Jacques Derrida,* 325–27.

9. Derrida at least twice refers to Augustine as "my compatriot." Cf. *Circumfession,* 18, 46.

10. Cf. *Sylloge Inscriptionum Graecarum,* ed. W. Dittenberger, vol. 1 (Leipzig: apud S. Hirzelium, 1915–1924), 241 (line 103), records a fourth century B.C. Delphic inscription wherein *kanna* refers to a writing instrument. In a related sense, *canna* also forms the basis of "canal." Cf. *Thesaurus Linguae Latinae,* vol. 3 (Leipzig: B. G. Teubner, 1906–1912), 223–25, s.v. canalis; and the *Oxford Latin Dictionary* (Oxford: Clarendon Press, 1968), 263, s.v. canalis. Derrida, *Circumfession* 10, compares the pen with which he writes to a syringe which once removed blood from one of his crural veins.

11. I think here of various *canones* along with their relationship to *regulae,* as in the early Christian *regula fidei* or monastic *regulae,* but also of canonicity in relation to defining the books of Scripture. Cf. *A Patristic Greek Lexicon,* ed. G. W. H. Lampe (Oxford: Clarendon, 1961), 701–702, s.v. kanon; A. Blaise, *Dictionnaire Latin-Français des auteurs chrétiens* (Turnhout: Brepols, 1954), 127–28, s.v. canon; *Lexikon für Theologie und Kirche,* vol. 5 (Freiburg: Herder, 1996), 1177–84, s.v. Kanon. Cf. *Circumfession,* 47: "no matter, writing is only interesting in proportion and in the experience of evil, even if the point is indeed to 'make' a truth in a style, a book and before witnesses." For some of Derrida's views concerning what it means to "transgress" limits or norms, cf. his article "The Principle of Reason: The University in the Eyes of Its Pupils," *Diacritics* 13 (1983): 3–20, especially 17. But since "Plato's Pharmacy" this dynamic is also fundamental to Derrida's reading of philosophical texts. Cf. Caputo, *Deconstruction,* 80–82. On the grammatical, literary, and philosophical background of canon, cf. *Paulys Real-Encyclopädie der classischen Altertumswissenschaft,* ed. by W. Kroll, vol. 20 (Stuttgart: J.-B. Metler, 1919), 1873–78, s.v. Kanon; and H. Oppel,

"KANON: Zur Bedeutungsgeschichte des Wortes und seiner lateinischen Entsprechung," *Philologus*, Supplementenband 30 (1937): 1–108. On the development of the term in connection with canon law, cf. L. Wenger, *Canon in den römischen Rechtsquellen und in den Papyri: Eine Wortstudie*, Situngsberichte der Österreichischen Akademie der Wissenschaften, Philosophisch-Historische Klasse, Bd. 220, Abhandlungen 2 (Vienna: Hölder-Pichler-Tempsky, 1942). Various lexicons provide examples of the semantic links between the terms in several languages. Cf., in particular, the *Thesaurus Linguae Latinae*, vol. 3, 261–62, s.v. canna; 272–275, s.v. canon; *A Greek-English Lexicon*, ed. H. G. Liddell and R. Scott (Oxford: Clarendon Press, 1940), 874, s.v. kanna; 875–76, s.v. kanon; and the *Oxford English Dictionary*, s.v. canon and cannon.

12. R. Lim's chapter "The Containment of the *Logos*," in *Public Disputation, Power, and Social Order in Late Antiquity* (Berkeley: University of California Press, 1995), 215–29, traces the subversion of public debate in favor of a growing obsession with written records and documents during fourth- and fifth-century doctrinal struggles over the definition of Christian orthodoxy. "The living voice of public disputation was nearly silenced by the insistent voice of written authorities at the Council of Ephesus in A.D. 431. From then on, the sway of the *logos* in formal councils was eclipsed by consensual procedures that centered on written evidence read aloud by *notarii* and episcopal *sententiae* reacting to these documents" (220). Cf. also H. C. Teitler, *Notarii and Exceptores: An Inquiry into Role and Significance of Shorthand Writers in the Imperial and Ecclesiastical Bureaucracy of the Roman Empire: From the Early Principate to c. 450 A.D.* (Amsterdam: J. C. Gieben, 1985).

13. Bennington and Derrida, *Jacques Derrida*, 1.

14. G. Bennington, "Derridabase," in Bennington and Derrida, *Jacques Derrida*, 8.

15. Bennington and Derrida, *Jacques Derrida*, 1.

16. Ibid.

17. Derrida, *Circumfession*, 154–55.

18. Caputo, *Prayers*, xviii. Elsewhere in *Prayers*, Caputo comments, "So *Circumfession* tells the surprising story of Derrida's conversion from . . . secular texts and languages to a certain Hebrew, to his life of faith and passion, of prayers and tears" (285).

19. Derrida, *Circumfession*, 154. Compare his statement with Augustine, *Confessiones* 10.3.4: "there are many people who have read my works or know me only by hearsay. None of these have laid their ears to my heart, though it is only there that I am whoever I am."

20. *Circumfession*, 3.

21. Ibid., 10–15; 194: "uncircumcised piece of writing."

22. Bennington, "Derridabase," 3–4.

23. Ibid., 188–91.

24. Cf. Derrida, *Circumfession*, 122.

25. Cf. Derrida, *Circumfession*, 19: "I am not writing about Saint Georgette, the name of my mother, whom her brother sometimes used to call Geo." At *Circumfession*, 46, Derrida likens Geoff's "theologic program" to a "maternal figure of absolute knowledge." Cf. also ibid., 30–31.

26. Cf. ibid., 13: "and it's as though Geoff, very close, pronounce it Djef"; 16–17: "not even the theologic program elaborated by Geoff who remains very close to God, for he knows everything about the 'logic' of what I might have written in the past . . .

who you would be tempted to compare to Augustine's God when he asks whether there is any sense in confessing anything to him when He knows everything in advance."

27. Cf. ibid., 13, 31: "G. whom I love and admire, as will rapidly have been understood, whom I prefer, oh yes, and I could never have accepted, jealous as I am, to write a book, a book about me, with anybody else"; 36: "for even if I wanted to break his machine, and in doing so hurt him, I couldn't do so, and anyway I have no desire to do so, I love him too much."

28. There are numerous examples, but note, for example, that at the point in his text where Bennington begins to discuss "The Sign" in Derrida's thought ("Derrida-base," 22– 23), Derrida recalls that his dying mother could no longer remember his name: "and therefore for the rest of her life I no longer have a name . . . and when she nonetheless seems to reply to me, she is presumably replying to someone who happens to be me without her knowing it." (*Circumfession*, 22).

29. The issue of self-knowledge in Augustine is the subject of renewed controversy. R. Williams, "The Paradoxes of Self-Knowledge in the *De Trinitate*," in *Augustine: Presbyter Factus Sum*, ed. J. T. Lienhard, S.J., E. C. Muller, S.J., and R. J. Teske, S.J. (New York: Peter Lang, 1993), 121–34; and idem, "*Sapientia* and the Trinity: Reflections on the *De Trinitate*," in *Collectanea Augustiniana: Mélanges T. J. van Bavel*, ed. B. Bruning, M. Lamberigts, and J. Van Houtem, vol. 1 (Leuven: Augustinian Historical Institute, 1990) (*Augustiniana* 40:1–4, 317–32); L. Ayres, "The Discipline of Self-Knowledge in Augustine's *De Trinitate* Book X," in *The Passionate Intellect: Essays on the Transformation of Classical Traditions Presented to Prof. I. G. Kidd* (New Brunswick, New Jersey: Transaction Press, 1995), 261–96; and J. Milbank, "Sacred Triads: Augustine and the Indo-European Soul," *Modern Theology* 13 (1997) 451–74, challenge recent presentations of self-knowledge in Augustine. Williams and Ayres are unconvinced by scholars such as E. Booth, "St. Augustine's *notitia sui* Related to Aristotle and the Early Neo-Platonists," *Augustiniana* 27 (1977): 70–132, 364–401; 28 (1978): 183–221; 29 (1979): 97–124; idem, "St. Augustine's *De Trinitate* and Aristotelian and Neo-Platonist Noetic," *Studia Patristica* (papers presented at the Seventh International Conference on Patristic Studies, Oxford, 1975), vol.16, part 2, ed. by E. A. Livingstone (Berlin, Akademie-Verlag, 1985), 487–490; and idem, *Saint Augustine and the Western Tradition of Self-Knowing* (Villanova, Pa.: Villanova University Press, 1989); and by G. P. O'Daly, *Augustine's Philosophy of Mind* (London: Duckworth, 1987), of the degree to which the character of self-knowledge in Augustine will abide comparison with Descartes. Meanwhile, Ayres and Milbank oppose the close alignment of Augustine with Platonic interiority as found in C. Taylor, *Sources of the Self: The Making of Modern Identity* (Cambridge: Cambridge University Press, 1989), 127–42. Clearly, Augustine's descriptions of the nature and function of certainty about himself vary among his different treatments of the question, which he examines against the backdrop of a range of ancient philosophical skepticisms. Nevertheless, these descriptions yield an Augustinian position on self-knowledge which endows it with an assured metaphysical status, different as this is both in structure and in function from that found in Descartes. *Circumfession* assumes this to be the character of self-knowledge for Augustine, and I see no reason to challenge the assumption. For a fresh discussion of the approaches to self-knowledge uniting and separating Augustine and Descartes, cf. B. Stock, *Augustine the Reader: Meditation, Self-Knowledge, and the Ethics of Interpretation* (Cambridge, Mass.: The Belknap Press of Harvard University Press, 1996), 243–78; and now S. Menn, *Augustine and Descartes* (Cambridge: Cam-

Robert Dodaro

bridge University Press, 1998). For a helpful, clear statement of the *status quaestionis* of Augustine's relationship to "Platonic" philosophies, cf. R. D. Crouse, "*Paucis mutatis verbis:* St. Augustine's Platonism," in *Augustine and His Critics*, ed. R. Dodaro and G. Lawless (London and New York: Routledge), forthcoming.

30. Cf. J. Rist, *Augustine: Ancient Thought Baptized* (Cambridge: Cambridge University Press, 1994), 145–47.

31. Cf. Augustine, *Confessiones* 10.1.1 (CSEL 33/1.226): "uolo eam [ueritatem] facere in corde meo, coram te in confessione, in stilo autem meo coram multis testibus." All translations of *Confessiones* are taken from *St. Augustine, The Confessions*, trans. by M. Boulding, ed. by J. E. Rotelle (New York: New City Press, 1997). Hereafter, references to Augustine's *Confessiones* will be placed in parentheses within the text.

32. Augustine's admission in the first part of this statement, literally translated as "I want to do truth," depends upon John 3:21 ("But the one who does truth comes to the light"), which he cites partially in the preceding sentence. Derrida plays on the expression *ueritatem facere* suggesting thereby that "there is no truth beyond the truth one 'does,' the truth one 'makes' of oneself" (Caputo, *Prayers*, 290, referring to Derrida, *Circumfession*, 47–49).

33. R. J. O'Connell, *St. Augustine's Confessions: The Odyssey of Soul* (Cambridge, Massachusetts: The Belknap Press of Harvard University Press, 1969), especially 120–34.

34. The reference to 10.1.1 is manifested by the allusion once again to John 3:21. Cf. CSEL 33/1.274: "etiamne id restat, ut ipse me seducam et *uerum non faciam* coram te in corde et lingua mea?"

35. Cf. above, n. 32.

36. *Pace* Boulding, *St. Augustine* (cf. above, n. 31), 280 n. 176. Cf. J. J. O'Donnell, *Augustine, Confessions, Volume III: Commentary on Books 8–13; Indexes* (Oxford: Clarendon Press, 1992), 238.

37. Derrida, *Circumfession*, 10–12.

38. *Cruor*, blood as it flows from the body as distinct from *sanguis*, the blood within the body. Cf. ibid., 6.

39. Cf. ibid., 10: "leaving me nothing more to do, the inside of my life exhibiting itself outside, *expressing* it before my eyes, absolved without a gesture, dare I say of writing if I compare the pen to a syringe."

40. This *cruor* is alliterated to "crude word" (ibid., 3), and thus associated with Geoff's attempt to extract (like blood) the essence of Derrida's thought: "a circumference licking me with a flame and that I try in turn to circumvent, having never loved anything but the impossible, the crudeness I don't believe in, and the crude word lets flow into him through the channel of the ear, another vein, faith, profession of faith or confession, belief, credulity, as though I were attached to him just to look for a quarrel by opposing a naive, credulous piece of writing which by some immediate transfusion calls on the reader's belief as much as my own." (ibid., 3–4); "then the glorious appeasement, at least what I call the glorious appeasement . . . should expose outward, and thus to its death, what will have been most alive in me" (ibid., 12–13).

41. Ibid., 3.

42. One thinks again of pen/stylus as *canna/canon*: canon/cannon.

43. Derrida, *Circumfession*, 11–12.

44. Ibid., 13.

45. Cf. ibid., 6.

46. Cf. ibid., 155: "but she must have known that the constancy of God in my life is called by other names, so that I quite rightly pass for an atheist"; 314: "that secret truth, that is to say, severed from the truth." Cf. Caputo, *Prayers*, 284, 290–91.

47. J. Milbank, *Theology and Social Theory: Beyond Secular Reason* (Oxford: Basil Blackwell, 1990), 402.

48. Ibid.

49. Ibid., 403.

50. Ibid., 402.

51. Cf. E. Rebillard, "Orthodoxie, Ecriture et doctrine chrétienne: propositions pour une approache processuelle de l'orthodoxie à propos de la controverse pélagienne sur la grâce," in *Définir, maintenir et remettre en cause l'«orthodoxie» dans l'histoire du christianisme*, Communications présentées au colloque des 5–8 juin 1998, ed. A. Romano and E. Rebillard (Rome: Ecole française de Rome), forthcoming. Cf. also J. P. Burns, "Augustine's Role in the Imperial Action against Pelagius," *Journal of Theological Studies*, n.s. 30 (1979): 67–83. Fundamental for consideration of Augustine's action against the Pelagians is O. Wermelinger, *Rom und Pelagius. Die theologische Position der römischen Bischöfe im pelagianischen Streit in den Jahren 411–432* (Stuttgart: Anton Hiersemann, 1975); and idem, "Neuere Forschungskontroversen um Augustinus und Pelagius," in *Internationales Symposium über den Stand der Augustinus-Forschung*, ed. C. Mayer and K.-H. Chelius (Würzburg: Augustinus-Verlag, 1989), 189–217. Cf. also Brown, *Augustine*, 353–64.

52. Ibid., 418–19.

53. In this connection, cf. also the criticism offered by R. Williams, "Saving Time: Thoughts on Practice, Patience and Vision," *New Blackfriars* 73, no. 861 (June 1992): 319–26.

54. Cf. Augustine, *Confessiones* 10.42.67 (CSEL 33/1.277): "Quem inuenirem, qui me reconcilaret tibi? ambiendum mihi fuit ad angelos? qua prece? quibus sacramentis? multi conantes ad te redire neque per se ipsos ualentes, sicut audio, temtauerunt haec et inciderunt in desiderium curiosarum uisionum et digni habiti sunt inlusionibus. elati enim te quaerebant doctrinae fastu exserentes potius quam tundentes pectora et adduxerunt sibi per similitudinem cordis sui conspirantes et socias superbiae suae potestates aeris huius, a quibus per potentias magicas deciperentur, quaerentes mediatorem, per quem purgarentur, et non erat. diabolus enim erat transfigurans se in angelum lucis." (Whom could I find to reconcile me to you? Should I go courting the angels? With what prayer or by what rites could I win them to my cause? Many have there been who tried to make their way back to you and, finding themselves insufficient by their own powers, had recourse to such means as these, only to lapse into a fancy for visions that tickled their curiosity. They were deservedly deluded for they sought you in arrogance, thrusting out their chests in their haughty knowledge instead of beating them in penitence; and so they attracted to themselves the spiritual powers of the air as their true kin, fit accomplices and allies of their pride. These spirits used magical powers to beguile their clients, who were seeking a mediator to purge them of their impurities, but found none; for there was no one there but the devil, disguised as an angel of light.)

55. Augustine's remarks concerning Neoplatonist theurgy at *Confessiones* 10.42.67 are typical of his treatment elsewhere (especially in *De ciuitate Dei*, Book 10), and are based on a rivalry with theurgy which, in the late fourth and fifth centuries, offered a

challenge to Christian eucharistic theology. Cf. R. Dodaro, "*Christus sacerdos*: Augustine's Preaching against Pagan Priests in the Light of *S. Dolbeau* 26 and 23," in *Augustin Prédicateur (395–411)*, *Actes du Colloque International de Chantilly (5–7 septembre 1996)*, ed. G. Madec (Paris: Etudes augustiniennes, 1998), 377–93, which concerns especially the arguments marshaled by Augustine against theurgy as a sacramental *system* in his *Sermo Dolbeau*, 26 (*Sermo Mainz*, 62), recently published in Augustin d'Hippone, *Vingt-six sermons au peuple d'Afrique*, ed. F. Dolbeau (Paris: Institut d'Etudes Augustiniennes, 1996), 366–417. On Neoplatonic theurgy as a religious and philosophical system, cf. especially H.-D. Saffrey, "La théurgie comme phénomène culturel chez les néoplatoniciens (IV$^e$-V$^e$ siècles)," *Recherches sur le néoplatonisme après Plotin* (Paris: Vrin, 1990), 51–61 (*Koinonia* 8 [1984]: 161–71); P. Athanassiadi, "Dreams, Theurgy, and Freelance Divination: The Testimony of Iamblichus," *Journal of Roman Studies* 83 (1993): 115–30; and now G. Shaw, *Theurgy and the Soul: The Neoplatonism of Iamblichus* (University Park, Pa.: Pennsylvania State University Press, 1996).

56. Cf., for example, *Codex Theodosianus* 16.10.17–18 (A.D. 399); 15.1.41 (A.D. 401). Cf. Augustine, *De ciuitate Dei* 18.54.1, and O. Perler (en collaboration avec. J.-L. Maier), *Les voyages de saint Augustin*, (Paris: Etudes augustiniennes, 1969), 391–95: "Les événements antipaïens de 399 à Carthage." R. Markus, *The End of Ancient Christianity* (Cambridge: Cambridge University Press, 1990), 115–21 offers a concise view of the developments during A.D. 399–401.

57. Cf., for example, Augustine, *Epistula* 50 to the municipal councillors at Sufes in the Roman African province of Byzacena in the aftermath of a such a riot. In A.D. 399, following the promulgation of an edict of the Emperor Honorius which ordered Gaudentius, the *comes* of Africa, to destroy pagan idols and temples at Carthage (cf. *Codex Theodosianus*, n. 56), Augustine preached *Sermo* 62 in which he urged Catholics at Carthage to show restraint in opposing pagan rituals. He again urged Catholics to avoid such provocations in *Sermo* 24, which he preached at Carthage in A.D. 401. Cf. also *Epistulae* 90, 91, 103, 104, concerning religious rioting at Calama in the Roman African province of Numidia in A.D. 408. R. Markus, *The End of Ancient Christianity*, 113, rightly points out that in *Sermo* 62 Augustine was engaged in "crowd management." Yet he abhorred pagan religious observances and fully supported repressive imperial legislation against it. But cf. P. Garnsey, "Religious Toleration in Classical Antiquity," in *Persecution and Toleration*, ed. W. J. Shields (Oxford: Clarendon Press, 1984), 1–27, who argues soberly that standard modern views of religious toleration found no place among either Christians or pagans in late antiquity. Cf. also F. Paschoud, "L'intolerance chrétienne vue et jugée par les païens," *Cristianesimo nella Storia* 2 (1990): 545–77, who finds that fourth-century pagans were as intolerant as Christians. P. Brown's "The Limits of Intolerance" in *Authority and the Sacred: Aspects of the Christianisation of the Roman World* (Cambridge: Cambridge University Press, 1995), 29–54 endorses both Garnsey's and Paschoud's viewpoints (33–34), yet cautions that we need to pay far greater attention to *paideia* and to the "canon of decorum" which established codes of conduct for the negotiation of religious practice among the social and political elite of the era (40), and less attention to philosophical debates and to the character of imperial legislation in order to evaluate religious intolerance with a more historically accurate viewpoint. Brown argues that, in effect, the practical intolerance may have been less harsh and comprehensive than the written sources seem to suggest.

58. Cf. Augustine, *Epistulae* 185.25 and 93.17.

59. Cf. Augustine, *Epistula* 185.26.

60. Cf. Augustine, *Confessiones* 10.36.59 (CSEL 33/1.270–271): "Sed numquid, domine, qui solus sine tyfo dominaris, quia solus uerus Dominus es, qui non habes dominum, numquid hoc quoque tertium temptationis genus cessauit a me aut cessare in hac tota uita potest, timeri et amari uelle ab hominibus non propter aliud, sed ut inde sit gaudium, quod non est gaudium? . . . itaque nobis, quoniam propter quaedam humanae societatis officia necessarium est amari et timeri ab hominibus, instat aduersarius uerae beatitudinis nostrae ubique spargens in laqueis euge, euge, ut dum auide colligimus, incaute capiamur et a ueritate gaudium nostrum deponamus atque in hominum fallacia ponamus, libeatque nos amari et timeri non propter te, sed pro te." (Is it possible, Lord—this I ask of you who alone hold sway without trace of pride, because you alone are the true Lord who owe fealty to no other—is it possible that the third category of temptation has left me in peace, or ever can leave me in peace throughout my life in this world? This is the temptation to want veneration and affection from others, and to want them not for the sake of some quality that merits them, but in order to make such admiration itself the cause of my joy. . . . The enemy of our true happiness therefore lies in wait for those of us who by reason of our official positions in human society must of necessity be loved and feared (*timeri*) by our fellows. On every side he scatters popular plaudits to trap us, so that as we eagerly collect them we may be caught unawares, and abandon our delight in your truth to look for it instead in human flattery. So the affection and fear we receive come to be something we enjoy not for your sake but in your stead.)

61. Cf. above, n. 7.

62. Cf. especially, M. G. Mara, "Le Confessioni di Agostino: una confluenza di raggiunte convizioni," *Augustinianum* 36, no. 2 (1996): 495–509, especially 505–509: "Polemica anti-donatista."

63. Cf. Augustine, *In Iohannis euangelium tractatus* 33; *Sermones* 13.4–5; 302.14; *Epistula* 153.9–15; *Enarrationes in Psalmos* 50.9–11.

64. Cf. Augustine, *Sermo* 13.7: English translation by E. M. Atkins in *Augustine: Select Letters and Sermons*, ed. R. J. Dodaro and E. M. Atkins (Cambridge: Cambridge University Press), forthcoming.

65. Cf. Augustine, *Confessiones* 1.9.15.

66. Cf. Augustine, *De ciuitate Dei* 4.4. English translation adapted from H. Bettenson, *Augustine: Concerning the City of God against the Pagans* (London: Penguin Books, 1972), 139. Note the use that Noam Chomsky makes of this text in examining the labeling of Palestinians as terrorists. Cf. N. Chomsky, *Pirates & Emperors. International Terrorism in the Real World* (Montréal and New York: Black Rose Books, 1991), 9.

67. Cf. R. Dodaro, "Eloquent Lies, Just Wars, and the Politics of Persuasion: Reading Augustine's *City of God* in a 'Postmodern' World," *Augustinian Studies* 25 (1994): 77–138, especially 105–112.

68. Petilian, Donatist bishop of Cirta, regarded Catholic offers of negotiation as "war waged with kisses." Cf. Augustine, *Contra litteras Petiliani* 2.17.38.

69. Correction and punishment are core themes in Augustine's work. Cf. T. J. van Bavel, "Correctio, corrigere" and "Correptio, corripere," *Augustinus-Lexikon*, vol. 2, fasc. 1/2: *Cor-Deus*, ed. C. Mayer (Basel: Schwabe & Co., 1996), respectively at 22–27 and 35–39.

70. I say "either he *or* his church" because the two sets of judgments cannot always be said to have coincided. In the controversy with Pelagius and his companions, Augustine and other African bishops pursued condemnation until Zosimus, bishop of Rome (A.D. 417–418), finally issued his *Epistula "Tractoria"* in June/July 418. In this letter he condemned Pelagius and Celestius for heresy. The action provoked a schism among eighteen Italian bishops including Julian of Eclanum. Among the best general accounts is that of F. G. Nuvolone and A. Solignac, "Pélage et Pélagianisme," *Dictionnaire de Spiritualité*, vol. 12:2 (Paris: Beauchense, 1986), 2889–942. But cf. also the studies indicated above, note 51, along with Perler, *Les voyages*, 328–45; C. Pietri, *Roma Christiana. Recherches sur l'Eglise de Rome, son organisation, sa politique, son idéologie de Miltiade à Sixte III (311–440)* (Rome: Bibliothèque de l'Ecole française d'Athènes et de Rome, 1976), 1222–44, and now M. Lamberigts, "Augustine and Julian of Aeclanum on Zosimus," *Augustiniana* 42 (1992): 311–30.

71. Cf. especially, Zosimus, *Epistula* 2 (*Collectio Avellana* 45 [CSEL 35.99–103]), which is also known as *Epistula "Magnum pondus."* This is the strongest of Zosimus's letters to the African episcopate, and charges them with calumny, citing the example of Susanna (Daniel 13). Cf. also idem, *Epistula* 3 (*Collectio Avellana* 46 [CSEL 35.103–108]), known as *Epistula "Posteaquam a nobis."* For discussion of both letters, cf. Brown, *Augustine*, 360–61, and especially Wermelinger, *Rom*, 143–46, and Lamberigts, "Augustine," 318–23.

72. *De correctione Donatistarum.* Cf. Augustine, *Retractationes* 2.14.

73. The Conference of Carthage was held from 1–8 June A.D. 411 in the presence of more than 500 bishops, Donatist and Catholic. Augustine took part as one of seven Catholic representatives. From the outset, the Donatists rightly understood the Conference, which had been convoked by the emperor Honorius, as a pretense for their condemnation. As expected, the imperial legate Marcellinus ruled in favor of the Catholics. An appeal to the emperor Honorius produced on 30 January 412 an even harsher edict by which Donatist clergy were ordered into exile outside North Africa (cf. *Codex Theodosianus* 16.5.52).

74. Referring to the petition of the Lord's Prayer, "forgive us our debts, as we forgive our debtors." Cf., Matthew 6:12; Luke 11:4.

75. Augustine, *Epistula* 185.38. English translation as in Dodaro and Atkins, *Augustine.*

76. Cf. Augustine, *Confessiones* 7.20.26.

77. Ibid. 7.21.27 (CSEL 33/1.166–167): "Itaque auidissime arripui uenerabilem stilum spiritus tui et prae ceteris apostolum Paulum, . . . et coepi et inueni quidquid illac uerum legeram, hac cum commendatione gratiae tuae dici, ut qui uidet non sic glorietur, quasi non acceperit, non solum quod uidet, sed etiam ut uideat—quid enim habet quod non accepit?"

78. Culminating at *De praedestinatione sanctorum* 5.10 [A.D. 429].

79. Augustine, *Sermo* 13.1 (CCL 41.177). "Audiamus Apostolum iudicantem terram: *Non sic pugno,* inquit, *tamquam aerem caedens, sed castigo corpus meum et in seruitutem redigo, ne forte aliis praedicans ipse reprobus efficiar."*

80. Ibid.

81. Augustine, *Sermo* 13.2 (CCL 41.177): "exsultare ei, non sibi."

82. Ibid.: "Si autem putaueris quod ab illo quidem homo es, a te autem iustus es, non seruis Domino in timore, nec exsultas ei in tremore, sed tibi in praesumptione."

83. Ibid. Cf. Exodus 20:1–7; Deuteronomy 5:6–21.

84. Augustine, *Sermo* 13.3 (CCL 41.179): "ut in illo inueniaris qui in te peristi. Non enim potuisti in te nisi perdere te; nescis inuenire te, nisi ille qui fecit te quaerat te."

85. Augustine, *Sermo* 13.4 (CCL 41.179): "Iudicant enim terram reges, duces, principes, iudices."

86. Augustine, *Sermo* 13.8 (CCL 41.182): "Hanc in corde retinens homo in homines dilectionem, esto iudex terrae. Et ama terrere, sed dilige. Si superbis, superbi in peccata, non in hominem. . . . Sed adhibeantur poenae. Non recuso, non interdico, sed animo amantis, animo diligentis, animo corrigentis."

87. Augustine, *Sermo* 13.7 (CCL 41.181–182): "Prius iudica de te, ut de penetrali conscientiae securus procedas ad alterum. In te ipsum redi, te attende, te discute, te audi. . . . Si bene audisti, si recte audisti, si in audiendo te iustus fuisti, si tuae mentis tribunal ascendisti, si graues tortores adhibuisti timoris, bene audisti si sic audisti, . . . Sic audi et proximum tuum."

88. Cf. Augustine, *De trinitate* 8.9. Augustine's concept of justice requires that love of neighbor does not stand in competition either with self-love (cf. Matthew 12:33) or with love of God, because "true love" consists in "loving the other either because they are just or so that they might become just" (*De trinitate* 8.9). Thus, living justly means loving one's neighbors in a way that aids them in living justly by enabling them to love themselves, their neighbors, and God in the manner prescribed by divine law and by the example of Christ (*De trinitate* 8.10). Cf. R. Canning, *The Unity of Love for God and Neighbour in St. Augustine* (Leuven: Augustinian Historical Institute, 1993), 231, 295–313; and Williams, *Sapientia*.

89. Augustine, *Sermo* 13.8–9.

90. Cf. Augustine, *In epistulam Iohannis ad Parthos tractatus decem* 7.8; PL 35.2033. There are parallel texts in Augustine, which are indicated by A. Clerici, *Ama e fa' quello che vuoi* (Palermo: Edizioni Augustinus, 1991), 58–63. Clerici lists four: *In epistulam Iohannis ad Parthos tractatus decem* 10.7; *Sermones* 163B.3; 56.17; and *Expositio epistulae ad Galatas* 57. To Clerici's parallel texts, I would evidently want to add *Sermo* 13.9.

91. Theories concerning the circumstances and dating of these sermons are advanced by A.-M. La Bonnardière, *Recherches de chronologie augustinienne* (Paris: Etudes augustiniennes, 1965), 51–53; and by Perler, *Les voyages*, 451. But cf. P. Agaësse, *Saint Augustin, Commentaire de la Première Epître de S. Jean*, Sources Chrétiennes 75 (Paris: Cerf, 1961), 7–14. A series of repressive edicts enacted by the emperor Honorius in A.D. 405 declared the Donatists "heretics" in legal terms, banned their religious assemblies, and confiscated those private homes which were used for such meetings, threatened the Donatist clergy with exile and their accomplices with harsh floggings. Donatists were also denied certain rights concerning contracts and inheritance. Cf. *Codex Theodosianus* 16.5.37; 16.5.38; 16.5.39; 16.6.3–5; 16.11.2, bearing in mind the reservations expressed by Brown, *Authority*, 29–54.

92. Cf. Clerici, *Ama* 54–58. In one of the parallel texts cited by Clerici, Augustine exhorts his listeners regarding the obligation to forgive enemies, "But if you do forgive him . . . get rid of the hate, I say, from your heart, not the severity. 'What if the one who is asking pardon has to be punished by me?' Do what you will (*fac quod vis*). I imagine that you love your son even when you are beating him. You pay no attention to his tears under the strokes of the cane. . . . All I'm saying is, you must rid your heart of hatred" (cf. Augustine, *Sermo* 56.17). English translation by E. Hill, *The Works of Saint*

Robert Dodaro

*Augustine: A Translation for the 21st Century*, Part III, Vol. 3: *Sermons 51–94*, ed. by J. E. Rotelle (New York: New City Press, 1991), 104–105.

93. Cf. especially K.-H. Lütcke, *«Auctoritas» bei Augustin* (Stuttgart: W. Kohlhammer, 1968); idem, "Auctoritas," in *Augustinus-Lexikon*, vol. 1, ed. C. Mayer (Basel: Schwabe & Co, 1986–1994), 498–510, especially 507–509; P.-T. Camelot, "Autorité de l'Ecriture, autorité de l'Eglise: A propos d'un texte de saint Augustin," in *Mélanges offerts à M.-D. Chenu, maître de théologie* (Paris: Vrin, 1967), 127–33, which offers an interpretation of Augustine, *Contra epistolam Manichei quem uocant fundamenti* 5 (CSEL 25/1.197): "ego uero euangelio non crederem, nisi me catholicae ecclesiae conmoueret auctoritas." Cf. also J. Merdinger, *Rome and the African Church in the Time of Augustine* (New Haven: Yale University Press, 1997), especially Part II (63–208), which presents a fresh account of the complex relations between African Catholic bishops and successive bishops of Rome.

94. Augustine's arguments against Neoplatonists, Donatists, and Pelagians are identified above. To these should be added the following texts which also employ 1 Corinthians 4:7: *Confessiones* 13.14.15: on Manicheans, especially in the context of the sections preceding and following; *De diuersis quaestionibus octaginta tribus* 69.7; *De trinitate* 14.21: on Arians; *De ciuitate Dei* 17.4.7–8: on Jews. Cf. Connolly, *Augustinian Imperative* 63–90, especially 83–85, which analyzes the structure of confession/conversion in regard to Augustine's pursuit of the Pelagians in a manner similar to the argument offered here.

95. Cf. Augustine, *Sermo Dolbeau* 26.36 (ed. Dolbeau, *Vingt-six* 394): "Immundae quippe animae ea ipsa magna immunditia est per seipsam se putare posse purgari. Sed de illis qui nulla idola coluerunt neque aliquibus chaldaicis aut magicis sacris sese obstrinxerunt, temere aliquid dicendum non est, ne forte nos lateat quod eis aliquo modo saluator ille reuelatus sit, sine quo saluari nemo potest" (It is indeed a great uncleanness of the unclean soul, thinking it can purify itself all on its own. But one must not say anything rashly about those who have not worshipped any idols, nor bound themselves over to Chaldean or magical rituals, in case perhaps it has escaped our notice how the saviour, without whom nobody can be saved, has revealed himself to them in some manner or other.) English translation by E. Hill, *The Works of Saint Augustine: A Translation for the 21st Century*, Part III, Vol. 11: *Newly Discovered Sermons*, ed. J. E. Rotelle (New York: New City Press, 1997), 208. Cf. A. Solignac, "Le salut des païens d'après la prédication d'Augustin," in *Augustin Prédicateur (395–411), Actes du Colloque International de Chantilly (5–7 septembre 1996)*, ed. G. Madec (Paris: Etudes augustiniennes, 1998), 419–28; Dodaro, *Christus Sacerdos*.

96. Augustine, *De trinitate* 15.51 (CCL 50/A.534): "Ad hanc regulam fidei dirigens intentionem meam quantum potui, quantum me posse fecisti, quaesiui te et desideraui intellectu uidere quod credidi et multum disputaui et laboraui. Domine deus meus, una spes mea, exaudi me ne fatigatus nolim te quaerere, sed quaeram faciem tuam semper ardenter. Tu da quaerendi uires, qui inueniri te fecisti et magis magisque inueniendi te spem dedisti. Coram te est firmitas et infirmitas mea; illam serua, istam sana. Coram te est scientia et ignorantia mea; ubi mihi aperuisti suscipe intrantem; ubi clausisti aperi pulsanti. Meminerim tui; intellegam te; diligam te. Auge in me ista donec me reformes ad integrum." English translation by E. Hill, *The Works of Saint Augustine: A Translation for the 21st Century*, Part I, Vol. 5: *The Trinity*, ed. J. E. Rotelle (New York: New City Press, 1991), 436.

97. Cf. Augustine, *De trinitate* 1.14; 1.22; 2.2; 2.3; 2.17; 8.1; 15.49; 15.51.

98. Cf. Augustine, *De trinitate* 8.1 (CCL 50.269): "seruata illa regula ut quod intellectui nostro nondum eluxerit a firmitate fidei non dimittatur."

99. Cf. Augustine, *De trinitate* 8.8 (CCL 50.277): "prius autem quam intellegamus credere debemus." Cf. E. TeSelle, "Crede ut intellegas," *Augustinus-Lexikon*, Vol. 2, Fasc. 1/2: *Cor-Deus*, ed. C. Mayer (Basel: Schwabe & Co., 1996), 116–19.

100. Similar to the conclusion of *Confessiones* (13.38.53). Cf. U. Duchrow, "Der Aufbau von Augustinus Schriften *Confessiones* und *De Trinitate*," *Zeitschrift für Theologie und Kirche* 62 (1965): 338–67.

101. Cf. Augustine, *De libero arbitrio* 3.18.52; 3.19.53 (*De natura et gratia* 67.81; 29.33); *De peccatorum meritis et remissione* 2.2.2; *De perfectione iustitiae hominis* 1.1; *De ciuitate Dei* 10.24; 20.6.1; *Retractationes* 1.9.6. Cf. Rist, *Augustine* 135–40.

# four
# Desire of God

Richard Kearney

In *On the Name* (1995), Derrida writes: "The desire of God, God as the other name of desire, deals in the desert with radical atheism."[1] In what follows, I wish to tease out some of the issues thrown up by this arresting statement. When we speak of the desire of God, do we mean our desire for God or God's desire for us? Or both? And if, as Derrida suggests, the desire of God deals with radical atheism, is it possible to reconcile this desire with theism?

## I

Making the wager that it *is* possible to speak of a genuinely theistic desire of God, I will suggest that this requires us to distinguish between two different ways of desiring God—namely, *onto-theological* and *eschatological*. First, what I refer to as the onto-theological paradigm construes desire as *lack*—that is, as a striving for fulfillment in a plenitude of presence. Here desire expresses itself as a drive to be and to know absolutely. *Conatus essendi et cogniscendi.* This relates back to the biblical tales of Adam's Fall and the Tower of Babel— what Genesis, and later the Talmud, referred to as the "evil drive" (*yezer hara*) to be God by refashioning Yahweh in our own image.[2] It is also, no doubt, what I John had in mind when it warned against the "lust of the eyes" for what shines and seduces—a theme taken up by the Pauline preference for what is "unseen" over what is "seen" (Romans 8:18), and again in the Augustinian critique of the "concupiscentia occulorum": the ocular-erotic drive to appropriate the ephemera of the visible universe. At its most sophisticated, this lust of the eyes took the form of an obsessive epistemological curiositas with regard to absolute knowledge. "This empty curiosity is dignified and masked by the names of learning and science," wrote Augustine. " . . . it is called in the divine language the lust of the eyes. . . . Hence also men proceed to investigate the concealed working of nature beyond our ken, which it does no good to know and which men want to know only for the sake of knowing."[3]

This influential passage of Augustine prefigured a whole legacy of suspicion toward the desire for absolute knowing, culminating (as Heidegger noted in his 1920–21 Winter Semester lectures) in Luther's fulminations against the "fornicating of the spirit"—the fornicatio spiritus which seeks to reduce God to a possession of metaphysical vision (visio dei).[4] The attempt by certain philosophers to objectify the deus adventurus into an onto-theological object is nothing but a "desire to dominate and master," argued Luther, for such philosophers "elevate their own opinion so high into the heavens that it is no longer difficult for them . . . to make judgments about God in the same way that a poor shoemaker makes a judgment about leather." So doing, they prefer "power to weakness," the superbia and securitas of speculative constructions to everyday acts of faith. Thus the futural coming of the kingdom finds itself compromised—as does the eschatological yearning invoked by Paul when he described the desire for the kingdom as "hope for what we do not see" (Romans 8:25).[5] Viewed from such a Pauline perspective, the ontology of presence (ousia) is a travesty of the parousia still to come (abousia).

This Judeo-Christian critique of onto-theological desire is, however, by no means reducible to a rejection of desire per se. The Nietzschean verdict that "Christianity gave eros poison to drink" is not quite as self-evident as it seems. On the contrary, the destruction of onto-theological desire might be more properly conceived as a spur to transcend our captivation by all that is (ta onta) for another kind of desire—a desire for something that eye has never seen nor ear heard. That is to say, eschatological desire. Here we might cite the great erotic psalms and canticles which speak of human desire for the Creator as "flesh fainting for God" (Psalm 63); or as an expectant bride yearning for her bridegroom—a biblical genre extending to the erotico-ecstatic writings of many Jewish and Christian mystics, not least of all Augustine himself when he speaks of the erotic restlessness of the soul in search of God—"inquietum cor nostram." Here Augustine addresses God as impassioned lover: "You shed your fragrance about me; I drew breath and now I gasp for your sweet odour. I tasted you and now I hunger and thirst for you. You touched me and I am inflamed with love" (Confessions, Bk 6).

Richard Kearney

What is perhaps most telling here is the active-passive character of this divine desire. Augustine reveals the *double genitive* at work in the "desire of God." It is because the Creator has first shed fragrance and touched Augustine that Augustine is inflamed with passion. Augustine's desire of God is a fervid *response* to God's desire of Augustine. But one of the most revealing verses on this paradox of divine desire—echoed here in Augustine—is surely the Song of Songs 3:1–4 where the anxious, expectant seeking of the lovestruck bride is reversed into a *being-found*, that is, a *being desired.* Here the desire of God is a "hound of heaven" that hunts and finds you, a disguised angel or sentinel who finds you out by asking "where are you?"—"Who goes there?"—and you reply, "Here I am! It is me." The lover of God, this verse tells us, exists in the accusative as well as the nominative. "The bride speaks of her beloved: upon my bed at night I sought him whom my soul loves; I sought him but found him not; I called him, but he gave no answer. So I said to myself, 'I will rise now and go about the city, in the streets and in the squares; I will seek him who my soul loves.' . . . I sought him, but found him not. The sentinels *found me*, as they went about the city. I asked, 'Have you seen him whom my soul loves?' Scarcely had I passed them, when I found him whom my soul loves." It is only *after* the bride has passed the sentinels who "found" her, that she finds *Him* whom her soul loves.

God, it seems, is the other who seeks me out *before* I seek him, a desire beyond my desire, bordering at times, in the excess of its fervor, on political incorrectness! "You have searched me and you know me Lord. . . . You search out my path and are acquainted with all my ways. . . . You hem me in, behind and before, and lay your hand upon me. . . . Where can I flee from you? If I ascend to heaven, you are there; if I make my bed in Sheol, you are there. If I take the wings of the morning and settle at the farthest limits of the sea . . . your right hand shall hold me fast" (Psalm 139). A hot God if ever there was one! This desire of God is no mere deficiency or privation but its own reward —positivity, excess, gift, grace. "Those who seek the Lord *lack* no good thing" (Psalm 34). Why? Because such desire is not some gaping emptiness or negation (as Sartre and certain existentialists held) but an affirmative "yes" to the summons of a superabundant, impassioned God—"Here I am. Come. Yes, I will. Yes, I will. Yes."

This desire beyond desire I call *eschatological* to the extent that it alludes to an alterity that already summons me yet is not yet, that is already present yet always absent (Philippians 2:12), a *deus adventurus* who seeks me yet is still to come, unpredictably and unexpectedly, "in the twinkling of an eye" (I Corinthians 15:52). "Like a thief in the night" (I Thessalonians 5:2).[6]

But how account for this puzzling phenomenon of desire before and beyond desire—this hyperon/proteron of eschatological eros? I propose to hazard something of a philosophical guess in what follows by adverting to two of the leading thinkers of so-called postmodernity—Levinas on eschatological

114

desire in *Totality and Infinity* (1961) and Derrida on the "desire of God" in *On the Name* and related texts.

## II

Levinas's major work *Totality and Infinity* opens with a definition of eschatology and proceeds, in one of the initial sections, to a phenomenological description of desire. A question immediately arises about how these two terms—eschatology and desire—are related. And it does not take long to realize that, for Levinas, both have the same *ethical* structure—namely, a relationship with the other "beyond the totality."

By "totality," Levinas means "being" as it is encompassed by history, reason, representation, horizon, and power—in brief, *ontology*. Totality, Levinas explains, is all that can be thought and said in terms of "objectivity." This includes the object-presences of representation—as evinced in the *libido dominandi* of speculative epistemology. But it also extends to a) the *archeological* obsession with first causes (a retrospective account of desire running from Neoplatonic metaphysics right through to Freudian psychoanalysis) and b) the *teleological* drive toward a final end (a prospective account of desire proffered by the Hegelian-Marxist model of history). By contrast, Levinas defines *eschatology* as a relationship of desire which breaches the totality of being, opening up what he terms "infinity." "It is a relationship," he explains, "with a *surplus always exterior to the totality*, as though the objective totality did not fill out the true measure of being, as though another concept, the concept of *infinity*, were needed to express this transcendence with regard to totality, non-encompassable within a totality."[7]

Levinas suggests, rather boldly, that a phenomenology of desire holds the key to this eschatological infinity. He thus confronts us with the paradox that the infinite is inscribed *within* our historical experience of totality precisely as a "trace" which betrays that which is "beyond" it. This trace, he argues, is evinced, first and foremost, by *desire* and *responsibility*—desire of the other and responsibility for the other. Eschatological desire is, in short, desire of the infinite.

Contrary to the judgment of history in which Hegel wrongly saw its rationalization, eschatology calls for a different kind of judgment, one which breaks with the totality of wars and empires, one which (*pace* Hegel) does not envisage the end of history within the totality of being. Throwing down the gauntlet to Hegel in the opening arguments of his Preface, Levinas writes: "The eschatological, as the 'beyond' of history, draws beings out of the jurisdiction of history and the future; it arouses them in and calls them forth to their full responsibility. Submitting history as a whole to judgment, exterior to the very wars that mark its end, it restores to *each instant* its full signification in that very instance. . . . [I]t is not the *last judgment* that is decisive, but the *judgment of all the instants of time* (my italics), when the living are judged."[8] Here, already, Levinas touches on one of the most puzzling features of the desire of God—its yearning for an eschatological kingdom *beyond history* while welcoming the coming of what comes *in each instant!*

The way we get from totality to infinity is, Levinas suggests in the first chapter of *Totality and Infinity*, by following the way of desire. Here, in a section entitled "Desire for the Invisible," Levinas describes a desire for the absolutely other whom we cannot see, consume, or represent. This desire is not only different from biological *need*, but from all dialectical concepts of eros considered as *lack* driving toward fulfillment (e.g., desire as unconscious libido in Freud-Lacan or as struggle for power and recognition in Hegel-Kojève. One thinks especially of Kojève's canonical definition of desire as an "emptiness that wants to be filled by what is full").[9]

Let me briefly rehearse some decisive turns in Levinas's presentation. We begin our existence in sensible immediacy and familiarity—a *chez soi*—only to be turned toward an "elsewhere," an "otherwise," an other. Desire thus arises as an inaugural and initiating movement toward an other-than-self, and this other cannot be reduced to a thing that one needs or consumes—the bread I eat, the water I drink, the land I appropriate. Things one possesses in this manner are not "absolutely other."

So far, Levinas merely confirms the standard Hegelian distinction between desire and need. But he then marks his departure from the dialectical account of desire as a longing for some coveted lost object. The desire that Levinas calls *metaphysical* (and sometimes eschatological) tends toward something entirely different. "The metaphysical desire does not long to return, for it is desire for a land not of our birth, for a land foreign to every nature, which has not been our fatherland and to which we shall never betake ourselves."[10] This is not the desire of absolute consciousness to return to its own essence. Nor, in spite of Levinas's respect for certain forms of Zionism, is it a promised land that could ever be occupied. No, this most fundamental desire of all desires, *prior* to all needs and inclinations, is the desire of the good.

Here Levinas turns from Hegel to Plato. Heeding the Socratic preference for Diotima over Aristophanes in *The Symposium*, Levinas claims that metaphysical desire "desires beyond everything that can simply complete it. It is like goodness—the Desired does not fulfill it, but deepens it."[11] The desired is like the good precisely because it cannot be possessed, because it is invisible, separate, distant, different, transcendent. This is not to say that desire is without relation, only that it is related to a desired that is never *given*, to an otherness that is absolute precisely because it absolves itself from the intentionality of adequation and appropriation. In other words, desire is a relation that is unequal to itself, asymmetrical.

The desired of eschatological desire exists before memory and beyond anticipation. It is immemorial and unimaginable, exceeding the horizons of historical time. But if the desired good gives itself thus from "beyond" history, it is nonetheless inscribed, as vigilance and summons, in each instant of our existence. It is incoming at all times. It is, moreover, on embracing this eschatological paradox that Levinas goes beyond Plato.

In contrast to both Hegelianism and Platonism, it is not the accomplishment of knowledge but its very inadequacy (*inadequatio*) which exposes the inordinateness of our desire for the absolutely other. This exteriority of the desired vis-à-vis the desirer cannot, however, be understood in terms of horizontal questing—as an endless restlessness that satiates itself in some dialectical infinity. Exhausting every "passion of the possible," it marks an ethical relation to the infinite as *verticality*—transcending all dialectical models of *Wesen* and *Gewesen*, of *anamnesis* and *amnesis*, of *Möglichkeit* and *mögen*. Invoking the language of the Torah, Levinas writes: "For desire this alterity, non-adequate to the idea, has a meaning. It is understood as the alterity of the Other and of the Most-High. The very dimension of height is opened up by metaphysical desire."[12] But this elevation of desire toward the Most-High does not imply (as one might think) a Platonic elevation to a transcendental hinterworld. On the contrary, the experience of height arises, once again, *in the midst of* my relation to the concrete living other. The good *beyond* finds itself inscribed *between* one and another. Desire here again reveals itself not as deficiency but as positivity. Not as *manque-à-être* but as grace and gratuity, gift and surplus, less insufficiency than the bursting forth of the "more" in the "less."[13]

## III

We have seen how an eschatological understanding of desire seeks to chart a course beyond both the Hegelian and Platonic dialectics of desire. In the fourth and final part of *Totality and Infinity*, Levinas embraces this challenge under such headings as "The Ambiguity of Love," "Phenomenology of Eros" and "Subjectivity in Eros."

Levinas here acknowledges the rapport between intersubjective desire and language. Desire is at once language and that which exceeds language. The "erotic" is the "equivocal" par excellence—a simultaneity of need and desire, of concupiscence and transcendence, which reaches the interlocutor and goes beyond him. Eros—as word inscribed in flesh—discloses the "ambiguity of an event situated at the limit of immanence and transcendence."[14] It highlights the oscillation between the Hegelian tale of eros as return-to-origin and Plato's vision of metaphysical elevation. Levinas states the equivocation thus: "Love remains a relation with the Other that turns into need, and this need still presupposes the total, transcendent exteriority of the other, of the beloved. But love also goes beyond the beloved. This is why through the face filters the obscure light coming from beyond the face, from what *is not yet*, from a future never future enough."[15]

This future never future enough signals the messianic advent of eschatological infinity. But if "love" of the other bears ambiguous witness to this on the plane of affective or sexual immanence, it is desire as such which points us toward transcendence in its absolute exteriority. *Desire beyond love* would thus appear to be a higher ethical relation to the other than *desire with love*. Though Levinas never spells this out it seems a logical consequence of his reasoning in this section and one quite in keeping with his trenchant critique of "love" in his 1954 essay "Le Moi et la Totalité": "*L'amour c'est le moi satisfait par le toi, une société à deux, société de solitudes. . . . L'amour ne contient pas la réalité sociale. . . . Le 'tu' véritable n'est pas L'Aimé, détaché des autres. Il se présente dans une autre situation. La crise de la religion dans la vie spirituelle contemporaine tient à la conscience que la société déborde l'amour, qu'un tiers assiste blessé au dialogue amoureux, et qu'à l'égard de lui, la société de l'amour elle-même a tort. . . . Tout amour—à moins de devenir jugement et justice—est l'amour d'un couple. La société close, c'est le couple.*"[16] If love stops short at couples and coupling, desire cuts through toward the irreducible other.

But we are compelled to ask here if it is possible ever to fully separate out the strands of desire and love that mesh so intimately in the term eros? Can one desire the infinite—including infinite justice—without first loving the finite desired flesh in front of us? Can one desire the alterity of goodness without loving *human* others? Can an eschatology of eros ever be wholly disengaged from an intersubjective relation of one-with-another?

## IV

In the section "Phenomenology of Eros," Levinas attempts to tease out some of these puzzles. First, he offers a phenomenological description of the feminine erotic as epitome of *equivocation*—the simultaneity of the clandestine and the exposed, of not-yet-being and being, fragility and weight, violability and inviolability, modest inwardness and profane nudity. But the feminine already signals a secession from Hegel's master-slave dialectic. The feminine remains untouchable in the context of voluptuosity, "not as a freedom struggling with its conqueror, refusing its reification and its objectification, but a fragility at the limit of non-being wherein is lodged not only what is extinguished and is *no longer*, but what is not yet."[17]

From this account of the feminine as oblique witness to an eschatological not-yet, Levinas moves on to a phenomenology of the *caress* (echoing Sartre's analysis in Part 3 of *Being and Nothingness*). He here construes the caress as an erotic surge into the invisible, a transcendence in and through the immediately sensible—what he calls future in the present, "seizing upon nothing, soliciting what ceaselessly escapes its form toward a future never future enough, in soliciting what slips away as though it *were not yet*."[18] This is why Levinas insists, with Hegel and Sartre, that desire is not adequately understood in the terminology of subject and object, consciousness for- and in-itself, possibility and actuality. The erotic, Levinas avers, is not reducible to the *Bildungsprozess* of a subject giving and seeking meaning. Already in the erotic we glimpse the epiphany of the face as eschaton of exteriority; we begin to understand that being-for-the-other escapes the dialectic of antecendence and finality, in that in existing for another I exist otherwise than in existing for me. This erotic epiphany is the portal to ethics itself, the carnal trace of *goodness.*

Levinas is in fact taking issue here with a long tradition—running from the Stoics to Hegel and Sartre—which argued that desire and ethics are opposed. Levinas also appears to take his distance at this point from a herme- neutical approach to eschatological desire as advanced by Ricoeur in *Freud and Philosophy* (1960).[19] For Levinas the signification of the *face* is presup- posed by and makes possible the symbolism of the *sign.* Ethics *precedes* her- meneutics. In this sense even the "double-meaningness" of eros presupposes the face: The feminine is erotic by virtue of the inversion of the face in the ambiguous play of lust. Lust is the mixing of the metaphysical and the ani- mal. In the "lasciviousness of erotic nudity one plays with the Other as with a young animal."[20] In its feminine epiphany, says Levinas, the face that I desire dissimulates, alludes, allures with innuendo, speaks by not speaking. But it is by virtue of this very indirection and obliquity that *eros* represents a sort of *via negativa de profundis* in which voluptuosity breaches the master-slave dialectic of power and project. "Nothing is further from *Eros* than possession. In the possession of the Other I possess the Other inasmuch as he possesses me: I am both slave and master. Voluptuosity would be extinguished in possession."[21]

It is here, finally, that Levinas chooses to replay Hegel's desire of desire *against itself.* For while admitting that voluptuosity aims not at the Other but at the other's voluptuosity—voluptuosity of voluptuosity—he reads this not as a struggle for self-recognition but as *trans-substantiation* through the engen- dering of a child! Here erotic love seeks what is to be engendered—the "in- finitely future"—where same and other are not fused or balanced but, "beyond every possible project, beyond every meaningful and intelligent power—en- gender the child."[22]

Let us pause at this rather startling turn in Levinas's argument. Levinas is speaking here, we must remind ourselves, in eschatological rather than merely biological terms. Engendering the child goes beyond questions of genes and genealogy, of primogeniture and property rights, beyond even the ontological *Eigentum* of *Ereignis* and *Eigentlichkeit.*

And so, Levinas argues, if desire begins in voluptuosity it excels in *pater- nity.* And this excellence is the very opposite of a *privatio* or *steresis.* Paternity, insists Levinas, allows the lover who "loves the love of the Beloved" to return to himself while at the same time moving beyond himself in the coveting of the child, both other and myself. We are here before a new category: the paternal relation with the child as a "desire that is not extinguished in its end nor appeased in its satisfaction."[23]

The transcendence of trans-substantiation—marked by paternity—is one where the I is, in the child, an other, itself as another, one-for-another. The child is the stranger, as Levinas reminds us (invoking Isaiah 49), who is me as a *stranger to myself.* But the future of the child could not come to pass from beyond the dialectical horizons of power were it not, we repeat, for the erotic encounter with the other as feminine—an encounter which breaks the relation with the future as a solipsistic project of the subject, as a power of mastery over possibilities, replacing it with a very different relation to the future which Levinas calls "fecundity." (At the mention of fecundity, all card-carrying Platonists, Hegelians, and Sartrians clear the room!)

## V

In fecundity the subject finds itself again as the self of an other and not only as itself alone: There is a leave-taking of one's former self as "virile and heroic I," a reversal of one's initial subjectivity into infinite recommencement. *Eros* goes toward a future which *is not yet.* Lured by the alterity of the feminine, it leaves behind the imperial subject which from every adventure returns to its Ithaca, like Ulysses. Finding itself the self of an other, erotic subjectivity remains a future by transcending absolutely in fecundity. This freedom of absolute commencement opened up by fecundity has, Levinas claims, nothing to do with a subordination of desire to some impersonal or neutral force—such as "Hegel's universal" or "Freud's unconscious."[24] "It is precisely as itself that the I is, in the relation with the other in femininity, liberated of its identity. . . . In the I being can be produced as infinitely recommencing, that is, properly speaking, as infinite."[25] Thus, in contrast to Heidegger's being-toward-death, Levinas (like Arendt, whom he seems never to have read) here promotes the idea of beginning-again-through-the-birth-of-another—ethics as natality rather than as mortality, as the yes of woman rather than the *nom-du-père,* as *autrement qu'être* rather than *manque à être.*

And so out of the ambiguity of voluptuosity, which remains a quest of desire even in profanation, we discover the fecundity of "infinite being" as a being that is forever *recommencing,* establishing a relation with the child as the other that is not power over the future but a relation with the absolute future of infinite time. In fecundity the obsessive neurosis of the self seeking to repeat itself or return to itself is breached, inaugurating, in the relationship with the alterity of the child, the time of the other as alteration of one's very own substance, the time of a "third" exploding the lovers' *société à deux.*

Accordingly, through a phenomenology of voluptuosity-paternity-fecundity, the desiring self moves from *reiteration* of the self as ego to *initiation* into the enigma of oneself-as-another; it rediscovers within the very depths of voluptuosity a movement of transcendence outward to an Other beyond its power and knowledge.[26] Levinas concludes his phenomenology of desire at this point by reasserting the eschatological infinity of desire: "The Other is not a term: he does not stop the movement of Desire. The other that Desire desires is again Desire; transcendence transcends toward him who transcends—that is the true adventure of paternity, of the transubstantiation which permits going beyond the simple renewal of the possible in the inevitable senescence of the subject. Transcendence, the desire for the Other, the goodness correlative of the face, founds a more profound relation: the goodness of goodness. Fecundity engendering fecundity accomplishes goodness . . . the gift of the power of giving, the conception of the child. Here the Desire which in the first pages of this work we contrasted with need, the Desire that is not a lack, the Desire that is the independence of the separated being and its transcendence, is accomplished—not in being satisfied and in thus acknowledging that it was a need, but in transcending itself, in engendering Desire."[27]

In paternity, as Levinas concludes in a related passage, desire is maintained as "insatiate desire, that is as goodness."[28]

## VI

So what are we to make of all this? The most arresting claim in Levinas's analysis of voluptuosity-fecundity-paternity is that it is desire that keeps love vigilant and asymmetrical. With regard to paternity, we might conclude that the parent loves the child in a way that the child can never be expected to love the parent, but only its own child in turn in the *next* generation—in a future never future enough. The parent who seeks to appropriate the child's desire, making the child return to the parent who engendered it, like Chronos devouring his offspring, twists fecundity back onto itself and forfeits the eschatological infinity of desire. Desire of the other as separate and transcendent is desire as gift rather than appropriation. It is the refusal of incest—the renunciation of *Sittlichkeit* (as family or tribal closure). Desire thus engenders an ethics of asymmetrical fecundity: an ethics that finds its epitome in the desire of God.

But aporias abound. Is eschatological desire ever really possible, we might ask, or is it always deferred to some messianic moment of peace—a future never future enough? Is not the desire we invariably encounter as erotic love, voluptuousity, and fecundity fundamentally at variance with a metaphysical desire for the invisible? Is not paternity—as desire through surplus, selfhood through otherness, recommencement through rupture—not itself an *impossible way of being*, replacing human time with the "messianic time" of "prophetic eschatology"? Or as Levinas himself puts it: Is the eschatological time of eternity—which fecundity and paternity desire—"a new structure of time, or an extreme vigilance of the messianic consciousness"?[29] This problem, Levinas concedes, "exceeds the bounds of this book."[30] Perhaps indeed of any book. For the very hyperbolic excess of Levinas's ethics is, arguably, the very token of its impossibility. An impossibility which prompts John Caputo to claim that "the work of Levinas comes over us today like the voice of a Jewish prophet . . . inspiring a prophetic postmodernism. We are awed, shocked, even scandalized by the sublimity, by the excess, of what Levinas demands, which is clearly too much. . . . What Levinas asks is not possible."[31]

## VII

Let us now look to Derrida for some indication of a response to this impossible dilemma. We return here to his statement: "The desire of God, God as the other name of desire, deals in the desert with radical atheism."[32] The most immediate difference with Levinas here is Derrida's linking of the desire of God with atheism. By locating the desire of God in an atheistic context, Derrida appears, on the face of it, to be reversing the Levinasian position. But what exactly does Derrida mean by atheism? Firstly, he does *not* mean a *dismissal* of the God phenomenon per se but a general openness to an alterity without name, without identity, without the historical givenness of a specifically revealed deity—Jewish, Christian, Muslim, etc. This general disposition toward an alterity to come, understood as unforeseeable advent and event, Derrida calls the "Messianic"—in contradistinction to any particular "messianism" of positive revelation.[33] Atheism, then, is less a refusal of God as such, for Derrida, than a renunciation of a specific God (or Gods) as condition of possibility of a God still to come, still to be named.

We might recall here Derrida's suggestion in *On the Name* that the "most consequent forms of declared atheism will have always testified to the most intense desire of God."[34] Or his observation that "like mysticism, apophatic discourse has always been suspected of atheism" (citing the example of Angelus Silesius suspected by Leibniz).[35] It is, tellingly, on foot of this latter passage that Derrida goes on to ask "Who speaks to whom?" in the "desire of God." "If atheism, like apophatic theology, testifies to the desire of God . . . in the presence of *whom* does it do this?"[36]

What exactly is this desire of God of which Derrida speaks? Let's begin by stating what it is *not*. It differs, most obviously, from the "desire of the proper" operating within a thematics of identity and possession.[37] Desire of God goes beyond the desire to have, to know, to see (*avoir, savoir, voir*). It goes beyond also the "fratricidal desire" of rivalry and *ressentiment* invoked by Augustine in the *Confessions* in his discusssion of sibling rivals at their mother's breast; or by Derrida himself in his allusion to coveting his own elder brother's drawing in *Memoirs of the Blind*.[38]

Desire of God is, Derrida says, not just some insatiable human questing but another voice of apophasis foreign to every "anthropotheomorphic form of desire"—a desire which carries with it "its own proper suspension, the death or the phantom of desire." "To go toward the absolute other," asks Derrida, "isn't that the extreme tension of a desire that tries thereby to renounce its own proper momentum . . . of appropriation?"[39]

This seems very close to what Levinas called *eschatological* desire—a messianic disposition of attention and vigilance, as noted above, transcending the onto-theological nostalgia for original causes and first foundations. Derrida appears to deepen this parallel in his analysis of "*désir et trouble*" in "Archive

Fever"[40] where he deconstructs the archeological desire which burns fever-
ishly for the trace of the primordial beginning, the archive, the *arche*, the
aboriginal origin, the inaugural source. This is the oldest desire, he claims, not
only of archival history but of metaphysics itself—to know, for once and for all,
how it was in the beginning, *in principio, en arche*. This archeological-archival
desire spells trouble, however. It provokes another kind of fever, turning
passion to malady and mania, "for we are thereby driven beyond the archive
to the *arche*, pushed past the slow labor of working with traces, of patiently reconstructing competing versions of memory, in order to displace the trace with
*la chose même*, to displace the general archive with living memory and pure
presence."[41]

But Derrida goes further. Where Levinas could be said to have exempted
certain forms of metaphysical and theological desire from his critique of
presence, Derrida is uncompromising. For deconstruction, Levinas is still *too
metaphysical*. At strategic junctures, Levinas lapses back into the most classical (Neoplatonic) metaphysics, a lapse which prompts Caputo to comment
that "Levinas is vulnerable to all of the criticisms that beset metaphysics, for
this is metaphysics indeed, a metaphysics of the Good not the true, a metaphysical ethics, not a deontology, but metaphysics still."[42] So Derrida (like
Caputo) deconstructs Levinas by taking the metaphysics out of him.

Even negative theology, which shares the same passion for the impossible
as deconstruction, is too specific here in closing down options of radical alterity.[43] For Derrida, negative theologies are not immune to archive fever; they
simply replace the theistic essentialism of onto-theology with a higher and
more rarefied form of hyper-essentialism. Whereas negative theologians—
from the pseudo-Denys to Meister Eckhart and Marion—desire the *"tout
autre"* in the name of a biblical-monotheistic God, deconstruction desires of
the wholly other as *every* other, regardless of its theistic pedigree. An all-in-
clusiveness summed up in the claim—*tout autre est tout autre*.

It is by virtue of this radicalization, this unconditional openness to *every*
other regardless of its identity, that Derrida speaks of a "desire beyond desire":
an atheistic desire in the "other voice," gesturing toward an "absolute other," a
*tout autre* irreducible to the language and limits of anthropo-theo-morphism.
So if Derrida continues to speak of a "desire of God" (as he does) he has in
mind an impossible God of such indeterminate and undefined alterity that it
always remains to be invented. This *à-Dieu* of pure invention is what Derrida
calls the "messianic," namely, a non-lieu of absolute passion and passivity, of
incessant waiting and welcome, preceding and exceeding every historical
revelation of a specific Messiah (the "messianisms" of Judaism, Christianity,
Islam . . . ).

## VIII

In *The Prayers and Tears of Jacques Derrida* (1997), John Caputo equates
this non-locatable "desire beyond desire," this messianic beyond messianism,

123

with deconstruction itself. Deconstruction is the desire for the impossible as impossible, that is, for what is beyond all our intentional horizons of possibility. Indeed Caputo implies that this messianic inventiveness may be just that bit *more* respectful of radical alterity than any of our revealed religious eschatologies. Desire beyond desire is, after all, precisely beyond the "desire of the proper"[44] which draws the Gift "back into the circle of a proper or identifiable Giver which gives us a proper or identifiable Gift."[45] That is why desire beyond desire remains desire for a Godless God—a God still to be invented.[46]

The desire beyond desire is divested, it seems therefore, of all *specific* "horizons of waiting."[47] It keeps all options open. Like the Messiah itself, the time to *faire vos jeux*, cast your die, make your wager, nail your colors to the mast, choose your specific faith, never seems to arrive. Deconstruction is like waiting for Godot—not just in two acts but forever (*go deo*). And here again, we are well beyond negative theology. For if it is true that certain negative theologians and mystics—notably Eckhart—prayed God to rid them of God, they had no doubt that it was the God of Judeo-Christian revelation that they were praying to. Not so with deconstruction. Deconstructive faith is a leap into the dark. Radical atheism.

But in not wishing to exclude any other-to-come is not deconstruction opening itself to the risk of indiscrimination? In *On the Name*, Derrida puts us to the pins of our collars on this vexed question. He writes: "The other, that is, God or no matter who, precisely, any singularity whatsoever, as soon as every other is wholly other. For the most difficult, indeed the impossible, dwells there: there where the other loses his name or is able to change it in order to become no matter what other."[48] But here precisely is the problem—the changing of the messianic other into "every other"? If every other is wholly other, does it still *matter* who or what exactly the other is? Derrida deepens the dilemma at this point, contaminating theology with a dose of teratology, "One should say of *no matter what or no matter whom* what one says of God or *some other thing*" (my italics).[49] And this "some other thing" as we learn in *Given Time* also includes things *neither* divine *nor* human—this is a "wholly other form of alterity: one or other persons but *just as well places, animals, language* (my italics)."[50]

If we thought Kierkegaard was making the question of identifying "who speaks when God speaks" difficult in *Fear and Trembling*, we hadn't yet read Derrida! Caputo offers a gloss on this difficulty, countering that what might *appear* like indifference—every other is the same as every other—is in fact its opposite: a scrupulous attention to the singularity of each other before me in flesh and blood, here and now. "The wholly other is any singularity whatever, whoever, whose this-ness we cannot lift up, cannot generalize, cannot universalize, cannot formalize, any singularity which fixes us in this place so that we cannot look away. . . . Every singularity is a wholly other whose alterity should be respected, not assimilated to the same, not subsumed under the universal."[51]

But can the problem be put to bed so quickly? In thus rightly resisting the temptation to reduce the alterity of every other to the rubric of species and genus, to the identifiable features or fingerprint of a nameable being, is deconstruction (or Caputo's version of it) not, in spite of itself, removing the very criteria whereby we distinguish and differentiate one kind of other from another—divine from human, good from evil, true from false? Are we not in fact confounding the otherness of God with everything and everyone that is not-God, thereby compromising God's unique transcendence? In the name of a God of desire beyond desire, do we not perhaps lose something of the God of love who takes on very definite names, shapes, and actions at very specific points in time, the God of *caritas* and *humilitas* who heals specific cripples and tells specific parables, who comes to bring life here and now and bring it more abundantly? (In fairness, we should also take into account Derrida's reference to "love" in *On the Name* as the "infinite renunciation which in a certain way *gives itself back to the impossible*").[52]

At this juncture, we might recall those figures in sacred history who received a call from God, insisted on some kind of sign, and were granted one. So it was with Gideon who said to the Angel of God who appeared to him under the oak of Ophrah: "Show me a sign that is you who speaks with me" (and he was shown one). So it was with Jacob who wrestled with God's angel through the night until it spoke its name—Israel. So it was with Moses and the burning bush; with Isaiah and the "still, small, voice"; even with Abraham (*pace* Kierkegaard) on Mount Moriah—for the sign that it was the God of goodness who summoned Abraham, and not some evil impostor, was that God intervened and commanded Abraham to replace Isaac with a sacrificial lamb.

So too it was with Christ who, while refusing to convert stone to bread, nonetheless revealed himself as the son of God through acts of healing and love. Even after his death, the resurrected Messiah acknowledged the human need for "signs" of recognition—making himself known to Magdalen as "teacher" (*rabounai*), to Thomas as wounded, to Peter on Lake Tiberias as fisherman, to the disciples on the road to Emmaus as eucharist (the sharer of bread). The passage in Luke is telling here: "They *recognized* him in the breaking of the bread . . . their eyes opened and they *recognized* him." And it is only on foot of this sign that they realized, retrospectively, that "their hearts had been burning inside them while he had spoken to them on the road, explaining the Scriptures" (Luke 24:30–35). It is through a specific sign of identification—the epiphany of broken bread—that the Messiah reveals itself and, at the same time, reveals to the disciples their own desire of God, the burning passion in their hearts for something still beyond them. Here, it is through the *identifiable* eucharistic act of sharing bread that the desire of God is made manifest—*shown* even though it cannot be *said*.

What I find telling in these various incidents is that God needs to be *recognized* for us to be able to say that it is indeed God we desire (and not some idol, simulacrum, or false prophet). That is, presumably, why it is not sufficient for the bride in the Song of Songs to aimlessly wander the streets at night, seeking and desiring "him who her soul loves." She can only find whom she is seeking when God's sentinels *find her* and respond to her burning question "Have you seen him whom my soul loves?" It is because our desire is human that we have to see to believe, that we need signposts and signals on our night journey, sentinels to guard and guide us on our undecidable way toward the absolute other. For without such spiritual guides, without such teachers of wisdom, story, and interpretation, how are we to practice what Ignatius calls "discernment of spirits"—discriminating between good and evil specters, between those thieves that come in the night to rob and violate and those who come to heal and redeem?[53]

## IX

By seemingly releasing the "desire of God" from any particular tradition of revelation and narrative, does deconstruction not make it difficult for us to address this human need to identify God, to look for at least *some* sort of credentials before taking him in—or being taken in? In prizing God free from both onto-theology (where idols abound) and from the biblical messianism with which Levinas and the negative theologians still affiliate themselves, does deconstruction not leave us open to *all* comers?

Derrida acknowledges the terrifying riskiness of undecidable-unidentifiable "newcomers" when he concedes that we have no way of telling the difference between the demonic and divine other. "For pure hospitality or pure gift to occur there must be absolute surprise . . . an opening without horizon of expectation . . . to the newcomer whoever that may be. The newcomer may be good or evil, but if you exclude the possibility that the newcomer is coming to destroy your house, if you want to control this and exclude this terrible possibility in advance, there is no hospitality. . . . The other, like the Messiah, must arrive whenever he or she wants."[54] Indeed, for Derrida it is precisely because we do not see or recognize who the other is that *faith* exists. "If we refer to faith, it is to the extent that we *don't see*. Faith is needed when perception is lacking. . . . I don't *see* the other, I don't *see* what he or she has in mind, or whether he or she wants to deceive me. So I have to trust the other, that is faith. Faith is blind."[55]

This God of absolute faith would be a God of absolute desire—but also a *"tout autre* without face."[56] A God not only of discretion but of absolute "secrecy." A God not only reserved in terms of its coming but an "impossible, unimaginable, un-foreseeable, unbelievable ab-solute surprise."[57] Yet—I repeat—how can we ever recognize a God stripped of every specific horizon of memory and anticipation; how can we ever give *content* to a faith devoid of stories and covenants, promises, alliances, and good works? How can we fully trust in a God devoid of all names (Yawheh, Elohim, Jesus, Allah)? Or whose only real other name is "desire"? If the powers of human vision and imagination are *so* mortified by the impossible God of deconstruction—leaving us "without vision, without truth, without revelation"—then must not our encounter with the "coming of the other" find itself not only blind but empty as well? We might be tempted to put to Derrida here the question he put so adroitly to Levinas in "Violence and Metaphysics"—how is alterity to be *experienced* as other if it surpasses all our phenomenal horizons of experience?

Let me try to spell out further the radicality of deconstruction on this point. If *tout autre* is indeed *tout autre*, what is to prevent us saying yes to an evil alien as much as to a transcendent God who comes to save and liberate? Is there really no way for deconstruction to discriminate between true and false prophets, between bringers of good and bringers of evil, between holy spirits and unholy ones? How do we tell the difference, even if it's only more or less? How do we decide—even if we can never *know* (for certain), or *see* (for sure) or *have* (a definite set of criteria)? Blindness is all very well for luminary painters and writers, for Homer and Rembrandt, but don't most of the rest of us need just a *little* moral insight, just a *few* ethical handrails as we grope through the dark night of postmodern spectrality and simulacritude toward the "absolute other," before we say "yes," "come," "thy will be done"? Is there really no difference, in short, between a living God and a dead one, between Elijah and his "phantom,"[58] between messiahs and monsters?

Caputo has this to say about deconstruction's duty to oblige the monstrous, to accommodate the undecidable: "The figure of the future is an absolute surprise, and as such, Derrida says, something 'monstrous.' To prepare for the future, were it possible, would be to prepare for a coming species of monster, 'to welcome the monstrous *arrivant*, to welcome it, that is, to accord hospitality to that which is absolutely foreign or strange.' Whatever arrives as an 'event,' as an absolute surprise, first takes 'the form of the unacceptable, or even of the intolerable, of the incomprehensible, that is, of a certain monstrosity' (*Points*, 386–87)."[59] Alterity as absolute surprise is absolutely unprepared for: "It is only when the 'come!' calls for something it cannot know or foresee that the come really has passion. Jacques' secret, if there is one, lies on a textual surface, inconspicuous by its superficiality, without a martyr to bear witness, without a revelation to unveil it, without a second coming or even a first. It is always to come."[60]

But can we square such unconditional fideism with the messianic cry of Psalm 34: "Taste and *see* the goodness of the Lord"? If it is true, as Caputo claims, that "*différance* does not love you or even know you are there . . . when you pray, do not say thanks"[61]—if this is true, how can we reconcile Derrida's *Dieu du désir* with the biblical God of love who knows every hair on our head and to whom we give thanks for what is given?

To make these monster-matters even more perplexing, we might cite Joseph Campell in *The Power of Myth:* "The monster comes through as a kind of God. . . . By a monster I mean some horrendous presence or apparition that explodes all of your standards for harmony, order and ethical conduct. . . . That's God in the role of destroyer. Such experiences go past ethical . . .

judgments. Ethics is wiped out. . . . God is horrific."[62] This claim is itself disturbingly congruent with Simon Critchley's chilling suggestion in his analysis of subjectivity-as-substitution (as a structure of possession by an alterity that can be neither comprehended nor refused): "Does not the trauma occasioned in the subject possessed by evil more adequately describe the ethical subject than possession by the good? Is it not in the excessive experience of evil and horror . . . that the ethical subject first assumes its shape? Does this not begin to explain why the royal road to ethical metaphysics must begin by making Levinas a master of the literature of horror? But if this is the case, why is radical otherness goodness? Why is alterity ethical? Why is it not rather evil or an-ethical or neutral?"[63]

## X

Derrida is in fact painfully, terrifyingly, aware of these difficulties of judgment. He goes to considerable lengths to address them. He makes it very clear, for example, that the desire beyond desire is a desire for justice. ("Justice is desirable through and beyond right and law," he writes in *Specters of Marx*; and he adds, elsewhere, "letting the other come is not inertia open to anything. . . . [D]econstruction cannot wait").[64] Indeed, having ostensibly released the "desire of God" from the ethical constraints of biblical affiliation, Derrida seems to redress this somewhat by reintroducing a certain complementarity of the messianic and messianism. The messianic needs messianism in the final analysis as much as messianism needs the messianic. Perhaps deconstruction, like the Freudian version of psychoanlaysis analyzed by Derrida in *Archive Fever*, is really a form of "Jewish science" after all? (That at least is a hypothesis entertained, if not endorsed, by Caputo: "All this talk in deconstruction about a messianic promise, about praying and weeping over something to come, about faith in something unforeseeable, does that not draw upon—even quite transparently—a Jewish archive? . . . Is deconstruction not the product of a Jewish mind?").[65]

Caputo appears (at times) to reinscribe Derrida within a specific tradition of "messianism"—what he terms a "certain Jewish Augustinianism" extending to those wandering prophets and ankhorite desert fathers who desired a God without being, beyond being, otherwise than being. And in response to the objection that deconstruction evacuates God completely of God, Caputo replies that it is precisely the "haze of indefiniteness" which deconstruction's "faith without faith" provokes in us, which nourishes "the urgency and passion of decision."[66] But can we be so sure? Can we draw a line in the sand between deconstruction as desertification of God and desertion of God? Can we dance and sing and pray before the God of deconstruction? Can we desire God without *some* recourse to narrative imagination? Without some appeal to tradition(s)? Without some guide for the perplexed?

In *Given Time*, Derrida returns to this abiding dilemma. He explains here that the "desire beyond desire" is always bound to a double injunction—to respond to the gift *and* to the economy of exchange. He says: "It is a matter—desire beyond desire—of responding faithfully but also as rigorously as possible both to the injunction or the order of the gift ("give"/*donne*) *as well as* to the injunction or order of meaning (presence, science, knowledge). *Know* still what giving *wants to say, know how to give,* know what you want to say when you give, know what you intend to give, know how the gift annuls itself, commit yourself even if commitment is the destruction of the gift by the gift, give economy its chance."[67]

In other words, desire beyond desire—as precisely that desire for the gift beyond the commerce of daily transactions—both *is* and *is not* outside the circle of exchange; just as the messianic—as "desire of God"—both is and is not outside the circle of messianism. This confession of double injunction allows Derrida to concede that the "overrunning of the circle by the gift, if there is any, does not lead to a simple exteriority that would be transcendent and without relation."[68] On the contrary, it is this very exteriority that sets the circle going. Ultimately, the desire of God can never step completely outside of the circle of desire as *vouloir, amour, envie, attente, conatus, concupiscentia* —and, with Levinas in mind, we might add: *voluptuousity, paternity, fecundity.*

## Conclusion

Returning to our introductory citation from the Song of Songs, we might say that while God's lover will always continue to seek and desire him whom her soul loves, she has already been found, because already sought and desired, by him whom her soul loves. Her desire thus occupies a middle space, a two-way street between action and passion, yearning and welcome, seeking and receptivity. I suspect that Derrida's "desire of God" goes somewhat in the direction of this double genitive. A doubling back of desire well captured in the advice given to Nathanaël in Gide's *Nourritures Terrestres: "Que ton désir soit moins une attente qu'une disposition à l'accueil."* (Let your desire be less expectation than a readiness to receive.) But Derrida might well qualify this by adding that, when it comes to God at any rate, you rarely have one without the other. *Attente* and *accueil* are the two Janus faces of desire. Why? Because desire responds to the double demand of eschaton and eros. God's desire for us—our desire for God. "It's not a question of one or the other," as Caputo rightly reminds us, "but of inhabiting the distance between the two with as much grace and ambiance and hospitality as possible."[69]

What, we might ask finally, has all this to do with postmodernity? Given the postmodern proliferation of phantoms and false prophets, ranging from the spectral simulacra of the mass media to the virtual realities of the World Wide Web (where the highest number of Internet hits registered in the last year pertain to extraterrestrial "aliens"), Derrida's puzzling over the phenomena of undecidable others—ghosts, hallucinations, substitutions—could not be more timely. Our age is not just one of *mondialatinization* but of *mondi-alienation*—"aliens" are everywhere: at the borders of the United States and Europe; landing in wheatfields in Santa Rosa from outer space; assuming all kinds of extraterrestrial masks and makeup on our multiplex silver screens. One only has to recite last year's box office hits to realize the exponential extent of this cultural paranoia: *Mars Attack, Men in Black, The Fifth Element, Independence Day, Contact,* not to mention the multi-million-dollar re-release of the *Star Wars* series. Never, arguably, has it been more necessary to separate mass-media fantasies from real-life others who call us to a justice and democracy to come.

Derrida's own response to this postmodern dilemma would seem to be twofold—*believe* and *read!* In spite of our inability to know for sure "who speaks" behind the many voices and visages that float before us, now present now absent, now here now elsewhere, Derrida tells us that we must continue to trust and have faith. "*Je ne sais pas, il faut croire,*" as the refrain of *Memoirs of the Blind* goes. But if our belief is blind, and each moment of faithful decision terrifying, we can always be helped by the vigilant practice of meticulous, rabbinical reading. We must never abandon our responsibility to read between the lines:

> In order to overcome hallucination we have to listen to and closely read the other. Reading, in the broad sense which I attribute to this word, is an ethical and political responsibility. In attempting to overcome hallucinations we must decipher and interpret the other by reading. We cannot be sure that we are not hallucinating by saying simply "I see." "I see" is, after all, just what the hallucinating person says. No, in order to check that you are not hallucinating you have to read in a certain way.

In what way, we might ask? "I have no rule for that," Derrida humbly concedes. "Who can decide what counts as the end of hallucination? It is difficult. I too have difficulties with my own work."[70]

But in spite of these avowed difficulties, Derrida has done more than most other living philosophers—theist or atheist—to make us sensitive to the three calls of God: *donne, pardonne, abandonne.* The problem is that these calls are, for deconstruction, always made in the dark where the need to discern seems so impossible. So my final question is: How do we read in the dark?

## DISCUSSION WITH RICHARD KEARNEY

*John D. Caputo.* In Richard Kearney's written text he cited, but he did not read, this passage from *The Prayers and Tears of Jacques Derrida,* "It is not a question of one or the other, but of inhabiting the distance between the two with as much grace and ambiance and hospitality as possible." The distinction between the messianic and the messianisms is a tension that we inhabit and it would never be a question of choosing one or the other. With that in mind, let me briefly make three points.

(1) The notion of justice as *à-venir* refers structurally to the vulnerable; to the victim, not the producer of the victim. It would never be the case that the "other" one to come would be Charles Manson, or some plunderer or rapist. The very notion of the to-come refers to the one who is not being heard, who is silenced, victimized by the existing structures. It will always be the case that someone is being injured by the present order, so that the worst injustice would be to say that present order represents perfect justice.

(2) We are always situated within concrete historical traditions and structures. The point of a distinction like that between justice and law, or the messianic and the concrete messianisms, is to prevent the existing traditions, which are all we have, from closing in upon themselves, from becoming monoliths. There is no such a thing as the one tradition, which is always rife with conflicts, silenced voices, and the prestige of the "tradition" is implicated in the dead bodies it produced in order to establish itself. Still, all we have is traditions, languages, cultures, social and institutional structures, our legacies, and we must both mourn everything that has been erased in those traditions and pray for the justice that these traditions promise. Deconstruction seeks to inhabit the tension between mourning and the promise, between recognizing that this is the only world I have and appreciating its finitude, keeping it open to what it cannot foresee. I can only inhabit my tradition justly if I appreciate that it is blind and that it tends structurally to close itself off from its other.

(3) I am worried about Richard Kearney's desire for criteria. I think we have situated decisions in contexts and traditions, about which we need to know as much as possible. But there comes a moment when all our knowing, all our study of norms and standards, fails us. Then there comes the moment that I understand deconstruction to be describing, that moment of singularity in which we need to choose. This is not decisionism, because it does not have to do with an autonomous ego making a wild leap, but a profound responsibility to everything in that situation which has hold of me. I am at that moment, in that *Augenblick*, on my own. I don't think that mixes me up with Charles Manson, but demands an act of radical responsibility in a singular situation in which I cannot excuse myself by saying that I am just doing what the rules require.

**Richard Kearney.** I agree. How could I not agree with my host? I agree with Jack's reading in *The Prayers and Tears of Jacques Derrida*. We are fellow travelers. But I still think there are difficulties. There is a certain madness of decision, a holy madness, which you invoke, which is so difficult and so terrifying and so risky that it needs the counterbalancing gesture of prudence, of law, of reading. Deconstruction is open to the victim, because deconstruction is justice. That is true. But there are moments in the deconstructive enterprise when it is not as simple as Mother Theresa going out into the streets of Calcutta and identifying suffering victims. There is a real sense of risk in deconstruction that the other who comes may destroy your house. Hospitality, to quote Derrida, may turn into "wild war and aggression." Pure hospitality, pure openness to the incoming of the other, is dangerous unless it invokes certain criteria, unless it is contingent as Kant insisted—Derrida discusses this in *Cosmopolites*[1]—on certain *conditions* of hospitality, for example, that the visit of strangers be temporary, nonviolent, and law-abiding. Now that is already not very hospitable because you are laying down certain criteria. But it is a recognition that if we were to actually practice absolute hospitality toward the absolute other, *sans vision, sans verité, sans révelation*—we might be opening the door to the monster who destroys our house, to wild war and aggression. I think that there is that difficult moment of absolute terror, of fear and trembling in deconstruction, which in a way is somewhat sanitized by simply saying, in the heel of the hunt, "It is not any other, it is only the other as victim." I think that makes it too quick and too easy. There is something utterly radical in deconstruction that calls, in my opinion, for the countervailing and the counterbalancing gesture of reading, law and prudence.

*Jacques Derrida.* As you can imagine, it is really impossible to address such difficult questions by improvising. I wanted to thank you especially because I was overwhelmed by the lucidity with which you pointed to the difficulties, my own difficulties, and you were fair enough to mention also the fact that I was trying to face the difficulties without really hiding or dissimulating them. So just a few words, which will not be proportionate to what you said.

Your last question was, "How do we read in the dark?," referring to what I said in Dublin. How could we read, properly speaking, read, if not in the dark? If we read, if reading was simply seeing, we would not read. When I say we read in the dark, I do not mean that we have to read without seeing anything, but that the essential feature of reading implies some darkness. That is what distinguishes reading from seeing, from perception. You can transfer this law to the relationship between knowledge and faith, and to the question of criteria that you were addressing. If I were simply perceiving a text, I would not read it. No doubt, I read it while looking at it, seeing something in it. Even if I close my eyes, I see something visible in it. This visibility is indispensable. Even if I read in my memory, if I were blind, this visibility is indispensable, but it is not constitutive of the act of reading. I read to the extent that I exceed visibility. So we always read in the dark, and write in the dark, not only, as I sometimes do, when I try to write down a dream and I wake up and it is totally illegible. We have to read in the dark, and this is a general law which accounts for all the questions that you raise.

To go back to the problem of hospitality that Jack mentioned a moment ago, as you know, I am aware that you can not found the politics of hospitality on the principle of unconditional hospitality, of opening the borders to any newcomer. I am aware of those problems. What I mean is that when we control a border, when we try to discriminate, when we try to find criteria to discriminate between the enemy and the friend, or between the monster and the god, then the indispensable act of knowing, discriminating, adjusting the politics, is indispensable, no doubt, but it is a way of limiting hospitality. We have to be aware that, to the extent that we are looking for criteria, for conditions, for passports, borders and so on, we are limiting hospitality, hospitality as such, if there is such a thing. I'm not sure there is pure hospitality. But if we want to understand what hospitality means, we have to think of unconditional hospitality, that is, openness to whomever, to any newcomer. And of course, if I want to know in advance who is the good one, who is the bad one — in advance! — if I want to have an available criterion to distinguish between the good immigrant and the bad immigrant, then I would have no relation to the other as such. So to welcome the other as such, you have to suspend the use of criteria. I would not recommend giving up all criteria, all knowledge and politics. I would simply say that if I want to improve hospitality, and I think we would agree about that, if I want to improve the conditions of hospitality, the politics of hospitality, I have to refer to pure hospitality, if only to have a criterion to distinguish between the more limited hospitality and the less limited hospitality. So I need what Kant would call the regulating idea of pure hospitality, if only to control the distance between in-hospitality, less hospitality, and more hospitality. This could also lead us beyond Kant's own concept of hospitality as a regulating idea.

So at some point I have to take into account the need for criteria but without really believing that this need for criteria has an essential link to hospitality, or to the relation to the other as such, or to the singular other. And I would like to follow this thread in order to go back to what was finally the center of your concern, which as you know I share. I'm going to read in the dark. At some point you ask, "Where do we draw a line in the sand between deconstruction as desertification of God and as desertion of God?" There is no line. As soon as you look for a line, a clear line between desertification and desertion, between an authentic God and a false God or false prophet, as soon as you look for this — and you cannot help looking for this — but as soon as you rely on this desire, or as soon as you think you have gotten this criterion, that is the end of faith. You can be sure that God has left. When you are sure it is the real one, and that you have a criterion to identify Him, you can be sure that in that case you have the desert, the bad one. I am not here pleading for, advocating faith or religion, I'm just analyzing a structure. As soon as you have or think you have this line that you want to draw in the sand between desertification of God and desertion of God, as soon as you have it or think you have it, you've lost it. You've lost what you're looking for. So you have to resist this resistance to this openness to a possible monstrosity and to this evil. What is difficult — and I confess this difficulty and I experience it as you do — occurs when, taking what I just said into account, you nevertheless have to make decisions, for instance political decisions, ethical decisions. Then you have not only to discover but to produce criteria, to invent politics, for instance, and

Richard Kearney

you have to negotiate between this absolute non-knowledge or indeterminacy, which is a necessary openness to the singularity of others, and the necessity of criteria, politics, ethics, and so on. So you have to negotiate between what is non-negotiable and what has to be negotiated. And this is a terrible moment. You said this better than I can. But this is the moment of decision. You have to make a decision not simply to open your house, that's not the decision, you open your house to anyone, this is pure hospitality, it requires no decision. It's impossible but it requires no decision. Now if you close the border and the house, no decision either, no hospitality. The decision occurs when you want to reach an agreement between your desire for pure unconditional hospitality and the necessity of discrimination. It is filtering. I don't want to host anyone who would destroy not only me but my wife and children. For this decision, I have no criteria. That's what makes a decision a decision. If I had criteria, a set of norms, that I would simply apply or enforce, there would be no decision. There is a decision to the extent that even if I have criteria, the criteria are not determining, that I make a decision beyond the criteria, even if I know what the best criteria are, even if I apply them, the decision occurs to the extent that I do more than apply them. Otherwise it would be a mechanical development, a mechanical explicitation, not a decision.

So there must be a decision, not in the sense of decisionism, as Jack said. But what is the difference? Here I go back to the point of departure in your lecture, "the desire of God," with a double genitive. Whose decision is it? If it is my decision, my own decision, meaning by that a possibility which lies in myself, a potentiality—"I am able to make such a decision"—this would mean the decision would be mine because it would simply follow my own habitus, my own substance, my own subjectivity. It would look like a predicate of myself. The decision follows from what I am. If I give because I am generous, the gift is a predicate of my generosity, of my nature, so it would be my decision because it would follow what I am myself, my own subjectivity. For this very reason, the decision wouldn't be a decision. So here we reach the most difficult point, where a responsible decision, to be responsible, must not be mine. My own decision, my own responsible decision, must in myself be the other's; if it's simply mine, it's not a decision. When I say that a decision must be the other's in myself, I do not mean that I am irresponsible, that I am simply passive or simply obeying the other. I must deal with this paradox. That is, my decision is the other's. Otherwise we will fall into Schmitt's decisionism in which the notions of subject, of will, of the sovereignty of the subject are again revalidated or confirmed. No, we have, not to account for, but to experience the fact that the freest decision in myself is a decision of the other in myself. The other is in me, the other is my freedom, so to speak. You can transfer what I'm saying about decision to desire. The desire of my desire is not mine. That's where desire stops. If my desire for the other, for the *tout autre*, were simply *my* desire, I would be enclosed in my desire. If my desire is so powerful in myself, it is because it is not mine. That does not mean that I'm simply passively registering or welcoming another's desire. It simply means that I experience my own desire as the other's desire. Of course, God, what may be called God's desire, is part of this scenario. When I say in French *tout autre est tout autre*, which is difficult to translate, this does not mean, as you say, inclusiveness. It means simply that every other, without and before any determination, any specification, man or woman, man or God, man or animal, any other whatever is infinitely other, is absolutely other. That is the only condition for the experience of otherness. This sentence is virtually an objection to Levinas, of course, for whom *le tout autre* is first of all God. Every other is infinitely other. That is not a logic of inclusion but, on the contrary, a logic of alterity.

I would add just one last point, because this *tout autre est tout autre* is also the axiom of what I call messianicity. I am not sure I would say, as perhaps Jack Caputo has said, that messianism is on the side of war and messianicity is on the side of peace. I do not know if he said that literally. Of course, there is always a risk of war with messianicity; messianicity is not peace. I would not identify messianism in the classical sense as the experience of wars. But again, according to the same logic of contamination, if I make reference to the Messiah, to the tradition of messianisms in our culture, in order to name messianicity, it is in order to keep this memory. Even if messianicity is totally heterogeneous to messianism, there is this belonging to a tradition, which is mine as well as yours. I do not refer to it the way you do here, but it is our language, our tradition, and I would try to translate one into the other without erasing the heterogeneity of the two. Thank you.

**Richard Kearney.** I want to thank Jacques Derrida and Jack Caputo for their responses to my tentative and perhaps provocative talk. I am grateful. I want to say something about the necessity of the work they are doing—these micrological worryings about the need for decision and the appreciation of how difficult is the question of discernment, and whether it is possible or impossible. What is punctually so important about this work, and why it intrigues me, is that at the level of our contemporary social imaginary, there is a need for discernment and discrimination which the academies and universities are not taking on. When I referred, at the end, to *mondialienation*, I had in mind a tendency to see the other as alien, to demonize the other. I think that this has a lot to do with political constellations, with end of the Soviet Union and other traditional enemies. I think that the whole problem of the immigrant and the victim, which is at the center of Jacques Derrida's recent reflections on hospitality, on cosmopolitanism, on Kant, and of course of Caputo's book *The Prayers and Tears of Jacques Derrida*, is absolutely essential, lest the other become invariably the scapegoated monster. That is certainly becoming a very real problem for us in Europe today, where there is a growing problem of closure to the other. I am sure, if it has not already become a problem here in the United States, it will become one—the problem of how one can relate openly and hospitably and justly to the other, without demonization. When I look at the films and the videos that are capturing the popular unconscious

Richard Kearney

and social imaginary, what I see is a culture of paranoia, of fear of the other, and an inability to be able to tell the difference between the victim and the aggressor. That sort of radical confusion requires the close, micrological, quasi-rabbinical reading of deconstruction as a close attention to detail and singularity, without rushing to premature verdicts. That is the great virtue of Derrida's and Caputo's most recent work.

## NOTES

1. Jacques Derrida, *On the Name*, ed. Thomas Dutoit (Stanford: Stanford University Press, 1995), 10.

2. See my analysis of the *yezer hara* in the first chapter of *The Wake of Imagination* (London: Routledge, 1994), 37–53.

3. Augustine, *Confessions*, trans. R. Pine-Coffin (New York: Penguin, 1961), 174–80, 245–47.

4. See John Van Buren, *The Young Heidegger—Rumor of the Hidden King* (Bloomington: Indiana University Press, 1994), 189f.

5. See Saint Paul, "We live by faith, not by what is seen. We consider not the seen but the unseen" (Romans 8:25; I Corinthians 5:7, 4:18). See also Van Buren, *The Young Heidegger*, 179f.

6. We must be ready, Scripture tells us, "for the Son of Man is coming at an unexpected hour" (Matthew 24:44). See Van Buren, *The Young Heidegger*, 190: "The Coming will arrive only in the Kairos, the moment, the 'fullness of time.' . . . The time and content of this arrival are not objectively available in advance to be expected (*erwartet*), represented, and calculated, but rather are to be determined only out of the Kairos itself which will happen with 'suddenness.' . . . The situation of the parousio-kairological temporalizing of the believer/God relation is thus a futural Second Coming (*Wiederkunft*) that is textured by a having-been and that will be determined only out of the incalculable eye-opening moment of arrival."

7. Emmanuel Levinas, *Totality and Infinity* (Pittsburgh: Duquesne University Press, 1969), 23. My use of this archeology/teleology distinction is derived from Paul Ricoeur, *Freud and Philosophy: An Essay on Interpretation*, trans. Denis Savage (New Haven: Yale University Press, 1970).

8. Ibid., 23

9. In his *Introduction to Hegel's Phenomenology of Spirit*, trans. J. H. Nicholas (New York: Basic Books, 1969), Alexander Kojève describes the notion of desire-as-lack as follows: "The I of desire is an emptiness greedy for content; an emptiness that wants to be filled by what is full, to be filled by emptying this fulness, to put oneself—once it is filled—in place of this fulness, to occupy with its fulness the emptiness caused by overcoming the fulness that was not its own" (38).

10. Levinas, *Totality and Infinity*, 33–34.

11. Ibid., 34.

12. Ibid., 35. Such desire is also, for Levinas, the possibility of freedom—freedom *from* the reign of hunger and fear, dominion and power; freedom *for* the desire of the absolute other whose trace is the face of this other before me.

13. Emmanuel Levinas, *De Dieu qui vient à l'idée* (Paris: Vrin, 1986), 87.

14. Levinas, *Totality and Infinity*, 254.

15. Ibid., 255.

16. Emmanuel Levinas, *Entre Nous* (Paris: Grasset, 1991), 30–31.

17. Levinas, *Totality and Infinity*, 258.

18. Ibid.

19. Ricoeur, *Freud and Philosophy*, 20f.

20. Levinas, *Totality and Infinity*, 263.

21. Ibid., 265.

22. Ibid., 266.

23. Ibid.

24. Ibid., 272.

25. Ibid.

26. Ibid., 276–77.

27. Ibid., 269.

28. Ibid., 272.

29. Ibid., 285.

30. Ibid.

31. John Caputo, "Hyperbolic Justice" in *Demythologizing Heidegger* (Bloomington: Indiana University Press, 1993), 200–201.

32. Derrida, *On the Name*, 80.

33. Jacques Derrida, *Specters of Marx*, trans. Peggy Kamuf (New York: Routledge, 1994), 167–70.

34. Derrida, *On the Name*, 36.

35. Ibid., 35–36.

36. Ibid., 35. When Derrida speaks of atheism we must, of course, take it with a pinch of fine salt, while still taking him at his word. In *Sauf le nom* (*On the Name*, 35), Derrida alerts us to the porous boundaries between theism and atheism. He notes, for example, that the *apophasis* of certain kinds of negative theology "at times so resembles a profession of atheism as to be mistaken for it." He goes on to observe that "like a certain mysticism, apophatic discourse has always been suspected of atheism" (citing the example of Angelus Silesius suspected by Leibniz). Derrida then introduces the rather startling idea that if apophasis inclines almost toward atheism, might it not be the case that, on the other hand, "the extreme and most consequent forms of declared atheism will have always testified to the most intense desire of God" (36). On foot of this arresting hypothesis, Derrida distinguishes between two kinds of *desire of God* (his italics)—1) the notion of desire at its most "insatiable" (therefore as lack seeking fulfillment) "according to the history and the event of its manifestation or the secret of its nonmanifestation" (presumably in the history of the revealed monotheistic "messianisms," for example) and 2) another voice of apophasis which seems foreign to every "anthropotheomorphic form of desire." Of this second desire—beyond desire—he writes: "But isn't it proper to desire to carry with it its own proper suspension, the death or the phantom of desire? To go toward the absolute other, isn't that the extreme tension of a desire that tries thereby to renounce its own proper momentum, its own movement of appropriation?" (37). On the basis of this distinction, Derrida identifies the equivocal double genitive operative in the "desire *of* God"—"does it come from God in us, from God for us, from us for God" (37)? And this, in turn, leads on to the crucial—and, for Derrida, ultimately unanswerable—question to *whom* is the discourse of the desire of God addressed? In other words, "if atheism, like apophatic theology, testifies to the desire of God, if it avows, confesses, or indirectly signifies, as

in a symptom, the desire of God, in the presence of *whom* does it do this? (37, my italics). In short, "who speaks to whom?" (37). It is perhaps telling that Derrida proceeds, having posed this impossible question, to analyze the role of testimony, revelation, confession, memory, and time in Dionysius the Areopagite and Augustine (who "haunts certain landscapes of apophatic mysticism," 40). Derrida also makes telling comments about the paradoxical "desire of God" in the writings of Levinas himself in *Adieu: A Emmanuel Levinas* (Paris: Galilée, 1997), 76–79, 113, 179–82, 185.

37. Jacques Derrida, *Given Time, I: Counterfeit Money*, tr. Peggy Kamuf (Chicago: University of Chicago Press, 1991), 21–22.

38. Jacques Derrida, *Memoirs of the Blind: The Self-Portrait and Other Ruins*, trans. Pascale-Anne Brault and Michael Naas (Chicago: University of Chicago Press, 1993), 36.

39. Ibid., 37. Where Levinas finds himself in contradiction with himself on the question of the identity of the "other"—on the one hand pleading ignorance regarding the ethical origin of the other, on the other identifying it as God; on the one hand suggesting that the other is a singular and unique human other, on the other, that he/she is a trace of the divine absolute—Derrida turns this very undecidability into a deconstructive "aporia." For Derrida, desire of God *is* impossible for the simple reason that we can never tell if the desired one is God or not. Elsewhere—*Given Time*, p. 5—Derrida equates desire with a *desire to give* (that which one does not have) which is *impossible*. Hence desire becomes the desire of the impossible. And this resurfaces, later in the same text, as the desire to exit from the economy of the circle—that is, of "time as a circle" (8). Once again, Derrida leaves us with an impossible question: "Why would one desire, along with the gift, if there is any, the exit? Why desire the gift and why desire to interrupt the circulation of the circle? Why wish to get out of it (*en sortir*)" (8)?

40. Jacques Derrida, *Archive Fever: A Freudian Impression*, trans. Eric Prenowitz (Chicago: University of Chicago Press, 1996), 52.

41. John Caputo, *The Prayers and Tears of Jacques Derrida: Religion without Religion* (Bloomington: Indiana University Press, 1997), 364–65. "Pure presence" is, after all, what Derrida calls "absolute evil—absolute life, fully present life, the one that does not know death and does not want to hear about it" (*Specters of Marx*, 175).

42. Caputo, "Hyperbolic Justice," 200–201.

43. Caputo, *Prayers and Tears*, 3. See also the contrasting position of Jean-Luc Marion in "In the Name: How to Avoid Speaking of Negative Theology." Marion argues that negative theology is less onto-theological than Derrida supposes. Citing Denys the Areopagite's claim in *The Divine Names* (VII, I, 865c) that "what is praised multiply under multiple names is said to be anonymous and ineffable by the Scriptures," Marion suggests that this opens a "third way" beyond the simple affirmation and negation of names, a "beyond" where words assume a purely pragmatic function—"au-delà de tout nom et de toute dénégation de nom . . . la parole ne dit pas plus qu'elle ne nie—elle agit en se reportant à Celui qu'elle dé-nomme" ("In the Name," p. 29 [Richard Kearney was working with the untranslated version of "In the Name."—Eds.]). As such, the "hyper" (beyond) of negative theology "rétablit ni l'essence, ni la connaissance, mais les transgresse en vue d'une louange de ce qui précède et rend possible toute essence" ("In the Name," p.29). Which is another way of saying that the "hyper" of essence is in fact an otherwise than essence or being (that is, beyond onto-

theology understood as a metaphysics of presence). And all that is thus considered beyond or other than being—as non-being and non-presence—operates, for Denys (and Marion)—according to the modality of desire: 's'il est permis d'ainsi parler, même le non-étant désire le bien qui se trouve au-dessus de tous les étants . . . même le non-étant participe du beau et du bien . . . tous les étants . . . et tous les non-etants se trouvent dans le beau et le bon sur un mode qui dépasse l'essence (*hyperousias*)" (*Divine Names*, IV, 3, 697a; IV, 7, 704b; IV, 10, 705d). Marion derives the following insight into the "desire of God" from this position: "L'horizon de l'être reste régional, parce qu'il laisse par définition hors de lui les non-étants. Or il est toujours possible de les prendre en considération, puisqu'ils se réfèrent au bien, même en n'étant pas, sur le mode du '*désir.*' Donc la première (et dernière) des dénominations de Dieu devra se tirer de l'horizon du bien, plutôt que de celui de l'être, étant entendu que même cette dé-nomination n'atteint pas Dieu en propre, ni au propre" ("In the Name," p. 31). (Even Aquinas had this to say [as negative theologian] about the hyper-link between love-desire and God-goodness: "God, because he is infinite, cannot be captured in any way. . . . But he who loves more, because he desires more, will see God more perfectly and be more happy" [*Summa Theologiae*, I. Q 129.6]). See also Aquinas's discussion of desire and the formula associated with the Pseudo-Denys: "*bonum est diffusivum sui*"). Marion develops this "God beyond being" (*Dieu sans l'être*) into a "theology of absence" which articulates itself as a "pragmatics of the word" which attests to the God-Good "beyond being" by an action of listening/attention and desire/love ("In the Name," p. 32, 36–37). But if the "third way" of de-nomination safeguards God "beyond every proper name," it also acknowledges the mystery of God's omnipresence in the world—"Dieu se connaît en toutes choses et aussi à part de toutes choses. Dieu se connait par connaissance et aussi par inconnaissance" (*Divine Names*, VII, 3, 872a). Thus while respecting the invisibility and inaccessibility of God—according to the Scriptural ordinance that no one can see the face of God (John 1:8; Exodus 33: 20)— Marion accepts that we nonetheless need some kind of vision, even if (as Gregory of Nyssa realized) such "seeing is to be found in non-seeing" (*Vie de Moise*, II, 163). Even negative theology then has recourse to some kind of narrative imagination—albeit in the modality of *quasi* and *sicut*. So that when Paul acknowledges that God reveals himself "not only in (his) presence but as much in his absence" (Philippians 2:12), he does not deny the necessity—and desirability—of *some kind of presence*, albeit a *quasi*-presence. But Marion himself stops short of embracing the full consequences of this position. Rather than looking to hermeneutic retrievals and re-imaginings of biblical narratives and stories—the lives of prophets and apostles, of saints and martyrs (not to mention Abraham, Moses, Jacob, and Jesus)—Marion holds fast 1) to the *viae nega-tivae* of the great mystical theologians (Denys, Athanasius, Basil, Gregory of Nyssa) and 2) to the mystical-phenomenological intuition of the "saturated phenomenon" whose very excess can be neither seen, known, spoken, nor imagined, and whose very su-perabandance surpasses predication and nomination. It is perhaps here, indeed, that both Derrida's deconstruction and Marion's theology of absence-distance tend—in their agreed repudiation of the "metaphysics of presence"—to underestimate the need for some kind of critical discernment—based on informed judgment, hermeneutic memory, narrative imagination, and rational discrimination. Their common reaction to the excesses of onto-theology might be said to entail its own form of excess—an excess of absence answering to the excess of presence. Thus while Marion demarcates his own position from the atheistic stance of Derrida's deconstruction—by stating that the donating intuition "(ne) ferait défaut auquel cas on pourrait bien rapprocher la théologie négative de l'athéisme ou la mettre en concurrence avec la déconstruction" ("In the Name," p. 40)—he nonetheless pushes the intuition of divine saturation to the point of sheer incomprehensibility and irrationalism—"l'excès d'intuition s'accomplit sous la figure de la stupeur, voire de la terreur que l'incompréhensibilité nous impose" ("In the Name," p. 41). For the theist Marion, no less than for the atheist Derrida, we are left with the dilemma of "holy madness," how to judge between true and false prophets, between good and evil ghosts, between holy and unholy messiahs.

44. Derrida, *Given Time*, 21–22.

45. Caputo, *Prayers and Tears*, 165. While Caputo concedes that "deconstruction and a certain religion have both been scared by the same (messianic) ghost," he clearly prefers Derrida's response to that of the revealed eschatological messianisms: "We cannot forget that the distinction between the messianic and the concrete messianisms is always a political distinction for Derrida, one that spells the *difference between war and peace*, the war that Christianity has waged relentlessly on Judaism, and all the wars among the determinate messianisms. That is perhaps the point of this distinction in the first place. For the history of Western politics, and of the relations between the West and the Middle East is and has been, from time immemorial, a history of wars waged in the name of the several messianisms, the incessant battle to take Mount Moriah. The *concrete messianisms have always meant war, while the meaning of the messianic is, or should be, shalom, pax.* . . . What room is there, in this Christian messianic eschatology, for Jews and Arabs, for Africans and immigrants, for *Gastarbeiter* and native populations?" (190–191, my italics). The choice between the messianic and messianism is clear for Caputo—peace or war.

46. Caputo outlines the conundrum thus: "Derrida, 'who rightly passes for an atheist,' is an atheist who has his own God, and who loves the name of God, loves that 'event,' and what 'takes place' or eventuates in that good name. He has no desire (it goes against *everything* that deconstruction is and desires), to prevent the event of that 'invention'" (4). Indeed, deconstruction is nothing other than this desire of invention itself. "Getting ready for the 'invention' of the other, covenanting (*con-venire*) with its in-coming (*in-venire*), initialing a pact with the impossible, sticking to the promise of inalterable alterity, *tout autre*—that, says Derrida, 'is what I call deconstruction.' . . . That is his passion" (*Prayers and Tears*, 4). This insistence on the irreducible alterity and unpredicatablity of the Messiah may help explain why it is that the first to declare Jesus as Messiah are not his apostles (as one would expect) but *demons!* Jesus insists, tellingly, that they remain silent about his identity, as in Luke 4, for example: "In the synagogue there was a man who had the spirit of an unclean demon, and he cried out with a loud voice, 'Let us alone! What have you to do with us, Jesus of Nazareth? Have you come to destroy us? I know who you are, the Holy One of God.' But Jesus rebuked him, saying, 'Be silent and come out of him!'" (Luke 4:31–36). See also Luke 4:40–42: "Demons also came out of many, shouting: 'You are the Son of God!' But he rebuked them and would not allow them to speak, because they knew that he was the Messiah." How is it that holy and unholy spirits seem to recognize each other so immediately in this way? Are the Scriptures actually suggesting that the premature desire to identify and name the Messiah is in fact demonic? That reserve, discretion, and silence (or what Kierkegaard called the "indirect communication" of going "incognito") are the most appropriate responses to the kerygma of the Messiah?

47. Jacques Derrida, *Points . . . : Interviews, 1974–1994*, ed. Elisabeth Weber (Stanford: Stanford University Press, 1995), 41.

48. Derrida, *On the Name*, 74. This is why Derrida's religion is a "religion without religion" (*Given Time*, 49)—which means, in his own words, a religion "sans vision, sans verite, sans revelation" ("On a Newly Arisen Apocalyptic Tone in Philosophy" in *Raising the Tone of Philosophy: Late Essays by Emmanuel Kant, Transformative Critique by Jacques Derrida* [Baltimore: Johns Hopkins University Press, 1993], 167). As such, the "come" of deconstructive desire is a response to a plural and quasi-apocalyptic summons (*envois*) which addresses without message and without destination, without sender or decidable addressee, without last judgment, without any other eschatology than the tone of the "viens" (ibid.). Caputo reads this passage—correctly I believe—as Derrida's way of distinguishing deconstruction's "apocalypse *sans* apocalypse" from any specific apocalypse of the Judeo-Christian-Islamic kind: "This apocalypse without any vision, verity or un-veiling, this apocalypse *sans* apocalypse, is not John's, which calls determinately and identifiably for Adon Yeshoua. . . . This apocalypse without apocalypse belongs to and opens up a messianic time without any messianisms, without Yeshoua or any other identifiable Messiah, Jewish, Christian, Islamic. . . . (As 'aleatory errance') it moves by chance, not by a logic, not even a Heideggerian eschato-logic, whose *Spiel* is that the *Geschick*, gathering itself together in the unity of a *legein*, drives itself into an end-time, and then flips into another beginning" (*Prayers and Tears*, 99–100).

49. Ibid., 73.

50. Derrida, *Given Time*, 71.

51. Caputo, *Prayers and Tears*, 52.

52. Derrida, *On the Name*, 74.

53. *Who* is it I desire when I desire my God? *Who* comes when the other comes—unexpectedly and unpredictably like a thief in the night? Surely the first question for any vigilant and invigilating Messiah is—"*Who* do you say that I am?" It is also worth recalling here that in the very passage where St. Paul invokes the Lord coming like a thief in the night, he calls for sober and en-lightened vigilance: "But you, beloved, are not in darkness, for that day to surpise you like a thief; for you are children of light and children of the day; we are not of the night or of darkness. . . . So, let us keep awake and be sober" (I Thessalonians 5:5–6).

54. Jacques Derrida, "Hospitality, Justice, and Responsibility" in *Questioning Ethics*, ed. Richard Kearney and Mark Dooley (London: Routledge, 1998).

55. Ibid.

56. Jacques Derrida, "Foi et Savoir: Les Deux Sources de la Religion aux limites de la simple raison," in *La Religion*, ed. Jacques Derrida and Gianni Vattimo (Paris: Ed du Seuil, 1996), 31.

57. Caputo, *Prayers and Tears*, 73. One of the main reasons why Derrida insists—hyperbolically—that "*tout autre est tout autre*" is, Caputo argues, to safeguard the messianic from being reduced to any single face or faith, for that would imply a sectarian God who takes the side of one belief against others. (Caputo's thinking here is remarkably similar to scruples expressed by Heidegger in his "skeptical" and "deconstructive" refusal to embrace a specifically Catholic, or indeed Christian, world-view for fear it would limit our openness to what is still to come. See Van Buren, *The Young Heidegger*, 337–40). That is why for deconstruction the Messiah has many faces and never actually comes. Deconstruction thus respects the "desire of God" by keeping

desire constantly alive, primed for the incessant in-coming and in-vention of the other. But we might reply to Caputo here that if it is true that the Messiah may come at every instant, this does not mean that whatever/whoever comes in every instant is messianic. If we refuse to take sides or to judge—according to some sort of ethical criteria however approximative—that some others are less genuinely messianic than others, do we leave ourselves with any answer to those manic-psychotic visionaries who claim to hear the voice of God calling them to acts of cleansing sacrifice—David Koresh, Jim Jones, Peter Sutcliff, Charles Manson? Or, more complex still, have we any answer to those official, eminently law-abiding inquisitors who executed heretics (Christ, Stephen, Bruno, Joan of Arc, Jean Huys) out of some mistaken obedience to what they believed was a messianic voice calling to them in the night? These are puzzling and troubling questions indeed, provoked and addressed (if not resolved) by the scrupulous work of thinkers like Caputo and Derrida himself, both of whom remain fully attentive to these radical problems. See especially Caputo's spirited and sophisticated responses to the charge that deconstruction lacks "criteria" to judge between just and unjust others in *Modernity and Its Discontents*, ed. James L. Marsh, John P. Caputo, and Merold Westphal (New York: Fordham University Press, 1992), 18–22, 127–30, 178–94. In my "Postscript" to *Poetics of Modernity: Toward a Hermeneutic Imagination* (Atlantic Highlands, N.J.: Humanities Press, 1995) and my "Epilogue" to the second edition of *Poetics of Imagining: Modern and Postmodern* (Edinburgh: Edinburgh University Press, 1998), I continue my hermeneutic exchange with deconstruction on this vexed issue of ethical criteria, judgment, and discernment. For making this issue a live and urgent one I am indebted to the recent work of Caputo and Derrida.

58. Jacques Derrida, "Shibboleth: For Paul Celan," trans. J. Vilner, in *Word Traces: Readings of Paul Celan*, ed. Aris Fioretos (Baltimore: Johns Hopkins University Press, 1994), 102–103. One must recall here, however, that in his repeated efforts to show that "deconstruction is justice" (i.e., ethical), Derrida himself does tend to identify the messianic "other" who calls and comes as *victim* (see his "Wears and Tears" chapter of *Specters of Marx*) rather than just *any* other at all (e.g., oppressors and executioners). Caputo puts the dilemma thus: "The mistake is to think that deconstruction cannot oppose cruelty or oppression because then it could be 'excluding' or 'marginalizing' someone, viz., the oppressors . . .[that] the homicidal rapist, the plunderer, a violent military, all that is just the 'Other' and deconstruction recommends openness to the Other." The error here, according to Caputo, is to construe deconstruction in an excessively "formal" sense, thereby paying no attention to the "substantive merits" of what kind of power is in place (i.e., just or unjust, democratic or totalitarian). "Exclusion and marginalization," Caputo concludes, "are never merely formal ideas (but) always have to do with damaged lives and disasters. . . . People who produce victims are not the 'Other' to whom we owe everything" (*Against Ethics* [Bloomington: Indiana University Press, 1993], 119). But the problem for deconstruction is perhaps precisely that its very character is "formal" rather than "substantive," as witnessed in Derrida's repeated denials that deconstruction is a program dealing with how we should behave or what we should do in our everyday world of "substantive" practices and decisions. (Indeed, it could be argued that Levinas is less "formal" than Derrida to the extent that he does identify the "Other" in specifically biblical allusions to "the widow, the orphan, the stranger"). It is true, of course, that Derrida holds that the other is always embedded in a specific language, history, or society as bearer of a "proper name" with his/her unique perspective of the "here, now,

at this point," etc. But surely is it not simply the singularity and uniqueness of every other (with his/her proper name and perspective) that helps us substantively distinguish between whether they are *good or evil?* (Hitler too was a unique, singular individual with a proper name and perspective). Admittedly, Derrida could be said to be attempting to "deformalize" the question of justice somewhat in identifying the "other" as "refugee," "nomad," "exile," "emigre," "Jew"—in brief, as the displaced and disenfranchised victim whose cry for justice may sometimes require the suspension or revision of the law. But these remain largely indeterminate characterizations (e.g., we are all potentially "Jews" to the extent that we become exiled from the logocentric fold), and we also encounter continuing problems of discernment in that several acts of slaughter have been carried out by individuals or groups that consider themselves victimized and dispossessed of their original rights (rightful homeland, rightful heritage, etc.)—Basques, Ulster Catholics, Palestinians, ultra-Zionists, Azeris, Serbs, Iraqis, Sudetan Germans, etc. In an essay entitled "Hyperbolic Justice," Caputo aligns Derrida's deconstructive justice with the "myth of the smallest singularities . . . of the smallest hair on your head, of the least among us" (in *Demythologizing Heidegger,* 200–201). But in so doing, Caputo is once again re-inscribing Derrida's open-ended deconstruction in a specifically biblical tradition of discernment—a line of re-inscription which ultimately leads Caputo to identify the Derridean "Other" not only with the "Jew (as) placeholder for all those who have no place," but more specifically with "Jesus the Jew" who gives justice to the "man with the withered hand" (*Prayers and Tears,* 230–31). "Flesh is the locus of obligation," insists Caputo in *Against Ethics* (127). And one might add, *suffering* flesh, for Caputo confirms the claim that the flesh of the stranger that obliges us is always that of the victim, not the victimizer (119). However, even Caputo's more specified, substantified and deformalized version of deconstructive ethics, is *still,* arguably, *too* hyperbolic—still not sufficiently prudent about the need for normative limits and narrative instantiations.

59. Caputo, *Prayers and Tears,* 74.

60. Ibid., 102.

61. Ibid., 169.

62. Joseph Campell, *The Power of Myth* (New York: Doubleday, 1988), 222. One finds a similar invocation of mythic divinities who call and come in terror and darkness *irrespective of ethical distinctions between good and evil* in certain texts of the later Heidegger, e.g., when he even speaks of the "good of evil" or the "primal mythical force of might." See Van Buren, *The Young Heidegger,* 371–77, 382–85, 392–94. Van Buren concludes with this troubling critical question: "So we can ask roughly what, according to the later Heideggger's preparatory sketches and drafts, is supposed to be coming in this second coming? Are we simply to call out: *Komm, Viens,* Come! Thy kingdom come, thy will be done?" (392). By contrast, I John calls for a critical discrimination between good and evil spirits, between "spirits of truth" and "spirits of error": "Beloved, do not believe every spirit but test the spirits to see whether why are from God; for many false prophets have gone out into the world" (I John 4:1). This vigilance is in keeping with Jesus' warning to his disciples: "Beware that you are not led astray; for many will come in my name and say, 'I am he!' and, 'The time is near!' Do not go after them" (Luke 21:8). A similar admonition is issued, later in Luke, to keep vigilant watch for the second comer: "Be on guard so that . . . the day not catch you unexpectedly like a trap. Be alert at all times, praying that you may . . . stand before the Son of Man" (Luke 21: 34–36).

63. Simon Critchley, *Very Little . . . Almost Nothing: Death, Philosophy, Literature* (London: Routledge, 1997), 80. Ricoeur issues a related, if less frontal, critique of Levinas's rejection of all forms of memory, narrative, and history in *Autrement: Lecture d'Autrement qu'être ou au-delà de l'essence d'Emmanuel Lévinas* (Paris: Presses universitaires de France, 1997), 12–14, 25, 38–39. Ricoeur identifies a performative contradiction in Levinas's simultaneous invocation and disqualification of narrative memory: "Avec la justice ne peut-on espérer le retour du souvenir, au-delà de la condamnation du mémorable? Sinon, comment Emmanuel Levinas aurait-il pu écrire le sobre exergue: 'A la mémoire des êtres les plus proches'" (9).

64. Derrida, *Specters of Marx*, 175; and "Psyché: Inventions of the Other" in Jacques Derrida, *Acts of Literature*, ed. Derek Attridge (New York: Routledge, 1992) and in *Reading de Man Reading*, ed. Lindsay Waters and Wlad Godzich (Minneapolis: University of Minnesota Press, 1989), 55. While acknowledging the element of "madness" involved in all attempts to judge and decide when confronted with the impossible demand for justice, Derrida also acknowledges the need for prudence. This is the double bind of judgment when faced with the competing demands of justice and law (rights). Justice requires the law just as law demands justice (see Derrida, "Force of Law: "The Mystical Foundations of Authority," in *Deconstruction and the Possibility of Justice*, ed. Drucilla Cornell, Michael Rosenfeld, and David Gray Carlson [New York: Routledge, 1992]; *Politiques de l'amitié* [Paris: Galilée, 1995]; and Caputo's illuminating analysis, "The Epoch of Judgment" in *Against Ethics* [1993]). See also, in this regard, Derrida's insistence in "Psyché: Inventions of the Other" that for the coming of the wholly other a "kind of resigned passivity for which everything comes down to the same is not suitable" (55). In his later writings, in the eighties and nineties, Derrida does recognize the need of deconstruction to curb the endless drift of deferral and deferment—especially when he acknowledges that, from an ethical point of view, "deconstuction cannot wait"; that the demand for justice is here and now, in each instant of judgment and decision. But while Derrida is aware of the dilemma of reconciling the wholly other who surprises us with the necessity for anticipatory horizons and practical decisions, he doesn't (arguably) go far enough in illuminating this. The difficulty of moderating madness with prudence still remains. The dilemma of how to judge between alterities, between something specifically "messianic" which brings peace and justice and not just "anything at all," remains unresolved. Caputo's current work on a new meta-noetics of meta-phronesis is a pioneering attempt to grapple with this fundamental ethical problem of deconstruction. We might also look for some direction here in Gadamer's hermeneutical dialectic between novelty and tradition: "We welcome just the guest who promises something new to our curiosity. But how do we know the guest whom we admit is one who has something new to say to us? Is not our expectation and our readiness to hear the new also necessarily determined by the old that has already taken possession of us?" ("The Hermeneutical Problem," in *The Continental Philosophy Reader*, ed. Richard Kearney and Mara Rainwater, [London: Routledge, 1996], 115). But even Gadamer's dialectical hermeneutics needs to be supplemented by a critical hermeneutics capable of discerning between good and evil ways in which tradition too can "take possession of us."

65. Caputo, *Prayers and Tears*, 263.

66. Ibid., 63. One could cite here, in support of Caputo's reading, the eschatological paradox of desire as *both* insatiate *and* overabundant, as *both* searching *and* saturated. See, for example, Psalm 78: "They ate and were filled. The Lord gave them

what they wanted: they were not deprived of their desire," or again, Psalm 21: "You have given him his heart's desire." This could be said to correspond to the deconstructive paradox that the messianic is always deferred but is also a desire and demand for justice here and now, a justice that "cannot wait"!

67. Ibid., 30.

68. Ibid. Derrida makes a similar concession, we might add, when he acknowledges the need for infinite justice to be tempered by finite laws and approves Kant's recommendation to make hospitality conditional when it comes to the question of offering refugees political asylum in one's state. Thus while Kant argued for universal hospitality as the condition of perpetual peace—what Derrida calls *"unconditional or pure hospitality which does not seek to identify the newcomer, even if he is not a citizen"* (my italics)—Derrida acknowledges the practical wisdom of Kant's insistence on certain conditions of hospitality, e.g., that the visit of strangers be temporary, and that the strangers be non-violent and law-abiding. For Kant knew, observes Derrida, that *"without these conditions hospitality could turn into wild war and aggression"* ("Hospitality, Justice, and Responsibility" and also his essays *Cosmopolite de tous le pays, encore un effort!* [Paris: Galilée, 1996]; *Adieu: A Emmanuel Levinas* (Paris: Galilée, 1997], 69f, 91f; and *De l'hospitalite/avec Anne Dufourmantelle invite Jacques Derrida à répondre*, [Paris: Calmann-Lévy, 1997], especially 29f). In other words, if deconstruction—understood as impossible justice, gift, and hospitality—is indeed another name for "desire beyond desire," it too has its limits. It might also be noted here that the "other" who threatens war and aggression is not always the "outsider" seeking entry but may well be a projection of alien unconscious fears and fantasies *within ourselves* (e.g., scapegoating, witch-hunting, ethnic cleansing, show trials, Cold War paranoia, UFO phobia, xenophobia, racism).

69. Caputo, *Prayers and Tears*, 173.

70. Derrida, "Hospitality, Justice, and Responsibility," 78.

## DISCUSSION

1. Jacques Derrida, *Cosmoplites de tous les pays, encore un effort!* (Paris: Galilée, 1997).

# Overcoming Onto-theology

Merold Westphal

> *We go to church in order to sing, and theology is secondary.*
> —*Kathleen Norris*[1]

Not long ago I participated in a conference on biblical hermeneutics. It asked about the relation between trust and suspicion for Christians reading the Bible. The keynote addresses by Walter Brueggemann and Phyllis Trible were brilliant. But for me the highlight of the conference was the workshop led by Ched Myers, whose radical reading of the gospel of Mark is one of the finest pieces of biblical interpretation I have ever read.[2] To be more precise, the highlight was the moment in the middle of the workshop when he had us sing.

He was developing the claim that biblical interpretation in the service of some relatively closed theological system (there are many) and biblical interpretation in the service of some species of historical criticism (there are many) are not as different as either side would like to think. Both are best understood in terms of the Marxian analysis of the fetishism of commodities; for they turn the text into an object to be mastered by the interpreter for the advantage of the interpreter, a source of theoretical treasure to be accumulated and owned. (Elsewhere I have described this as the King Midas theory of truth.)

In the middle of the argument, Myers stopped and said it was time to sing. But first we would have to clap, and soon all forty of us were clapping rhythmically. (If you know anything about Christians in the Reformed tradition, you know that we were participating in a performative refutation of Hume on miracles!) Then he began to sing

> O Mary, don't you weep, don't you mourn.
> O Mary, don't you weep, don't you mourn.
> Pharaoh's army got drownded.
> O Mary, don't you weep.

The second time through we all joined in; then he would sing the verses and each time we would join in again on the refrain.

I didn't want the singing ever to end. But when it did, Myers invited us to reflect on the phenomenon of American slaves singing about the liberation of Jewish slaves three thousand years earlier, a story they had made their story, and he asked us who Mary might be. We realized right away that first and foremost it was the mother of Jesus at the foot of the cross. Blissfully ignoring the realities of time's arrow, the American slaves were seeking to comfort Mary with the song of the Exodus, reminding her, as it were, of her own song, the Magnificat. Our leader did not have to point out that by singing the old spiritual and reflecting on it we were making the story of Miriam and Moses our story too, opening ourselves to be seized once again by its message of hope (insofar as we are oppressed) and judgment (insofar as we are oppressors).

Almost immediately I thought of Heidegger's critique of onto-theology. He thinks it is bad theology because we "can neither pray nor sacrifice to this god [of philosophy]. Before the *causa sui*, man can neither fall to his knees in awe nor can he play music and dance before this god" (ID, 72).[3] It seemed that as we joined the slaves in their song we had overcome onto-theology without even trying. For while we were not singing and dancing—that would be too much of a miracle to expect of Christians from the Reformed tradition—we were singing and clapping before the God who drownded Pharaoh's army.

The onto-theological God enters the scene "only insofar as philosophy, of its own accord and by its own nature, requires and determines how the deity enters into it" (ID, 56). The God to whom we were singing had entered the scene without the imprimatur of the learned, saying

> I have observed the misery of my people who are in Egypt; I have heard
> their cry on account of their taskmasters. Indeed, I know their sufferings,
> and I have come down to deliver them. (Exodus 3:7–8)

We should not be surprised to read that Miriam sang and danced with tambourines before this God who threw horse and rider into the sea without consulting *ta meta ta physica* or the *Wissenschaft der Logik* (Exodus 15:20–21).

Miriam and the American slaves did not need to overcome onto-theology. They were never tempted by it. The situation is more complex for us, even if (heaven help us) we are ready to sing and clap, if not quite to sing and dance, with them. We have immersed ourselves in traditions where onto-theology is at work, and we have listened as Heidegger has thematized and named a practice whose purest, but by no means only, forms are those of Aristotle and Hegel.[4] Perhaps, however, we have not listened carefully enough. For Heidegger's term is often bandied about in a manner not supported by the text.

It will be useful to recall how in the fifties, here in the United States, the term 'communist' came to mean "anything to the left of my right-wing position." Then, in the sixties, and no doubt inevitably, 'fascist' came to mean "anything to the right of my left-wing position." The U.S. Congress, it turned out, was made up wholly of communists who called themselves Democrats and of fascists who called themselves Republicans. The terms 'communist' and 'fascist' were not used to inform but to inflame, not to assist sober analysis but to avoid the hard work of analysis by resorting to name-calling.

The term 'onto-theology' is all too often used in this way. Without too close a look either at how Heidegger uses the term or at the specifics of the discourse to be discredited, 'onto-theology' becomes the abracadabra by which a triumphalist secularism makes the world immune to any God who resembles the personal Creator, Lawgiver, and Merciful Savior of Jewish, or Christian, or Muslim monotheism. The only religion that escapes the Lord High Executioners who speak as Heidegger's prophets is religion that is pagan/polytheistic, pantheistic, or a/theistic (with or without the slash).

When this happens, the Pascalian character of Heidegger's critique is overlooked. It is not directed toward the God of the Bible or the Koran, before whom people do fall on their knees in awe, pray, sacrifice, sing, and dance. It is a critique of a metaphysical tradition that extends from Anaximander to Nietzsche and includes Aristotle and Hegel as high points (WM/1949).[5] It is also a critique, by extension, not of theistic discourses as such, but of those that have sold their soul to philosophy's project of rendering the whole of reality intelligible to human understanding. Their fault does not consist in affirming that there is a Highest Being who is the clue to the meaning of the whole of being. It consists in the chutzpa of permitting this God to enter the scene only in the service of their project, human mastery of the real.

As a restatement of the ancient question, "What has Athens to do with Jerusalem?", Heidegger's critique is a reminder of how hard it is to sing "the Lord's song in a foreign land" (Psalms 137:4), in this case that Greco-Germanic land of which Heidegger himself was to become so fatally enamored.[6] As such it is an invitation and challenge to theology to be itself, to refuse to sell its birthright for a mess of philosophical pottage. Reminding the theologians of the Pauline question—"Has not God let the wisdom of this world become foolishness?"—Heidegger asks, "Will Christian theology make up its mind one day to take seriously the word of the apostle and thus also the conception of philosophy as foolishness?" (WM/1949, 276; cf. IM, 6: "From the standpoint of faith our question [of being] is 'foolishness.'"). Perhaps this is why several years later Heidegger would write, "If I were yet to write a theology — to which I sometimes feel inclined — then the word *Being* would not occur in it. Faith does not need the thought of Being. When faith has recourse to this thought, it is no longer faith. This is what Luther understood." And perhaps this is why Jean-Luc Marion has tried to think God without Being.[7]

It is thus a mistake, I believe, to identify the God of onto-theology simply as "the omnipotent, omniscient, and benevolent God" or as "the God who divinely, eternally pre-contains all things in a mind so immense that all creation is but a supplemental *imago dei*, a simulacrum of the Infinite and Eternal, which means Infinitely and Eternally the Same," even with the further claim that this is an "excessively Eleatic idea of God which has overrun the biblical traditions ever since Philo Judaeus decided that Yahweh needed to square accounts with Greek ontology, the result being that Greek ontology settled the hash of Yahweh and Elohim."[8]

There is a lively and legitimate debate about whether we should speak of God in this way. But, at least in the Christian traditions (I cannot speak for the Jewish and Muslim), the primary motivations for attributing omniscience, including foreknowledge, to God are biblical rather than philosophical, even if the vocabulary in which the matter gets discussed is, for better or worse, often Hellenic. Further, Kierkegaard is surely, with Heidegger, one of those who calls Jerusalem back to itself from Athens by contrasting the God of the philosophers with the God of living faith. But his Climacus presupposes the God just described as onto-theological when he says that reality is a system for God, though not for us human observers.[9] In a similar manner, Climacus insists that God is capable of the philosophy of world history to which Hegel aspires, though we, including Hegel (as long as the latter has not become God) are not. There is a metanarrative; it's just that we aren't in on it.[10] We may have access to aspects of it on a need to know basis, but that gives us far less than philosophy requires for its purposes; for its need to know is the absolute need posited by objectivity, while the believer's need to know is the limited need posited by subjectivity.

Kierkegaard helps us to see that the onto-theological gesture consists not in positing a God who differs radically from us by satisfying the requirements of Hegel's Logic and Philosophy of World History, who sees the world synchronically as system and diachronically in terms of a grand metanarrative. It consists in positing such a God as an excuse for making the claim that we can occupy the divine perspective on the world, or at least peek over God's shoulder. Spinoza let the cat out of the bag when he acknowledged that philosophy needs to see the world *sub specie aeternitatis*. There is all the difference in the world, the difference, say, between Kierkegaard and Hegel, or Pascal and Spinoza, between affirming that there is such a point of view and claiming that we (the intellectual elite, whether we call ourselves philosophers or theologians) can embody it. With Kierkegaard and Pascal one could fall on one's knees in awe before such a God, but only so long as there is an infinite, qualitative difference between that God and ourselves. Perhaps onto-theology consists in the pride that refuses to accept the limits of human knowledge.

The debates over whether there is indeed such a divine knower and whether such ideas are appropriate to a particular religious tradition can continue unabated. (They are likely to do so with or without our permission.) The critique of onto-theology has little if anything to contribute to them. For it is directed not at *what* we say about God but at *how* we say it, to what purpose, in the service of what project. It might seem as if any affirmation of God as Creator, a necessary condition, I should think, of any authentic Jewish, Christian, or Muslim faith, is an onto-theological gesture; for it implies that the whole of being is ultimately to be understood, insofar as we can understand it, with reference to the Highest Being. But the believer might speak as follows.

> In affirming God as Creator I am affirming that there is an explanation of the whole of being and I am pointing in the direction of that explanation; but I am not giving it, for I do not possess it. To do that I would have to know just *who* God is, and just *how* and *why* God brings beings into being out of nothing. But both God's being and God's creative action remain deeply mysterious to me. They are answers that come loaded with new questions, reminding me in Heideggerian language that unconcealment is always shadowed by concealment, or in Pauline language that I only see "through a glass, darkly" (or "in a mirror, dimly," I Corinthians 13:12). My affirmation of God as Creator is not onto-theological because it is not in the service of the philosophical project of rendering the whole of being intelligible to human understanding, a project I have ample religious reasons to repudiate.[11]

Not only might the believer speak this way. With or without help from Pseudo-Dionysius, theologians such as Augustine, Aquinas, Luther, Calvin, and Barth have spoken this way. All of them have insisted, with or without help from Rudolf Otto, that the God of the Bible and of their theologies is Wholly Other in an epistemic sense as being the *mysterium*. I must confess, with all the contrition I can muster up (which, I confess, is not much), that I get too much fun out of reminding my Thomist and Calvinist friends of these themes in their masters and suggesting that the latter are Kantian anti-realists, insisting that our knowledge of God is not an instance of the *adequatio rei et intellectus*. For they strongly insist that as humans our knowledge of God suffers from qualitative and not merely quantitative limitations and that we do not know God as God knows God, as God most truly is, as unmediated presence to the intellect. But if they are Kantian anti-realists, they are not onto-theologians. They are trying to make the best sense they can of their faith, but they have not bought into the project of making the whole of reality intelligible to human understanding with help from the Highest Being. Far from grudgingly conceding the epistemic transcendence of God to Dionysius and Otto, they go out of their way to insist upon it as being of the highest religious significance. They agree with the twentieth-century psalmist who sings, "I cannot worship what I comprehend."[12]

In developing this argument I have appealed to the distinction Climacus makes in *Concluding Unscientific Postscript* between the *what* and the *how* of our theological affirmations.[13] Does this work for Heidegger as well? I will try to show that it does, that when he protests against letting God enter the scene only on philosophy's terms, it is the *how* rather than the *what* of theological assertion that is his target.

For Jewish, Christian, and Muslim monotheism, God is the Creator. This means that God is not created. The devout child, brought up in one of these traditions, knows how not to look for an answer to the question, "And who created God?" The child will not say that God is an uncaused cause or is *causa sui*, though after a couple of courses in philosophy she might come to think that such language expresses quite nicely what she has believed from childhood. When Heidegger praises "the godless thinking which must abandon the god of philosophy, god as *causa sui*" by suggesting that it is "thus perhaps closer to the divine God . . . more open to Him that onto-theo-logic would like to admit" (ID, 72), is he telling our young believer that she must give up her faith in God as Creator? I think not. I think he is warning her that the language she is about to adopt for expressing that faith is dangerous, that it comes from a land foreign to that faith, and that in its native habitat it is part of a project antithetical to that faith. Appropriation of some sort may be unavoidable, but it is always dangerous.

We could begin to make this point by noting that Heidegger has no special resources for showing that there is no loving, personal Creator, and that he does not appeal to such traditional attempts to show this as the argument from evil in the world or a positivistic interpretation of the natural sciences. But it is not necessary to do this because Heidegger is quite emphatic that this is not what he is up to. "For the onto-theological character of metaphysics has become questionable for thinking, not because of any kind of atheism, but from the experience of a thinking which has discerned in onto-theo-logy the still *unthought* unity of the essential nature of metaphysics" (ID, 55). While insisting that the biblical words, "In the beginning God created heaven and earth" are not an answer to the philosophical question of being, Heidegger notes that this does not settle the ontic question of their truth or falsity (IM, 6).

Further, in the *Letter on Humanism*, he writes, "With the existential determination of the essence of man, therefore, nothing is decided about the 'existence of God' or his 'non-being' . . . Thus it is not only rash but also an error in procedure to maintain that the interpretation of the essence of man from the relation of his essence to the truth of Being is atheism." He then quotes a passage from *Vom Wesen des Grundes*, "Through the ontological interpretation of Dasein as being-in-the-world no decision, whether positive or negative, is made concerning a possible being toward God." After rejecting the hasty conclusion that philosophy doesn't decide for or against the existence of God because it is "stalled in indifference," he insists that he is only trying "to think into the dimension in which alone that question can be asked. . . . Only from the truth of Being can the essence of the holy be thought. Only from the essence of the holy is the essence of divinity to be thought. Only in the light of the essence of divinity can it be thought or said what the word 'God' is to signify" (LH, 229–30; see ER, 91 n. 56).

Attributing to Nietzsche Kierkegaard's distinction between New Testament Christianity and Christendom, and recognizing that his own critique is a confrontation with Christendom as a cultural phenomenon, Heidegger insists that such a confrontation "is absolutely not in any way an attack against what is Christian, any more than a critique of theology is necessarily a critique of faith" (WNGD, 63–64).

It is in the light of statements like these, I believe, that we must understand Heidegger's repeated insistence on the atheistic character of philosophy.[14] I have argued elsewhere that this atheism is methodological rather than substantive,[15] but perhaps 'methodological' is not the best term in relation to Heidegger. It would be better to say that philosophy is atheistic in his view, not because it takes an ontically negative stand on the question of God's reality but because it asks ontological questions that are prior to all ontic questions and neutral with respect to all ontic answers. Even if we suspect that this notion of philosophy's neutrality is an ironical relic of modernity's Enlightenment notion of reason as pure, uncontaminated by the particular commitments that give to traditions their positivity, we can recognize that Heidegger's critique of onto-theological thinking neither presupposes nor argues for the unreality of an uncreated Creator.

Why then, does he get so apopleptic at the notion of God as *causa sui*? Negatively speaking, it is because God as *causa sui* and *causa prima in a certain context* "corresponds to the reason-giving path back to the *ultima ratio*" (ID, 60). To put it more briefly, the *how* of onto-theology is calculative-representational thinking. Because it is "the onto-theo-logical constitution of metaphysics" (ID, 42) with which we are dealing, the critique of onto-theology is one way to talk about the task of overcoming metaphysics. But metaphysics is both calculative and representational thinking. Sometimes Heidegger lumps them together to make it clear that they are two sides of the same coin (EPTT, 377; cf. OM, 100). Elsewhere he discusses them separately, speaking of calculative thinking to emphasize the project of modern technology (the will to power become the will to will) and speaking of representational thinking to emphasize the theoretical foundations of modern technology, not just in modern science but in classical metaphysics going all the way back to Plato and Aristotle.

The goal is to have the world at our disposal (*verfügbar, zur Verfügung stehen*, etc.), in the one case practically, in the other theoretically. It is the latter need that makes philosophy, long before modern philosophy, "a technique for explaining from highest causes" (LH, 197). Heidegger's fullest account of representational thinking as placing the world at our cognitive disposal is *The Principle of Reason*. It is Leibniz who hatches this egg, but it has been incubating since Plato and Aristotle (PR, 4, 53, 118, 121). It begins as the demand for reasons (PR, 22–30). But as the demand for completeness (PR, 32–33), since an unexplained explainer leaves things ultimately unexplained, the principle of reason becomes an appeal to God as *ultima ratio* (PR, 26, 101, 117, 125).

One can even say that for metaphysics, constituted in this way as onto-theology, "God exists only insofar as the principle of reason holds" (PR, 28). This goes beyond the evidentialist posture that will only believe in God if pure reason can prove God's existence. God's raison d'être has become to make it possible for human reason to give ultimate explanations. This is what Heidegger means when he says that "the deity can come into philosophy only insofar as philosophy, of its own accord and by its own nature, requires and determines that and how the deity enters into it" (ID, 56). God is at the beck and call of human understanding, a means to its end of making the whole of being intelligible in keeping with the principle of reason. In order to place the world at the disposal of human theory (and practice), it becomes necessary to place God at our disposal as well. But there is no awe, or singing, or dancing before such a factotum. And if there is any clapping, it will have the form of polite applause. "Please join me in welcoming The Ultima Ratio."

Heidegger's objections to the calculative-representational thinking that places not only the world but God as well at our disposal are more Kierkegaardian than Kantian. What we lack is not so much the power to pull off this project (though, of course, we do) as the right to attempt it. The "swaggering comportment" (DT, 81) of this "unconditional self-assertion" (LH, 221; cf. WNGD, 68, 101) issues in an "insurrection" and "assault" (WNGD, 100), a "monstrousness" (QT, 16) that makes us into the "tyrant of Being" rather than the "shepherd of Being" (LH, 210). We become "that which places everything in relation to *itself*" (OM, 87). "Man becomes that being upon which all that is, is grounded as regards the manner of its Being and its truth. Man becomes the relational center of that which is as such. . . . [M]an contends for the position in which he can be that particular being who gives the measure and draws up the guidelines for everything that is" (AWP, 128, 134). In short, calculative-representational thinking is hubris on a world historical scale.

We have already seen that God is part of this world that revolves around "man" (Heidegger does not note the gendered character of the humanism he criticizes). This is where the specifically religious character of Heidegger's critique comes to the fore, for "even God can, for representational thinking, lose all that is exalted and holy, the mysteriousness of his distance" (QT, 26).

For Heidegger, philosophy not only begins in wonder but must never lose touch with the awe, wonder, and even dread we experience before the mystery that metaphysics as onto-theology seeks to demystify.[16] This is every bit as crucial for any theology that would remain religiously significant.

In postmodern contexts, onto-theology is one of the seven deadly sins. But one is not necessarily committing onto-theology when affirming God as *causa sui*. It is not as if after Heidegger philosophy somehow knows better than to affirm the reality of an uncreated Creator. But it is dangerous to do so in the language of *causa sui*, for this language has its provenance in a project that can be traced from Anaxagoras to Nietzsche (for the project survives the death of God) and that is deeply antithetical both to authentic philosophy and to authentic theology. This project is the *how* that turns the *what* of Jewish, Christian, and Muslim monotheism into onto-theology, leaving us with the God of the philosophers instead of the God of Abraham, Isaac, and Jacob.

The critique of onto-theology by name belongs to Heidegger II.[17] But at least implicitly it can be found in Heidegger I and even earlier. There is, of course, that passage early in *Being and Time* where Heidegger reminds us that Being is not a being and that thinking Being consists "in not 'telling a story'— that is to say, in not defining beings as beings by tracing them back in their origin to some other beings, as if Being had the character of some possible entity" (BT 26, translation modified). Early and late, metaphysics is the forgetfulness of Being, and that theme is part of the critique of onto-theology. But not the best part, nor the part that has a bearing on how theology can avoid lapsing into onto-theology (for theology does not come home to its proper task by making the question of being prior to the question of God). The most compelling themes in that critique can be, and in Heidegger often are, developed independently from the ontological difference.

Accordingly, it is to a different text from Heidegger I that I turn, namely the 1927–28 lecture, *Phenomenology and Theology*. Heidegger tells us that it is guided by the notion of phenomenology given in ¶7 of *Being and Time*. But even more important for understanding the lecture are: the notion of knowledge as a founded mode of being-in-the-world (BT, ¶13); the notion of assertion as a derivative mode of interpretation (BT, ¶33); and the distinction between *Zuhandenheit*, the ready-to-hand, and *Vorhandenheit*, the present-at-hand or objectively present (BT, ¶15, 16, 33).[18] In other words, we are dealing with a critique of the primacy of the theoretical. As a project of rendering the whole of being intelligible in accordance with the principle of reason, onto-theology presupposes and practices the primacy of theoretical reason.

Heidegger quotes Luther's definition of faith as "letting ourselves be seized by the things we do not see" and adds his own negative and positive account: "[F]aith is not something which merely reveals that the occurring of revelation is something happening; it is not some more or less modified type of knowing. Rather, faith is an appropriation of revelation. . . . *Faith is the believing-understanding mode of existing in the history revealed, i.e., occurring, with the Crucified*" (PT, 10). But this means that since "theology is constituted by thematizing faith" (PT, 11), it "is not speculative knowledge of God" (PT, 15).

This does not mean that faith and theology should be given the non-cognitivist interpretations familiar from positivist or Wittgensteinian contexts. Faith is a *"believing-understanding mode of existing,"* and it stands in relation to something actual. Heidegger's believer surely believes that "in Christ God was reconciling the world to himself" (II Corinthians 5:19). But with Luther, Heidegger refuses to allow faith to be understood as the *pistis* which Plato puts on the lower half of the divided line. We misunderstand faith terribly if we assume that the believer really wants to be an onto-theologically constituted metaphysician, but failing to be part of the intellectual elite settles for a second-class, "more or less modified type, of knowing."[19]

Every positive science concerns a domain that is "already disclosed," prior to any "theoretical consideration," in a "prescientific manner of approaching and proceeding with that which is." Science always presupposes this "prescientific *behavior* [*Verhalten*]" (PT 7, emphasis added). For theology as a positive science, faith is the "prescientific *behavior*" in which the *Sache* that concerns it is "already disclosed." In the case of Christian theology, what is disclosed is above all "Christ, the crucified God" (PT, 9). Of course, faith is dependent on revelation for its *positum*, but that does not mean that faith is simply the assent to new information. Rather "existence struck by this revelation becomes aware of its forgetfulness of God. . . . [B]eing placed before God means that existence is reoriented in and through the mercy of God grasped in faith. . . . [The believer] can only 'believe' his existential possibility as one which human existence itself is not master over, in which it becomes a slave, is brought before God, and is reborn. . . . *Faith = Rebirth*" (PT, 10). It is immediately after this account of faith as an existential paradigm shift that Heidegger identifies with Luther's understanding of faith as opposed to the Platonic reading whose *Wirkungsgeschichte* has distorted so many discussions of faith and reason.

Faith is the "appropriation" of revelation and theology is the "thematizing" of faith (PT, 10–11). Hegel thinks the task of thematizing faith belongs ultimately to philosophy and that it consists in transforming faith into absolute knowledge by translating *Vorstellungen* into *Begriffe*. But this is just Plato's divided line translated into German. Heidegger is too Lutheran to buy into this project (from one who professed to be a Lutheran!). He has learned from another Lutheran (Kierkegaard) that it trivializes the appropriation of revelation in which existence is re-oriented and the believer reborn by replacing this task with a speculative task that is at once too easy and too elitist to be anything but an enemy of faith.

So, when he tells us "Theology is not speculative knowledge of God" (PT, 15), he has two things in mind. First, the task of theology is not to "found and secure faith in its legitimacy, nor can it in any way make it easier to accept faith and remain constant in faith. Theology can only render faith more difficult" (PT, 12).

Second, this is because the goal of theology "is never a valid system of theological propositions" but rather "concrete Christian existence itself." Because faith is both the motivation and justification of theology, "this objectification of faith itself properly has no other purpose than to help cultivate faithfulness itself. . . . Every theological statement and concept addresses itself *in its very content* to the faith-full existence of the individual in the community; it does *not* do so subsequently, for the sake of some practical *'application'"* (PT, 12). In other words, because its goal is the *praxis* of the believer as a distinctive mode of existence, *"theology in its essence is a practical science."* Unlike onto-theology, theology properly understood is "innately homiletical," but not "due to any accidental requirements which demand, say, that it apply its theoretical propositions to a practical sphere" (PT, 14–15). The apostolic kerygma that "in Christ God was reconciling the world to himself" is already the entreaty, "be reconciled to God" (II Corinthians 5:19–20).

Theology arises out of a "prescientific behavior" and has as its goal what we might call postscientific behavior. It is as if Heidegger is saying, "I have found it necessary to deny theory in order to make room for practice." Of course, as we have seen, the denial of theory is not its abolition but its *Aufhebung*, its teleological suspension, its re-inscription in a context where it is neither the *arche* nor the *telos*, neither the *terminus a quo* nor the *terminus ad quem*.

This polemic against the primacy of the theoretical is found as early as the 1920–21 lectures, *Einleitung in die Phänomenologie der Religion.* By contrast with the 1927–28 lecture, Heidegger even denies that philosophy (in this case as a phenomenology of religion) should think of itself as a science (GA, 60 3, 8–10, 15, 17, 27, 29, 35). This is because it seeks to be faithful to experience, which relates to the world in its *Bedeutsamkeit* rather than to "objects" (GA, 60 8–16). We have here a clear anticipation of the distinction between *Zuhandenheit* and *Vorhandenheit*, whose importance for the later lecture has already been suggested.

It might be objected that in the later, explicit critique of onto-theology, Heidegger links it to calculative-representational thinking, the essence of modern technology. Thought is too closely linked to a certain practice. With Heidegger I, by contrast, it seems that the linkage of knowledge to action is an important desideratum. So how can the earlier emphasis on the embeddedness of knowing in doing, both in general and specifically in the life of faith, be an anticipation of the later critique of instrumental reason?

But we must not interpret the distinction between *Bedeutsamkeit* and objects, or between *Zuhandenheit* and *Vorhandenheit* only in utilitarian terms, nor allow the famous hammer of *Being and Time* to turn Heidegger into a crude pragmatist. We radically misconstrue our being-in-the-world when we portray it as an objective pole made up of facts whose only job is to obtain and a subjective pole whose only job is to mirror these facts.[20] Attention to the use of a tool helps us see this; but we need something like the Aristotelian distinction between *praxis* and *poiesis* to indicate that our concernful dealings with beings which are positively or negatively meaningful in relation to our projects are not necessarily instrumental. A theoretical or representational interpretation of our being-in-the-world is as inadequate to the "Hammerklavier" Sonata as it is to the hammer, to say nothing of the word of the Lord which is "like a hammer that breaks a rock in pieces" (Jeremiah 23:29). Or, to put it a bit differently, God is not a tool; but both as *fascinans* and as *tremendum*, the *mysterium* is *Bedeutsamkeit* and not mere object, is *zuhanden* and not merely *vorhanden*. Before such a God one can fall on one's knees in awe.[21]

But the onto-theological project commits the fallacy of misplaced concreteness. It abstracts the cognitive dimension of the religious life and gives it essential primacy. In each of the three dimensions of its relation to human action it is a danger to faith. 1) For the sake of absolute conceptual mastery, it seeks to free knowledge from its rootedness in pretheoretical practice so that it can become self-grounding. In this way it gets itself stuck to the epistemological tar baby that has paralyzed so much of modernity. 2) When mathematical physics replaces theology as the queen of the sciences, pure theory discovers that it has wonderful technological applications.[22] Heidegger's critique of God as the highest value is a reminder that the technological attitude can rub off onto faith, that piety can degenerate into an instrumental religion in which God becomes a means to our ends (WNGD, 105). 3) In its more overtly theological modes, onto-theology finds that it has cut itself off from the modes of appropriation, singing and dancing, for example, that constitute living faith.

In relation to *Phenomenology and Theology*, however, there is a more serious objection. Theology becomes onto-theology when Jerusalem sells its soul to Athens by buying in on the latter's project. Within Christian history, the critique of onto-theology belongs to a tradition of dehellenizing repristination. Heidegger explicitly links his critique with Luther, and thus, by implication, with a tradition that looks back to Augustine and ahead to Pascal, Kierkegaard, and Barth.[23] He seems to confirm Jerusalem's declaration of independence from Athens when he writes, "On the grounds of its specific positive character and the form of knowing which this determines, we can now say that theology is a fully autonomous ontic science" (PT, 16), not, of course, in relation to the revelation upon which it depends, but in relation to the other sciences.

But a problem arises when he immediately asks specifically about the relation of this science to philosophy as the ontological science. Theology needs philosophy, he says, but neither for its *positum*, revelational content, nor for some rational legitimation. Rather, "all basic theological concepts . . . have as their *ontological* determinants meanings which are pre-Christian and which can thus be grasped purely rationally." Thus, for example, the theological concept of sin must be understood in terms of the ontological interpretation of guilt, presumably as found in *Being and Time* (PT, 17–18; cf. LH, 229–30, cited above).

At first Heidegger calls this relation one of guidance, but then he describes it no fewer than nine times as "correction" (*Korrektion, Korrektiv*, PT, 19–20). In this connection he reminds us that faith is "the mortal enemy of the *form of existence* which is an essential part of *philosophy*" by virtue of an "*existentiell opposition* between faithfulness and a human's free appropriation of his whole existence" (PT, 20).

As a Christian thinker, Marion is more than a little nervous at this suggestion that theology must be corrected by philosophy. The idea that Heidegger might help free our thinking of God from the question of being and its close link with the onto-theological project turns out to be illusory.[24] Under Heidegger's tutelage "every theology remains subject to the question of Being." By virtue of his own attempts at overcoming metaphysics, he seems to side with Luther, Pascal, and Barth in their attempt to overcome the Babylonian captivity of faith to philosophy; but this is only to substitute a new philosophical master for the old ones. When Marion looks the (Trojan) gift horse in the mouth, what he sees is an "ontic independence, which implies an irreducible ontological dependence. . . . It seems that the question of 'God' never suffered as radical a reduction to the first question of Being as in the phenomenological enterprise of Heidegger."[25] Heidegger makes theology autonomous vis-à-vis chemistry, but not vis-à-vis Heidegger!

Why shouldn't Marion be offended? Why should Christian theology submit itself to correction from a life form that is its "mortal enemy" and that employs "pre-Christian" and "purely rational" concepts as its tools?

But perhaps the matter isn't quite that simple. Let us take a closer look at the role Heidegger assigns philosophy vis-à-vis theology to see whether there remains a possibility of theological appropriation rather than the either/or of capitulation/repudiation. First, Heidegger says that the ontological meanings philosophy furnishes are "pre-Christian" and can be grasped "purely rationally." As already indicated, it is surprising to hear Heidegger appeal to pure reason. The repudiation of the view that philosophy can embody the view from nowhere is central to his critique of Husserl and Dilthey, and, indeed, to his whole corpus. So we can turn our attention to the notion that Heidegger's ontology is "pre-Christian."

At this stage of the game (the twenties) it is not so much the pre-Socratics that concern us as Aristotle, who plays a significant role in the development of the hermeneutics of facticity that becomes ontology in *Being and Time* (see GA, 61; GA, 63; and PIRA). But, as Van Buren, Kisiel, and others have shown, Heidegger draws very heavily on a variety of Christian sources, including the Pauline epistles, in trying to break the stranglehold of pure theory on the life of faith. So perhaps the correction to which Heidegger subjects theology is in significant measure self-correction rather than imperialistic hubris. My account of the critique of onto-theology, both early and late, has focused on just those features for which this is most arguably the case, features that are separable both de jure and often de facto from the project of thinking being.

Second, Heidegger claims that the corrective guidance philosophy offers to theology is purely formal, and he invokes the notion of formal indication (*formale Anzeige*) that plays such an important part in his earlier work (PT, 19–20).[26] Hegel once told a similar story. The contents of theology and philosophy, he solemnly intoned, are the same. The only "corrective" philosophy supplies concerns its form—and this from a philosopher whose Logic insists on the inextricability of form and content. Kierkegaard has taught us to laugh loudly (so as to keep from crying) at this pretense under which Hegel seeks to subject Christian faith to the canons of autonomous human reason. A similar laugh should greet Heidegger's "Who me? I'm only concerned with questions of form. All the content comes from the Christian *positum.*"

Except . . . Heidegger derives his formal indications, not from pure reason but hermeneutically; and, as we have just been reminded, the texts he reads are very largely Christian texts. So once again, we are free to look for those elements that are authentically theological; and once again these may not revolve around the ontological difference. Further, just to the degree that the heart of onto-theology concerns the *how* rather than the *what* of discourse about God, there is something formal about what is at issue.

Finally, we are told that the "demand" for philosophy to play a corrective role in relation to theology "is not made by philosophy as such but rather by theology" (PT, 20). There may be a touch of megalomania here. Just as Heidegger later would think that the National Socialist movement desperately needed him to clarify its identity and would freely turn to him if it understood both its own and his greatness, so here he thinks that (Christian) theology needs him and is most fully itself when it turns to him for correction.[27] Still, just to the degree that Heidegger's critique has genuinely theological origins, as we have been noting, it makes sense to see "correction" as self-correction and the demand for a critique of onto-theology as arising from a theology that recognizes its own onto-theological tendencies and sees these as temptations to be resisted.

My project is to appropriate Heidegger's critique of onto-theology for theistic theology, for religiously significant discourse about the personal Cre-

159

ator, Lawgiver, and Merciful Savior of Jewish, or Christian, or Muslim monotheism. Because appropriation is always recontextualizing it is always both
affirmation and negation; it is a little bit like an Hegelian *Aufhebung*, though
without the implication of logical or conceptual necessity. That is why for each
of the three themes just discussed in relation to philosophy's "correction" of
theology, I found something to reject (à la Marion), and something to preserve
from Heidegger. This has led to the notion that theology must submit itself to
the discipline of Heidegger's critique, now understood as prophetic self-criticism. And this may seem to run counter to the argument that the critique of
onto-theology concerns its *how* and not its *what*, an argument apparently
directed toward getting theology off the hook of Heidegger's critique. So let me
try to clarify.

When I address an issue like this I always have two audiences in mind, one
quite secular (or at least anti-theistic), the other rather traditionally theological, often in a Thomistic or Calvinist way.[28] To the first I say, "The critique in
question is very powerful, but closely examined it does not do the work you
would like it to do. It does not discredit theistic discourse as such, does not
make the world safe from the God of Abraham, Isaac, and Jacob (and Moses,
and Jesus, and Mohammed). It only discredits certain forms that discourse
can/has/does take(n)." To my Thomist and Calvinist friends I say, "Don't get
too comfortable. While the critique in question does not do the work its anti-
theist enthusiasts would like it to do, it has a lot of legitimate bite. Moreover,
there are good theological reasons to take it seriously, for it identifies and
critiques ways in which the most orthodox God-talk becomes idolatrous."

The main argument of this essay has been addressed to the first audience.
I have argued that both the explicit critique of onto-theology in the forties and
fifties, and important anticipations of it from the twenties are directed toward
the *how* rather than the *what* of our God-talk and that they have more the spirit
of Pascal than that of positivism. That is to say, they do not provide or seek to
provide a philosophical case against belief in a personal Creator (as is all too
often implied); they rather seek to keep open the space for religiously meaningful God-talk by resisting the "metaphysical" tendency, whether found
among philosophers or theologians, to imprison theological discourse within
a primacy of theoretical reason under the rule of the principle of sufficient
reason. What is necessary to overcome onto-theology is not the abandonment
of theistic belief but the avoidance of this temptation to have God at our
disposal, conceptually speaking.

This reading weakens Heidegger's critique, I think, only for those who
have hoped it would do for continental philosophy what positivism once did
for analytic philosophy. It still retains plenty of force not only against such
paradigmatically onto-theological systems as those of Spinoza and Hegel but
also against what we might call onto-theologies of the right, more popularly
known as fundamentalisms. While the latter may not speak the language of
sufficient reason and *causa sui*, they do treat God as being at their disposal

conceptually (it's scary how much they know about what God is up to) and convert this quite quickly into the project of having the world at their disposal practically as well. Theocracy legitimizes itself onto-theologically.

Between these extremes we can locate two other sites where Heidegger's critique has force against onto-theological tendencies which may not have prevailed so completely but which are nevertheless very real. Closer to the fundamentalist end of the spectrum are those theologies, Protestant and Catholic, which are sometimes designated 'scholasticism'. This term has negative connotations precisely when its use points to onto-theological tendencies to which theistic discourse can, but need not, succumb.

Closer to the other end of the spectrum, ironically to be sure, are certain invocations of negative theology. Marion speaks of the discourse "that disqualifies or deconstructs the very notion of God; this discourse consists in speaking of God in order to silence him, in not keeping silent in order to silence him. . . . [I]t does not see the difference between silencing and keeping silent."[29] But silencing God is one way of having God at our disposal and protecting ourselves against being seized by what we do not see. The act of protesting against onto-theology can become an onto-theological gesture.

As we move away from the extremes toward cases like these last two we move into situations that are at once ambiguous and closer to home. Because of their ambiguity we need to look closely to determine just where and to what degree God-talk becomes the arrogant humanism that puts God at our disposal; and in light of the distinction between the *how* and the *what,* we should not expect to be able to answer these questions simply in terms of propositional content. Because these sites are closer to home we need to look closely to see to what degree our carefully crafted critique is directed at ourselves.

So far I have spoken as if overcoming onto-theology means 1) learning correctly to identify it and 2) learning to avoid it. But, at least for the theistic discourses that primarily concern me, learning to avoid means learning to speak of God otherwise than onto-theologically. Something must be said, however briefly, about the positive meaning of this overcoming. We can take Heidegger's implicit slogan, "I have found it necessary to deny theory in order to make room for practice," as our key.

For a gloss on the positive meaning of denying theory, I turn to Wagner's *Lohengrin.* It can be read as a tenth-century *Shane.* The hero rides into town, takes care of the bad guys, and then rides off into the sunset, alone. But I propose reading it as a retelling of the story of Cupid and Psyche. Motivated by the desire to rule, Ortrud turns Gottfried, rightful heir to power in Brabant, into a swan by means of sorcery. She then persuades her husband, Telramund, to accuse Elsa, the young boy's sister, of his murder. (This will clear the path to power for Ortrud and Telramund.) The matter is to be settled by combat.

When no local knight is willing to defend Elsa's honor, the magnificent Lohengrin arrives in a boat pulled by a swan.

Needless to say, it is love at first sight between Elsa and Lohengrin, but to her he is more than her hero and husband-to-be. In language heavy with theological overtones, she calls him her *Retter* and her *Erlöser*. She gives herself to him totally.

> Mein Held, mein Retter! Nimm mich hin,
> *Dir geb' ich Alles, was ich bin!*

Lohengrin, whose name is not yet revealed within the drama, asks Elsa to promise never to ask his name or country.

> Nie sollst du mich befragen
> Noch Wissen's Sorge tragen,
> Woher ich kam der Fahrt,
> *Noch wie mein Nam' und Art!*

Elsa promises solemnly to honor this request, and at Lohengrin's request, repeats her promise to obey his command (*Gebot*). He vindicates her by defeating Telramund, and in ecstasy she repeats

> *Nimm alles was ich bin!* (Act I/Scene III)[30]

But now Ortrud's shame adds desire for vengeance to her lust for the throne. Standing between Satan and Iago, she plants the seeds of doubt in Elsa. Her lover came by magic. How does she know he won't leave her and disappear just as quickly? (Doesn't every Shane leave a woman behind, weeping?) Shouldn't she know his name? At the end of the second act, Telramund, once again Ortrud's dupe, accuses Lohengrin of sorcery and publicly challenges him to reveal his name. Lohengrin says that he will do so only in response to a demand from Elsa, but she renews her pledge.

> Mein Retter, der mir Heil gebracht!
> Mein Held, in dem ich muss vergeh'n!
> Hoch über alles Zweifels Macht
> *Soll meine Liebe stehn!* (2.5)

For a third time she insists that trusting love shall triumph over the doubt born of *Wissen's Sorge*.

At the beginning of the final act we hear the familiar wedding march and then the lovers are alone in the bridal chamber. Almost immediately their ecstatic joy is disturbed by Elsa's request to know her lover's name. At first she says it was so wonderful to hear him say her name and she wants to return the favor. "You can tell me," she says, "I won't tell anyone else." He warns her that she is on the verge of ruining everything and pleads with her to let love prevail over doubt as she has promised.

Then we learn how effective Ortrud's intimations have been and what really motivates Elsa's doubt. She is afraid that some day Lohengrin will tire of

her and leave her. He came by magic and she seeks some magic to bind him to her. The ancient linkage between knowing the name and the ability to conjure, only hinted at earlier, now becomes explicit.[31] Elsa's *Wissen's Sorge* is not born of self-giving love but of the desire to be in control, to have Lohengrin at her disposal.

He tells her that he is Lohengrin, son of Parsifal and a knight of the Grail. The magic that brought him to her would have left them together forever if she had trusted him. But it requires all knights to return to the temple of the Grail once their identity is known. The swan returns and is restored to Elsa as Gottfried. But Lohengrin sails away, leaving Elsa to cry out in anguish and pass out in her brother's arms.

In C. S. Lewis's retelling of the Cupid and Psyche story, the demands of walking by faith and not by sight are even stronger. As Psyche tells her sister about the god to whom she has been married and with whom she lives in a magnificent palace, she explains, "Oh, Orual . . . not even I have seen him— yet. He comes to me only in the holy darkness. He says I mustn't—not yet—see his face or know his name. I'm forbidden to bring any light into his—our— chamber."[32] To make matters worse, although they are standing right in front of the palace, Orual cannot see it. It is hard to know whether to say that Psyche's God-relation takes place in hidden inwardness or in hidden outwardness. But even the site of their communion is invisible and inaccessible to her unbelieving sister.

Whether it is just the name that is forbidden, or in addition that the beloved is not allowed to see her lover's face, the challenge of faith is the same: The believer is called upon to sustain a beautiful and loving relationship through trust in a lover about whom she remains significantly (though not totally) in the dark and who, though he gives himself to her freely, is not at her disposal. The relationship is destroyed when the beloved succumbs to *Wissen's Sorge* and insists on Enlightenment, on dissipating the darkness of mystery with the light of human knowledge, on walking by sight and not by faith.

To be able to resist this temptation, faith must deny theory, or, to be more precise, the primacy of insight. For such faith, Plato's divided line and Hegel's modern version thereof as the movement "beyond faith" to knowledge are not the ascent from that which is inferior (body, senses, epistemic risk, opinions available to the many) to that which is superior (soul, intellect, the certainty of sheer presence, insights available to the culturally elite); they are rather the withdrawal from the site at which alone is possible a loving, trusting relation with a God before whom one might sing and dance (or at least clap).

This love, this trust, this relationship—these are the practice for the sake of which it was necessary to deny theory. This is not to abolish theology. It is to see that theology's task is to serve this life of faith, not the ideals of knowledge as defined by the philosophical traditions Heidegger variously calls calculative-representational thinking, metaphysics, and onto-theology.

Who knows better than Pseudo-Dionysius the importance of silence before the mystery of God? Yet he also knows that the life of faith is very vocal, and he spends much of his time, especially in *The Divine Names*, telling us, not how not to speak about God, but how to speak about God. It is as if he can hear his audience asking again and again, "But if the point of our discourse about God is not to pull (or push) God out of the cloud of unknowing, into the light of sheer presence, what is the point of it?" To which he replies, again and again, "In a word: praise." For praise is an essential component in the practice of faith. We accompany our "wise silence" with "songs of praise."[33] For Marion it is because God is *agapē* and gift that "predication must yield to praise." We receive the gift of love in silence. "Only then can discourse be reborn, but as an enjoyment, a jubilation, a praise."[34]

"We go to church in order to sing, and theology is secondary." One way to see how far we have overcome onto-theology is to ask how strongly we are inspired by our theology to sing songs of praise to the God who triumphed over political, economic, and cultural oppression when "Pharaoh's army got drownded."[35]

## DERRIDA'S RESPONSE TO MEROLD WESTPHAL

*Jacques Derrida.* Without pretending to get to your central point, I would just ask a minor and humble question, which perhaps has to do, not with what you said, but with the virtual strategy of your paper. I refer to two statements of yours. At the beginning you said, "Miriam and the American slaves did not need to overcome onto-theology; they were never tempted by it." Could you clarify this? What is the evidence that they were never tempted by it? Are you not presupposing that onto-theology is simply confined within a speculative, academic, or specialized discourse? I am not sure that Miriam and American slaves did not need to overcome onto-theology, that they were never tempted by it, or that they should never be tempted by it—perhaps in terms of politics. That is one side of the question. The other side of the same question would have to do with another statement that you made at the end of your paper, when you said "not only against such paradigmatically onto-theological systems as those of Spinoza and Hegel, but also against what we might call the onto-theology of the right, more popularly known as 'fundamentalisms'." And later, "theocracy legitimizes itself onto-theologically." Are you sure of that? Do not you think that there is some possible fundamentalism which could use the deconstruction of onto-theology for its purpose? That some fundamentalism could use strategically the tools of Heidegger in a deconstructionist critique of onto-theology? You see, perhaps there is more than one fundamentalism. And here the strategy of these politics must be perhaps a little more complicated than that.

*Merold Westphal.* Thank you. I was assuming that onto-theology is something that happens only at a fairly high level of reflection and almost exclusively in what we think of as academic contexts. That is why I let Miriam and the slaves off so easily. Your question as to whether that is a legitimate assumption is an interesting one and I will have to think about that some more. I do not have an immediate response to it. There is a sense in which what I referred to as fundamentalist onto-theology is not exactly the academic versions that we are familiar with, but I think they do occur at a high level of a self-reflective need to legitimate social practices and social hegemonies. I think that any fundamentalism that invoked deconstruction or other kinds of finitist analyses in their own project would have lost something that for most of the fundamentalisms that I know anything about is very important. Whether they could continue and survive and still be something like themselves I do not know. It is an interesting thought. My experience is that the closer one gets on the spectrum to fundamentalism, the more immediate and the more emotional is the negative reaction to the sort of suggestions that I have been making today.

*Jacques Derrida.* The reason I associate these two points is that perhaps onto-theology for Heidegger is not simply a critique of theology, not simply an academic discourse, but a real culture.

*Merold Westphal.* Yes, if technology is the metaphysics of the atomic age, then onto-theology is all over the place.

## NOTES

1. *Dakota: A Spiritual Geography* (New York: Ticknor & Fields, 1993), 91.

2. *Binding the Strong Man: A Political Reading of Mark's Story of Jesus* (Maryknoll, N.Y.: Orbis, 1988).

3. Works of Heidegger will be cited in the text and notes by means of the following abbreviations:

AWP—"The Age of the World Picture," in *The Question Concerning Technology and Other Essays,* trans. William Lovitt (New York: Harper & Row, 1977).

BT—*Being and Time,* trans. John Macquarrie and Edward Robinson (New York: Harper & Row, 1962).

CT—*The Concept of Time,* trans. William McNeill (Oxford: Blackwell, 1992).

DT—*Discourse on Thinking,* trans. John M. Anderson and E. Hans Freund (New York: Harper & Row, 1966).

EPTT—"The End of Philosophy and the Task of Thinking" in *Basic Writings,* ed. David Farrell Krell (New York: Harper & Row, 1977).

ER—*The Essence of Reasons,* trans. Terrence Malick (Evanston, Ill.: Northwestern University Press, 1969).

GA—*Gesamtausgabe,* followed by volume number.

GA 15—*Seminare* (Frankfurt: Klosterman, 1986).

GA 60—*Phänomenologie des religiösen Lebens* (Frankfurt: Klosterman, 1995).

GA 61—*Phänomenologische Interpretationen zu Aristotles: Einführung in die Phänomenologische Forschung* (Frankfurt: Klosterman, 1985).

GA 63—*Ontologie: Hermeneutics der Faktizität* (Frankfurt: Klosterman, 1988). Translation by John Van Buren, Indiana University Press, 1999.

HCT—*History of the Concept of Time: Prolegomena,* trans. Theodore Kisiel (Bloomington: Indiana University Press, 1985).

ID—*Identity and Difference*, trans. Joan Stambaugh (New York: Harper & Row, 1969).

IM—*Introduction to Metaphysics*, trans. Ralph Manheim (Garden City: Double-day, 1961).

LH—"Letter on Humanism," in *Basic Writings*.

MFL—*The Metaphysical Foundations of Logic*, trans. Michael Heim (Blooming-ton: Indiana University Press, 1984).

OM—"Overcoming Metaphysics," in *The End of Philosophy*, trans. Joan Stam-baugh (New York: Harper & Row, 1973).

PIRA—"Phenomenological Interpretations with Respect to Aristotle: Indication of the Hermeneutical Situation," trans. Michael Baur in *Man and World*, 25 (1992).

PR—*The Principle of Reason*, trans. Reginald Lilly (Bloomington: Indiana Uni-versity Press, 1991).

PT—*Phenomenology and Theology*, in *The Piety of Thinking*, trans. James G. Hart and John C. Maraldo (Bloomington: Indiana University Press, 1976).

QT—"The Question Concerning Technology," in *The Question Concerning Technology*.

WM/1929—*What Is Metaphysics?* in *Existentialism from Dostoevsky to Sartre*, ed. Walter Kaufmann, 2nd ed. (New York: New American Library, 1975).

WM/1943—Untitled postscript to WM/1929 in Kaufmann, *Existentialism*.

WM/1949—"The Way Back into the Ground of Metaphysics," Introduction to WM/1929 in Kaufmann, *Existentialism*.

WNGD—"The Word of Nietzsche: 'God Is Dead,'" in *The Question Concerning Technology*.

4. Kant uses the term 'onto-theology' to describe the attempt to prove the exist-ence of God "through mere concepts, without the help of any experience whatsoever. . . ." *Critique of Pure Reason*, A632 = B660. Heidegger's usage is quite different.

5. Aristotle is the paradigm of onto-theology in WM/1949, just as Hegel is in ID.

6. For a critique of this infatuation in Heidegger's work, see John D. Caputo, *Demythologizing Heidegger* (Bloomington: Indiana University Press, 1993).

7. Marion cites the Heidegger passage from GA 15, 436–37 in *God without Being*, trans. Thomas A. Carlson (Chicago: University of Chicago Press, 1991), 61. Converse-ly, Heidegger writes, "Someone who has experienced theology in his own roots, both the theology of Christian faith and that of philosophy, would today rather remain silent about God when he is speaking in the realm of thinking" (ID 54–55). For Marion's suspicion that this silence is itself, ironically, metaphysical and an expression of the will to power, see *God without Being*, 54–55, 60.

8. The first quotation is from Hent de Vries, "Adieu, à dieu, a-Dieu," in *Ethics as First Philosophy*, ed. Adriaan T. Peperzak (New York: Routledge, 1995), 218. The second and third quotations are from John D. Caputo, *The Prayers and Tears of Jacques Derrida: Religion without Religion* (Bloomington: Indiana University Press, 1997), 113. Caputo is speaking here in a Derridean perspective, which is not the problem, for Derrida's critique of the metaphysics of presence and Heidegger's critique of onto-theology are deeply akin. Another example: When Levinas expresses his reservations about "the factitious transcendence of worlds behind the scenes," (*Otherwise than Being or Beyond Essence*, trans. Alphonso Lingis [Dordrecht: Kluwer Academic Pub-lishers, 1991], 4–5), John Llewelyn says he is "endorsing Nietzsche's proclamation of

the death of the God of onto-theology. . . ." *Emmanuel Levinas: The Genealogy of Ethics* (New York: Routledge, 1995), 150. On page 156 Llewelyn identifies "onto-theological transcendence" with "a God of the *Jenseits*, the Beyond," as if theism were automatically onto-theological.

9. *Concluding Unscientific Postscript to Philosophical Fragments*, vol 1, trans. Howard V. Hong and Edna H. Hong (Princeton: Princeton University Press, 1992), 118.

10. *Postscript*, I, 141, 158. While Climacus finds it necessary to emphasize the difference between the human and divine perspectives, he finds no need to deny the reality of the latter. So, when Caputo writes, "Cast in a deconstructive slant, God is . . . not the eternal but the futural" (*Prayers and Tears*, 113), Climacus responds, "For an existing person, is not eternity not eternity but the future, whereas eternity is eternity only for the Eternal, who is not in a process of becoming? . . . [T]he *eternal* relates itself as the *future* to the *person in a process of becoming*" (*Postscript*, I, 306–307). The implication is that the phrase "not the eternal but the futural" projects onto God the limitations of the human condition.

11. For a sophisticated version of such an argument in the context of natural theology, see Brian Leftow, "Can Philosophy Argue God's Existence?" in *The Rationality of Belief and the Plurality of Faiths*, ed. Thomas Senor (Ithaca: Cornell University Press, 1995). In conversation, Leftow has put it this way: "When I offer a version of the cosmological argument I find to be sound, I am trying to prove the existence of God, not to explain the world." On the inextricability of unconcealment and concealment, Heidegger quotes Hamaan as saying, "Lucidity [*Deutlichkeit*] is a suitable apportionment of light and shadow." *The Principle of Reason*, trans. Reginald Lilly (Bloomington: Indiana University Press, 1991), 9.

12. Leslie F. Brandt, *Psalms/Now* (St. Louis: Concordia Publishing House, 1973), 175.

13. This distinction is crucial to Climacus's notion of truth as subjectivity. For my analysis in the context of this larger theme, see *Becoming a Self: A Reading of Kierkegaard's Concluding Unscientific Postscript* (West Lafayette, Ind.: Purdue University Press, 1996), pp. 114–33.

14. See the Aristotle lectures of GA 61, 196–97; PIRA, 367; CT, 1; HCT, 79–80; MFL, 140.

15. See Merold Westphal, "Heidegger's *Theologische Jugendschriften*," *Research in Phenomenology* XXVII (1997): 247–61.

16. See, for example, WM/1929, 251, 256; WM/1943, 260–64; DT, 55, 63–68, LH, 199; PR, 54–55, 61–62, 68.

17. Or, if you like, to Heidegger II and III. See Reiner Schürmann, *Heidegger on Being and Acting: From Principles to Anarchy* (Bloomington: Indiana University Press, 1987), 12–18.

18. Marion will suggest an even stronger dependence of the lecture on *Being and Time*. See *God without Being*, 66–69.

19. When Levinas distinguishes his own critique of onto-theology from Pascal's, it is because he surprisingly assumes that Pascal assimilates faith to opinion on Plato's divided line. See "God and Philosophy," *Collected Philosophical Papers*, trans. Alphonso Lingis (Dordrecht: Martinus Nijhoff, 1987), 155. But cf. the reference to "reasons that 'reason' does not know" on 172.

20. Nietzsche writes, "We are not thinking frogs, *nor objectifying and registering mechanisms with their innards removed . . .*" (emphasis mine). *The Gay Science*, trans. Walter Kaufman (New York: Random House, 1974), second edition preface, section 3.

21. Reference to awe suggests that our concrete being-in-the-world has an affective side that must not be overlooked. In "Hermeneutics as Epistemology," in *Blackwell Guide to Epistemology*, ed. Ernest Sosa and John Greco (Oxford: Blackwell, 1999), 415–35, I trace the double reduction in *Being and Time* from the merely theoretical to both the practical and the affective, a "reduction" which, unlike Husserl's, seeks to recapture the natural standpoint. The account of *Befindlichkeit* in paragraphs 29–30 of *Being and Time* belongs to the early, implicit critique of onto-theology. "The fear of the Lord is the beginning of knowledge" (Proverbs 1:7).

22. We have just seen Heidegger explicitly deny that "application" is the right way to think the relation of theory to practice in theology.

23. On the importance of Luther, Pascal, Kierkegaard, and, in this connection, both Paul and Augustine, see John Van Buren, *The Young Heidegger: Rumor of the Hidden King* (Bloomington: Indiana University Press, 1994); Theodore Kisiel, *The Genesis of Heidegger's Being and Time* (Berkeley: University of California Press, 1993); and the essays by Van Buren and Kisiel in their jointly edited volume, *Reading Heidegger from the Start: Essays in His Earliest Thought* (Albany: SUNY Press, 1994).

24. It is worth noting in this connection that Pseudo-Dionysius points to a God beyond being because he is a proto-Kantian who sees 'being' as a category of human understanding that is inadequate to the divine reality. See *Pseudo-Dionysius: The Complete Works*, trans. Colm Luibheid (New York: Paulist Press, 1987), 49–50, 53, 63, 135, 138, 263.

25. *God without Being*, 68–69.

26. For the meaning and importance of this concept, see all three of the works cited in note 23.

27. It would seem that Heidegger had more luck with the theologians than with the Nazis on this score, as is seen in the work of Bultmann and in volumes such as *The Later Heidegger and Theology*, ed. James M. Robinson and John B. Cobb, Jr. (Westport, Conn.: Greenwood Press, 1979).

28. This is true, for example, in my treatment of the critique of religion of Marx, Nietzsche, and Freud in *Suspicion and Faith* (New York: Fordham University Press, 1998). I adopt a similar posture in relation to Derrida's critique of the metaphysics of presence, which I take to be very closely related to Heidegger's critique of onto-theology.

29. *God without Being*, 55. Cf. Feuerbach's analysis of those who declare God unknowable so that God's existence "does not affect or incommode [them]. . . . The alleged religious horror of limiting God by positive predicates is only the irreligious wish to know nothing more of God, to banish God from the mind." Ludwig Feuerbach, *The Essence of Christianity*, trans. George Eliot (New York: Harper & Brothers, 1957), 15.

30. I am assimilating *Lohengrin* to a long tradition of allegorical readings of the Song of Solomon, according to which the relation of beloved to lover no longer concerns the relation of woman to man but the believing soul (male or female) to God. Thus Mary's "Here am I [*me voici*], the servant of the Lord; let it be with me according to your word" (Luke 1:38) makes her a model, not of ideal womanhood, but of devout

humanity. This is perhaps most easily seen by hearing her words echoed in those of her son, "[N]ot my will but yours be done" (Luke 22:42).

31. Martin Buber interprets Israel's request (anticipated by Moses) to know the name of their deliverer as a desire for magical power. Accordingly, he interprets the famous answer of Exodus 3:14 not as "I am who I am" but as the promise "I shall be there" with the meaning "You do not need to conjure Me, but you cannot conjure Me either." *Kingship of God*, trans. Richard Scheimann (New York: Harper & Row, 1967), 104–107. Cf. *The Prophetic Faith* (New York: Harper & Row, 1960), 27–29 and Gerhard von Rad, *Old Testament Theology*, trans. D. M. G. Stalker, vol. 1 (New York: Harper & Row, 1962), 179–84.

32. C. S. Lewis, *Till We Have Faces* (Grand Rapids: Eerdmans, 1966), 123.

33. *Pseudo-Dionysius: The Complete Works*, 50–51. Dionysius echoes an older tradition. For example, Cyril of Jerusalem writes in the fourth century, "But some one will ask, If the divine Being is incomprehensible, what is the good of the things you have seen saying? Come now, am I not to take a reasonable drink because I cannot drink the river dry? Of course I cannot bear to fix my gaze upon the sun in its strength. But is that any reason for not glancing up at him if I need? . . . I praise and glorify our Maker, seeing that 'Let everything that hath breath praise the Lord' is a divine command. I am now trying to glorify the master, not to expound his nature, for I know quite well that I shall fall far short even of glorifying him as he deserves. . . . For the Lord Jesus comforts me for my insufficiency by saying, 'No man hath seen God at any time.'" *The Catechetical Lectures*, VI, 5 in *Cyril of Jerusalem and Nemesius of Emesa*, vol. IV of *The Library of Christian Classics*, ed. William Telfer (London: SCM Press, 1955), 128–29.

34. *God without Being*, 106–107. Cf. Krzysztof Ziarek, "The Language of Praise: Levinas and Marion" *Religion and Literature* 22, no. 2–3 (Autumn 1990): 93–107.

35. This essay was supported by a grant from the Pew Evangelical Scholars Program, which I am pleased to acknowledge with gratitude.

# Fragments

## The Spiritual Situation of Our Times

David Tracy

### Modernity and the Discontents

If postmodernity is to avoid the essentialism it hopes to rout, it must first admit that there is no such phenomenon as postmodernity. There are only postmodernities. If modernity is to escape the trap of totalization it has unintentionally set for itself, not only must it demand modernity as political democratic pluralism (the Enlightenment's signal achievement and still unfinished project) but also admit that there is a plurality of modernities.

By this shift to the plural for modernity I do not refer only to the obvious differences between the forms of Western modernity and other forms of modernization, especially in Asia. To understand our cultural situation rightly one must expand the cultural horizons, including the philosophical and religious horizons, of the contemporary Western discussion beyond a Western sense of centeredness and a Western sense of its own pluralism toward a new global sense of polycentrism. For there is no longer a Western cultural center with margins. There are many centers now, of which the West is merely one. Moreover, once one drops the Western grand narrative, the continuities in that narrative begin to dissolve. To observe that necessary disillusion, recall the now familiar postmodernity versus modernity debate. What can this contemporary debate—a debate on two essentialisms—now mean? It is not only that within Western culture itself there are now several postmodernities. There are also several modernities. Indeed one can find in what is often named postmodernity as well as in the classical model of modernity itself—classical Enlightenment modernity which repressed the more flexible, more open, more fragmented culture of the fifteenth, sixteenth, and early seventeenth centuries—elements of that creative period of early modernity before the reified model of the Enlightenment became the model of modernity.[1]

Most forms of postmodernity are explosions of once-forgotten, marginalized, and repressed realities in Enlightenment modernity: the other, the different, above all in this essay, the fragments that disallow any totality system by demanding attention to the other, especially the different and the marginal other. These repressed elements were clearly far less marginal in early modernity, that too-seldom-studied singularity in most debates on modernity. The key phenomenon provoking new study is religion. Clearly it is time to re-open an otherwise exhausted debate on religion and modernity. It may well be, as several contemporary phenomenologists claim, that religion is the non-reductive saturated phenomenon par excellence. Indeed, I am convinced that this is the case. And yet even before that contemporary case can be made it may be necessary to clear the decks of some further cultural debris. Religion has always been the unassimilable (as distinct from conquered and colonized ) other of Enlightenment modernity. Any saturated form of the religious phenomenon had to be marginalized by the Enlightenment. It could not fit what counted as rational. Other developments in Western culture fought this marginality of religion: the Romantic discovery of symbols and archaic rituals; from the Western interest in Hindu excessive forms for the sacred to Buddhist insistence on formlessness; Scholem's researches into Kabbalah (indeed, that the scholarly recovery of Kabbalah undid the pretension to mastery of so rich and complex a heritage as Judaism is clearly not simply a modern ethical monotheism); the fragments of the divine in Kabbalah and, as it turns out, in rabbinic exegesis itself that undo that claim; or in the Jewish prophetic discourse recovered by Levinas to help one understand against the backdrop of the Enlightenment how the ethics of the other, not the self, is first philosophy.

All of the these religious phenomena, as distinct from the Enlightenment's notion of rational religion, are clearly other to the demands for intellectual closure in what will be allowed to count as rational in many forms of classical modernity. Why otherwise the bizarre parade since the late seventeenth century of the modern ways of naming God: that series of isms for naming God invented in modern philosophical and theological thought had very little if anything to do with God as a religious phenomenon and religion as a saturated sacred phenomenon. Those 'isms' were intended rationally to control the discussion of the ultimate religious other in any radically monotheistic reflection on God. But can the question of God really be controlled as a religious question by the modern discussion of deism, pantheism, modern atheism, modern theism[2] or even, in the best achievement of modern Western religious thought, panentheism from Bruno to Hegel to Whitehead?

Even before the categories of the other and the different became such central philosophical, cultural, ethical and religious categories for many, Western thinkers sensed the temptation to reduce all reality to more of the same (Foucault) or at best to the similar, which too often served as an ever-more-tattered codpiece for more of the same: the onto-theo-phallo-logical system of Western classical modernity. First sensing this totalization of Enlightenment thought, the German romantics, especially Schlegel, privileged the metaphor 'fragments' over any totality and interpreted religion in its richer symbols and mythical forms rather than the Enlightenment 'isms' for God, especially deism. But beyond the early Romantic groping after fragments that helped to challenge the stranglehold of every modern totality system lay the two greatest unveilers of modernity's secret dream to be the logos of its own onto-theology, namely Nietzsche and Kierkegaard. Is there anyone better than Kierkegaard at exposing the bizarre drive to totality of all modern rationalist idealist systems and of Christendom alike? What Kierkegaard showed was that Christendom as a triumphant totality system could not and cannot survive any true experiment with authentic Christian living. Indeed Kierkegaard will do almost literally anything to break through the reified ice of Enlightenment and Christendom alike. He will write under pseudonyms (there is no Kierkegaard, there is only Johannes Climacus, Judge William, the Seducer, Don Juan, et al.). Kierkegaard will forge a new indirect discourse for the sacred to undo any claim to adequacy of direct discourse in the idealist version of totality. He will try any genre—diaries, music, exercises, dialogues, edifying discourses, narratives. He will try anything except a system. Kierkegaard's famous charge to Hegelian systems applies to all modern rational systems. If only Hegel had written the words "A Thought Experiment" at the beginning of all his books, then Kierkegaard would be the first, he says, to honor Hegel as the greatest of the modern philosophers. But Hegel of course did not.

Kierkegaard's paradoxically anti-Christian double, Nietzsche, plays the same fragmentation role for both Christendom and Enlightenment modernity alike but now with a hammer. When Nietzsche's hammer is too blunt a tool against Christianity and against Enlightenment modernity he too will try any form, any genre, any intellectual strategy to break out of the modern system. He forged style after style from his early essays to the quasi-gospel genre of *Thus Spoke Zarathustra* to genealogical analysis through aphorisms piled upon aphorisms to fragments juxtaposed with fragments in an increasingly desperate attempt to recover not merely the controlled rhetoric of Aristotle's topics but the out-of-control rhetoric of the tropes careening with joy (not despair) at the very edge of the modern abyss. Nietzsche, while clearly dialectical in his own understanding of difference, is not of one mind. He is clearly dialectally anti-Christian, is also clearly interested in and fascinated by the saturated, othering phenomenon of religion itself. Indeed Nietzsche was far more creative in religion and its saturation quality than many of its Romantic defenders. Religion, like Nietzsche himself, does not fit the modern totality system. It should not. For religion is something and somewhere else. At the very least, religion is, as William James named it, a disclosure of something more—more than classical modernity considered not merely actual (a relatively easy argument) but even possible. The contemporary argument on religion is not finally about actuality or even what is rendered possible by modern standards. The basic argument on religion is, as Levinas first made clear, about the possibility of impossibility.

But one need not stay with either the new or old Kierkegaard or Nietzsche to feel their fragmenting force anew. It becomes clearer and clearer that a dominant metaphor for twentieth-century Western thought both early and late, both radical, conservative, and postmodern is the metaphor of fragments. Fragments are our spiritual situation. And that is not so bad a place to be. It is with fragments that radical conservative critics may join postmodern critics, that theological and anti-theological critics may finally listen to one another. After the welcome collapse of the religious certainties of all modern totality systems, all see fragments as a sign of hope, perhaps (with Walter Benjamin and Simone Weil) the only signs of hope for redemption.

## Fragments: The Neo-Conservatives

There are three kinds of contemporary thinkers for whom the category 'fragments' is crucial: the first, the radical conservatives, see 'fragments' with regret and nostalgia as all that is left of what was once a unified culture; the second, the postmodernists, see 'fragments' as part of their love of extremes and as thereby emancipatory toward and transformative of the deadening hand of the reigning totality system, the rationality of modern onto-theology; the third group, of whom Walter Benjamin and Simone Weil are the most suggestive in the early twentieth century, see fragments theologically as saturated and auratic bearers of infinity and sacred hope, fragmentary of genuine hope in some redemption, however undefined. It is with Benjamin and Weil that I wish to ally myself. And yet when speaking of this surprising alliance of three such disparate groups there remains much to learn from the first two sets of thinkers, the radical conservatives (who are also usually countermodernists) and the radical postmodernists.

It is often difficult for postmodern thinkers to allow for the strange similarity in the midst of vast difference between the countermodernists and themselves. The differences are real and clear for all to see: Who can combine Leo Strauss and Lyotard despite the sometimes surprising analogies in their critiques of modernity? Who can think of Hans-Georg Gadamer and Julia Kristeva together? Surely they are entirely different and yet possess surprising similarity in their analyses of the narrowness of modern methods and rationalities. All these thinkers, in very different ways, make appeals to classic texts and movements as intense fragments set loose to undo the reign of the modern systems.

Or consider perhaps the most curious case of all, T. S. Eliot.[3] This once singularly important conservative critic was for a while a kind of Emersonian sage of much of anglophone literary criticism and cultural reflection. In one of the most remarkable and too-seldom-reflected-upon collapses of influence in our time, the reputation of Eliot as critic and thinker is now in tatters. In many ways Eliot's world is a world well lost. For it is now clear that Eliot's earlier anti-Semitism has marred beyond retrieval many of his works of cultural high criticism. This is so especially, but not solely, in the case of his notorious essays *After Strange Gods* and even in some of the imagery of his early poetry. Moreover the very bitterness surfacing in Eliot's form of nostalgia for a lost unity can seem to suggest a certain meanness of spirit lurking just below the surface of many of his essays. Of course one still reads and will always read Eliot's brilliant individual literary essays on Dante or the metaphysical poets as distinct from his rejection of everything about the Romantics. However, Eliot's prose, save for such essays on individual literary works, is now on the whole best left unread. But Eliot's poetry is an entirely different matter. That poetry endures as one of the great testaments to the fragmented character of our times.

This is not only true of Eliot's early *The Wasteland*. That poem, exemplary for all of us whether we are countermodern or postmodern, stands as one of the signal witnesses of a civilization and a personal sensibility now in fragments and seeking for other fragments, in his famous words, "to shore up against our ruin." Even more significant in terms of the importance of the fragment for Eliot's poetry is his explicit Christian poetry, especially his *The Four Quartets*, the most misread and misinterpreted great poem of our times. If the Christian vision of *The Quartets* were to be read through the beclouded lens of Eliot's own more conservative essays defending at times something like a new Christendom, then all *The Quartets* would disclose is a fragile orthodox Christian world become a new nostalgic synthesis disguised to replace the fragmented world he portrayed in *The Wasteland*: C. S. Lewis set to verse perhaps. But the poetry should be read, and better heard, as non-totalizing but oddly moving and partly harmonizing fragments of music. Indeed the musical structure of Eliot's *Quartets* is the best example in all his poetry of his famed auditory imagination. That musical structure is not the structure of a closed harmony of a great Beethoven symphony but far more like the fragmentary structure of Beethoven's Quartets. The fact that the fragments never fully harmonize in *The Quartets* is stunning. For example, less explicitly but far more pervasively and subtly than in *The Wasteland* Eliot uses in *The Quartets* an Eastern, especially east Asian Buddhist sensibility to disclose a new meaning for fragments. These Buddhist moments occur not in single explicit quotation as in the fire sermon of *The Wasteland* but rather as a leitmotif interweaving and undoing any attempts at full harmonization. Indeed, even the Christian motif of incarnation in the wondrous and moving Christian passage of the *Third Quartet* becomes, after all, fragmentary, i.e., hints and guesses for the imagination.

*The Quartets* should always be read with the *Wasteland* and Joyce's *Ulysses* in mind. For Eliot, Joyce better than anyone (even the author of *The Wasteland*) understood modern history as a vast chaos and confusion, a nightmare from which we are attempting to awake. But Eliot could not and would not move with Joyce into the sheer play of language and difference in *Finnegan's Wake*, that favorite text of postmodernists. Eliot moved beyond *The Wasteland*, to be sure, and beyond his own and Joyce's earlier attempts at signifying fragments in a negative way in *Ulysses* for Joyce and *Ash Wednesday* for Eliot. Greek and Jew became opposites and met in a new myth of Ulysses for Joyce; Christianity properly rethought is where Greek and Jew finally meet for Eliot.

In *The Quartets*, unlike his more influential essays, Eliot's Christianity is not conventional at all. Indeed a great deal of the major imagery is Buddhist rather than Christian:[4] the central image of the entire poem "the impersonal still point" which grounds and yet Buddhist-like does not ground the poem; the ever-more-refined and more fragmentarily musical and more Buddhist sense of how the mind can be modified in its very ability to perceive at all by closely directed yet not tense, stoic attention to experience, including any experience in reading the poem itself; such close attention to the fragments of meaning become like the no-sense, not-nonsense, of the great Zen Koans. Any careful reading, like Eliot's own in his recording, can render problematic any commonsense or ontological, perhaps more exactly, onto-theological categories by destabilizing all Western ideas. As Cleo McNelly Kearns argues, the syntax of *The Quartets*, more subtly but just as insistently as the syntax of *The Wasteland*, continually breaks down and renders ambiguous and polyvalent, perhaps even over-determined, the subject, verb, object pattern by which the English language is usually spoken. In *The Quartets*, identity becomes either the 'they' of the masses in history, or the 'it happens' of Buddhist emptiness and fullness in the great pool imagery of the first Quartet, or the 'it gives' Christian incarnational imagery of the third Quartet. Saturated fragments all. Both sets of images, Buddhist emptiness and Christian incarnation alike, meet musically in the fourth Quartet but never merge into some final harmony. In the *Quartets*, Christianity does not provide a restored unity to our contemporary culture (as the essays had promised) but rather a renewed sense of the saturated fragments of gift, promise, body, and faith as a new kind of knowledge born of love. For myself that is the great gift of any classical retrieval of our traditions as achieved by all the truly radical conservatives of our age.

But just as surely, in *The Quartets* Eliot, here more like a postmodern thinker than a neoconservative, turns from Western to Buddhist imagery to help Westerners suspect all false consolations, even and sometimes especially 'God'. In Buddhist imagery and thought Eliot finds the cleansing power of a radical hermeneutics of suspicion of all stability, all identity, all analogical and dialectical attempts at unity. He realizes that whatever sense of Buddhism any of us may glimpse today will not be Buddhist enlightenment but can only be some auratic fragment as we too sense the reality of non-being in this moment, here, now. Consider Eliot's use of Buddhist imagery in the pool in the first Quartet. Is the pool empty or full? Is emptiness itself fullness? All these questions, provoking fragmentary images, are as stunning and as healing to our fragmented sensibilities as is Eliot's wondrous Christian fragmentary imagery of the "hint half guessed, the gift half understood, in carnation."

I do not suggest that in Eliot's *Quartets* opposites ever really meet. However it is always crucial to watch how Eliot in his greatest poetry brings opposites always to the verge of meeting and then breaks them off into a difference and finally into fragments that do not yield to any totality. After all, some of the postmodern thinkers, even Lyotard, move from a radical rejection of modernity (here read Habermas) to an almost ecstatic rediscovery of certain fragments of premodernity. Consider for example Lyotard's retrieval of fragments of early modernity as distinct from Enlightenment modernity. Consider Kristeva's recovery of the Christian love mystics from Bernard of Clarvaux to Jeanne Guyon, or consider how postmodern understandings of difference differ from or do not differ from classical modern dialectical and analogical strategies. Here the differences are clear but they are far less clear if one turns, as many now do, to the radically apophatic strategies of the negative theological traditions. Or consider Foucault's last radical turn in his history of sexuality when he discovered, despite his own earlier denials of the very possibility of a self, a new notion of caring for the self aided by fragments of the ancients available to him through the fine scholarship on ancient philosophy of Pierre Hadot and Peter Brown. These historians of the ancient world helped Foucault, the quintessential postmodern, to reconsider how to think anew with the fragments left by ancient Greeks and Romans.

### Fragments: The Postmodernists

Fragments first entered the postmodern sensibility through Bataille.[5] He hated modern rationality's domesticating power. He loved extreme fragments as excessive in regard to all order and transgressive of Enlightenment rationality. As contemporary thought has moved forward, often under the explicit banner of some version of postmodernity, Batailles's early love of excess, transgression, and the disruptive passions has expanded to the saturated fragments, always fragments, of the great love mystics of the tradition. That postmodern turn toward the mystics has yielded one of the most surprising developments in contemporary philosophical and theological thought: the amazing return of religion as the most feared other of Enlightenment modernity.

Since the eighteenth century Enlightenment religion has been the last taboo for modern thought. Religion is that other that cannot be assimilated but only at best correlated and, more usually, simply ignored or dismissed. Like the Jesuits of Voltaire's imagination, religion usually enters the rooms of modernity without warmth and leaves without regret. But postmodern visions seek out religion, most often in its most transgressive and excessive forms—such as the Christian love mystics; the Kabbalists; the Sufis; the apophatic thinkers like Dionysius, Marguerite Porete, or Meister Eckhart; or the uncontainable force of a religious phenomenon like Joan of Arc. Dorothy Day was surely correct when someone once called her a saint and she replied "Do not trivialize me." We all sense why religion has become so central a phenomenon to be described and analyzed in much postmodern thought and its successors: Religion never could be contained by modernity; it could only be conquered (as Feuerbach, Marx, and Freud insisted it must be) or it could be colonized as a once necessary but now overcome form for absolute knowledge as in Hegel and his idealist successors. Sometimes religion became pleasant narratives and symbols to help moderns feel again as they think their way toward some rational utopia. Religion usually appears in Enlightenment modernity as some other phenomenon than religion. Perhaps religion is ethics or bad science or disguised metaphysics. Perhaps religion was once real, even fierce, but is now just one more captive of onto-theo-logy.

The many strategies of modern thought to curtail religion range from benign neglect to indifference, from hostility to nonaggression pacts. All seem unable or unwilling to describe religion itself as an effect of a saturated, auratic othering phenomenon. The religious phenomenon seems most other to and different from all that counts as real and reasonable in modernity. The most explosive power in many forms of postmodern thought is the return of The Ultimate repressed by the Enlightenment—the return of religion as a phenomenon demanding new attention, new description, and, of course, new critique.

Religion, or at least the radical forms of religion, may first have entered postmodern thought as a surprisingly welcome harbinger of the postmodern love of extreme, transgression, and excess. But now the main attention on religion is elsewhere than simply on transgression and excess.[6] Principal philosophical and theological attention is devoted to how the traditions of radical apophatic negative theologies differ from contemporary understandings of difference and otherness; to how God is a radically religious phenomenon which cannot be controlled philosophically or theologically by the preferred modern strategy since the late seventeenth century, namely the rendering of God into a secretly non-religious phenomenon, a rational ism—deism, pantheism, panentheism, atheism, modern theism—and then arguing (on modern rational grounds alone) which ism is the most acceptable to a modern mind. The conclusion is often something like a fairly warm deism. Or notice how the new phenomenologists, especially in France—Jean-Luc Marion, Jean Louis Chretien, Michel Henry, and many others—follow the earlier lead of Paul Ricoeur and Emmanuel Levinas to find various saturated religious phenomena—spirit, gift, liturgy—and demand the most careful phenomenological description precisely as saturated auratic phenomenon and the most rigorous analytical demands on an unthought and unexpected possibility for modern minds, namely the possibility of impossibility. The strategies are of course many (and sometimes mutually contradictory) in the various new attempts at understanding religion. Religion and philosophy have found each other again as fragments to each other that do not and no longer wish to form a modern totality. But what of theology? Is it still, as Walter Benjamin once suggested, "wizened and best kept out of sight?" Hence the third use of the category 'fragments'—one which I do not hesitate to name theological, indeed, theological-spiritual.

## Theological-Spiritual Fragments

It has become a truism by now that modernism, whatever else it is, prefers the unfinished, the syntactically unstable, the semantically malformed. What Benjamin adds to this familiar portrait is something like a theological theory of the modernist image. The contemporary image is a fragment.[7] History may not yield to the continuity of narrative, nor to the intellectual hope of either an analogical or a dialectical imagination. History, including intellectual history, breaks up into images. Benjamin calls these images dialectical but it may be more accurate to his purposes and his strange messianism as a theory of catastrophe to name his work fragments as saturated images. The image Benjamin seeks to blast from past experience for present purposes is, as he himself states, dialectic at a standstill.

Above all one must avoid modernity's (not only Hegel's) central temptation: the drive to systematize, to render a totality system. To render any totality system present is to efface the fragment, the distinct and potentially explosive image in favor of some larger conceptual architectonic of which the fragment is now made a part.

What Benjamin attempted was not a representation of history but a reconstellation of historical images to show the diachronic relationship of certain fragments as images from a past epic to related images that proliferate for us in every present moment. Even the category of the historical context so central to the historiographer can become a kind of totality that should be first respected and then dissolved to allow for the present to experience the historical event as a radically unique saturated fragment of time. The fragment, especially the marginal fragment that recalls forgotten, even repressed memories of the suffering of the victims of history, are privileged by Benjamin over any conception of an historical totality. In Christian theological terms this can read as a privileging of Mark's fragmentary discontinuous non-closure, apocalyptic gospel grounded in fragments of the memory of suffering over the Luke/ Acts view of history as fundamentally structured like a continuous realistic narrative.

In the Jewish theological terms of Benjamin himself, a radically eschatological, indeed apocalyptic and messianic understanding of history yields (in keeping with the Jewish prohibition on speculation on the future) to Kabbalistlike fragments that are hints of redemption. Benjamin privileges modern writers like Baudelaire and Kafka on formal, never purely formalist, grounds.[8] Baudelaire for Benjamin invented a form for modern poetry: a form that reveals through the fragmentary form itself the brokenness and falseness of modern experience and the obfuscation of all singularities in the nineteenth century's deceptively continuous modern bourgeois experience. Kafka, even more, shows that in his fragmentary parabolic, not symbolic, forms how one may be able to feel one's way to some slight hint of redemption, even if that redemption is neither understood (there is no theory of redemption in either Kafka or Benjamin) nor even fully experienced save through the unsettling fragments in Kafka's strange parables.

Benjamin's own essays take the same fragmentary form: an attempt to let the fragments speak for themselves and thereby generate new tension and meaning as they work with and against every other fragment in a new constellation of fragments, or at times phantasmagoric collage. Benjamin's farewell not only to all modern totality systems but even to the aura of all classical organic and symbolic works curiously parallels T. S. Eliot's journey in his poetry (but never in his essays) from a sheer constellation of fragments and images in *The Wasteland* (to shore us up against our ruin) to the fragmentary auratic "hints and guesses" of Christian redemption to the ultimate fragment—the hint half guessed, the gift half understood—the incarnation in *The Quartets*.

By concentrating on fragments the all-too-familiar modernity versus postmodernity debate of our day could finally shift. At least it can if three crucial moves are made. First, shift focus from the debate between the eighteenth-century Enlightenment model of modernity and the late-twentieth-century postmodern celebration of excess and transgression to the fragments left by modernity and postmodernities alike, especially the great fragmentary attempts of early modernity and the new debate on apophatic theology in the late twentieth century.

Second, let go of the hope for any totality system whatsoever. Focus instead on the explosive, marginal, saturated and, at times, auratic fragments of our heritages. Do this not, in conservative fashion, to shore up against our present ruin (although that too can of course be a noble response) but rather in the manner of Walter Benjamin and Simone Weil: Blast the marginalized fragments of the past alive with the memory of suffering and hope; remove them from their seemingly coherent place in the grand narratives we have imposed upon them. Learn to live joyfully, not despairingly, with and in the great fragments we do indeed possess.

Sometimes this search—this intellectual, and I do not hesitate to say spiritual, search—must demand a destructive moment, a moment not merely of critique but of radical suspicion of all totalities by means of finding the spiritual fragments that expose any pretense to totality. Consider Kant. Why is radical evil the fragment that blasts away all remaining optimism of reason of the three critiques? Why is radical evil the fragment that even Kant's great critiques could not contain? Thus did Kant, the quintessential and greatest of the moderns, fully notice in his later essays that the fragments of history and religion are far more theoretically significant than he originally thought. Why did Hegel—even at the end of his life, after not only the *Phenomenology of Spirit* but the *Logic*—find it necessary to rethink and reformulate again and again (as the distinct editions of his final lectures in the philosophy of religion clearly show) the two religious fragments that kept rendering the Hegelian system unstable as a system: a Judaism the Hegelian system could contain only by the lie that after the biblical period Judaism had become a dead religion; a Buddhism which Hegel himself kept trying over and over again to understand and to contain within a system?[9] But as he clearly sees and implicitly admits, it cannot be thus contained.

And surely it is time to move beyond the saturated fragments hiding as land mines in all the early classical modern systems to the greater flexibility and modesty, the speculative fragmentary power of such extraordinary early modern thinkers as Nicholas of Cusa, with his pluralistic sensibility, his mysticism of limit, his explosion of all scholasticism by articulating the distinct great modern notion of infinity as glimpsed in his retrieval of certain fragments of Eckhart and Dionysius and the whole apophatic tradition—for Cusanus the apophatic tradition is to be interpreted not merely as an expression of the limits of our intelligence (as with the later Kantians) but as a sign of the very excess of intelligibility in infinity and excess of intelligence in the radical incomprehensibility of God. God's incomprehensibility for Cusanus is never merely a sign (as with such later thinkers as Kant and Jaspers) of our own finitude and limits but of God's very excess and positive incomprehensibility, related always to an infinite universe, never a closed cosmos.[10]

Should we not also free Giordano Bruno[11] from the imprisonment that the nineteenth-century idealist thinkers accorded him as the first modern rationalist and realize instead his extraordinary ability to try every possible form, including highly fragmentary forms, to produce his new vision of an infinite universe? The fragmentary kabbalistic and hermetic elements in Bruno's vision are now clear—and just as clearly disallow the false rationalist reading of him as the first modern totality thinker.

And then there is Pascal. At the very end of early modernity and with Enlightenment modernity on its way, who else saw so clearly the possibilities and devastating limits of modernity? The very category of infinity, so alive and liberating for Cusanus and Bruno, remained alive for the great mathematician. At the same time, Pascal sensed the terror of the silence of infinite space. He understood the full power of mathematics and science and all the works of the "order of intelligence." At the same time he grasped the radical difference of the saturated, auratic order of charity: Pascal did not leave a system. He left something far more valuable—penseés, concentrated reflections, saturated images—fragments. Perhaps it is time, at the end of Enlightenment modernity, to rethink the fragments of the thinker who foresaw the extraordinary possibilities and equally extraordinary limits of modernity and to understand his devotees to penseés — to fragments.

## Derrida's Response to David Tracy

*Jacques Derrida.* I would like to share with you certain concerns I have regarding the concept of fragment. First of all, allow me to refer to the title of this conference, "Religion and Postmodernism," and, if I may, to reflect on myself. I know that I sometimes used the word "religion," in a not very complex way, such as ethics with a few stories added. But I never, ever used the word "postmodernism."[12] I know that it is a word which is used to embrace a number of people, sometimes including myself, sometimes. But I never felt that this was a concept that I could rely on. Now, with the concept of fragment, the way that you used it, I started to form a hypothesis about my own hesitation to use the word "postmodernism." One nasty form of the question I wanted to ask you is, Who finally in the premodern, modern, or postmodern era escaped fragmentation? If no one, not even Hegel, if the fragment is everywhere, what is the help of this periodization? Now, again in reference to my own difficulties in using some words, I also have difficulty with the concept of fragment. Not because I am on the side of system or totality, but because my guess is that you cannot dissociate fragment from the system. As you yourself recalled, the dominant metaphor of modern and postmodern times (if it is a metaphor), fragment, is not a number of things with which you have associated it — with singularity, for example, or with aphorism and parable. A fragment means literally a broken totality, not simply interruption. There are interruptions which are not fragments. The figure of a fragment implies a broken whole and, as you wonderfully phrased it, with a hint of redemption, of the reconstitution of totality. One of the reasons I do not use the word fragment is precisely the hint of the memory of totality, the desire to reconstitute the system and the totality. It is still a part of the totality. From that point of view, it is essentially conservative. You have shown this in the work of Eliot. It is a work of mourning for totality and for the system. I am not sure that today everything which resists totality or system is devoted to or turned toward the fragment. I would dissociate the aphorism and the fragment. If we apply this concept to literary forms, I am not sure that every aphorism is a fragment. That is one question. As you know, Blanchot has a powerful discourse on the necessity of the fragment, and he used the word fragment. I am a little suspicious of the authority of the system or totality in the fragment, which is a potential totality and keeps in itself some authority, sometimes oracular and prophetic authority. The hidden mastery which sometimes is located in the fragmentary form is for me an object of suspicion. I remember that Blanchot, who was sensitive to this, replied to me that, well, perhaps we should avoid what in the fragment implies the ruse of authority. When you write in the form of a fragment, you imply, well I have more to say, I have a system in the back of my head, and I am here in a position of authority. I am not sure that I would widen the concept of fragment the way you did. It might be of no help to periodize, to provide a scansion in history. That is why I started with the concept of postmodernity. I am not sure what this word means and I am not sure that it is useful to understand what is going on today. Because postmodernity is an attempt to build, to periodize the totality of history within a teleological scheme. I do not say this in order to say that we should give up the hope for a hint of redemption That is the logic I tried to refer to last night. Once you know what the hint of redemption is, you lose the hope. The hope for redemption must go through renunciation. I am a little anxious about the reconstitution of teleology in history, or in the religious hope for redemption, through this praise of the fragment. Of course, I, with some others, write in a form which is not completely harmonious, but it is not fragmentary either. I would say that what is going on today—in religion, in art, in philosophy, in thinking—is a way of inventing gestures which are not subject to totality or to a loss of totality, to the nostalgia and work of mourning for totality. Of course, that is impossible. We cannot simply stop mourning and nostalgia, but then something else is perhaps at work, but this "perhaps" is not in tune with "postmodernity" or with the "fragment." Thank you.

*David Tracy.* I would like to say two things. I also have no particular desire to provide periods. They are simply heuristic categories that come and go. My point in mentioning them is my own belief that in the usual debate, where singulars are used instead of plurals, there is too narrow an understanding of modernity that ignores completely the form modernity took, the much more interesting, flexible form, often privileging the fragment, of early modernity, which is different from the eighteenth century forward. There is a difference between modern thinkers, like Kant or Hegel, in classical modernity, who repressed the fragment, and Cusa, who has no such hesitation. Paul de Man found it useful to see those who thought that you have to search for where the problem is, for what is being repressed or suppressed, and others who, like Cusa in my opinion, do not have such a problem. The very distinction between two such kinds of thinkers, both legitimately called modern, is worth pursuing. I wanted to say the same thing about someone who is thought to have the first totality system in modernity, namely, Bruno, although, in fact, when you examine his work, that is not so.

Secondly, and this is the more important question, which has to do with teleology, you say that the fragment is always the fragment of a totality system and therefore always presumes a teleological view of the whole, whether of history or of religion. There is great truth to that. I was privileging a particular understanding of fragment, namely Benjamin's (and also, I think, Simone Weil's), which notion is by no means a fragment of a totality system. It is purely messianic, purely an understanding of the hint of redemption, like Rosenzweig's before him. I was also highlighting how in the Christian case Mark's

Gospel must be taken more seriously into account than it usually is, if you only have a Lucan-tempted teleology of history. Eschatology, if it is to be taken seriously, as it is in Judaism and Christianity, can never be a teleology. In a conservative thinker like Eliot, fragment does not turn out to be fragmentation, an always-already-happened. Even Incarnation becomes in Eliot the "hint half guessed, the hint half understood," and it is that that returns an eschatological, even messianic notion to Eliot's use of fragment. That exactly parallels Benjamin's messianic, which insists upon the disruption of eschatology and moves against teleology. That notion of fragment, which I called theological, could either be a naming of God or a refusing to name God, refusing a theory of redemption. The recovery of the eschatological fragment is anti-teleological. The closest Judaism comes to teleology is in the Jahwist stories, and in the New Testament in Luke, which becomes Luke-Acts. In Luke, you have a continuous narrative, and it is, as Hans Frey says, history, a realistic narrative. You do not have this in Mark, Matthew, or in the peculiar meditative form that John takes. It is for that reason that I think there is exactly the danger you speak of, if it is used non-eschatologically. That is why Benjamin is so good at this.

*Jacques Derrida.* Perhaps it is only a question of your use of words. Of course, I would also carefully distinguish between teleology and eschatology. My question was about the use of the word fragment. In eschatology, you may have interruption, disruption, something unfinished, and in that sense something fragmentary. I have the feeling the fragment is not simply disruption or an unfinished something. It is something finished, and it refers to the totality from which it comes. If you take the fragment out of this common use, then I have no question. But it is often the case, especially in literary criticism, that we think of the fragment as a totality, as self-sufficient.

*David Tracy.* I quite agree with you. If I am right, in the two examples I gave, of Eliot and Benjamin, that is not the case, and there is something peculiar in each of them that disallows that becoming the case, which is also why I spoke of "what is often called postmodernity." It is a notion of excess and transgression, initially, and it becomes far more important and interesting when it becomes, as it has throughout this conference, a third way. Any way that explicitly names God as the negative theology tradition tries to do, or as does Luther's hidden theology, is not talking about totalities, because God is not a totality. The fragments of the divine reality that are explicitly spoken of in the Kabbalah do not mean fragments of a totality or a return to a totality. They mean God, which perhaps must remain un-nameable, but certain aspects of which can be seen in the fragments. I think that is why Benjamin was obsessed by the notion. He was a great reader of German Romanticism, but his notion of fragment, like Eliot's, was a notion that lends itself to an eschatological—Jewish, Christian, or Islamic—theological reading, not simply a fragment of a totality, although I admit that is the more usual reading.

*Jacques Derrida.* When you refer to the usual way it is used, there are two possibilities. Either the fragment is a piece, taken out of the whole, or it is a symbol, two broken pieces. In both cases, the fragments are pieces of the totality. That is the common use of the metaphor.

*David Tracy.* That is the common use of the metaphor. But I think that you would agree, especially in view of what you say about messianism, that it is not the common use of the metaphor in any messianic religion or eschatology, in which the fragment is not related to a totality. It is related to something barely nameable, something incomprehensible, the name that must not be spoken.

## NOTES

1. See Hans Blumenberg, *The Legitimacy of the Modern Age* (Cambridge, Mass.: MIT Press, 1983) and Louis Dupré, *A Passage to Modernity* (New Haven: Yale University Press, 1993).

2. Michael J. Buckley, S.J., *At the Origins of Modern Atheism* (New Haven: Yale University Press, 1987).

3. I regret that, because of copyright laws, I am unable to give extended quotations from *The Wasteland* and *The Quartets*. Reading a copy of these texts for this section would prove very helpful.

4. For a penetrating study, see Cleo McNelly Kearns, *T. S. Eliot and Indic Tradition: A Study in Poetry and Belief* (Cambridge: Cambridge University Press, 1987).

5. George Bataille, *Theory of Religion*, trans. Robert Hurley (New York: Zone Books, 1992). The most sophisticated analyses of the fragment in the French tradition may be found in the work of Maurice Blanchot.

6. See, inter alia, Jean-Luc Marion, *Prolégèmene a la charité* (Paris: Presses universitaires de France, 1991).

7. I have been strongly influenced in this section by the brilliant study of Benjamin's notion of dialectical image in Michael Jennings, *Dialectical Images: Walter Benjamin's Theory of Literary Criticism* (Ithaca: Cornell University Press, 1987). The more theological-spiritual reflections are my own.

8. Walter Benjamin, "On Baudelaire," in *Collected Writings*, ed. Marcus Bullock and Michael W. Jennings (Cambridge, Mass.: Harvard University Press), 361–63.

9. Georg Wilhelm Hegel, *Lectures on the Philosophy of Religion*, 3 vols., ed. and trans. E. Spiers and J. Burden Sanderson. (London: Routledge & Kegan Paul, 1968).

10. See, especially, the texts (and introduction) in *Nicolas of Cusa: Selected Spiritual Writings* trans. and intro. by H. Lawrence Bond (New York: Paulist Press, 1997).

11. Most recently, see Karen Silvia de Léon-Jones, *Giordano Bruno and the Kabbalah* (New Haven: Yale University Press, 1998).

12. Derrida certainly does not use the word "postmodern," but he will occasionally mention it while keeping his distance from it. See *The Politics of Friendship*, trans. George Collins (London & New York: Verso, 1997), 151. [Eds.]

# Apostles of the Impossible

## On God and the Gift in Derrida and Marion

John D. Caputo

In a series of groundbreaking texts published over the last twenty years, Jean-Luc Marion proposes to stretch phenomenology to the limits of its highest possibility, to the limits of an impossibility, to the possibility of something "impossible," something declared off limits by the "conditions of possibility" imposed by modernity and onto-theology.[1] He proposes a radical phenomenology of a saturating *givenness*, a phenomenological description of an event, or the possibility of an event, of bedazzling brilliance, given without being, visited upon us beyond comprehension, leaving us stunned and lost for words. "Deconstruction," if this is a word Marion can use, plays the preparatory role of undoing the conceptual constraints and preconditions imposed by metaphysical concepts, dismantling the onto-theological impediments which dull the glow of this event and stop up its overflowing givenness.

Jacques Derrida, no less in love with the impossible than Marion, no less its zealous apostle, is wary of such saturating givenness. For Derrida, *the* impossible is something that is *never given*, that is always deferred. Deconstruction is a call for the coming of something unforeseeable and unprogrammable, a call that is nourished by the expectation of something *to come*, structurally to come, for which we pray and weep,[2] sigh and dream. Deconstruction is (like) a deep desire for a Messiah who never shows (up), a subtle spirit or elusive specter that would be extinguished by the harsh hands of presence and actuality. The very idea of a Messiah who is never to show and whom we accordingly desire all the more is the very paradigm of deconstruction. The structural impossibility of his being given (*étant donné*, to borrow Marion's felicitous phrase) is just what makes this Messiah possible, just what nourishes our desire and keeps the future open. This impossibility is not the doom and gloom of deconstruction; it is not an end but a beginning, for *we begin by the impossible*. Indeed the end would only come if the Messiah were actually to show up, for what would then be left to hope for? In what could we have faith? What could we desire? (*Inquietum est cor nostrum.*) So, instead of a phenomenology of the bedazzling brilliance of givenness, deconstruction is "writing in the dark," groping like a blind man feeling his way with his stick (or stylus), producing at most a self-interrupting, quasi-phenomenology of "blindness" and of expectant faith—*il faut croire*[3]—in something coming, I know not what, something I cannot see, something *tout autre*. (Through a *glas* darkly.)

Thus, from time to time in the course of this exchange, one catches sight of two different *messianic figures*, sometimes hovering in the background, sometimes plainly in view, which are figures of two different experiences of the impossible and of two different *faiths*. The first is that of a Messiah who has pitched his tent among us in the flesh, who has been *already given*, a figure of transfiguring glory, the icon of the invisible God, an impossible gift of God. Faith here is the gift of having the eyes to see his invisible glory. The other is the darker figure of a Messiah who is still to come, unimaginable, unprefigurable, who is *never to be given*. If he said to be *sans l'être*, this does not mean that he is beyond being, or does not have to be, but rather, like a specter, that he neither is nor is not but is yet to come. For his very not-yet-coming is the way to keep the future coming and open with expectation, to keep alive our faith and hope in something impossible. Here the gift of faith means a faith in the gift, where faith means that we *lack* the eyes to see and must feel in the dark.

So I will construe this exchange as a debate between two apologists for the impossible or, shall we say, in keeping with the religious theme of the conference, two apostles of the impossible, which must seem an odd debate to some inasmuch as the laurels go to the one whose thought is more impossible, for both discussants agree that the impossible is what they love. One is reminded of the standard set by Johannes Climacus in the *Concluding Unscientific Postscript*: the madder and more paradoxical (the more impossible) the belief, the greater the passion and the truth! For the lover of the merely possible is a mediocre fellow.

The first section of this paper concerns the question of the *hyperousios*, of presence and givenness in mystical theology, addressed in Marion's paper "In the Name" and Derrida's response; the second section takes up the problem of presence, givenness and phenomenality in the aporia of the gift, discussed in "On the Gift."

## Saving the Name of God: Deconstruction and Mystical Theology

### Hyperessentialism

Derrida claims that deconstruction is not negative theology because, despite the felicity of its rhetoric and the resourcefulness of its strategies, negative theology, however *negative* it may be, is always a *theology*, and as such committed to a positive, hyperbolic hyper-affirmation of hyper-essential being (*hyperousios*), viz., God, while *différance*, however ineffable it may be, is not God. He does not speak against negative theology, nor is he opposed to hyperbolic affirmations, or to the name of God, which is one of the names he is most concerned to save. He is simply trying to differentiate deconstruction from negative theology. He does not consider negative theology a "failure" whose mistakes he must be careful to avoid. Indeed, Derrida would consider it as much a "congratulation" as an "accusation" to be called a negative theologian (*Psy.*, 545/HAS, 82),[4] and he goes so far as to say that he does not trust any discourse that is not touched by negative theology (*Sauf*, 81/ON, 69).[5] His interest in *Sauf le nom*, a more recent and a deeply affirmative study, is not to undermine or confound negative theology but to "translate" it, or generalize it, so that we may all come to appreciate its general import for the "other," or *tout autre*, wholly other, *whoever* or *whatever* that may be, no matter whom (*n'importe: Sauf*, 90/ON, 73), whether or not one happens to be a believer in the concrete religions of the Book. For *every* other is *wholly* other (*tout autre est tout autre*) (*Sauf*, 92/ON, 74). This way of "translating" negative theology, far from constituting an assault, is set forth precisely in the interest of *saving* its name, saving it for everyone, not just Christian Neoplatonists. So if Derrida and Marion are two apostles of the impossible, Derrida is a more Pauline figure, who wants all the *gentiles*, the *goyim*, to share in the good news, while Marion is more Petrine and insistent on a straiter gate. Still, in the interests of clarity, Derrida wants to avoid any confusion of deconstruction with negative theology.

But, on Marion's telling, Derrida "attacks" ("In the Name," p. 29) negative theology and this "attack" is important to Derrida because Derrida is feeling "threatened" and attacks in order to defend himself. For, by offering its own negation of presence, "mystical theology"—the term Marion prefers to "negative theology," as that phrase occurs only in a chapter heading in Pseudo-Dionysius's *Mystical Theology*, and even then in the plural, and was probably supplied by the redactor—represents a "serious rival," "perhaps the only one possible," to deconstruction, which Derrida must thus beat back. For Marion, deconstruction is engaged in a war with mystical theology over which of the two is to have "final pre-eminence" in the deconstruction of presence. Derrida, Marion thinks, is worried that mystical theology will steal deconstruction's thunder as a critique of presence while at the same letting God back in the door, putting us in the presence of God by way of its very critique of presence. Marion does not take issue with Derrida's disclaimer that deconstruction is not "mystical theology," but he presses the claim that whatever good deconstruction does is already done by the deconstructive element implicitly at work in mystical theology. Most important, Marion vigorously contests the claim that mystical theology is a hyper-ousiology which remains "in submission to the privilege of presence" ("In the Name," p. 29).

On his part, Derrida might wonder if Marion, too, is feeling threatened and sees an attack where there is none, attacks in order to defend himself. For, as Marion points out, Derrida's description of mystical theology as a hyper-essentialism seems to be nothing more than the traditional understanding — perhaps the only one possible — of the *via eminentiae*. By "denying being" of God, mystical theology does not mean — God forbid! — to deny, denounce or renounce God. God without being does not mean being without God. Mystical theology does not forbid us access to the presence of God, but by raising God up beyond every name in heaven or on earth, including the name "being" or the predicate "presence," thereby affirms God all the more purely and sublimely (*hyper*). If the creature is called "being," Meister Eckhart says, we will call God a pure nothing. If the creature is called nothing, we will call God pure being. We can let God be (*lassen*) God, keep God safe (*sauf*) as God, only if we concede that God eludes our names and confounds our comprehension. Mystical theology, one might say, is always going about the Father's business.

But if that is so, then, from Derrida's point of view, the business of the *via eminentiae*, the matter that matters most to mystical theology, is to save the eminence of God. Thus for Derrida the *via eminentiae* would represent a celestial version of a classical *"economy,"* like the higher, holier economy described at the end of *The Gift of Death* (DM, 95ff./GD, 101ff.).[6] Every negation in mystical theology is a good investment, having been expended in order to yield the higher return of the *hyperousios*, repaying us with the presence of God *eminentiore modo*. The negations made in this mystical economy are not expended "without reserve," which means they do not represent a pure "loss;" rather, they are precisely the best way to "save" and praise the name of God, to allow God to be God, in all God's splendor and height (*hyper*). That way of saving the name of God, Derrida argues in *Sauf le nom*, itself a dialogue in several voices, is the dominant voice of mystical theology, its safest voice, but always just *one* of its voices, while he himself is interested in its other, riskier voices, which he associates with *khora* and desert errancy. That is why Derrida says in his response to Marion's paper that he does not consider mystical theology to be just one thing — it has a "multiplicity of voices" (*multi-*

*plicité des voix: Sauf,* 15–16/ON, 35)—and he does not entertain a single
"thesis" about it but sorts among its several voices.

The question on which this debate between Derrida and Marion about
mystical theology turns, then, must be sharpened and clarified by distinguishing the different issues involved. Derrida characterizes mystical theology as a
*hyperessentialism,* not a denial but a *higher (hyper)* affirmation of being or
presence (*ousios*), and as such an *economy* in which nothing is lost, every
negation being returned with (infinite) interest. Marion responds by defining
hyper-essentialism in terms of the "metaphysics of presence," which is in turn
strictly defined, and arguing that mystical theology is not a "metaphysics of
presence," but he does not raise the question of "saving" or economy. Marion
adamantly rejects "hyper-essentialism" if this is interpreted in terms of the
"metaphysics of presence," but he clearly wants to embrace some other interpretation of the *hyperousios,* which belongs to the literal vocabulary of Pseudo-
Dionysius, an interpretation that escapes the metaphysics of presence. That is
the work his notion of "givenness" is called upon to perform. So then there are
several questions moving through this debate. In addition to the one Marion
presses, "Is mystical theology a *metaphysics of presence?*" it is no less important
to ask: "Is mystical theology a mystical *economy?*" This also involves pressing
the question of just what *hyperessentialism* means, whether it is identical with
the "metaphysics of presence," which means we need to know just what the
"metaphysics of presence" is. Only then can we ask and answer the question,
"Is mystical theology a hyperessentialism?"[7]

### The Third Way

According to Marion's argument in "In the Name," Derrida is assuming
that we are forced to choose between two ways, affirmation and denial, and
given that limited choice mystical theology opts in the end for affirmation over
denial. By remaining stuck in this binarity, Marion contends, Derrida betrays
his ignorance of the "third way" (eminence) which lies at the heart of Pseudo-
Dionysius's *Mystical Theology.* Marion calls the third way "*dé-nomination*"
because it takes the form of un-naming or non-naming (de-naming, as in
defusing). Lying beyond both affirmation and negation, de-nomination represents a final and more radical possibility transcending even the opposition
between truth and falsity, the central binarity upon which the whole logic of
metaphysics turns. On Marion's reading, when the third way negates negation
itself, this does not eventuate in a still higher affirmation which thereby wins
the day over negation, but passes beyond the sphere of naming, affirmatively or
negatively, beyond naming altogether, into un-naming, hence into nameless
anonymity. In *dé-nomination* we nominate or denominate God, we say God's
name, speaking to or of or in the name of God, but in just such a way as to undo
this naming, to break with every predicative assertion about God.

The word "denomination," we should observe, has a remarkable polysemy in English usage. It has a *religious* meaning, that of a confessional denomination, like the Southern Baptist Convention, and a *monetary* meaning, as a form of currency, like a ten-dollar bill. Hence to say in English that mystical theology deals in "denomination" would implicate it in economics and currency, in good investments and bad, and also implicate it in various confessional, denominational conflicts, in religious communions and excommunications, the wars, figurative and literal, among what Derrida calls the concrete messianisms.

One of the most interesting arguments Marion makes in his provocative paper is to insist that the third way represents a qualitative change which passes beyond the *apophantic*, the sphere of predication, to which the play of affirmations and denials (*apophatic/kataphatic*) is confined, into what Marion calls the purely *pragmatic* sphere, which is therefore not a higher affirmation but beyond affirmation. By pragmatics, Marion means two things: [W]hen the name of God is used in mystical theology, it is not used to predicate anything of God, to determine "what" God "is," but simply to *refer* to God and to *praise* God. In the third way, "God" means something like "(Praise) God," "Hallelujah, praise the Lord!" For Marion, the pragmatic sphere is a sphere of pure praise and pure prayer but not predication, pure reference but not meaning. There is a fundamental or structural distance between meaning and reference such that, in the name God, the two can never coincide or even slightly overlap. This is a crucial point on which Derrida and Marion are also divided. For Derrida, we do not praise just anything by saying just anything to or about it. We praise what we have in some way been motivated to call praiseworthy, and direct our prayers where we have some idea they will go, to the Father, e.g., so that the *hymnein* has something to do with an *apophansis*. That is because prayer and praise are significant (*semantikos*) even if they are not apophantic, that is, either true or false (*Psy.*, 572–74 n./HAS, 136–38 n.16). (This is an interesting point that might come back to haunt Derrida, if we may say so, inasmuch as his "pure messianic," to which we say *"oui, oui"* must be also protected from apophantic determinability and seems to protect the structural distance between sense and reference.) Thus, from Derrida's point of view, Pseudo-Dionysius praises the Trinity of divine persons, not the devil, despair, and disobedience, and he prays to God, not mammon. This is the same point Derrida made in "Violence and Metaphysics" regarding the *tout autre*: by the *tout autre* Levinas certainly means *quite precisely* other people, and he certainly did not mean rocks or horses, which means that Levinas had a fairly definite idea of what he meant by what is wholly other than anything we can mean or intend (ED, 187/WD, 138).[8]

Marion rejects Derrida's view that praise is contaminated by predication on the ground that no predicate or name adequately names God, as indeed no proper name adequately names any singularity whatsoever. However, from Derrida's point of view, that would demonstrate that sense and reference do not coincide, but it does not show that they do not partly overlap. It would not be necessary that the name spoken in praise by the mystical theologian imply an adequate comprehension of what it praises, but only that it would be "significant" and that we would have an adequate understanding that we are praising this rather than that. Indeed, this disagreement uncovers an interesting point of agreement. For Derrida, like Marion, we would not be likely to praise the *tout autre* if we *did* have an adequate comprehension of it, just because anything of which we have an adequate comprehension will not be *tout autre*. Knowing that the *tout autre* is incomprehensible, that it is *impossible* to comprehend the wholly other, would seem to be for Derrida the condition of possibility of something eminently praiseworthy, which would amount to what Derrida would call a "quasi-transcendental condition," that is, of both its possibility and its impossibility, of knowing and not knowing what we love and praise. The impossible is also is just what Derrida means by "experience" and by "deconstruction," which is, he says, "defined as the very experience of the (impossible) possibility of the impossible, of the most impossible, a condition that deconstruction shares with the gift, the 'yes,' the 'come,' decision, testimony, the secret, etc." (*Sauf*, 32/ON, 43). Experience is really experience when it is an experience of *the* impossible, not when it experiences the possible. Something is really happening, really is an event, is really interesting, only when it is *the* impossible that is happening, the possible being at most a mediocre fellow. Experience is experience, not when it conforms with the conditions of experience but when it shatters them, exposing us to what we did not see coming, taking us where we cannot go (*Sauf*, 94/ON, 75). That is what we love and desire, our *désir de l'impossible, désir de Dieu*. The point of Derrida's critique of the "metaphysics of presence" in his early writings is not skepticism but the affirmation of the *tout autre*, of the *l'invention de l'autre*, of the "incoming" of *the* impossible, which is why I am portraying Marion and Derrida here as fellow travelers on the road to the impossible.

Mystical theology, Marion argues, does not transpire in the sphere of Being or the horizon of presence at all,[9] but of the Good which is beyond, without, or otherwise than Being. For beings and non-beings alike desire the Good. Being and beings are what come forth from and return to the Good. *Esse prima creaturum*. But this is not to say that the Good supplies the secret or missing predication, the needed name which grasps or exhausts the unnameable God. We do not know "what" the Good "is," just because the Good is otherwise than and without Being and essence. "Good" is the *best* name we have for saying that God is above every name. To say "God is good," for Marion, belongs to the pragmatics of pure praise and reference, not the logic of predication. It is, as we said, like shouting "Hallelujah," as Merold Westphal argues elsewhere in this volume, like breaking out into song upon hearing the name of God. Better still, for Marion, it is not shouting, singing, or dancing, but listening to what "bountiful beauty bids" (*la bonté belle appelle, kallos kalei*), since, as he will argue, the name of God is not a name by which we name but a name by which we are named.

John D. Caputo

### Saving the Name of God

That theology has always sought to *protect* God from comprehension and knowledge is a point about which Marion and Derrida agree. That point made throughout by Marion is the very argument of Derrida's *Sauf le nom*. The names of God may be thought of as Husserlian arrows of intentionality that would wound God if they reached their target, Derrida says, from which God must be kept safe:

> It [the arrow] is everything save what it aims for, save what it strikes, even, indeed, save what it wounds; this is what makes the arrow miss even that which it touches, which thereby remains safe. (*Sauf*, 67–68/ON, 62)

In *one* of its voices, Derrida says, mystical theology is trying to *save* God from the arrows of knowledge, to cross its swords over the breast of God, to protect God and keep God *safe*.

> As if it was necessary both to save the name and to save everything except the name, *save the name*, as if it were necessary to lose the name in order to save what bears the name, or that towards which one goes through the name. (*Sauf*, 61/ON, 58)

By saving God from being brought to presence in the name, the name of God keeps God safe, a saving gesture which, on Derrida's terms, embodies the most sublime, divine economy, a "mystical economy." Unless we lose this name we will not save it. That is Meister Eckhart's famous and beautiful prayer, "I pray God to rid me of God." What could compensate us for the loss of God? What could save us if we lost the presence of God? Is not theology structurally an operation of saving, articulating a divine economy, an economy of salvation, a sacrificial economy of losing in order to save, dying in order to live? Unless a man lose his life, he will not save it. Unless I confess I do not comprehend God, I will not know the incomprehensible God.

Perhaps this deeper agreement is why Marion thinks that Derrida's "critique" of mystical theology can be turned around into a basis for properly understanding the true work of theology, which is true to itself precisely when it is *not* a "metaphysics of presence" *in the precise sense that Marion means this*, viz., a conceptual comprehension or a conceptual idol. For God is God if and only if God withdraws from our knowledge, in principle and not merely in fact. That confession of non-knowledge, Marion contends, is not a simple failure to know but an opening onto another form of knowledge where what is known of God is God's incomprehensibility. For anything we can know of God conceptually would not be God, not if God is greater than anything we can conceive, not if God always exceeds and overflows our comprehension, our conceptual knowledge. The name of God is meant to shield God from presence. To be sure, Derrida would not say anything different about the *tout autre*. We would not love, or say *oui, oui*, or call for the coming of a *tout autre* that we could comprehend, for that would be the incoming of the *same*, not the *tout autre*. Is not the *tout autre* the shore we never reach, always other than anything we can conceive or see coming? But in theology the *tout autre* goes under the *determinate* name of God, which it is the vocation of theology to save, whereas deconstruction says no more than *tout autre*. But in theology itself, for Derrida, God is truly God, is beyond God and *Gottheit*, only if God "slips away" (*dérober*) from the grasp of knowledge (*Sauf*, 56/ON, 56).

This new praxis or pragmatics of the divine names, Marion adds, is revealed in baptism: "Baptize them in my Name" means, according to a commentary by Gregory of Nyssa, that this "Name" is not a predicate by which God's essence is inscribed within the horizon of our understanding, but rather that we are to be inscribed within God's un-nameable Name, that we are to be included in the clearing opened by the Name. In mystical theology, the goal is to not to bring the name of God to presence but to silence that Name in order to let ourselves be named, of which Baptism is the exemplary operation. The name of God is not a name to say, but to hear. "The Name is not said; it calls" ("In the Name," p. 42).

### Givenness versus Presence

Marion's argument comes to a head in his concluding remarks on the "saturated phenomenon," and it is there, in my view, that the several questions of the "metaphysics of presence," "economy," and "hyper-essentialism" can finally be sorted out and a serious difference of opinion between Marion and Derrida uncovered. The saturated phenomenon can be defined in strictly Husserlian terms and precisely as the reverse of the "poor" phenomena with which Husserl passed his days, according to which an intention or intended meaning is never completely confirmed or fulfilled by the corresponding "givenness" or intuitive content. Thus "Budapest" is a relatively empty intention if I have never been to that city, less empty if I have spent a week there, and never completely fulfilled even if I have lived my whole life there. Like any idea, "Budapest" represents an "infinite" idea or intention, a regulative ideal, an "idea in the Kantian sense," to which no finite complex of intuitive content is ever fully adequate. For Husserl and Kant, "God" is the very paradigm of such an idea, as an intention of an "infinite being" which has no intuitive content at all and no hope at all of every acquiring any. In a provocative move, Marion turns the Husserlian analysis on its head and says that, on the contrary, in the case of God, and especially in the case of mystical theology, God "is" — or better, God "gives" — an overflowing intuition, a flood of intuitive content which "saturates" the intention, an excess of *givenness* (*Gegebenheit*) which the idea, intention, or concept simply cannot contain.

This is a very different possibility than the one that Derrida noticed in his reading of the *Logical Investigations*, viz., that Husserl had "discovered" (without taking any joy in it) the formal possibility of a completely empty or blind signifier, operating entirely in the absence of intuitive fulfillment, something that would be found, e.g., in formal systems that lack an intuitive interpretation, like non-Euclidean geometry, or even in nonsensicals like *abracadabra*.[10] Marion's more radical phenomenology turns Husserl's analysis on its head by pushing Husserl in a direction directly opposite to the one in which Derrida was leading him,[11] viz., the formal possibility of an absolutely plenitudinous givenness exceeding any possible intention. But phenomenology itself can only render a description of such a formal possibility, of a "revealability" which only historical "revelation" can actually give.[12] This inversion of Husserl, and of Kant as well, which extricates the phenomenon, as that which gives itself from itself, from the subjectivistic constraints and transcendental conditions imposed upon it by the modernist structure of subjectivity in Kant and Husserl, goes to the very heart of what Marion means by postmodernism.[13] The saturated phenomenon comes after the subject, after the reduction of the subject, after the reduction of modernity's subjective transcendental.

This Husserlian distinction provides Marion with a new way of describing the "three ways" of mystical theology, a way of casting them in neo-Husserlian or neo-phenomenological terms. (i) *Affirmation*: When I say "God is good" this proposition draws the meaning or intention "good" from the given but finite goodness of creatures in order to confirm partially and incompletely God's infinite goodness. (ii) *Negation*: When I say "God is not good" the meaning or intention of the goodness of God infinitely surpasses the goodness of anything given in ordinary ("poor") experience. (iii) *Eminence*: The excess of intuitive givenness overflows and saturates the intention, so that it "means" something like "God! Goodness! Hallelujah!" That is a saturated phenomenon. We fail to comprehend God, not from a lack of givenness, as in Husserl and Kant, but from an excess in givenness, surplus. Deconstruction—and atheism (Marion likes to associate these two)—compare to mystical theology only on the level of the second way, of negation, Marion contends, not the third way. Deconstruction and atheism are for him geniuses of negation, skilled only in the way of saying *no* and *not*. While it is true that deconstruction would dissociate itself from the plenitudinous givenness of the third way, Marion's point sits uneasily with Derrida's constant and unrelenting affirmation of *the* impossible, the affirmation of the *tout autre*, the *viens, oui, oui*, particularly in the work since 1980. But for Derrida, to affirm the impossible is not to affirm infinite givenness.

With everything other than God, Marion contends, we always mean or intend more than is actually given to us, and our experience is always forced to play catch-up with our intention. But with God, more is given to us than we can ever mean or say, so that words and concepts are always at a loss to express what has been given. With the name of God, the shortcoming has to do with the failure of the concept, intention, or signification, which is always limited and imperfect, not with givenness, which is excessive and overflowing. Thus for Marion everything turns on distinguishing *presence* from *givenness*, on keeping them apart, precisely in order to confine the notion of "presence" to the "metaphysics" of presence, which means to the order of intention, meaning or concept. Thus for Marion mystical theology escapes the "metaphysics of presence" because he identifies the metaphysics of presence with the rule of the concept, which is for him the rule of idolatry. The metaphysical concept makes an idolatrous claim to a conceptual grasp of God by reducing God to the proportions of the concept. Instead of putting us in the presence of the inconceivable God, the concept cuts God down to the size, and the grasp, of the concept, which is why the concept is an idol. So for Marion to say that God is "given" but God is "not present" means to say that God gives himself in a way that exceeds our reach or our grasp, that God cannot be conceived according to the terms set by a metaphysical concept; it is to say that we are given access to God by God's own self-giving or givenness, beyond or without a concept. Thus by insisting that God is *absent* from the *concept*, what Marion calls "denomination" keeps God's *givenness* safe from the "metaphysics of presence."

### *Hypergivenness, Hyperessentialism, and Economy*

This raises the question of whether what Derrida means by "presence" is confined to what is *conceptually* grasped, presented or represented. It would seem that, from Derrida's point of view, by redescribing the *hyperousios* in terms of givenness rather than presence, Marion does not remove mystical theology from hyper-essentialism so much as he shifts the site of hyper-essentialism from "presence" to "givenness." But for Derrida an excess of givenness is no less hyper-essentialistic than an excess of presence. Derrida would be the first one to say—he said it from the start—that the *hyper* in *hyperousios*, the height and sublimity of its *ousia*, is such that it cannot be spoken or conceptually grasped because it is too present, hyper-present, meta-present, for our words to express or for our concepts to comprehend. That loss of words, he said, is a recourse mystical theology allows itself, which Levinas, who lodges the point of contact with the wholly other in language itself, is denied (ED, 170/WD, 116). For Derrida, that is the dominant (but not the only) voice of mystical theology, which, he says, is not narrowly metaphysical or ontological but "meta-metaphysical, meta-ontological" (*Sauf*, 80/ON, 68), and this in the service of saying and saving the truth of the name which it both says and unsays. Now if, like Marion, one wishes to confine the term "presence" to the poor presence of what is made present in and through the narrow constraints of a metaphysical concept, in order to distinguish that from the inexpressible and inconceivable excess of givenness which marks the plenitude of the *hyperousios*, then one may say the *hyperousios* is too *given* for our words and concepts to keep up with. Whether one defines the *hyperousios* in terms of hyper-presence, the excess of presence in the general sense, or in terms of hypergivenness, the excess of givenness over intention, it seems that one remains within the framework of what Derrida calls "hyper-essentialism," that is the superabundant self-presenting of God, the deeper, saving operation of the God beyond God, without Being, otherwise than essence, higher than being. Either way, it seems, Marion would be embracing what Derrida calls the dream of presence without *différance*, the dream of something that transpires *outside* of language, whereas for Derrida, dreaming always arises *within* language, as the dream of language for the *tout autre*. For language is structured by the *"viens, oui, oui."*

One way to see that, from Derrida's point of view, what Marion is describing in "In the Name" still belongs to what Derrida calls hyper-essentialism is as follows. For Derrida, Marion is proposing a neo-phenomenology of hyper-fulfillment and hypergivenness, which is a very adroit and fascinating neo-Husserlian (or hyper-Husserlian) way to describe hyper-essentialism, whose deftness and dexterity Derrida clearly admires. But it would be for Derrida no less an *economy*. On Derrida's interpretation, the very structure of the *hyper*— of the movement of *hyper, über, epekeina, ultra, au-delà, sans (Sauf, 73/ON, 64)*—is economical: [I]t loses in order to save; it is a way to make God *safe* so that God is not absolutely lost. God without being does not mean being without God. Mystical theology for Derrida—and one could argue that he has Meister Eckhart, Thomas Aquinas, and Angelus Silesius on his side on this point—is a mystical economy. That is what mystical theology always says about itself whenever it comes under fire by the police of orthodoxy, as it quite regularly does. The *Process* against Meister Eckhart is marked by the Meister's repeated assurances to the ecclesiastical apparatchiks with whom he dealt that he is not denying God but protecting the purity of God. When I say that God is nothing, a pure nothing, not even a little bit, Eckhart told the inquisitors, I am saying that God has the *puritas essendi*, with the felicitous ambiguity of both purity *of* and purity *from* being. The French syntagma *"plus d'etre,"* as Derrida says, captures that ambiguity quite economically (*Psyché*, 552/HAS, 90). The negation, delimitation, or deconstruction of the concept of God is always going about its Father's business (*en tois tou patros*), always obeying the commandment to avoid carving the golden calves of sharply defined concepts. It stands with Moses against Aaron, smashing the tables of metaphysics in its outrage over the idols the onto-theologians have erected for their worship. It always labors in the service of keeping God safe, of protecting God from the arrows and idols of intentionality. As such, these negations are good investments whose yield is infinite, ways of forgoing the coins of finite conceptual comprehension in order to save God's incomprehensibility and thereby receive an infinite reward (*merces*). The conceptmongers have already had their reward in their conceptual systems and have closed themselves off from the infinite "gift" granted in the "denomination" (monetary sense) of infinite givenness, which neither moth nor rust will consume nor thieves steal (cf. DM, 92–93/GD, 97–98). That is the classic economy of salvation.

Furthermore, Derrida can enlist the support of Meister Eckhart and Angelus Silesius, who claim that mystical theology is indeed a *higher affirmation* of God's *Überwesen*, and that that is just the force of the *hyper* or *über*.[14] Marion has very adroitly shifted the third way from a *modus praedicandi*, an affirmative "predication," the affirmation of a finite and conceptually determinate predicate of God, into a *pragmatics*, a praise and a prayer. But, as Derrida reads Silesius and Eckhart, that is precisely a higher way to say *yes* to God and God's self-giving. In Derrida's terms, in the pragmatic sphere we say "God— *oui, oui!*" which has the ring of affirmation. God is the first yes—*Jah* (yes)-*weh*, Silesius quips in German—a positive or affirmative and not a negative infinity, the purely affirmative self-giving of God, while the creaturely yes is a second yes—*oui, oui*—made in response to God's generous self-donation. "*Jahweh spricht immer 'Ja',*" to cite the mystical pun of Angelus Silesius that Derrida loves. That higher, non-predicative, non-conceptual affirmation rises up above the determinate affirmations and negations, the determinate speech-acts and acts of judgment made by the subject. This affirmation, which takes place, according to Meister Eckhart, not in the "faculties" of the soul (intellect, will) but in its very "ground," is called *Gelassenheit*, a deeply affirmative assent to God's advent, a deep *amen*, which is for Eckhart the mystical meaning of Mary's *fiat mihi secundum verbum tuum*. When the angel addressed her, Mary said yes, not no. When God knocks at the soul's door, when God addresses His Word to us, the soul says yes, *fiat mihi, amen*, and God is born in the soul (Eckhart), given to the *interloqué* (Marion), affirmed in a hyperbolic affirmation, *oui, oui* (Derrida). "The Name is not said; it calls"—and the creature answers yes, *oui, oui, fiat mihi secundum verbum tuum, amen*.

### With or Without God

Marion thinks of Derrida and deconstruction as atheistic, and, to be sure, Jacques Derrida says of himself that "I quite rightly pass for an atheist" (*Circon.*, 146/*Circum.*, 155).[15] But, given the considerable attention Derrida has recently paid to the name of God, and to his "religion about which no one knows anything" (ibid.), this question requires further reflection. In my view, deconstruction itself, if it has a self, apart from the person of Jacques Derrida, is neither theistic nor atheistic. Deconstruction is a certain way of thinking about things, and not only thinking but doing, which keeps itself intensely alert to the contingency of what it thinks, and this not from a sense of skepticism or even *epoche*, but in order to keep itself open to the coming of the most unforeseeable, unimaginable, to the *l'invention de tout autre*. This structure of absolute hope and expectation, of the maximalized expectation of what he calls the "event," of what is coming or incoming (*l'in-vention*) Derrida is now happy (after an initial hesitation) to call the "*messianic*."[16] Hard as this may be for some to hear or to bear—whether they are for or against deconstruction— deconstruction is through and through a messianic affirmation of the coming of the impossible. Or again—I am trying to make this as intolerable as possible for the learned despisers of religion—deconstruction is a generalized form of, and a repetition of, what is going on in religion. Now in mystical theology, in the religions of the Book, *the* impossible comes and goes under the determinate name of "God" (as opposed to humanity, history, the classless society).

What Derrida tries to do in *Sauf le nom* is to examine what that means and what significance mystical theology holds for everyone, even if one is not a card-carrying, service-attending member of one of the religions of the Book. What is its *general import* even if one has not seen the inside of a church or synagogue or temple since childhood?

So the difference between deconstruction and the religions of the Book is not reducible to the difference between atheism and theism. Rather, it can also be seen in terms of the difference between a more general indeterminate messianic and the specific, determinable, doctrinal messianisms of Judaism, Christianity, and Islam. (Indeed as Zarathustra's heady discourses make plain, atheism too can take the form of a determinate messianism.) Derrida is not a learned despiser of religion but a lover of a religion without religion. Hence, deconstruction differs from the Christian mystical theology of Pseudo-Dionysius or of Meister Eckhart as an *indeterminate* differs from a *determinate* affirmation of *the* impossible. For Derrida is always asking with St. Augustine, *quid ergo amo cum deum meum amo:* "What do I love when I love my God?" (*Circon.*, 117/*Circum.*, 122). What Derrida loves about that question is that it *assumes that* one loves God, and it searches to understand *what* one loves when one loves God. For Derrida, the name of God has a certain uncontainable *translatability*, so that we are never sure whether the name of "God" is an example of the name of "justice," or whether justice is an example of God. Deconstruction lacks the authority to resolve that undecidability, the name of "literature," Derrida will say, having already begun (*Pass.*, 89 n.12/*ON*, 142–43 n.14),[17] which means that we are always subject to a certain unstoppable translatability and undecidability. That is also the difference between religion in the conventional sense, the religions of the Book, the religion in terms of which Derrida is rightly described as an atheist, and what Derrida calls a "religion without religion," (*DM*, 53/*GD*, 49) that is, a religion which is informed by the general and translatable structure of the religious without taking up the determinate content of any of the specific religious translations or "denominations." About this religion without religion, far from being a learned despiser, Derrida is a veritable defender of the faith, as is clear from *Memoirs of the Blind*. Derrida's religion, then, is very un-denominational, by keeping a safe distance not only between itself and any of the concrete messianisms (Christian, Jewish, Islamic) of the religions of the book, but also between itself and any monetary denominations, that is, economies—whereas Marion is interested in a very Christian economy.

But if Derrida is so far from feeling threatened by mystical theology that he distrusts any discourse that is not touched by mystical theology, then just what *is* Derrida saying about God? We have contended that Marion and Derrida are agreed in regarding the "intention" or the "concept" as an "arrow" which is aimed at the heart of God from which God must be "shielded" (*Sauf*, 91–92/*ON*, 74) or kept "safe." For Marion, who is thinking in terms of the Christian Neoplatonism of Pseudo-Dionysius, this is because the arrow of intentionality is too weak and narrow to penetrate or comprehend the infinite givenness of God; it would compromise the infinite incomprehensibility of God who has utterly saturated the intention "God" in a plenitude of givenness. But for Derrida, who is thinking in Jewish and *messianic* terms, not those of Christian Neoplatonism, the arrow takes aim at God and never reaches God precisely because the name of God is the name of what we love and desire, of that for which we pray and weep, something *tout autre* which is not "present," not only in the narrow sense of conceptual presentation advanced by Marion, but also not *given*. For Marion the signifier "God" is flooded by givenness; for Derrida it is a dry and desert aspiration for I know not what. *Inquietum est cor nostrum.*

What matters most of all for Derrida is what is *neither* present *nor* given, what is structurally *never* present or given, whose givenness or presence is always *to come.* The name of God for Derrida is not the name of, and does not safeguard, the *excess or surplus of givenness* but the name of what is *never given*, the excess of what is always promised, hoped for, prayed and wept over. It is the name of the future, of what keeps the future open, of what "keeps hope alive," to borrow a phrase from Jesse Jackson. It is the name of the structure of the future which is not merely a foreseeable future present, but a future beyond the horizon of foreseeability and possibility, an impossible future always "to come." Derrida is not here drawing upon atheistic resources but upon an old rabbinic tradition discussed by Blanchot that Derrida mentions in *The Politics of Friendship*, according to which the coming of the Messiah must never be confused with his actual presence.[18] If the Messiah were to appear somewhere, incognito and dressed in rags, and someone who penetrated his disguise were to approach him, he would ask the Messiah, "When will you come?" For that is the very structure of what we mean by the Messiah. Were the Messiah actually to become present, what would there be to hope for? What would be left of the future? Or of history? Even the history of Christianity, where it is believed that the Messiah has *already* come, is opened up by the question, "When will he come *again*?" As the Thessalonians seem to have been the first to learn, "Christianity" opens up with *différance*, with the deferral of this *second* coming, this coming *again*. For it belongs to the very idea of the Messiah to be always to come.

For Derrida, the "presence of God" does not mean, on the one hand, either God's historical givenness made flesh in a man or God's mystical givenness beyond intention in the soul, but neither does it mean, on the other hand, a cold and heartless atheism. For Derrida pursues a third possibility of his own, his own third way, where the presence of God means God's *coming* (*venue*), and the faith and hope and love of the future that this coming elicits, in particular, for a *justice* to come.[19] God is neither *simply* present or absent, neither *simply* given or not, for the name of God is the name of what is *to come.* God escapes the play of being and non-being, to be or not to be, for Derrida, because God is the specter of what is to come, the stuff of things to hope for

(Hebrews 11:1). Derrida's view is *theologically* suggestive inasmuch as he makes room for faith and confesses that we see always through a glass darkly, and that we are not face-to-face with givenness. For Derrida the presence of God is the coming of God, and the gift of God is a gift without givenness, *le don sans la donation*, not a gift of givenness but a faith in the gift to come.

It is opportune to mention here that while Derrida quite agrees with Marion that the meaning of the name of God is ultimately settled on the terrain of pragmatics, not apophantics, for Marion that means that the name of God is enacted in praise and liturgy, but for Derrida it means that it is enacted in peace and justice. *The impossible*, which we love and desire, is for Derrida a justice, indeed a democracy, to come. The question of radical social and political justice is, to my knowledge, never mentioned by Marion although, as Regina Schwartz points out, there is a powerful thematic of justice stirring in the notion of loving one's enemies.[20] The tendency of discussions of the confrontation of Derrida and Marion to be preoccupied with the question of mystical theology obscures the genuinely religious import of deconstruction, which is its prophetic import. This is a point that I have developed at length in *The Prayers and Tears of Jacques Derrida*. Derrida's discourse about the name of God has to do with prophetic justice, not Christian Neoplatonism. The name of God for Derrida has a prophetic not an apophatic force, and is more Jewish than Christian, more religious than theological, more concerned with the ethico-politics of hospitality than with mystical or negative theology.

These differences are not clarified by dividing things up into theism and atheism, by forcing a simple decision about whether one stands with or without God.[21] If the difference between Derrida can in part be considered in terms of the difference between Jewish and Christian, it is better thought of as the difference between a more generalized structure which Derrida borrows from the Hebrew and Christian scriptures, which he calls the messianic in general, and the specific or concrete messianisms. These differences are sharpened in the roundtable "On the Gift," where the focus is on the gift and givenness.

## The Gift With/out Givenness:
## Givenness and the Aporia of the Gift

In "On the Gift," the focal issue between Marion and Derrida is once again the question of givenness and presence, and once again they share a mutual concern, to save the gift in the face of the aporia which they both agree is well formulated in *Given Time*.

### Marion's Phenomenology of the Gift

In order to situate the debate that transpires in the roundtable it is necessary briefly to sketch Marion's analysis of the gift and his critique of Derrida, which forms the background of this discussion. For this purpose, I follow

Marion's 1994 essay entitled "Outline of a Phenomenological Concept of the Gift," since the critique of Derrida in *Etant donné* does not differ materially from this essay.[22] For Marion, the gift must be removed from the horizon of "economy" — this we learn from Derrida — and re-conducted or "reduced" to the horizon of "givenness" (French: *donation*; German: *Gegebenheit*), bracketing everything alien to the gift in order to think it in terms that are proper to it. Specifically, that means laying aside the metaphysical schema by which a donor (*causa agens*) produces an effect in a recipient (*causa finalis*) through the material and formal cause of the gift-object (Esq., 76–77). This causal-metaphysical schema, which confines the gift within the sphere of influence of the principle of sufficient reason, will be turned on its head by an analysis that catches up both the donor and the recipient in the sweep or momentum of the gift (*don*) itself, which is itself caught up in the momentum or horizon of *donation*. This is demonstrated point by point by three reductions.

(1) Reduction *to* the lived experience of the *donor*: [I]f the lover gives a ring to the beloved, the ring is but a token of what is truly given, an icon of the love, which means that the finite, visible surface of the ring is possessed of an overflowing and invisible depth. The donor gives a gift not by the simple transfer of an object or a being (the ring) but by regarding the ring as "giveable" (*donable*). Giveability itself arises only when the donor recognizes a duty (*devoir*) to give, an "obligation to give" (*obligation de donner*), which breaks the spell of autarchy — "I do not owe anyone anything" — and I own up to the debt I owe the other (Esq., 86). For the donor is already a recipient and obligated to give in virtue of an anterior gift. The gift is born in the recognition of being in debt. This is not an *ontic* obligation to a previous donor (Esq., 88) but an "ontological," or better, let us say, a "me-ontological" duty to *donation* itself by whose spell the donor is held captive. By arguing that the donor is obliged by the "gifting"[23] of the gift itself to give, Marion wants to establish that the donor does not precede the gift as its cause, but in so doing, for this will become important, he does not hesitate to insert duty and obligation into the heart of the gift.

(2) Reduction *to* the experience of the *recipient*: By an analogous structure, a recipient is not someone who merely receives a transfer of property but someone who agrees to sacrifice one's autonomy, agrees to be put in debt by the gift, graciously to accept a debt of gratitude. Once again, this is decided not finally by the recipient but by the gift itself which "by its own allure and prestige decides the recipient to decide himself for it" (Esq., 88). Marion's position reminds one somewhat of the Maori conception of the *hau* (spirit) of the gift which by a force of its own keeps the gift in circulation discussed by Marcel Mauss.[24] (3) Reduction *to* the *gift* itself: Accordingly, the gift itself is not the "physical counterpart" of the gift, the token ring, e.g., nor is it the joint effect of a giver who decides to give and of a receiver to receive. Rather the gift itself prompts both donor and recipient to enter into the sphere of giving, to "give in" (*adonner*) to itself, to the gift, to grow "addicted" to it. Giver and

recipient are less the subjective agents of the gift than subjects subjected to, swept up in and acted upon by it (Esq., 89), subjects who come after the gift.

This analysis can be "confirmed," Marion says, by observing the extent to which each of the three elements can be in turn reduced, suspended, or put out of play, "as far as possible," so as to allow the primacy of the gift, and its gifting, the fullest play. The reduction *to* the elements of the gift is now confirmed by a reduction *of* them. For the gift has a kind of *ex opere operato* quality for Marion—it works by itself—prior to the agency of the donor or recipient, rather like a Catholic sacrament. Or like the primacy of the *Spiel* over the *Spieler* in Gadamer, or like the primacy of the work of art over the artist and observer in Heidegger's "Origin of the Work of Art," or like the blossoming of the rose which blossoms without why, *sine ratione*, in Heidegger's *Der Satz vom Grund*. There follows then the sorts of examples Marion gives in the roundtable (and in *Etant donné*[25]) of gifts *without* givers or recipients, and even of gifts without gifts. There can be a gift without a recipient if I give a gift to someone who rejects my gift, as when I love my enemy who rejects my love. While my enemy thereby does himself a disservice he serves the purpose of a phenomenology of giving by allowing the gift of love to rise up all the more purely (Esq., 91). There can also be a gift without a gift itself, where the gift now appears to be taken in the positivistic and reified sense which is precisely excluded by the reduction *to* donation. Giving without a gift is found when the lover gives his invisible love without a visible token, without a ring. The lover gives his love but he does not give a *thing*, something *present*.

Finally there can be a gift without a donor, when, e.g., the donor makes an anonymous gift so that the recipient cannot identify the source. That allows Marion to formulate a radical view of the gift which has both a Levinasian[26] and Anselmian ring of infinite unpayable debt: The limit case of the gift arises when a recipient finds himself unable to identify the donor whom he could repay and is put indissolubly in debt, rendered insolvent (*insolvable*), in debt without limit to he knows not what, with a debt that arises before consciousness. Indeed, consciousness itself, the self, arises precisely as a consciousness of a debt that it cannot pay off, "guilty" (*schuldig*) by its very being, Heidegger would say, summoned into consciousness, Marion would say, by an "indebting givenness" (*la donation endettant*) (Esq., 93). Marion thus invokes the language of Heidegger and Levinas to express the "gift" of creation, of being called by a voice one never heard. Given this analysis, Marion concludes, we can push the paradox of the gift to its greatest extreme: The gift, reduced to givenness, decides itself to give itself as an insolvent debt remitted to an enemy (Esq., 93).

Derrida is introduced into this argument as an opponent of the phenomenology of the gift, a poser of an aporia that produces a "disturbing result" (Esq., 79) from which the gift must be rescued, an "objection" which makes *donation* disappear, leaving it in contradiction with itself (Esq., 77), unable to think itself (Esq., 80). Derrida blocks the way to the gift, diverts and deroutes us (*déroute*) from *donation*, by placing a seemingly insuperable aporia in its way: [I]f the gift appears, it is absorbed into economy; if it does not appear, that closes down the phenomenality of donation.[27] However, Marion hopes to show, phenomenology is not trapped by this melancholy aporia, "even if that appears to be the conclusion Derrida draws" (Esq., 80). But Marion draws a further conclusion of his own from his presentation of *Given Time*, viz., that the result of Derrida's analysis is entirely negative, that the impossibility of the phenomenal appearing of the gift as such, and thus of any *phenomenology* of the gift rigorously conceived, involves the impossibility of the gift pure and simple. What Derrida has demonstrated is but a first and completely negative result in Marion's view. Derrida's "objection" to the gift "only (*seulement*) establishes the condition under which the gift is impossible" without in any way showing that "what thus becomes impossible merits the name of gift" (Esq., 82).

Marion will steer his way around Derrida's "objection," which declares the gift impossible, by showing that what is made impossible by Derrida's analysis is precisely *not the gift*. The gift lies somewhere else—in the horizon of *donation*—where Derrida did not think to look, because Derrida's analysis begins and ends within the horizon of economy, from which it is unable to depart. "What is it missing here?" Marion asks, to which he answers: "The renunciation of the economic horizon of exchange in order to interpret the gift beginning with the horizon of donation" (Esq., 82–83). Once that change of horizon is put in place, the solely negative results of Derrida's analysis may be turned on its head and we may show the "remarkable fecundity" (Esq., 80) of this deconstructive "objection." This solely negative condition of impossibility may be transformed into a positive condition of possibility. The very conditions of this aporia can be turned to a positive account and made to issue in a phenomenological concept of the gift.

### Blindness and the Phenomenology of the Unapparent

Richard Kearney opens the roundtable by trying to press the "denominational" difference between Derrida, as a "quasi-atheistic, quasi-Jewish deconstructor," and Marion as a "hyper-Christian, hyper-Catholic phenomenologist." In an exchange that greatly entertained those who heard it, which perhaps reflects a concern Marion sometimes displays not to be consigned to a denominational theology, Marion explained that he is no longer interested in the religious meaning of the gift and is now at work on a pure phenomenology of the gift in terms of its "givenness," while Derrida rejoined that he himself is very interested in the Christian theology of the gift. His project, Marion explains, goes back to the Husserl of the *Logical Investigations* and the distinction made there between intention and givenness, which it is now his goal to radicalize. The project is to describe the phenomenon—of the gift, in particular, and any phenomenon generally—neither as an "object" constituted by a transcendental subject (Husserl), nor as a being projected in terms

John D. Caputo

of Dasein's understanding of Being (Heidegger), but, more simply and unconditionally, as *given*. This horizon of givenness opens up the full spectrum of the gift, ranging from the Husserlian modes of givenness of the "poorest" phenomena up to the overrich givenness of the highest "saturated" phenomena ("On the Gift," pp. 55–58).

For Derrida, on the other hand, the very idea of the gift, its very possibility, and he is not sure that it *is* possible, makes Marion's project of a "phenomenology of the gift" questionable, and this for two reasons. (1) *Phenomenology* is not necessarily a phenomenology of the "gift." There is no "semantic continuity," Derrida says in the roundtable, between (a) phenomenological "givenness," which means givenness to intuitive consciousness, whether as *giving* intuition (*gebende Anschauung*) in the Husserlian sense, or as *intuitus derivativus* in the Kantian sense, the *datum* or *factum* of the phenomenon, and (b) the "gift," which from a phenomenological point of view represents a specific class of phenomena involving intentional notions like generosity and gratitude. For Derrida, the gift is a limit concept, a special and highly aporetic notion which is not equivalent to simply being in some way "given." The kitchen table, e.g., does not begin to annul itself from the very moment that it is given as a table, as does the gift. Behind Marion's phenomenological gesture, which would entail making everything a gift, Derrida suspects a theological motive, a theology of gift, of the whole of creation as gift, of the gift of grace, etc., a motive which in other contexts Marion takes no pains to conceal. Still none of this is said, Derrida insists in the roundtable, *against* phenomenology, the gift, religion, or the *donum dei*. Indeed, he would think, this is the best way he knows to *save* them.

(2) *Gifts* do not admit of a strict "phenomenology." For Derrida, the very structure of the gift is such that, far from offering a "saturating" givenness, the gift is *never* given, and to the extent that it *is* given and *identified as such*, as *given*, it tends to annul itself as a gift. In his well-known analysis in *Given Time*, Derrida argues that as soon as the subject is *identified* as either a donor or a donee, the subject experiences a sense of self-gratification or of gratitude, which unavoidably sets in motion the circular dynamic of a debt to be repaid, of generosity to be recognized, thereby and precisely to that extent annulling the gift. So the very thing that makes it possible for the gift to "appear," to acquire "truth" and "phenomenality," viz., identifiable generosity and gratitude, and an identifiable gift, tend to make it *impossible*, to annul it as a gift. Some of the most profitable exchanges in the roundtable are devoted to clarifying this "impossibility." For Derrida, the very structure of the gift is aporetic and Marion is certainly right in the "Outline of a Phenomenological Concept of the Gift" to present Derrida as the philosopher of the aporia of the gift. But that aporia does not spell the end of the gift, or what Derrida calls in the roundtable its "absolute impossibility," but its beginning, its impulse, setting the dynamics of the gift in motion. "Let us begin through (*par*) the impossible" (DT, 17/GT, 6), not "with" the impossible, but *through* it or *by* it;

204

let us be set in motion and impelled by the impossible. For the impossible is what we truly desire and the "aporetic," that "no-way-to-go," is where we are most deeply desirous of going. "Go where you cannot go, to the impossible," Angelus Silesius said. "What I am interested in," Derrida says in the roundtable ("On the Gift," p. 72), "is the experience of the desire for the impossible, that is, the impossible as the condition of desire. . . . We con-tinue to desire, to dream, *through* the impossible." *The* impossible stirs our desire, feeds our faith, and nourishes our passion; *the* impossible is such stuff as dreams as made of. It is just when we see that it is *impossible* that our hearts are set afire and we are lifted up above the horizon of pedestrian possibility. For Derrida, we must not lose our faith in the impossible, which is also our hope, our love, our faith in the gift. The gift, *the* impossible, *viens, oui, oui!*

Accordingly, the point of Derrida's analysis will be missed, and Derrida will be mistaken as a critic of the gift, a suspicious opponent who poses "ob-jections" to the gift, unless one appreciates the unique dynamic of *the* impos-sible in deconstruction, around which his entire defense of the gift, his effort to *save the gift* is built. While Marion does regard Derrida as a critic of the gift in *Etant donné* and in the "Outline," that is not the view he takes in the roundtable, which is I think one of the more significant features of this discussion. "I think," Marion says, "I never said that *you* [Derrida] thought the gift was impossible" ("On the Gift," p. 62). Still, Derrida is presented in these published texts as posing important "objections" to the gift whose upshot is completely negative, which result in showing "only" (*seulement*) that the gift is impossible, results that must be turned against themselves if the friends of the gift are to take a single step forward. Derrida's ultimate mistake, Marion argues in those texts, is to allow the gift to be trapped by the horizon of economy and of presents/presence, and to have cut off the possibility of a gift outside economy. While we are to be grateful to Derrida for supplying a pow-erful demonstration that economy renders the gift impossible, Marion will now show that what Derrida thus declared impossible is precisely *not* the gift (Esq., 82), is everything except (*sauf*) the gift, which belongs to a different horizon altogether, outside or beyond economy, to which Derrida never lifts his eye. The gift which Derrida declares dead is an idol, while the possibility of the true gift remains to be understood. Marion will thereby turn Derrida's critique around and exploit its "fecundity" which Derrida evidently did not suspect, a move which, Derrida might be inclined to think, simply allows Der-rida to make the point Derrida intended all along. Thus, in just the way Mar-ion takes Derrida to launch an "attack" upon mystical theology whose mis-takes deconstruction must avoid, so he takes Derrida to present an "objection" to the gift, which objection Marion must answer. But from Derrida's point of view, deconstruction does not attack the name of God or mystical theology, but tries to keep it safe, nor does deconstruction try to nullify the gift but rath-er it shows that the conditions under which it is possible tend also to nullify it as a gift. In the end, Derrida wants to save those precious names, of God and the gift, and he daily prays and weeps for a Messiah to come to save both them and us.

In the roundtable Derrida protests that Marion makes against him the same objection that Derrida made against Marcel Mauss in *Given Time*: Derrida is said by Marion to discuss everything *except* the gift, having reduced the gift entirely to the horizon of an economic exchange. To which Derrida responds, "I did exactly the opposite" ("On the Gift," p.59). So Marion's critique is to be turned around: Deconstruction does not criticize everything except (*sauf*) the gift, but deconstruction means to make the gift *safe* (*sauf*). Derrida insists that it is impossible for the gift to "exist" *as such*, to be "present" or make an "appearance" as such, to be *identifiable* as such, and that it cannot be the subject of any "phenomenology" in a rigorous sense, but he never concluded from this to its "absolute impossibility," that there is absolutely no gift. On the contrary, the gift arises precisely in or though the "experience of this impossibility." Derrida's precise point of disagreement with Marion, then, is not that Derrida thinks there is no gift but that Derrida thinks there is no *phenomenology* of the gift, not *as such*, about which there is considerable discussion in the roundtable. For Derrida, from the moment and to the extent that the gift appears or acquires identifiable phenomenality as a gift, the gift begins to annul itself and to be drawn back into the circle of economy. Gift-giving for him must always be undertaken as a kind of never-ending struggle against economy, eventuating in certain momentary *interruptions* of economy, moments of madness, in which the time of the gift—the *Augenblick*—is given, something like the saving moments of skepticism in which *le dire* interrupts *le dit* in Levinas. Save/safe the gift, *sauf le don*.

Accordingly, for Derrida, any such "phenomenology of the gift" as one may propose could only be at best a *self-interrupting* phenomenology, a phenomenology of a phenomenon about which, at the crucial moment, we blink or even go blind. For at the crucial moment of the gift, instead of being visited by a *hypergivenness* or *hyper-appearance*, the gift must above all *not be given*, not appear. That is the beautiful, maddening, and impassioning aporia of the gift: [T]he very thing that would make it possible makes its appearance impossible. Marion is quite right to describe the "phenomenology of the gift" as a "phenomenology of the un-apparent" (Esq., 79), an expression borrowed from Heidegger's Zähringen Seminar, which Marion wants to take as a model of the phenomenology of the gift. Heidegger argued that the genuine *Sache* of phenomenology is not the being that appears, but its Being, which does not appear. Similarly, Marion will argue that the real business of the phenomenology of the gift, which is the gifting of the gift in its givenness (*donation*, *Gegebenheit*), will appear precisely with the disappearance of the gift, that is, of the ontico-causal agencies of giver, recipient, and the gift-object (cf. RD, 60–61). This means that, for Marion, the very lack of appearance of the gift is a phenomenological event. The "phenomenology of the unapparent" means that the visible or phenomenal gift—which is neither a being nor an object—

is bracketed in favor of the horizon of givenness (Esq., 79).[28] For "givenness" to arise, the gift must not appear, for the moment that the gift does appear, the gift is swallowed up in the horizon of causal agency and exchange and the horizon of givenness is wiped away.

But for Derrida, were there to be a phenomenology of the gift, were any such thing possible, it might indeed be described as a phenomenology of the un-apparent, of what does *not appear*, but that would mean a phenomenology of what is *not given*, not a gift in its givenness (*le don dans la donation*), but a gift without givenness (*le don sans la donation*). So the roundtable sometimes takes the form of a little tug of war between *sans* and *dans* (in English), the gift with or without givenness. Any such phenomenology of the unapparent would represent not the *appearance of the plenitude of givenness*, a supersaturating horizon of givenness appearing behind the disappearance of the gift, but the *interruption* of phenomenology and of givenness, not a saturating givenness but a blindness which blinks at the critical moment (*Augenblick*), like a player who, at a crucial moment, loses sight of the ball. For Marion, the gift is a matter of hypergivenness, while for Derrida it is a matter of never-givenness; for Marion, a matter of bedazzlement, for Derrida of blindness. In Derrida, this interrupted phenomenology would be a way of confessing the need for faith, a way of confessing "*il faut croire,*" which is the argument of Derrida's *Memoirs of Blindness*. That is why for Marion, "revelation" is defined in terms of "an excess of intuition" (Esq., 75), where for Derrida, revelation has to do with faith, with what eye has not seen nor ear heard.

In the last hour of the roundtable, Marion and Derrida return to the question of the status of phenomenology and, under the impulse of the discussion, their respective postures on phenomenology tend to flip in a curious way. Marion, who insistently defends a phenomenology of the gift, professes a disinterest in whether what he does is called phenomenology or not, while Derrida, long taken to be an antagonist to phenomenology, who distrusts the idea of a phenomenology of the gift, grows more protective of phenomenology's proper domain. "I remain," Derrida says, "a phenomenologist." Marion recognizes the importance of Derrida's objection concerning an equivocation on "gift" and "givenness," which do not necessarily coincide, a point which, as Marion points out, is also made against him by Paul Ricoeur. To those formidable complainants, Marion responds that he does not argue that gift and givenness coincide, that everything given is a gift, but the converse, that every gift is a given and must be thought in terms of givenness. Accordingly, he objects to the suggestion that he is trying to harness phenomenology to the service of theology by making every phenomenon a gift and then identifying the giver behind the gift, the cause of phenomena, viz., God. That is a misunderstanding, in part because Marion does not think of God as cause and in part because he does not say that every *Gegebenheit* is a gift, but that every gift must be understood in terms of *Gegebenheit*. The *Gegebenheit* of any everyday phenomenon is not a gift, but a gift is an excess of *Gegebenheit*.

John D. Caputo

The kitchen table is given, but the gift is *hyper-given* (for Derrida: the kitchen table is given, but the gift is *never given*). Marion is trying to reduce the gift to the horizon of givenness in order to be "fair" to certain phenomena by removing them from the horizon of causality, by letting them be as the given phenomena they are, without reducing them to objects for a subject, and without linking them up in a causal chain. That bears a striking resemblance to the project of what the later Heidegger calls *Denken*,[29] constituting a kind of *Gelassenheit* toward *Gegebenheit*. This may constitute a more radical "possibility" of phenomenology, or a "higher" phenomenology—this word "phenomenology" is not important, he says—but this is certainly not theology, says Marion, nor is it driven from behind by theology.

Still, Derrida rejoins, any such "phenomenology" as this must be of the sort that limits itself as a phenomenology. The phenomenology of the gift cannot strictly be called a "phenomenology" for exactly the same reason that Levinas's analysis of the "other" cannot be called phenomenology, viz., that at the precise moment of the "as such," of the Other *as such*, of the gift *as such*, the screen goes blank and the gift or the Other does *not* appear, not by a chance omission but structurally, in a way that is constitutive of what we mean by the Other or the gift. In just the way the Other who is given is not the Other, so the gift which is given is not the gift, and—this is an important point recently made by Robyn Horner[30]—the God who is given is not God. God, the gift and the *tout autre* share a common trait: They are each annulled from the moment they appear or are given, so that if they appear or are given then we may be sure that what appeared was not God, the gift, or the *tout autre*. So Derrida says he wants to speak "against phenomenology," or to "go beyond phenomenology," but to do so phenomenologically, "to find within phenomenology the injunction to go beyond phenomenology" ("On the Gift," p. 75).

### Catholic, Protestant, and Jewish Gifts

It is here that Richard Kearney's opening question about the "denominational" character of this debate, about the religious denominations of Derrida and Marion, their cultural and theological (or atheological) differences, becomes particularly pertinent. For Marion, a phenomenology of the inapparent seems to mean *the appearing of the invisible in the visible*, a sense that he is drawing in part from Levinas but still more from the "theological aesthetics" of the Catholic theologian Hans Urs von Balthasar and his theology of perception,[31] which is a source upon which Phillip Blond is also drawing in his introduction to *Post-Secular Philosophy*.[32] This means that the lover's invisible love shines through the visible gift of the ring, iconically, "sacramentally," just the way the *ousia* of the father is to be taken as an icon of his love for his sons and not idolized for itself, which is the mistake made by the prodigal son.[33] That is precisely what Janicaud regards as an illicit importation of the transcendent into phenomenology, a smuggling of the invisible into the visible. Merleau-Ponty died in 1961 and must have turned in his grave, Janicaud thinks, with the philosophy of the invisible that Levinas published in that same year. That is the crucial move made in Marion's new phenomenology: By displacing the finite, visible, and present gift, we are saturated by the hyperpresence or hypergivenness of the gifting of its unlimited and invisible givenness. Marion's position is nourished by a Catholic theology of the sacraments, a notion of Christ as God's *icon*, and a taste for medieval Catholic mystical theology and what Luther would call the *theologia gloriae*.

But for Derrida the sense of the "unapparent" is drawn not from this Catholic theology of perception but from a more Kantian and Protestant notion of the Idea and from an ultimately Jewish distrust of all images, whether idol or icon. For Derrida, the *non-appearing of the gift*, as opposed to the *appearing* of what is *hyper-given* to intuition or to ordinary experience, is to be compared to Kant's "thought" without a concept of an indeterminate *je ne sais quoi*, which regulates and motivates the ego as it moves through the conceptually determined and perceptually determinate intuitions of ordinary experience. We can "think" of the gift (desire it, dream of it, pray and weep over it) but we cannot "know" it, determine it conceptually (rather the way Marion thinks we can "know" that God is "incomprehensible"), nor does the gift present itself perceptually in the "manifold of experience." If it belongs to the "thought" of the gift that we cannot "know" it, then that means it is an object of "faith," and that we can only *do* it. A gift is something to *do*. So the way to save the "truth" of the gift—which has been delimited in *Given Time* on the basis of its non-appearance, is to see that the "truth" comes from *doing* the truth, *facere veritatem*, as Augustine says. That is why Derrida objects in the round-table ("On the Gift," p.72) that his view of truth is not as simple as Marion presents it in the "Outline" (Esq., 80–83). Derrida asserts that the "truth" of the gift—its "manifestation" or phenomenality—suffices to annul it; if the gift appears in its truth, that would result in its non-truth, the non-gift (DT, 42/GT, 27). But that is not the end of the story of truth, only its beginning. For Derrida does not exclude the *desire to realize* its truth in practice, to *do* the truth of the gift. Like Kant, Derrida finds it necessary to deny knowledge (truth) in order to make room for faith and doing the truth (which corresponds in Kant to the primacy of "practical reason") and this in order to *save* the gift. Aporias are made to be broken for Derrida, not to stop us in our tracks, but they are broken not by an adroit bit of theory but by a *deed*, by *going* where you *cannot go*, giving when you cannot give, giving what you do not have, an expression that Derrida says he loves very much. The gift is a pure thought without concept, but that is not a mere thought but a deed.

The Kantian analogy also leads into a Jewish analogy: The non-appearance of the gift is a feature of its *messianic* indeterminacy. We think/desire/dream of the coming of a gift/Messiah about whom we do not know a thing, for whom we can only pray and weep. Of any gift that is actually *given* we would always have to ask, "When will you come?" For any gift that is actually and identifiably *given* will set in motion the real and given circle of generosity and debts of gratitude, reciprocity and potlatches, eminent givers to whose generosity we owe a bottomless debt, privileged keepers and authoritative interpreters of the gift, etc. The "true gift" is as such always to come, and so has no truth in the sense of phenomenal manifestness or givenness, for it will always correspond to a desire. *Givenness* for Derrida will contact the gift to the actual circle of *real economies*, so to save the gift we must shield it from presence and that will also mean shielding it from givenness. For Derrida the giving of the gift is situated in a thinking/desiring of what will *never* be conceived or perceived, given or presented, so that the time of the gift is not only the *Augenblick*, the mad moment that defies economy, but the future, *à venir*, not the future present, the foreseeable future, but the absolute future. For Marion the gift is situated in a saturating givenness *without* being present or conceived, which is the work that is cut out by Marion for the hyper-givenness of the inconceivable saturating phenomenon.

### Partial Blackouts

While Derrida and Marion adopt fundamentally different views about givenness, they both agree that the gift requires a certain non-appearance or non-phenomenality, and hence their views are not simply or diametrically opposed. Marion's phenomenology of the gift might be described as a miti-gated phenomenology of the unapparent, putting in place only partial black-outs or partial reductions of one or two elements of the gift, but never blacking out all three of its elements at once. While we are bedazzled by Marion's hypergivenness, we are not to be left completely blind. Marion insists that a phenomenology of the gift, a reduction *to* the gift, is possible only if the "re-duction" *of* the gift is piecemeal, if it is not executed on all three elements of the gift at the same time, if it does not become absolutely or completely in-apparent. The energy of the gift, like one's appetite, is heightened by being starved or partially blocked. But Marion will not go gladly into that dark night of non-appearance that Derrida prescribes, and he struggles bravely against the failing of all the light. Marion thinks that to the extent that the gift tends to disappear its phenomenality is heightened, while Derrida would say that to the extent the gift appears it tends to make itself disappear. This is not a half full/half empty dispute. Marion enlists non-phenomenality in the service of phenomenality, while Derrida thinks that phenomenality tends to nullify the gift itself and that the pure gift requires non-phenomenality. The difference between the views is brought out by observing that, from Derrida's point of view, none of the examples of the reductions Marion gives in the roundtable, the "Outline," and *Etant donné* escapes the notion of economy or exchange in Derrida's sense. This is true precisely because and to the extent that the gifts Marion describes must necessarily retain *some measure* of consciousness, iden-tifiability, phenomenality, and manifestness, which are poison to the gift for Derrida.

(1) If I give something to my enemy, who rejects it, still, to the extent that

I am conscious of this operation of giving to an ungrateful (or anonymous) recipient, I will congratulate myself all the more vigorously for practicing an even higher and more selfless generosity, one which gives so purely as to do so without being thanked by, and can even endure being despised by, the recipient.

(2) If I leave my children or favorite charity an inheritance in my will, so that by the time the gift is received, the giver is gone, I will have thanked myself time and again for providing such a generous will that will ensure my happy memory. I may even have left precise instructions about where I wish them to place my statue or hang my picture in order best to preserve my blessed memory, while they in turn will feel eternally grateful (I hope)!

(3) A gift without something given: When a chief of state is sworn in, he is given no *thing*, except perhaps for a sheet of paper, a handshake, and some secret codes. But for Derrida, the institutional and structural *power* a chief executive is given is massive and obtrusively present and easily identifiable, which is why it repays with such enormous gratification the enormous egos of the people who seek high office. In order to shield the gift from being and presence, Marion is forced to trade on a positivistic sense of the gift, a pure spatio-temporal physical object (which is the gift that is suspended), which he calls the "physical counterpart" of the *real* gift, which is not suspended at all, thus undoing the example, which is supposed to represent the suspending of the gift. The reduction *to* the gift and the reduction *of* the gift trade on equivocal senses of gift and on equivocal senses of reduction. The suspension *of* the gift works only if we do not suspend the real gift but a stand-in which, as it were, takes the hit for the genuine gift. At this point, contrary to the earlier analysis (the reduction *to* the gift), Marion must refuse to admit *invisible* moral, symbolic, institutional structures like power, friendship, loyalty, preferences, or even time as "gifts," since they are not "present" as spatio-temporal physical objects. If I give you my loyalty or my time, I am not giving you any*thing*, i.e., any *object, thing,* or *being.* That positivistic blocking of the gift as *visible* thing allows the *phenomenology of the unapparent* to swing into action, allowing the *invisible* "horizon of givenness" to appear or "hyper-appear." But, from Derrida's point of view, a gift is real and has phenomenal presence, whether it is visible or invisible. Moral or symbolic gifts are every bit as "real," indeed even more real, *hyper-real* or *hyper-present.* They are, from Husserl's point of view, of no less interest (as ideal objects) to phenomenology and, from Derrida's point of view, no less *trapped by economy.* Moral gifts produce moral debts. It is not being visible or invisible that matters for Derrida, but being *identifiable* or *not identifiable.* Invisible moral gifts, no less than physical gifts, are identifiable as gifts and thus belong to the economy of exchange for Derrida (DM, 85–87/GD, 89–91). To give one's loyalty or one's time is for Marion a groundless "gift" without exchange and beyond visible presence and effective causality, outside the principle of reason. But for Derrida such a gift is no less *debt-ridden*, no less up to its ears in identity, debt, grounds, and reasons of an invisible, moral, and symbolic character.

### Economy and Debt

At this point it becomes clear that Marion and Derrida have very different conceptions of just what constitutes an "economy" of the gift, and that, whatever his dispute with the "metaphysics of presence," Marion is willing to settle for a *higher* economy, just so long as this economy that is not implicated in causality, in causal agents and effects. Marion does not dispute the contention that from the very moment that any of the three elements of the gift appear the *movement of debt* is set in motion. That does not present a problem to Marion because debt enters into the very *definition of the gift* for him—"donability," he says, means the duty (*devoir*) to give—while for Derrida debt is poison to the gift, *Vergiftung*, and the very *definition of economy*, which annuls the gift. For Marion to escape economy it is enough to give a non-objectivistic phenomenological description of the gift outside the *chain of the four causes*, while for Derrida the defining feature of an economy of exchange is the link or *chain between credit and debt*, even if the chain (*catena, cadeau*) is composed of invisible-moral links, not causal or objectivistic ones.[34] Marion's concerns are broadly Husserlian and Heideggerian, to avoid causal and objectivistic thinking, whereas Derrida has the *Genealogy of Morals* in mind. Derrida is worried about the contamination of *credere*, faith in the gift, by credit, which makes the gift a medium of exchange and so destroys its credibility as a gift, even and especially in celestial matters, which is the point of the analysis in the last chapter of *The Gift of Death*. Marion is worrying about causality, Derrida about credit.

While we were all grateful for a profound and genial discussion, the roundtable, alas, could not go forever and they could not discuss everything. But had the time of the gift of this discussion been greater, the one point that I would like to have heard next addressed is just this question of debt. For that, in my view, is central to the difference between Marion and Derrida. Marion and Derrida share very similar views of the "impossible," at least here, in the roundtable, and Marion's notion of what I called a partial blackout of the gift is comparable to Derrida's more severe notion that *any* presence of the gift draws it into an economy of exchange. But what most deeply divides Marion and Derrida, and the reason why any appearance at all of the gift, however partial, catches it up in economy for Derrida while not posing any problem of economy to Marion, is the appearance of debt. Even on this point, there is not total disagreement. Derrida and Marion share the view that the gift shatters the narcissism of the giver—and, as Marion points out, of the recipient, too. For even as the gift requires the donor to give up his greed, it also requires the recipient to give up his pride and independence, to be humble enough to accept. As Derrida says, and Marion seems to agree, where there are subjects there are only degrees of narcissism (*PdS*, 212–13/*Points*, 199) so the true gift must come after the subject.[35] But while both want to break up narcissism, they go about this in different ways. For Marion, narcissism is shattered by the recognition of a duty to give and of a debt of gratitude, while for Derrida the breakup of narcissism is a matter of *responsibility without duty or debt*. Is this a merely verbal difference or a substantive one?

For Derrida, a duty and obligation are inconsistent with the gift. If it is a gift, I am not obliged to do it; if it is an obligation, I am not making a gift. A duty is finite, rule-governed, coercive, and is measured by the law, whereas the gift is the unreserved affirmation of the other, of justice, and as such is unlimited. A duty should be paid off or discharged, whereas gifts should be multiplied. One can never give enough gifts, but it is absurd to say that we can never incur enough debt. Debts are destructive and we need to learn to manage debt. It would be more or less impolite to be polite out of duty, more or less unfriendly to be friendly out of duty (*Passions*, 22–23/ON, 8), and more or less ungiving to give a gift out of duty. I cannot be coerced to give or told to give according to a rule. If I am obliged to give a tithe, I am not giving but doing my duty, paying my fair share. What lies behind the gift for Derrida is not rule, measure, or coercion but "unlimited donatative affirmation" (*affirmation donatraice illimitée*). "*Il faut aller au-delà du devoir*," Derrida writes (*Passions*, 75 n.3/ON, 133). There is a kind of need or want or desire (*il faut*) to *exceed duty*, and if we can somehow save the notion of duty, for Derrida, then it must be a duty *without debt*. For the very idea of a gift, saving the gift, depends upon exceeding duty. A gift is everything except (*sauf*) duty and debt. The very idea of a gift involves not the duty to give but giving beyond duty. The gift is precisely what I am *not duty-bound to give*. Duty or debt is the necessary horizon of the gift, but only in the sense that the gift is what shatters or tears that horizon. Duty is what the gift requires—in order for its excess to have something to exceed. Otherwise the gift is not an excess but a way of measuring up to a standard. The excess of the saint makes no sense unless it exceeds debt and duty, unless it goes beyond what one is required to do, which is as far as the rest of us, who are not saints, ever get.

From Derrida's point of view, instead of immersing the gift in the element of donation, Marion sinks it in debt. Thus Derrida would want to know why, on Marion's own terms, by defining the gift in terms of duty, by confining it to the terms of duty, he has not introduced an *alien* horizon, a substance foreign to the terms of donation, which sends the gift tumbling back, not into causality, to be sure, but into the wider sphere of influence of the "principle of sufficient reason." For just as causality holds sway over objects or beings as the highest principle of speculative reason, so debt and duty hold sway over actions as the highest principle of practical reason. Duty and debt are the sufficient reasons we do things in the sphere of practical reason, even as causes are the sufficient reasons things happen in nature. But the gift must be like the rose, without why. A debt represents a disorder—and *ratio* comes from *reor*, arranging or ordering—a disequilibrium in the sphere of practical reason that doing one's duty corrects; a debt is an account that is out of balance which the discharge of duty restores. Doing one's duty makes sense, is rational, but a gift is an expenditure without reserve that no one can understand. Duty is a universal rational principle that can be promulgated and mandated, whereas a mandated gift is called extortion, a "payoff." When we are under a duty to give, when our boss asks for a "contribution" to the charitable cause chaired by his wife, we all understand that this is not a gift but a way of keeping one's job. That is why, from Derrida's point of view, there is nothing paradoxical about the ultimate paradox that Marion mentions: visiting upon your enemy an unpayable debt. Nothing makes more sense! It is one of the first principles *per se nota* of Wall Street capitalism. One can always explain oneself and give a reason when we are doing our duty and paying off a debt. But the knight of infinite giving suspends the principle of reason in a moment of madness and gives a gift, affirms the other, unlimitedly. *Il faut*, there is a need, a desire, a dream, to give donatively, not dutifully, out of love, not from a sense of debt. We do not dream of debts but of gifts; debts are matters for nightmares, not dreams. We are indeed addicted, *adonné*, to the gift, intoxicated by its divine madness, but we are not duty-bound to be addicted.

Marion would respond that we are indebted not to another donor but to *donation* itself, to the horizon of givenness by whose momentum giver and donee are carried along. By giving ourselves to giving, to the horizon of giving, we are carried by the life of *donation* to which we owe all. But that, from Derrida's point of view, would only seem to accentuate and intensify what is destructive about debt. It not only turns the gift (*le don*) to poison, but poisons *la donation*, the horizon of givenness itself. It is trouble enough to owe an identifiable debt to an identifiable creditor, but to situate the whole of life within an horizon of insoluble debt to an anonymous donor seems even worse. The gift ought to lift us up, not flatten and depress us. The debt mourns, but the gift pipes. It is very beautiful to say that we want to "give in" to the gift, to the horizon or the gifting of the gift, and displace the subjectivity of donor-caused subjects and recipient-produced subjects. But the whole (very Heideggerian) idea seems to be poisoned, from Derrida's point of view, if this over-arching *donation* or *Gegebenheit* is painted as a scene of boundless debt, leaving the recipient to sigh in a state of diffused and anonymous debt, instead of rejoicing in the state of grace. If we have been loved and given gifts, we ought not to be plunged into a horizon of infinite insolvent debt. For the Derrida of *The Gift of Death*, Marion plays into the hands of Nietzsche's barb about Christianity's *Geniestreich*, its stroke of genius. *Cur deus homo?* Because God must be paid what God is owed, and God wants blood, infinitely precious blood, to pay off an infinite, incalculable debt, to spill sacred sacrificial blood to offset the absolute insolvency of the sinner. It seems as if God saw everything He made and said that it was guilty and in insolvent debt, which calls for a blood economy. Who could believe that, Derrida asks with Nietzsche? (DM, 106–107/GD, 114–115) For a Derridean theology, it would seem that the God of gifts, the gift of God, and the gift of God in Jesus are to be thought not in terms of insolvent debt but in terms of giving without debt and in forgiving what debts accumulate (forgiveness is an issue that Derrida has recently been addressing in his lectures). Debts are for forgiving, not accumulating. According to the New Testament, the only calculation forgiving allows is that one should forgive seven times a day, and seventy times seven, that is to say, innumerably, countlessly, incalculably. That would seem to be, from Derrida's point of view, the real *Geniestreich* of Jesus.

### Khora and Confusion

At the end of this discussion, Richard Kearney, who has pressed the discussants throughout about the denominational distance that religion and theology create between Marion and Derrida, poses a question that is also central to their differences: How does each thinker address the element of incomprehensibility, of terror and stupor, of the monstrous, the *mysterium fascinans*, of a "wholly other" which one cannot simply domesticate and make one's own?

Marion responds to Kearney's question by invoking, quite like Derrida, a positive or productive conception of *the impossible:* If modernity and its metaphysics are constituted by the search for the possible and the conditions of possibility, then he is interested in the impossible, in what shatters the limits of possible experience in the pedestrian or quotidian sense, in what exceeds the expectations of metaphysics and confounds what metaphysics calls possible. Marion seeks a certain rendering, a phenomenological rendering, of this experience of the impossible, an attempt, as Augustine said, "incomprehensively to comprehend the incomprehensible," whose first step is to "deconstruct" the philosophical concepts that prohibit such an experience, and on this point, mystical theology and deconstruction are in agreement ("On the Gift," p. 74). Such an experience is to be described in terms of "the 'counter-experience' of bedazzlement, of astonishment or *Bewunderung*," of something we can see but cannot "designate as an object or a being," as "an event that we cannot comprehend." These counter-experiences are not here confined by Marion to strictly mystical experiences of God's givenness but are said to range over the most vivid and intense, the most important and indefinable experiences in our lives. Thus the scope of the "saturated phenomena" is wider than we might think. It is said to include birth and death, sickness and health, pleasure and pain, the work of art, the experience of the other person, in short, whatever cannot be neatly packed within the borders of an "object" or a "being."[36]

For Derrida, on the other hand, Kearney's question leads into another direction, not the dazzling excess of saturating givenness beyond Being, but the diffusiveness of *khora* below being and knowledge (*Timaeus*, 50b–52c). The difference between Marion and Derrida is at least partly defined in terms of the Platonic difference between *agathon* and *khora*. Kearney's question thus refers back to what Derrida calls in "How Not to Speak: Denials," "the *two* movements or *two* tropics of negativity" (*Psy.*, 563/DNT, 101), the symmetry and the ultimate undecidability between which—each is in its own distinctly different way incomprehensible and without being or presence—is a crucial element in Derrida's work.

The first movement or tropic follows the path of the *epekeina tes ousias,* the noble high road beyond being, knowledge and essence to the *agathon,* the name beyond every name, historically instantiated in the confluence of Christianity and Neoplatonism. That path of ascent, the mind's ascent to God, beyond being and beings, is the sense of the *sans* in Marion's *Dieu sans l'être.* Derrida on the other hand is headed out for a desert *sans,* following the scent of the second path, attempting to think the less prestigious, less reputable name *beneath* every name, not *agathon* but *khora,* which is not *hyper*-given but *hypo*-given, so that his *sans* is somewhat more at a loss to speak for itself. Historically, the *khora* refers to space in which the Demiurge inscribes the sensible likeness of the Forms in Plato's *Timaeus.* In several texts Derrida describes the "two voices" in which the *khora* is described by Plato. The one voice tries to reappropriate it as a philosopheme, either as a philosophical concept or as a metaphor, which allows it to be treated as a prototype of prime matter (Aristotle) or extension (Descartes). In the other voice, it is left to its dark, nameless, formless self, to its selfless *sans,* neither myth nor logos, eluding "all anthropo-theo-logical schemes, all history, all revelation, all truth" (*Khora,* 92/ON, 124), and that is the voice that interests Derrida. The *agathon* is the invisible splendor that permeates and animates the visible appearances, the uncontainable Beauty that shines through appearances in the *Symposium,* forming the majestic and dazzling setting of Marion's phenomenology of the unapparent, of the saturating phenomenon, which bedazzles us with its splendor. The *khora,* neither visible thing nor invisible form, lacks all such splendor, majesty, prestige, and beauty.

In the roundtable, Derrida says the *khora* even sinks below the level of history or historicization, humanization, anthropo-theologization. He means this, not in the sense that the *Timaeus* is not an historical document or that Plato's notion of *khora* is not locatable in the history of ideas, but in the sense that history too is something that is also, like the forms, inscribed in what Derrida means by *khora. Khora* is not an historical desert—it is not, e.g., the biblical desert—but the "desert in the desert" ("On the Gift," p. 76). *Khora* is a place of absolute "resistance" or "heterogeneity" to the formed structures, the constituted forms of history and culture, of the Western and non-Western, of philosophy and theology, of reason and revelation, of (religious) revelation (*Offenbarung*) and (Heideggerian) openness (*Offenbarkeit*), of Christianity, Judaism, or Islam. But this "non-something" is nothing to be taken lightly:

> It is also a place of non-gift which makes the gift possible by resisting it. ... The *khora* does not desire anything, does not give anything. It is what makes taking place or an event possible. But the *khora* does not happen, does not give, does not desire. It is a spacing and absolutely indifferent. (RT, 34)

*Khora*, Derrida says elsewhere, is a kind of surname for *différance* (*Khôra*, 95/ ON, 126), a kind of scriptorium for the inevitable inscriptions which constitute our institutions and structures, beliefs and practices, texts and deeds. "Deconstruction," if this is still the best word for what Derrida is up to, is an analysis of the contingency or fragility of what is thus inscribed in the "spacing" of *différance* or *khora*, of its historical, cultural, social, gendered, political formations, an analysis of how such formations are "forged" or built up, and how they can be built down or rebuilt. *Khora* does not give; it is a place of the non-gift, Derrida says. If anything, it un-gives, as the worm in the heart, the deconstructibility of every construction, the non-gift in the heart of the gift. It is a not a beneficent father or mother, not a giver of all good gifts, and so it is better addressed by the French *il y a* than the more seductive German *es gibt*: not "it gives," for *khora* does not give, but "it has (us), there," it takes place (*il a lieu*), "ashes there are there" (*il y a là cendres*). As a place of inscription, it is a condition of possibility; but as the disjointedness of spacing, it is a condition that also makes impossible, that allows what is built up to harbor its own unbuilding, its own deconstructibility.

This desert *khora* is I think a *saving* element in Derrida's thought, not a disheartening one, precisely because it blocks the way to fixing or determining in some unrevisable way what is given. *Khora* forces us to make our way by *faith*, construing shadowy figures which may turn out to be otherwise, beginning where we are in the midst of a web of institutions, structures, languages, and traditions. By virtue of *khora* we are forced to do the best we can, making our way by a kind of radical hermeneutics. That is not such a bad theology at all, but a rather sober theology of faith, for after all, as Kierkegaard (that master hermeneut of faith) said, there is something pagan about thinking the divinity of Jesus is written all over him, that it is *given*. But if Marion is willing to pass his forty days in this desert *khora*, this must also be in the interest of a theology of *Herrlichkeit*. He has his doubts about giving *différance* too much play. For Derrida, we must give *différance* its due, for it is in and through *différance* that we do what we have to do, which is always liable to come undone and unstuck, which for Derrida is why we are always work our works by faith and desire, by doing the truth. The fragility of our structures, the desert emptiness of our signifiers, are such stuff (*hyperstasis*) as faith is made of, our faith in what is to come, and this very desertification is the condition of keeping faith and hope and desire alive.

But, Derrida says, "I would like to translate the experience of this impossibility into what we call ethics or politics" ("On the Gift," p. 77). Now if ethics and politics have been traditionally reserved for the first way, if in Plato the just *polis* is the work of the *agathon*, in deconstruction ethics and politics are, if not the work of *khora*, since *khora* does not work, at least works always to be worked in *khora*, forced to cope with *khora*. That is because the demonstration of the contingency and deconstructibilty of our present institutions and structures is *always* undertaken messianically, with an eye to, and with a hope for, what is *to come, à venir.* In this Derridean "Re-public," justice does not sit serenely beyond being, essence, and time, at the top of a steep ascent, displaying its eternal pattern for mortals to mime, or, like a flood of givenness, swamp our poor, defenseless conceptions. Rather, like the Messiah, justice is always to come. Derrida is always worried that when someone lays claim to being laid claim to by a higher *hyperousios*, when they declare that they are called or laid claim to by a higher something or other, this higher, celestial hierarchy is liable to become a political one (*Psy.*, 91n/DNT, 134 n.9). The deconstructibility of every structure, the *khora* that infiltrates or un-forms every historical language and formation, keeps the future open, robs the present of too great an authority or prestige, prevents any current structure or event from declaring itself just, prevents the present order from presenting itself as justice itself. This is said not out of despair or nihilism, but just in order to let justice come, to let the gift come.

### Conclusion: Coming (Again)

For Marion, the destruction or deconstruction of every containing structure is undertaken just in order to prepare the way for a reduction to a pure and saturating givenness. "Modernity" and "subjectivity," "metaphysics" and "onto-theologic," are for him so many idols or impediments, so many humanly constructed barriers meant to contain, constrain, and cut off givenness, so many walls of presence that are to be rushed by *la donation*. "Deconstruction," if this word from a former professor at the Ecole Normale Supérieure is something that he can use at all, is a way to break down those walls, to break open those subjective or conceptual limits, a way to force these transcendental conditions to give way, like the walls of Jericho, to overfull transcendence, a way to let givenness give itself from itself in uncontainable overflow. For Marion, the Messiah has already come, hypergivenness has already overtaken us, and it is a question of having the eyes to see and the ears to hear and the songs to sing about what has already happened.

Derrida, on the other hand, seems a little intimidated by hyper-phenomenology, hypergivenness, and saturated phenomena. He wants to keep a safe distance from too much of this "hype," not only from a concern about the limits of phenomenology, but also because he is very wary of its politics. As a slightly black Algerian Jew, a *pied noir* who is always being made more welcome *elsewhere*, he is worried about anything with too much power, prestige, or authority. That is why the *khora*, as austere and ankhoral, as comfortless and desertifying as it is, gives him a certain cold comfort. For him the structure of *sans* and *au-delà*, of the "without" and the "beyond," which he also dearly loves, has to do not with *hypergivenness* but with *never-givenness*, with a messianic expectation of what is structurally to come. Deconstruction does not turn on a hypergivenness, where faith is itself a higher form of seeing, but on a faith, a hope, a love—very theological virtues!—a hope, a sigh, a dream, for what is not yet and can never be given. As Jacques says to Jackie, " . . . you have spent your whole life inviting calling promising, hoping sighing dreaming, convoking invoking provoking" (*Circon.*, 290–91/*Circum.*, 314).

Were the Messiah ever to show up, ever to pitch his tent among us in the flesh, in short, ever to be *given*, Marion would take this as be an event of excess and joy, a matter for prayerful praise—*Hallelujah*—whereas Derrida, approaching him cautiously, would ask, "When will you come?"

(Again.)

## NOTES

1. This chapter takes as its principal "texts" the exchange between Jacques Derrida and Jean-Luc Marion on the questions of God and the gift in the first two chapters of this volume. It was not presented at the Villanova conference.

2. To which might be added a third possibility (for it may not be a matter of choosing between these first two), viz., the figure of a Messiah who will come again, who even though he has come, perhaps even repeatedly, is not given now and so must come again.

3. See Derrida, *Memoirs of the Blind: The Self-Portrait and Other Ruins,* trans. Pascale-Anne Brault and Michael Naas (Chicago: University of Chicago Press, 1993); for a commentary, see Caputo, *The Prayers and Tears of Jacques Derrida: Religion without Religion* (Bloomington: Indiana University Press, 1997), 308–29. This work also provides the details of my approach to Derrida.

4. Psy.: *Psyché: Inventions de l'autre* (Paris: Galilée, 1987). HAS: "How to Avoid Speaking: Denials," in *Derrida and Negative Theology,* trans. Ken Frieden, ed. Howard Coward and Toby Foshay (Albany: SUNY Press, 1992), 73–142.

5. *Sauf: Sauf le nom* (Paris: Galilée, 1993) (ON: *On the Name,* ed. Thomas Dutoit [Stanford: Stanford University Press, 1995]).

6. DM: "Donner la mort" in *L'Éthique du don: Jacques Derrida et la pensée du don* (Paris: Métailié-Transition, 1992) (GD: *The Gift of Death,* trans. David Wills [Chicago: University of Chicago Press, 1995]).

7. For background on this issue, see Caputo, *Prayers and Tears,* 1–68.

8. ED: *Ecriture et la différence* (Paris: Editions de Seuil) (WD: *Writing and Difference,* trans. Alan Bass [Chicago: University of Chicago Press, 1978]).

9. Far from being the inalterable fate of theology, or mystical theology, Marion contends, the "metaphysics of presence" is actually a heresy. True theology is always a "theology of absence," not a metaphysics of presence. When the Arians claimed that God is knowable and revealed by the names God is given, they were condemned. Of course, Derrida would be just as much worried over this inclination to exclude or "condemn." Does not this condemnation of presence itself imply a desire for presence, for the self-presence of an authoritative and self-gathering *ekklesia?* Does it not imply a politics of presence, an onto-theo-politics, a policing operation from which theology does not sufficiently distance itself? In one of its voices, Derrida says, mystical theology tries to be a little too authoritative about the secret, to say that nothing or no one can oppose this because mystical theology speaks from the heart of the secret as from the heart of truth and of hyper-fulfillment (*Sauf,* 77–78/ON, 66–67). It is always the other

voice, the one that Derrida calls that of "hypercritique," where nothing is assured, neither philosophy nor theology, that interests Derrida more. See Jean-Luc Marion, *God without Being*, trans. Thomas Carlson (Chicago: University of Chicago Press, 1991), 153, where Marion sides with the power of the bishop to enforce the law if a theologian breaks with the consensus.

10. See Derrida, *Speech and Phenomena and Other Essays on Husserl's Theory of Signs*, trans. David Allison (Evanston, Ill.: Northwestern University Press, 1973), 88–104. See the Introduction to the present volume, section I. For a discussion of the relevant texts and the details of this complicated issue, see John D. Caputo, *Radical Hermeneutics: Repetition, Deconstruction, and the Hermeneutic Project* (Bloomington: Indiana University Press, 1987), 120–52.

11. See, e.g., Marion's somewhat unsympathetic account of Derrida, early on, on the "bottomless chessboard" in *L'idole et la distance* (Paris: Grasset, 1977), §18.

12. On this issue, in which Marion demonstrates the need for revealed "faith" even with so much phenomenological givenness, see "Métaphysique et phénoménologie: Une relève pour la théologie," *Bulletin de Littérature ecclésiastique* 94, no. 2 (1993): 189–206 ("Metaphysics and Phenomenology: A Relief for Theology," trans. Thomas A. Carlson, *Critical Inquiry* 20, no. 4 [1994]: 572–91).

13. Whatever his disagreements with Marion and Levinas, that is also pretty much what Phillip Blond means by postmodernism in his—shall we say?—lively "Introduction" to *Post-Secular Philosophy*, where Blond argues for a "theological realism" that involves a higher perception, allowing God somehow to make an appearance in the world after the blinders of modernism are lifted. Phillip Blond, "Introduction: Theology before Philosophy," *Post-Secular Philosophy: Between Philosophy and Theology*, ed. Phillip Blond (New York and London: Routledge, 1998), 1–66.

14. In his response to Marion's paper, Derrida goes to some length to document the attention he has paid to the third way. It is not something he missed because of a predilection for binary oppositions!

15. Circon: "Circonfession: Cinquante-neuf périodes et périphrases," in Geoffrey Bennington and Jacques Derrida, *Jacques Derrida* (Paris: Editions du Seuil, 1991) (Circum.: "Circumfession," in Geoffrey Bennington and Jacques Derrida, *Jacques Derrida* [Chicago: University of Chicago Press, 1991]).

16. See Derrida, *Psyché*, 11–62 ("Psyche: Inventions of the Other," trans. Catherine Porter, in *Reading de Man Reading*, ed. Lindsay Waters and Wlad Godzich [Minneapolis: University of Minnesota Press, 1989], 25–65).

17. *Pass: Passions* (Paris: Galilée, 1993) ("Passions: 'An Oblique Offering,'" trans. David Wood, in ON, 3–31).

18. Trans. George Collins (New York: Verso, 1997), 46 n.14. For more on this passage, and for a fuller commentary on the distinction between the messianic and the concrete messianisms, see *Deconstruction in a Nutshell: A Conversation with Jacques Derrida*, ed. John D. Caputo (New York: Fordham University Press, 1997), 24–25, 156–80, and Caputo, *Prayers and Tears*, 117–59.

19. This mention of the justice to come points to another problematic that is quite obscured by Marion, or at least by the confrontation of Derrida with Marion, one that I have developed at length in *The Prayers and Tears of Jacques Derrida*, that Derrida's discourse about the name of God has to do with prophetic justice, not Christian Neoplatonism. The name of God for Derrida has a prophetic, not a mystical, force,

and is more Jewish than Christian, more religious than theological, more concerned with the ethico-politics of hospitality than with mystical or negative theology.

20. Personal communication. See *Etant donné*, 128–29.

21. That is the title of one of Marion's earliest works, in which Marion clearly prefers to stand with the logic of with and to do without the logic of sans. Jean-Luc Marion and Alain de Benoist, *Avec ou sans Dieu?* (Paris: Editions Beauchesne, 1970). The text is a debate that Marion engaged in with Benoist.

22. Jean-Luc Marion, Esq.: "Esquisse d'un concept phénoménologique du don," *Filosophia della revelatione*, ed. M. Olivetti 72 (1994): 75–94.

23. While Marion wants to translate donation into English as "givenness," because he is himself translating the German *Gegebenheit*, "givenness" does not always work. Sometimes the neologism "gifting" captures his sense, and sometimes the transliteration "donation" itself.

24. Marcel Mauss, *The Gift: The Form and Reason for Exchange in Archaic Societies*, trans. W. D. Halls (New York: Norton, 1990), 10–11.

25. *Etant donné*, §§9–11.

26. Levinas says that the obligation to the other is a debt that increases the more it is repaid. Emmanuel Levinas, *Autrement qu'être ou au-delà de l'essence* (The Hague: Nijhoff, 1974), 14 (*Otherwise Than Being or Beyond Essence*, trans. Alphonso Lingis [The Hague: Nijhoff, 1981], 12).

27. The only possible escape Derrida allows himself in *Given Time*, according to Marion, is to say that sometimes it is not only a gift-object that is given and made present, but its "conditions" (life, time). But that represents only a modest improvement, Marion contends, because a "condition" is still a metaphysical and economic notion (Esq., 82).

28. It is the contention of Dominique Janicaud, who objects to a theological hijacking of phenomenology, that in Marion (and Levinas), this phenomenology of the unapparent is a way of smuggling the invisible transcendence of God into the phenomenology of perception. Dominique Janicaud, *Le tournant théologique de la phénoménologie française* (Paris: L'éclat, 1991). An English translation of this work is forthcoming from Fordham University Press. Janicaud has recently expanded this argument in *La Phénoménologie éclatée* (Paris: L'éclat, 1998).

29. I think that Marion depends heavily upon the later Heidegger, despite his critique of Heidegger's second idolatry in *God without Being*. Marion's "gift" looks a lot like the mystical rose that blossoms without why, free from the principle of sufficient reason and all causality, that Heidegger comments upon in *The Principle of Reason*, trans. Reginald Lilly (Bloomington: Indiana University Press, 1990), 32–40.

30. See Robyn Horner in "Rethinking God as Gift: Jean-Luc Marion and a Theology of Donation," a doctoral thesis at Monash University, Australia (1998).

31. See Marion, *L'idole et la distance* (Paris: Grasset, 1977), 15. See Horner, above, for the connection to Balthasar.

32. Hans Urs von Balthasar, *The Glory of the Lord: A Theological Aesthetics*, 7 vols., trans. Erasmo Leiva-Merikakis, et al. (San Francisco: Ignatius Press, 1982–90). See Phillip Blond, "Introduction: Theology before Philosophy," 1–66.

33. Marion, *God without Being*, 95–102.

34. In the debate over mystical theology, Marion narrows down the notion of "metaphysics of presence" to mean what is presented by the concept; in the debate

over the gift, "economy" is narrowed down to mean only a causal-objectivistic relation. These considerably narrower charges are easily eluded by the "givenness" of God in mystical theology, and of the gift in the phenomenology of the gift, but the broader problem of dealing with some sort of pure uninterpreted givenness without the play of *différance* remains.

35. PdS: *Points de suspension: Entretiens*, ed. Elisabeth Weber (Paris: Galilée, 1992). *Points: Points...: Interviews, 1974–94*, ed. Elisabeth Weber, trans. Peggy Kamuf et al. (Stanford: Stanford University Press, 1995).

36. See *Etant donné*, §23 and the final section of "Le Phénomène saturé," in *Phénoménologie et Théologie*, ed. Jean-François Courtine. (Paris: Criterion, 1992) ["The Saturated Phenomenon," trans. Thomas A. Carlson, *Philosophy Today: Studies in Phenomenology and Existential Philosophy*, vol. 21, ed. Leonore Langsdorf and John D. Caputo (Spring 1996): 103–124.]

# eight

# A Deconstruction of Religion

## On Derrida and Rahner

Michael J. Scanlon

Listening to Jacques Derrida at the roundtable discussion celebrating the new doctoral program in philosophy at Villanova University, I was amazed by his enthusiastic presentation of the "messianic" structure of experience as distinct from the "messianisms" of the religions of the Book. I was seated next to the current President of Villanova with whom I had taught theology in Washington for a number of years. We looked at each other with eyebrows arched in astonishment. Derrida had clearly evoked our common "transcendental" memories of the great twentieth-century theologian, Karl Rahner, whose work had shaped the tone and much of the content of the curriculum of the school where we had taught during the seventies and the eighties, the Washington Theological Union. As Derrida elaborated his reflections, I immediately jumped to what were to me intriguing connections between the great "postmodern" deconstructionist and the Roman Catholic "modernizer." In his own way Rahner had deconstructed religion and had developed from his own tradition a "religion without religion." Readers of this volume may find his theological deconstruction interesting.

Of himself Derrida says that he "rightly passes for an atheist." Although he has come to embrace the ethical demands of prophetic Judaism, he does not participate in the religious activity of Judaism or of any of the religious messianisms. For him the messianisms always lead to war. Their universal claims to having the ultimate truth pit them against one another and rule out peaceful coexistence — not to mention collaboration for the good of people. The tragic history of the "encounters" of the messianisms warrants Derrida's distancing. And yet Derrida is a peculiar atheist (all reflective atheists seem to have their own peculiar brand of atheism); maybe, like Ernst Bloch, he is "an atheist for God's sake" in his own way. Theologically literate he certainly is, and he remains quite interested in contemporary theological discussions — for example the tradition of negative theology about which he has spoken and written rather frequently of late. And he is certainly a man of "faith"!

To "modernize" Catholic theology Rahner borrowed Kant's notion of the "transcendental" and Heidegger's existential approach to time. He sought to fulfill the task given by the First Vatican Council to show the intrinsic connections among the many Christian doctrines in relation to human destiny. He was most enthusiastic in his reception of the Second Vatican Council's acceptance of a "hierarchy of doctrines" — a hierarchy to be assessed by relating the many doctrines to "the foundation of Christian faith." That foundation for Rahner is the Self-communication of God to the world. And God is the incomprehensible, ineffable Mystery. Any verbalization of God is infinitely distant from the Reality of God. To use Wittgenstein's distinction, God cannot be said, but God can be shown. To locate the divine showing in the world Rahner recalls Genesis 1:26 (human beings as image and likeness) as focused by Jesus Christ, as the necessary "moment" in the universal divinization of humanity through God's Self-bestowal in the Spirit.

Rahner was very concerned with the contemporary phenomenon of massive atheism. With the weakening of the socio-cultural supports for religion in the ongoing process of secularization he often spoke of believers as constituting a diaspora. He sought to reconcile his central belief in the universal salvific will of God with the many cultural "deaths of God." He deeply respected the atheist "of good faith," and he wanted to understand that good faith as the faith that saves. For him atheists of good faith could be anonymous believers. He had to make this case theologically, for "inculpable atheism" was a novel idea in light of traditional approaches to this issue.

For traditional theology faith was *the* necessary condition for salvation. But faith is the anthropocentric side of the coin whose theocentric side is revelation. If faith was to be understood as a real universal possibility, revelation must somehow be universal. The Catholic tendency to identify faith with "belief" led theologians to attempt to specify the minimal "content" of faith for it to be salutary. That God exists and that God rewards the good and punishes the evil seemed to constitute the minimal content of faith. The theology of Baptism distinguished explicit "water Baptism" from a "Baptism of desire" with the desire either explicit (in the case of the catechumen) or implicit (one would comply with the divine will if one knew it). The missionary movement to the world was energized by what was seen to be the necessity to bring some basic evangelical content to the millions outside the Christian pale. However, the modern expansion of the atheistic "mood" in a world becoming ever more self-consciously "secular" occasioned the need for further theological reflection on atheism. For Karl Rahner and others the traditional notion of "culpable atheism" (that adults could not maintain an atheistic viewpoint for an extended period of time—not to mention for a lifetime—without fault) was in need of significant nuance! For Rahner the question was could people without religion be "religious"?

To universalize revelation Rahner moved away from Vatican I's understanding of "revealed truths" to the contemporary understanding that revelation is the Self-revelation of God.[1] As transcendent Mystery God is immanent in the world. This universal presence is expressed in the biblical metaphor of the divine Spirit, God's "breath" as the world's divine "atmosphere." Never an "item" of experience, this Mystery is somehow "known" by all human beings—for Rahner (as for St. Augustine) God is the presupposition of all knowledge and, therefore, "known" in a preconceptual, athematic way. The religions of the world testify to this experience of "ultimacy" in their various, diverse ways.

To universalize faith Rahner turns to the traditional distinction between doctrinal faith (*fides quae creditur*) and personal faith (*fides qua creditur*). While the value sought by the former is "orthodoxy," the latter signifies "orthopraxy." For Rahner personal faith can be implicit—it can exist without doctrinal faith or "orthodoxy," whose whole purpose is to elucidate "orthopraxy." It would be one's personal response to the unknown Spirit of God, universally present as God's Self-Offer—in this case anonymously accepted as manifested though the person's lifestyle. While religious interpretation is important, in most human lives the experience of the Spirit takes place "in the warp and weft of everyday life, where responsibility, loyalty, love and so on are practiced absolutely, and where ultimately it is a secondary question whether such behavior is accompanied by any expressly religious interpretation."[2]

Jacques Derrida is a man of faith without religion, or, better, without religion in what Rahner would call the "categorical" sense. He embraces the messianic but without the messianisms (Judaism, Christianity, Islam). The latter, he is convinced and not without reason, always lead to war, as their verbal polemics become real *polemos*. For Derrida the messianic expectation is necessary if we are to speak of justice at all, and "deconstruction *is* justice." But what is the relationship between the messianic and the messianisms? In attempting to answer this question Derrida entertains two possibilities. The messianic is the general structure of experience, a "groundless ground" on which there have been revelations (Judaism, Christianity, . . .), so that the messianic becomes the "fundamental ontological" condition of the possibility of these religions. This possibility clearly resonates with Rahner's approach. For Rahner, the a priori is general, universal, transcendental revelation, identical with the presence of the divine Spirit in the world. The world religions are the a posteriori historicizations of this transcendental revelation. Perhaps it was this Rahnerian distinction that enabled the Catholic Church at Vatican Council II to show such a positive attitude toward these religions. Given this approach, the only way forward for religious people is genuine dialogue. Derrida, however, submits another possibility. The events of revelation that constitute the Jewish, Christian, and Islamic traditions are "absolute events, irreducible events which have unveiled this messianicity." With this possibility Derrida claims that these religions would not be "cases" of some religious a priori. These religions are irreducible "singularities," not particulars subsumable under a general category—like transcendental revelation! But without these messianisms we would know nothing about the messianic. For Rahner, of course, this "second possibility" is part of the first possibility—we know nothing of the a priori without the concrete a posteriori. For Derrida these answers remain a serious dilemma, given his deconstructive approach to transcendental thinking.

In response to Derrida's dilemma John Caputo offers the early Heideggarian notion of a "formal indication," a "kind of weak or fragile pointer at the lush complexities of the 'factical' messianisms."[3] Such a pointer does not subsume, enclose, or pre-contain particulars, "but simply points an indicative finger at 'singularities' that are beyond its ken." Thus, the messianic is not a "universal concept" that grasps or includes its particulars. It seems to me that Rahner would find this response congenial, for his "universal" or "transcendental revelation" is also not a concept grasping particulars. For Rahner the "universal" is a Gift, the divine Self-Gift to the world. This is not an epistemological foundationalism but a *theological foundationalism*, which fits nicely with Caputo's insistence that "the facticity or singularity" (of the messianisms) is not "conceived" or "grasped" but "entered into, given in to, by a certain practical or praxical engagement, which means that you can never 'get' it from the outside and you can never 'get into' it except by 'doing' it, *facere veritatem*" (Derrida's Augustinian approach to truth for deconstruction). Getting into or doing it, where *it* is God is only through the *praxis* of faith, hope, love, for God is the *cognoscibile operabile*, knowable only by doing the truth (or, better maybe, "making" the truth by changing the world).[4]

Derrida's religious language is testimony to the end of the secularism of modernity and the old Enlightenment. His new Enlightenment is an ethical retrieval of responsibility, an ethical stance that mediates his "religion without religion." Since religion is a language of hope, Derrida shares with Rahner an orientation to the future, not to the "future present" (the future of the present) but to the ultimate "advent." Both Derrida and Rahner are schooled in biblical eschatology in its prophetic and apocalyptic forms. The ethical Spirit of the prophets was a voice of indictment (Amos 5:18–24) together with a promise for the future, conditioned on the heeding of the indictment—a new exodus, a new covenant, a new David (a Messiah) to come in some "future present." By 200 B.C.E. this new act of salvation from God had not occurred, and it seemed more and more implausible, given Judaism's political weakness. By the time we reach the author of the book of Daniel a sense of despair has taken over, and out of this despair a new form of eschatology emerges, apocalypticism. This apocalyptic eschatology can be understood as the child of prophecy, prophecy in a new key, a sober key of hope against hope. The apocalyptic seer looks forward to a future which is no longer a "future present." It is rather an "Absolute Future," a future beyond the temporal movement of history as we know it. It is the future *of history*, rather than future history.

It is this apocalyptic (or "impossible") future that Derrida and Rahner both embrace, Derrida in the name of deconstruction, Rahner in the name of Christian hope. For Rahner God is the "Absolute Future," and Derrida's de-sertified religion requires the same impossible future. Derrida's religious mo-tifs—the promise, the democracy to come, justice, the gift, God—are all writ-ten under the sign of apocalyptic expectation. Derrida's prayer is "Come," "*Viens.*" As with all forms of apocalyptic, there is a "not yet," a waiting. But this waiting cannot mean procrastination. Justice, for instance, cannot wait. Jus-tice, like truth, must be done now even as we know that full justice will always be "not yet." Justice is neither a Platonic form nor a Kantian regulative idea— it is the impossible always ahead. The power of this apocalyptic justice is its demand for singular anticipations, all of them deficient, but all of them necessary. Justice is the Messiah who is always *venturum*, for if the Messiah were to come now or tomorrow, it would all be over. Derrida wants the Mes-siah to come, but he wants that coming to be infinitely postponed, like death.

For all their differences Derrida, the Jew who rightly passes for an atheist, and Rahner, the mystical-prophetic theologian who makes room for atheists, are both convinced that "faith is necessary." Both are consumed by a passion for the gift, the impossible gift—the Gift we cannot "get."

Rahner's form of messianism is the good news that God gives God away to the world. God is love, and love is Self-donation to the other. Derrida's affec-tion for his fellow countryman, Augustine, moved him when Augustine was quoted at the Conference on Religion and Postmodernism, *Imo quantus Deus est qui dat Deum* (Indeed, how much must he who gives God be God).[5] This "God who gives God" (a God associated in Derrida's faith with the promise, justice, the democracy to come) cannot *not* be evocative for our philosopher of deconstruction.

In the meantime Derrida has put his own spin on traditional God-talk. Not only is God "Wholly Other," but "every other is wholly other" (*tout autre est tout autre*). This radical alterity is also at the center of Rahner's religion in which love of God *is* love of neighbor. The Augustinian scholar Johannes van Bavel claims that in his theology of love Karl Rahner "closely follows Augus-tine's line of thought."[6] Van Bavel discovered an evolution in Augustine's thought wherein he moved from asserting a strong distinction between love of God and love of neighbor to an insistence on the practical primacy of love of neighbor. Indeed, in 407 C.E. Augustine went so far as to make a "daring inversion" of I John 4:8 and 16, "God is love" into "Love is God."[7] Among the far-reaching consequences of Augustine's inversion van Bavel mentions two: The first is that love is so much of one piece that it cannot be split up (it does not matter where our love begins, from God, from Christ, from neighbor, the outcome will always be the same); and the second is that love for neighbor is the absolute condition for love of God. This theology of love is not reductionist. Creator and creature are not identified. It is based on a radical interpretation of the Incarnation.

Derrida's religion is ethically mediated. Central to deconstruction is responsibility for the other. This alterity is a further connection between Derrida and his fellow countryman, Augustine, who is echoed in Karl Rahner. The latter two are representatives of a messianism which may justify a hopeful conclusion to this short essay. Maybe the messianisms are not necessarily violent.[8] The orientation of the messianic is toward an impossible future of hope. At their best the messianisms offer compelling visions of future peace and justice in their stories of God. It seems that our current post-secular mood might open us once again to messianisms more faithful to the messianic.

## NOTES

1. For Rahner's summary of the notion of revelation cf. *Foundations of Christian Faith,* trans. William Dych (New York: Seabury Press, 1978), 170–75.

2. Karl Rahner, *The Spirit in the Church,* trans. John Griffiths (New York: The Seabury Press, 1979), 27.

3. Cf. John Caputo, *Deconstruction in a Nutshell: A Conversation with Jacques Derrida* (New York: Fordham University Press, 1997), 177–78.

4. On the portrayal of God as the *cognoscibile operabile* (the "doable knowable"), as the object of knowledge that can be reached only by *praxis,* in Duns Scotus cf. Nicholas Lobkowicz, *Theory and Practice: History of a Concept from Aristotle to Marx* (Lanham, Md.: University Press of America, 1967), 74.

5. *The Works of Saint Augustine: A Translation for the 21st Century.* The Trinity. Part I, vol. 5, trans. Edmund Hill, ed. John Rotelle (New York: New City Press, 1991), 431 (26, 46).

6. Johannes van Bavel, "The Double Face of Love in Augustine," *Louvain Studies* 12 (1987): 121.

7. Ibid., 120.

8. For a lucid presentation of Derrida's thought on violence and religion cf. James K. A. Smith, "Determined Violence: Derrida's Structural Religion," *The Journal of Religion* 78, no. 2 (April 1998): 197–212. Smith, a doctoral student at Villanova University, concludes his study with a nice distinction between "the historical production of violence" and "the necessary production of violence" (211).

# Betting on Vegas

Mark C. Taylor

So what's the deal? Why are so many people, corporations, institutions, even governments betting on Vegas? What's its draw? What's at stake?

Las Vegas is the fastest growing city in the United States. The most popular retirement destination in the country, Vegas is home to eleven out of the twelve largest hotels in the *world*—and several bigger ones are being built at this very moment. From a western outpost of merely 4,500 settlers in 1945, to a city of one and a half million, this most unlikely oasis is a postwar phenomenon of unprecedented proportions. Why was Vegas created? How is its explosive growth to be explained? What does this city in the desert tell us about our past, present, and future?

I won't delay or defer—at least not yet. No, I'll put my cards on the table: My wager is that you cannot understand America today unless you understand Las Vegas; and if you cannot understand America, you cannot comprehend contemporary culture and the future it opens and/or closes. Nothing seems more obvious, more straightforward, more superficial than Vegas. And yet, appearances are deceptive—always deceptive. To understand Vegas, if, indeed, Vegas can be understood, you must not be dazzled by neon and overwhelmed by the din of slots. Vegas is never what it seems; that's its draw, or one of its draws. It revels in the unlikely, the implausible, even the impossible. In the city where everything seems possible, what is (the) impossible? Perhaps religion. What, after all, is more implausible than religion in Las Vegas? There are, of course, countless chapels, chapels that look like fast-food drive-thrus. But these tasteless one-stop wedding chapels, where ministers, priests, and rabbis give way to members of the world-renowned "Flying Elvises," seem to be more a parody or even a denial of religious beliefs and rituals. Negation and affirmation, however, can never be completely separated. In ways that are not immediately obvious, Las Vegas is a *religious* phenomenon—perhaps one of the most important religious phenomena in the United States. Contrary to expectation, what begins in Puritan New England reaches to a certain closure in the hot yet verdant sands of the Nevada desert. Las Vegas is where the death of God is staged as the spectacle of the Kingdom of God on earth. The stakes of Vegas, therefore, are higher—considerably higher—than even the biggest tunas realize.

Does all of this seem like an impossible bet? Do the cards seem stacked against such an implausible reading of the "city of sin"? Is the spectacle before you a put-on—yet another gesture of tiresome postmodern irony under the guise of exhausted academic respectability? Perhaps—perhaps not. After all— and all of this is after all—what would it mean to be certain in a world that has given us Las Vegas?

To trace the twists and turns of uncertainties that are growing as fast as Vegas, we must return to the source, or what once was considered the source, of civilization—the Nile—where we can explore pyramids that line its banks. Desert to desert, sand to sand, ash to ash: The question that remains in the midst of these pyramids is the question of the body or, more precisely, the question of the remains of an (un)certain body. What does the body become— what becomes of the body in Las Vegas?

Wandering through the Sphinx and entering the dark glass pyramid, latter-day nomads do not so much step through a looking glass as pass through an invisible screen and enter a space that is virtually cinematic. The Luxor Hotel boasts the largest atrium in the world—29 million cubic feet, big enough for nine 747 airplanes. Unlike every other hotel in Vegas, the Luxor's casino is not immediately obvious. The cavernous space, reminiscent of the pyramidal microchip structure housing the Tyrell Corporation in *Blade Runner*, is divided into several levels. Ascending a flight of stairs, one encounters another obelisk encircled by restaurants, gift shops, and three movie theaters with marquees announcing: "In Search of the Obelisk," "Luxor Live," and "The Theater of Time." These films or quasi-films from "Secrets of the Luxor Pyramid," written and directed by special-effects wizard Douglas Trumbull, who created, inter alia, *2001, Blade Runner, Stargate*, and *Back to the Future, The Ride.*

The Luxor complex creates a simulated immersive environment in which the cinematic morphs into the virtual. Film layered upon film generates a space in which passive observers of cinema become active players in virtual games that know no end. Trumbull proudly declares: "You're not just looking at the movie, you're in the movie; you become a character." In theaters strategically located within a structure that is a reproduction of a movie set that has never been built, the mechanical reproductions of the panorama and diorama are transformed into the electronic reproductions of telematic media. Like every typical Western narrative, "Secrets of the Luxor Pyramid" has three parts, which weave together past, present, and future to form a seemingly coherent whole. The film portrays an advanced pre-Egyptian civilization that has been forgotten for centuries. Within the frame of the film, everything traditionally associated with ancient Egypt is re-inscribed as a poor facsimile of the sophisticated technologies developed by an even more ancient people. One of the secrets of the Luxor is that what has long been considered the source of civilization is actually an imitation of an original, which has left virtually no trace. In this way, the trilogy reconfigures the space of the Luxor by recasting the hotel as a simulation of a simulation. Even at the source of the Nile, only a film of the original remains.

While it is obvious that this tomb buried in the Nevada desert is empty, it is not clear whether the absence of the body signifies that resurrection has occurred or that what seems to be the body proper is always the semblance of a body that is never present in the first place. Between the darkness of the simulated crypt and the light of Râ, figured by the beacon at the top of the hotel, lies the scene of virtualization where the real becomes immaterial and the immaterial becomes real. If the crypt is empty, the secret of the Luxor Pyramid is that there is no secret. In the absence of the secret, nothing remains to hide. Nothing.

Ascending from the depths of the structure, which now appears utterly superficial, one crosses the Nile, leaving behind camels and palm trees, and approaches the tunnel leading to The Strip. Having discovered the absence of the body at the base of the pyramid, the hieroglyphs decorating the walls now seem utterly indecipherable. When corpus is not grounded in corpse, signs become endlessly interpretable and, thus, are either completely meaningless or infinitely meaningful. Having once entered this tomb, there is "no exit"; everything remains inescapably cryptic.

Though the Luxor is unlike any other hotel, there is something strangely familiar about its "crypto-Egypto" architecture. Egyptomania is not, of course, new. From the moment Howard Carter opened Tutankhamen's crypt, the world has not been able to get enough of Egypt. Nor is the interplay of architecture and cinema, mediated by the imagery of Egypt, without precedent. Since the second decade of this century, Egypt has not only been the subject of countless films but has also provided guiding motifs for theme theaters ranging from Meyer and Holler's Egyptian Theater in Hollywood (1921) to Sony's 3–D IMAX theater in New York (1994).

These recurrent orientalist fantasies suggest readings of modern architecture that break with conventional critical wisdom. While the architects whose names are inseparable from the history of modernism were descrying ornamentation and stripping away decoration, other architects whose names have been long forgotten were designing and constructing spectacular movie palaces in which fantasy runs wild. From the 1920s to the 1960s, imaginative architects and speculative developers spared no expense in creating immersive environments, which effectively extended the screen beyond the stage to encompass the entire theater. Indeed, in some cases, the show even spilled onto the sidewalk and street. From decorated façades depicting Egyptian, Mayan, and French themes to the sleek curves of Art Deco and streamlined shapes appropriated from industrial design, the space of cinema became a riot of supplements in which ornament is not a crime. With the return of the repressed, the pure forms, white skins, and transparent walls of modernism no longer seem quite so functional and rational. Nor do the decorated sheds of postmodernism seem quite so innovative. If modernism has lessons to learn from Las Vegas, it is because Las Vegas has always understood modernism better than modernists themselves. Like the desires circulating through it, ornament never disappears even when it is repressed. The Strip strips bare the pretenses of modernism by exposing structure as ornament and form as figure rather than ground. If ground is figure and figure ground, foundations collapse revealing (impossibly) Ground Zero/Zero Ground. The site of this implosion is not the nuclear test site at the edge of town but the dark hole in the midst of the city, which clears (away) the ground for the (de)construction of the "Great Lite Way."

It was, of course, Robert Venturi, Denise Scott Brown, and Steven Izenor who first turned our gaze toward Las Vegas in their highly influential book, *Learning from Las Vegas*, which grew out of an architectural studio conducted at Yale in 1968. What eventually came to be known as postmodern architecture can be traced to the 1972 publication of this book. The importance of *Learning from Las Vegas*, however, extends far beyond the bounds of architecture. By focusing attention on the shifting relationships among structures, signs, and images, Venturi, Brown, and Izenor decisively shaped the conceptual landscape of postmodernism for almost three decades. But things have changed; the Vegas of the 1990s is not the same as the Vegas of the 1960s. As the end and beginning of the millennium approach, Venturi's once inventive postmodern architecture no longer seems adequate to the complex architecture of postmodernism.

*Learning from Las Vegas* presents a sustained attack on the architectural orthodoxy known as International Style, which had dominated design and construction in the United States since its introduction in the 1932 exhibition at the Museum of Modern Art curated by Philip Johnson and Henry Russell Hitchcock. Venturi and his associates issue what is, in effect, a manifesto in which they call for a more realistic and tolerant architecture that accepts "*existing* conditions" rather than an idealistic and moralistic architecture that rejects what is for the sake of what ought to be. The defining feature of the 1960s Strip and its architecture, they argue, is the circuit joining building, sign, and car. "The big sign and the little building," Venturi argues, "are the rule of Route 66. The sign is more important than the architecture." From this perspective, The Strip is the expressive embodiment of postwar American automobile culture. The structure and location of buildings determine and are determined by patterns of traffic flow. For Venturi, these developments signal a decisive break with the foundational tenets of modern architecture.

Ever sensitive to complexity and contradiction, Venturi correctly maintains that modernists affirm in practice what they deny in theory. While insisting that form follows function, modern architects implicitly appropriate the iconography of industrialism in a way that transforms structure into ornament. "Modern ornament," Venturi points out, "has seldom been symbolic of anything nonarchitectural." Since the symbolism of modernism refers to other architectural symbols, it is reflexive or self-referential. By contrast, in Strip architecture, Venturi argues, signs point beyond themselves by communicating information necessary for orientation in an ever more complex world. Underscoring the communicative function of signs in a text that suggests the source of the design feature that distinguishes both his own *Vanna Venturi House* (1963–65) as well as Philip Johnson's *AT&T Corporate Headquarters* (1979–84), Venturi argues:

> The sign for the Motel Monticello, a silhouette of an enormous Chippendale highboy, is visible on the highway before the motel itself. This architecture of styles and signs is antispatial; it is an architecture of communication over space; communication dominates space as an element in the architecture of the landscape. . . . A driver 30 years ago could maintain a sense of orientation in space. At the simple crossroads a little sign with an arrow confirmed what was obvious. One knew where one was. When the crossroads becomes a cloverleaf, one must turn right to turn left. . . . But the driver has no time to ponder paradoxical subtleties within a dangerous, sinuous maze. He or she relies on signs for guidance — enormous signs in vast spaces at high speeds.[1]

As this comment suggests, Venturi's postmodernist critique of modern architecture is, paradoxically, constructed around the quintessential modernist invention: the automobile. This is the argument's strength as well as its weakness. Any theory or architecture that remains bound to the car cannot escape the regime of Fordism and everything it represents. "Postwar Fordism has to be seen," as David Harvey insists, "less as a mere system of mass production and more as a total way of life." In a circuit of exchange mirrored by the reflexivity of the work of art, mass production produces mass consumption, which, in turn, reproduces mass production. The automobile is, in effect, the incarnation of the structure of self-referentiality that informs both modern and modernist practices of production and reproduction. Automobility is, of course, self-movement. Like an ancient Unmoved Mover who descends from heaven to earth, the automobile is moved by nothing other than itself. The dream of automobility is autonomy. To inhabit the automobile machine is to be integrated within a closed circuit in which all production is auto-production. The very proximity of self and machine creates an insurmountable distance between self and world. When automobility becomes a way of life, *machines à habiter* become glass houses whose windshields function like screens of non-interactive television and non-immersive cinema. To drive down The Strip in such a glass machine is to watch passively as the film unwinds and the spectacle unfolds.

But The Strip of the 1990s, unlike The Strip of the 1960s, is no longer built around the automobile. While cars do, of course, remain, Las Vegas Boulevard has become a pedestrian promenade. The shift from driving to walking reflects broader changes that have taken place in Las Vegas during the past three decades. The early years of postwar Vegas were dominated by two legendary figures: Bugsy Siegel and Howard Hughes. It was Bugsy, Los Angeles representative of the Chicago mob, who first had the extraordinary vision of creating a spectacular oasis in the midst of the Nevada desert. Though the bosses remained suspicious of Bugsy's ambitions, his relentless pursuit of his dream eventually led to the completion of the first major casino resort hotel. In the years after Bugsy's murder, the crackdown on illegal gambling in California made Las Vegas increasingly attractive to mobsters. There were intermittent efforts to clean up Vegas but the mob ruled the town until the late 1960s. All of this changed when, in 1966, Howard Hughes stole into Vegas in the dead of night and took up residence in the isolated penthouse of the Desert Inn.

Hughes is best known for the idiosyncratic paranoia that dominated the later years of his life. Paul Virilio goes so far as to describe Hughes as a "technological monk" whose life is a grotesque embodiment of the dystopic possibilities of contemporary culture. "Speed," Virilio writes, "is nothing other than a vision of the world, and for me Hughes is a prophet, a monstrous prophet, moreover, and I'm not really at all crazy about the guy, but he's a prophet of the technical future of society. That absolute inertia, that bedridden man, a universal bedridden man as I called him, that's what we're all going to become." This reading of Hughes not only represents a one-sided view of technology but also overlooks his important contributions to the transformation of Las Vegas. From his early involvement with Hollywood to his innovative development of flight simulators and high-tech amusements, Hughes projected a future for Vegas that broke with its seedy past. The realization of this future, however, required legislative actions, which could only be initiated by someone with Hughes's power and influence. Prior to the 1960s, Nevada state law limited gambling licenses to individuals. This restriction created enormous financial difficulties for anyone who wanted to construct a casino.

In most cases, individuals did not have the necessary capital to invest in an uncertain venture in the middle of the desert. Consequently, this state law had the unexpected effect of encouraging the illegal financing of casinos. One of the few organizations with enough money to bet on Vegas was the mob. Ever the canny businessman, Hughes recognized the financial opportunity created by legalized gambling. But he also realized that Vegas could not prosper as long as the mob ruled and legitimate business could not invest in the city. To create a more favorable climate for investment, Hughes developed a two-pronged strategy: First, he started buying hotels and casinos, and second, he began lobbying state legislators to enact a law that would permit corporations as well as individuals to secure gambling licenses. When the Nevada legislature eventually succumbed to Hughes's pressure, the Las Vegas of the 1990s became not only possible but almost inevitable.

As major corporations moved in, it immediately became obvious that financial viability required an expansion of Vegas's customer base. If there were to be any justification for the expenditure of funds necessary for the construction of new casinos and hotels, gambling would have to be made attractive to a broader range of people. To achieve this end, the new Las Vegas had to distance itself from its corrupt past. In devising strategies for developing Vegas, "legitimate" investors looked to Hollywood.

While Venturi and his colleagues had recognized certain similarities between Disneyland and the Vegas of the 1960s, they never could have anticipated the extent to which the appropriation of strategies deployed in theme parks has transformed today's urban space. From frontier villages and tropical oases to Mississippi riverboats and Mediterranean resorts, from medieval castles and the land of Oz to oriental palaces and the New York skyline, every hotel-casino is organized around a theme. Fantasies fold into fantasies to create worlds within worlds. The spectacular MGM Grand Hotel, whose 5,005 rooms make it one of the largest hotels in the world, "literalizes" the thematization of Vegas by replicating Disney World. Though ostensibly miming Disney's "original," MGM's theme park is significantly different from its prototype. While the Disney "imagineers" who designed EPCOT Center take pride in accurately representing our "small world" or "global village," the architects of MGM flaunt artifice by openly imitating an imitation for which there is no original. None of the nostalgia that pervades Disney World haunts Las Vegas. In Vegas, we forget that we have forgotten.

The primary motivation for this thematizing is, of course, economic. As I have noted, to attract people who never considered gambling, illegitimate vice had to be turned into legitimate entertainment. Moreover, the city had to be made hospitable to the middle class and their families. The Disneyfication of Vegas is intended to sanitize the city not so much by washing away its sin and corruption as by concealing it more carefully. Far from a den of iniquity, today's Vegas is supposed to create the façade of a user-friendly amusement park. When the hotel named New York, New York puts a Coney Island roller coaster between the hotel-casino and The Strip, the strategy guiding recent development is put on display for everyone to see.

These shifting financial incentives have brought changes in architectural programs. To create an environment appealing to a new clientele, architects had to develop design tactics that would convincingly integrate the fantastic and familiar. Between the 1960s and the 1990s, the pedestrian space of malls displaced the automobile space of the suburban strip. While most of these malls combined predictable design elements from arcades and department stores, which can be traced to the glass architecture that emerged in Europe during the nineteenth century, more venturesome developers sought to construct new environments for consumption by creating spaces in which shopping becomes spectacular entertainment. Vegas's new hotel-casino megaplexes borrow the most outlandish features of contemporary cathedrals of consumption and, as always, up the ante. The Vegas mallscape is not limited to the public interiors of giant hotels. In a certain sense, the entire Strip has become one big arcade or mall. No longer separated from the street by large parking lots, casinos crowd the sidewalk with façades that dissolve the boundary between inside and outside. When the thin film of glass dividing inner and outer dissolves, viewers are consumed by a spectacle that knows no bounds. The Strip has become an immersive environment in which the virtual becomes real and the real becomes virtual. In Vegas, as one of its leading citizens, Andre Agassi, proclaims from signs and screens, "It's all a matter [or, we might add, a non-matter] of image." As display screens dissolve into display screens to reveal endless dataspace, images become consuming, and "realities" are virtualized. Nowhere is the virtualization of reality more obvious than on the new Freemont Street. Long associated with the seedy side of old Vegas, Glitter Gulch recently has been transformed into what is, in effect, a gigantic computer terminal or virtual reality machine. Vegas city planners have, in effect, converted the train terminal, which inspired the glass architecture of the Parisian arcades, into a computer terminal to create the new space of the virtual arcade. Freemont Street is now covered with a 1500-foot computerized canopy with 1.4 million synchronized lights and lasers. To roam through Glitter Gulch is to discover the timely timelessness of terminal space.

In the space of the terminal, the architecture of postmodernism shifts. This shift involves a slipping away, which for Venturi and his followers is unimaginable. Though Venturi no longer believes in the foundational structures of modernism, he still has faith in signs. That is why he can call for an "architecture of communication" in which one still "relies on signs for guidance." But along today's Strip, even this faith becomes questionable. When signs consume the bodies that lend them weight, everything becomes (a "matter" of ) light. The ground that once seemed stable slips away, leaving nothing to fix meaning. This is the point, or one of the points, of the pointless pyramid and the sacrificial economy it figures. In an effort to grasp the point of the pyramid that has lost its point, I return to our point of departure — the Luxor Hotel.

The Luxor is, as I have noted, a monumental black glass pyramid. The tip of the pyramid — its point as it were — is the world's most powerful beam of light (315,000 watts), which, on a clear night, is visible 250 miles away. This tip is not black but is a miniature pyramid made of translucent glass. The juxtaposition of black and white glass combines with the interplay of the darkness and light of the pyramid to create vertiginous effects. Since the white point is invisible during the day, it looks as if the black glass pyramid has had its tip knocked off. At night, the massive black pyramid virtually disappears, leaving the small white pyramidal tip suspended in thin air as if it had no foundation. What flame burns atop this dark pyramid? What is its point? Why does it sometimes appear to be pointless?

"Pyramid" derives from the Latin *puramis*, which means "funeral pyre." "The erection of the pyramid," Derrida points out, "guards life — the dead — in order to give rise to the for-(it)self of adoration. This has the signification of a sacrifice, of an offer by which the all-burning annuls itself. . . . The sacrifice, the offer, the gift do not destroy the all-burning that destroys itself in them, they make it reach the for-(it)self, they monumentalize it." The pyramid, it seems, is a sacrificial altar. But who is sacrificed — what is sacrificed — on this altar? Is there a meaning to sacrifice? Is there a sacrifice of meaning?

Perhaps we can detect clues that will help to solve the mystery of the pyramid in the cryptic writings of an author whose texts are, in effect, hieroglyphs: Edgar Allan Poe. A diagram of a pyramid appears once in the writings of Poe: In his long "prose poem" entitled *Eureka*, he presents a visual aid to help the reader understand his abstract argument. The shape Poe traces recalls Dürer's well-known woodcut in which he depicts the pyramidal structure of visual perspective. Though seemingly self-contained, Poe's pyramid is actually a section of an all-encompassing sphere that figures the rhythms of the cosmic process. In his speculative poetics, the world and everything in it emerge from and return to a primordial unity that is the divine source of reality. The act o' creation through which the many emerge from the One involves a process c differentiation that Poe labels "radiation."

> Now a connection between these two ideas — unity and diffusion — cannot be established unless through the entertainment of a third idea — that of *radiation*. Absolute Unity being taken as a center, then the existing Universe of Stars is the result of *radiation* from that center.

Unity, in other words, is an unstable nucleus that erupts in a fiery explosion, generating the world of diverse appearances. It is as if Poe's "radiation" anticipates the fission that occurs one hundred years later at Ground Zero in the Nevada desert. The tip of the pyramid, which is the center of the sphere, is the point at which the real is totally present. The movement from center to periphery is marked by the dispersal of reality in a play of appearances. Appearances, however, are no more stable than their origin. Having originated in lack, appearances seek reunion with the One they are missing. Centrifugal and centripetal forces, however, are not equal. Since unity is "normal" and plurality "abnormal," Poe insists, "the tendency to return into the *absolutely* original — into the *supremely* primitive" cannot be resisted. Within this speculative economy, there is no expenditure without return.

The dialectic of "radiation" and "concentralization" entails alternative sacrifices, which, though reciprocal, are not symmetrical. Betting on the possibility of return, Poe longs for the sacrifice of sacrifice in which loss is lost. While it is undeniable that the realization of the many presupposes the sacrifice of the One, this loss is not fatal if the One can always be recovered. The return of, to, and on the One, however, is impossible apart from the sacrifice of the many. Fission must become fusion, which creates a meltdown. At the tip of the pyramid there is a flame, which not only radiates the sacrifice of the One but consummates the sacrifice of the many. The fire of consumption is a holocaust that consumes differences in an identity that leaves nothing but the trace of nothing.

Creation, fall, redemption . . . One, many, One . . . Identity, Difference, Identity. The story Poe tells in *Eureka* is the metanarrative that renders all narratives meaningful. For the detective who knows this tale, nothing remains indecipherable because everything has a point. The point from which this point is visible is the point of the pyramid. As Dürer suggests, this is the point of all vision, this is the point of every insight. In Poe's speculative poe-tic, ontology and epistemology are mirror images of each other. The tip of the pyramid is the center of vision around which everything is organized.

But what if this "story of the eye" is fiction? What if the eye always has a blind spot? What if wandering in the desert is not a passing phase but an endless condition? What if one can never reach the tip of the pyramid? What if the pyramid — as well as everything else — is pointless? In many of Poe's stories, tales, and poems the figure of unity is the South Pole, which, of course, marks the end of the world. Though it is always near, one never reaches the end. As (the) I approach(es), the end withdraws; where I am, it is not, and when it is, I am not. In "MS. Found in a Bottle," Poe recounts a horrifying tale of a ship wrecked while heading toward the ever inaccessible South Pole. The narrator adds a coda in which he confesses:

> To conceive the horror of my sensations is, I presume, utterly impossible; yet a curiosity to penetrate the mysteries of these awful regions, predominates even over my despair, and will reconcile me to the most hideous aspect of death. It is evident that we are hurrying onwards to some exciting knowledge — some never-to-be-imparted secret, whose attainment is destruction. Perhaps this current leads to the southern pole itself. It must be

confessed that a supposition apparently so wild has every probability of favor.[2]

The pyramid is something like the inverted image of the conical vortex, or, conversely, the fathomless abyss is an inverted pyramid. If the bottom of the cataract is inaccessible, or if the tip of the pyramid is missing, the cataract is groundless. The consequences of this confession are far-reaching. If there is a "never-to-be imparted secret," Poe's metanarrative unravels or becomes hopelessly tangled. A secret that is never imparted, a secret that is absolutely cryptic is indistinguishable from a secret that hides nothing. Instead of hiding the body that would solve every mystery, the pyramid becomes an empty tomb that marks the disappearance of the body. In the absence of a body, everything remains cryptic; detectives are condemned to blindness without insight, and hieroglyphs remain what they always have been—indecipherable because infinitely interpretable. To navigate the rough waters of "these awful regions," it is necessary to leave Poe behind and follow the ever-errant Bataille.

Bataille is endlessly fascinated by pyramids. Confirming what Poe suspects, he concludes that not all pyramids have a point. To make his point, Bataille reads Hegelianism against the grain by teasing out the implications of a fleeting observation in which Hegel notes but does not examine the explosion of the nuclear family and the economy (*oikos*) it presupposes.

> But if the universal thus easily knocks off the very tip of the pyramid and, indeed, carries off the victory over the rebellious principle of pure individuality, viz., the Family, it has thereby merely entered on a conflict with the divine law, a conflict of self-conscious Spirit with what is unconscious.[3]

According to the uneconomical reflections of Bataille, a pointless pyramid figures the sacrifice of meaning. Might Poe's "exciting knowledge—some never-to-be-imparted secret—whose attainment is destruction," then, anticipate the "non-knowledge" that Bataille detects at the heart of Nietzsche's gay science?

Pyramids, Bataille repeatedly insists, are inseparable from labyrinths. The foundations of these monumental structures are not solid but are intricate networks of cryptic subterranean passages. While dark labyrinths represent the confusion of earthly life, pyramids map escape routes by pointing to the bright light illuminating the world. Long associated with solar religion, pyramids reflect the triangular pattern of the sun's rays, which radiate creative power. Spanning the heavens and the underworld, pyramids are associated with birth as well as death. In one version of the Egyptian creation myth, the world first emerges in the shape of a pyramidal mound from Nun, who personifies the primordial ocean toward which Poe was always rushing. At the tip of this mound a lotus grows and from this lotus the Sun-god Râ-Atum emerges. Râ-Atum generates Geb, the Earth-god, and Nut, the Sky-goddess, whose offspring include, among others, Osiris and Isis, who prefigure the Christian drama of death and resurrection. By the VI[th] Dynasty, Egyptians believed that after death, the king, who is identified with the Sun-god, ascends to heaven to join Râ-Atum and travel through the night sky struggling against forces of darkness. Like the sign, the pyramid is the bridge that simultaneously brings together and holds apart different worlds. By representing the sacred mountain where order emerges from chaos, the pyramid forms the *axis mundi* that allows passage from earth to heaven. In a brief essay entitled "The Obelisk," Bataille summarizes the point of the pyramid:

> Each time death struck down the heavy column of strength the world itself was shaken and put into doubt, and nothing is less than the giant edifice of the pyramid was necessary to re-establish the order of things; the pyramid let the god-king enter the eternity of the sky next to the solar Râ, and in this way existence regained its unshakable plenitude in the person of the one it had *recognized*. . . . Thus, they assure the presence that never ceases to contemplate and dominate human agitation, just as the mobile prism reflects every one of the things that surrounds it. In their imperishable unity, the pyramids—endlessly—continue to crystallize the mobile succession of the various ages, alongside the Nile, they rise up like the totality of centuries, taking on the immobility of stone and watching all men die, one after the other: they transcend the intolerable void that time opens under men's feet, for all possible movement is halted in their geometric surfaces: IT SEEMS THAT THEY MAINTAIN WHAT ESCAPES FROM THE DYING MAN.[4]

In this way, the pyramid *fixes* time by tracing an escape from the labyrinth. "If one considers the mass of the pyramids and the rudimentary means at the disposal of their builders," Bataille concludes, "it seems evident that no enterprise cost a greater amount of labor than this one, which wanted to halt the flow of time." At the tip of the pyramid, time is supposed to become eternity.

But, as we have discovered, not all pyramids have a point; some are decapitated. If the point of the pyramid is to fix time by reversing temporal flow through a return to the eternal ground or origin of being, then the absence of the point marks the impossibility of return—or points to a different return which, though eternal, permits no escape from temporal flux. A pyramid of sorts triggered the ecstatic vision that marked the turning point in Nietzsche's life.

> The intensity of my feelings makes me both tremble and laugh. . . . I had cried too much . . . these were not tears of tenderness, but tears of jubilation. . . . That day I was walking through the woods, along the lake of Silvaplana; at a powerful pyramidal rock not far from Surlei I stopped.[5]

At precisely this moment, Nietzsche is blinded by the insight that *time returns eternally*. Nietzsche's notion of the eternal return represents a recognition of the irreversibility of time and the inescapable transience of everything once deemed unchanging. Never attempting to overcome time by returning the temporal to the eternal, Nietzsche acknowledges the eternity of time by collapsing the eternal in the temporal in such a way that every possibility of recovery vanishes. Bataille underscores the importance of Nietzsche's pointless point:

> In order to represent the decisive break that took place, it is necessary to tie the sundering vision of the "return" to what Nietzsche experienced when he reflected upon the explosive vision of Heraclitus, and to what he experienced later in his own vision of the "death of God": this is necessary in order to perceive the full extent of the bolt of lightning that never stopped shattering his life while at the same time projecting it into a burst of violent light. TIME is unleashed in the "death" of the One whose eternity gave Being an immutable foundation. And the audacious act that represents the "return" at the summit of this rending agony only wrests from the dead God his *total* strength, in order to give it to the deleterious absurdity of time.[6]

A pyramid with its tip knocked off is an altar of sacrifice. For Nietzsche, this sacrificial altar is the site of the death of the One that grounds Western metaphysics and thereby renders life meaningful. In the absence of God, who "gave Being an immutable foundation," there is no transcendental signifier to stop the play of signs. Signs can no longer be trusted or can no longer be trusted as they once were. When signs lose their foundation, the architecture of meaning shifts. "For it is the *foundation* of things," Bataille insists, "that has fallen into a bottomless void."[7] For Venturi and the postmodernism he represents, this foundationless architecture is inconceivable.

In a world that has lost the foundation it once seemed to have, why bet? Why take chances when there seems to be no possibility of return? We bet because we cannot do otherwise. Nothing remains but taking chances. *Nothing.* "The deleterious absurdity of time" is the trace of the death of God as well as all his delegates. The consumption of the body leaves the tomb empty and the labyrinth inescapable. The pointless pyramid is the altar of sacrifice where the potlatch of meaning is staged. This offering is the sacrifice of God, which, in a certain sense, leaves everything pointless. The death of God is, in effect, the death of the transcendental signified, which marks the closure of the classical regime of representation. Left to float freely, signs figure other signs in an errant play that is as endless as it is pointless. The point of this pointlessness is nothing—absolutely nothing. Vegas is *about* nothing—always *about* nothing. This, perhaps, is the spectacle or one of the spectacles staged on The Strip.

One goes to Vegas, I have suggested, expecting to win but comes away having learned how to lose. This loss is, however, a strange loss, for it is the loss of what we never possess. And yet, it is precisely this loss that puts play into play. Such loss can never be comprehended; it is always excessive—even prodigal. In this parable of prodigality that I have been retelling, the son does not return but, having sown his seed in seedy places, dies. When we search for the body, we find only the "pyramidal silence" of the empty tomb. The tomb, it seems, is empty not because resurrection has occurred but because the body has disappeared or has become nothing but the semblance of a body. When *corpus* no longer grounds corpus, meanings proliferate. The problem is no longer the absence of meaning but the excess of meanings.

Somewhere Nietzsche observes that when reality vanishes, we are not left with appearances but with something else, something other. Since reality and appearance are mutually constitutive, the disappearance of one is the transformation of the other. Though some artists, philosophers, and critics have long suspected that the real is little more than a fabrication constructed to deny its status as constructed, recent developments in electronic and telematic technologies disclose all "reality" to be virtual. Virtual reality is not merely a specific technology but is, more important, a trope for our current cultural condition. In the world on display in Las Vegas, the real becomes virtual and the virtual becomes real. For those who remain stuck in classical binaries and oppositions, "virtual reality" is an oxymoron. But the very ambiguity this self-erasing term harbors allows it to designate something like what Nietzsche suggests when he points to that which is *neither* reality *nor* appearance. The domain of the virtual is the boundary that simultaneously joins and separates "reality" and "appearance" by figuring disfiguring, and disfiguring figuring.

The pursuit of this ever-elusive limen that Vegas puts on display demands that we figure otherwise. Our calculations must become as iconographic as the world we inhabit and that inhabits us. To think differently, we must write differently, and to write differently, we must think differently. While we have been learning to think differently for many years, writing practices and the technologies they presuppose have remained virtually unchanged—even when authors claim otherwise. Though repeatedly insisting on the importance of difference and all it does not represent, we nonetheless remain caught in the eternal return of the same. Deconstructive strategies have become distressingly familiar and thus in all too many cases, we know the argument before we read the text. To overcome this critical impasse, if, indeed, it can be overcome, we must learn to write even more transgressively. Inc/Ink has become too limited, and pens no longer are sufficient; bits must become our ink. When bits are our "ink," we not only write with words but also with images and sounds. When intertextuality becomes hypertextual, nothing remains the same. *Nothing*. In the absence of final analyses, the closure of the book is about this nothing.

What is the lesson Las Vegas teaches us today—*ici, maintenant?* Nothing perhaps. Perhaps nothing. At least that's my wager, or one of my wagers. To bet on Vegas is to bet on nothing. And to bet on nothing is to bet on betting. Betting on nothing expects nothing in return. Absolutely nothing. This is, of course, a gamble—a huge gamble. But when everything becomes dicey, we are forced to confess that we have always been gamblers. It's all (a) crap(shoot). There you have it; I've laid *my* cards on the table. Now it's *your* deal; always *your* deal.

## DERRIDA'S DISCUSSION WITH MARK TAYLOR

*Jacques Derrida.* My question takes the form of a fiction. Could we imagine the same presentation, with the same apparatus, about the same technological and economical structure, with a different example, something else in the United States which would be indicative of the same state of technology, of capital? For instance, jails. Could you imagine the same thing with respect to American jails?

*Mark Taylor.* My first response, before you offered your example, was to say the floor of the stock market. That would be one place. Go back and look at the film *Wall Street*. The one thing we remember from that film is the line "greed is good." But that is not the interesting point in that film, it seems to me. The really interesting point is when Charlie Sheen comes bursting into the meeting that Michael Douglas is having with the Japanese investors to confront him about his betrayal, and Douglas responds with, "Where is your head, kid? Don't you know what is going on?" Notice all the art in the film. The buildings are filled with beautiful paintings and the house Douglas lives in is a Richard Meyer house. That is not accidental. At one point, he draws an explicit connection between art and money. He looks at a painting on the wall and asks, "Don't you realize that all this stuff is image—light." On the issues of prisons and light, Foucault only began to glimpse the scale of panopticism that is on display at Vegas. In a certain sense, part of what goes on in the prison is this kind of surveillance.

*Jacques Derrida.* But I mean real jails.

*Mark Taylor.* I know you do. But I want to say that part of what you begin to see on display in Vegas is surveillance. Surveillance in Vegas is amazing. Those casinos are virtual jails. There is not one move you make there that is not on display. Now I understand the difference between the casino as jail and real jails.

*Jacques Derrida.* But Vegas is not a real prison.

*Mark Taylor.* That way of putting it is too simple. The question we need to ask is, what is the relationship between so-called real jails and the kind of society or culture constructed around Las Vegas? I happened to be in Las Vegas the night the Rodney King verdict came down. It was a terrifying night. They had had racial riots in Vegas a few years before, and every cab driver assured you he had his gun and that everything was under control. It is all tied up with the Wild West, that mythology. It seems to me that part of what is given to us to think by what is on display at Vegas is precisely the kind of social structure that creates the prison industry. This may be one of the things that Vegas represses.

Mark C. Taylor

**NOTES**

1. Robert Venturi, Denise Scott Brown, and Steven Izenor, *Learning from Las Vegas: The Forgotten Symbolism of Architectural Form* (Cambridge, Mass.: MIT Press, 1972), 4.

2. Edgar Allan Poe, "MS. Found in a Bottle," *Poetry and Tales* (New York: The Library of America, 1984), 198.

3. G. W. F. Hegel, *Phenomenology of Spirit*, trans. A. V. Miller (New York: Oxford University Press, 1977), 286.

4. Georges Bataille, *Visions of Excess: Selected Writings, 1927–1939*, trans. Allan Stoekl (Minneapolis: University of Minnesota Press, 1985), 216.

5. Ibid., 219–20.

6. Ibid., 220.

7. Ibid., 222.

# Eating the Text, Defiling the Hands

## Specters in Arnold Schoenberg's Opera
*Moses and Aron*

Edith Wyschogrod

"A masterpiece always moves, by definition, in the manner of a ghost," its mode of temporalization, its timing, always out of joint, spectrally disorganizing the "cause" that is called the "original," Derrida tells us.[1] Can there be an "original" describing an event that has already occurred but that re-arises spectrally in the gap between theophany and inscription, the space between the golden calf and the tablets of the law (Exodus 32:19–20), between the idol as a physical artifact and writing? These questions are raised in the context of Arnold Schoenberg's opera *Moses and Aron*,[2] a masterpiece that, moving between music and text, purports to explore the relation of the Absolute as idea to the image that is alleged to manifest it. The complex of tensions between idea and image are brought forward through an innovative combination of speech, vocal, and instrumental music that I shall call Schoenberg's theosonics.

In what follows, I consider the relation between Moses, who insists upon the word in its ideality, and Aron, who maintains the necessity for its transposition into phenomenal manifestation, and the reversals their positions undergo. The complex of questions posed and suspended by the Mosaic traditions of phenomenality and ideality as manifested in the calf and the tablets, I argue, returns in Schoenberg's work as spectral re-enactments of older Jewish and Christian traditions exemplified in the comments on Moses in Maimonides' *Guide for the Perplexed* and in the brief remarks on Moses in Augustine's *Confessions*. I turn also to the process of semiotic idealization itself, i.e., the progressive understanding of textual inwardization first manifested in acts of ingesting the text described in a number of biblical passages. In what can be viewed as a countermove, I then consider a rabbinic tradition that contends that sacred food must be segregated from sacred text and that each confers sacred defilement, a "defiling of the hands." Against this backdrop, Schoenberg's Moses is shown, to borrow Derridean terms, as "the founder of the spirit of a people, . . . the figure of a revenant-survivant, a Ghost survivor" (*SoM*, 146). I maintain further that the effort to create a transcendent object in phonic and musical sound alters the Maimonidean and Augustinian perspectives that have been brought into Schoenberg's theosonics so that the feared images return to fissure the word. The unintended preservation of these older traditions re-arises spectrally not as an effort to perpetuate the past but, as the Frankfurt School's Theodor Adorno might put it, "at the vanguard of the new . . . in the interstices of the new."[3]

I shall forgo the temptation to examine the "ana-chronique" specter of Freud's Moses that haunts many contemporary accounts of Moses. Instead I shall focus upon the spectral re-arising of Jewish and Christian interpretations of Moses as they infiltrate Schoenberg's theosonics.

## A God without Images

It is not possible to enter into the complex intellectual and artistic influences on Schoenberg's work, nor to do more than allude to Schoenberg's innovative compositional techniques. It is however useful to note that Schoenberg attended closely to Schopenhauer's account of the relation between Idea (*Vorstellung*) and Representation (*Darstellung*) and to Schopenhauer's view that music reveals the inmost essence of the world as will. While Schopenhauer's perspective remains deeply embedded in Schoenberg's aesthetic, Schoenberg modifies Schopenhauer's assertion about music, arguing for the necessity of mediation, the translation of the Absolute into perceptually available content, even if such translation attenuates the power of the unrepresentable.[4] It is also likely that Schoenberg was aware of Hermann Cohen's widely disseminated view that God is the logical condition of reality and, as such, an idea. Nor could Helena Petrovna Blavatsky's theosophy and Rudolf Steiner's anthroposophy, teachings that stressed the notion of divine unity and influenced high modernist artists such as his friend Vasily Kandinsky, have escaped Schoenberg's notice.[5]

Yet it is important to see that *Moses and Aron,* first conceived as an oratorio in which the chorus played a leading role alternately reflecting the *vox dei* and the *vox populi*, a work in which numerous didactic exclamatory exchanges between the principals occurred, underwent significant revision as an opera. Moving from the more static oratorio form to the theatricality of opera, the miracles of Aron (Act 1) and the orgy before the golden calf (Act 2) were augmented and the speech of Aron in the unfinished third act, to which I shall have reason to recur, was conceptually modified to acknowledge the power of images.[6]

There is no reason to believe that a link with the sense-laden aspect of Schoenberg's Moses can be forged with the Moses of Numbers 10: 1–2, verses in which Moses is commanded by God to make two silver trumpets and given elaborate instructions as to their use. It is rather the Moses of halting speech and thaumaturgical power that Schoenberg sees as soliciting musical adumbration. His self-proclaimed identification with this Moses became more profound with the rise of Nazism whose potential he feared early on, a fear reflected in this theological declaration: "We [Israelites] know that we were chosen to think the thought of the one eternal, unimaginable, invisible God through to completion, in short to keep it alive! And there is nothing that can compare with that mission."[7]

The opera *Moses and Aron* is structured so that each protagonist dominates for a time only to be undone by the other. Moses and the voice from the burning bush do not sing but resort to a stylized song-speech, *Sprechstimme*, devised by Schoenberg to convey conceptual density and the abstractness of divine speech, whereas Aron's words are sung in fluid musical lines limited always by Schoenberg's twelve-tone row system, "rows or tones where no tone can recur before its turn comes, and then only subject to permutation."[8] The solo voices articulate a chain of transmission: From the burning bush comes God's voice heard as the voice of Moses and Moses' voice, in turn, issues from Aron. But the distinction between the personae of Moses and Aron blurs when, at the end of the last scene of the second act, the opera's original closing, Moses, exhausted, submits to an ineluctable contingency and materiality:

> Unimaginable God!/ Inexpressible many-sided idea,/ Will you let it be
> so explained?/ Shall Aron, my mouth, fashion/ this image?/ Then I have
> fashioned an image too,/ false,/ as an image must be./ Thus am I defeated!/
> Thus all was but madness that/ I believed before,/ and can but must not be
> given voice./ O word, thou word that I lack.[9]

Before Moses' final capitulation to the image, he depicts God as one who "is unseen, cannot be measured, everlasting and eternal because ever-present and almighty" (*MoA*, 44). In this context Moses appears to replicate the aniconic view of Jewish interpretation, the anathema pronounced upon the sacralization of the image, the elevation of its demonic potential into idolatry. As exemplified in Maimonides, the most serious theological error consists in the imputation of corporeality to God, an error that undergirds idolatry in that idolatry as he defines it is the idea that a particular form represents the agent between God and his creatures.[10] These errors are precipitated by the unfettering of a figural imagination required by ordinary mortals in order to render theological truths accessible but which disfigures this truth through figuration itself. Maimonides concedes that prophecy itself requires both the logical and imaginative faculties even if the rational faculty is to predominate. Restated in Adorno's terms, "pure" figuration is self-defeating "for it augments the chaotic moment lurking in all art as its pre-condition."[11]

Another danger of the hypertrophied imagination feared by Maimonides is its power to unleash a mixture of true and imaginary things.[12] In prophetic visions the *viva vox* of God is absent; when thought to be heard, it is only imagined to be present. Moses alone is exempt from the mediation of deceptive screening images: "All prophets are prophetically addressed through an angel except Moses our teacher, in reference to whom Scripture says, 'Mouth to mouth I speak to him.'"[13] This view seems to suggest that the danger of the golden calf lies in its ontological status as image, one in a series of images, an artifactual expression of an excess of imagination. But we shall see that a far more complex picture, one involving a series of idolatrous specters and their reversals, of simulacra restrained and unleashed, begins to emerge; that far from belonging to a panoply of images, the golden calf reflects a desperate effort to restrict the dissemination of images and the conjurations that give rise to them. At the same time, it is an attempt to substitute itself for the infinite semantic potential of writing, of a particular system of signs that is the law as incised upon tablets which are broken but which re-arise spectrally.

Consider again Maimonides' worry, his dread of the simulacrum, his fear that there may be no way to distinguish true from imaginary things. The Platonic principle that purports to select the true from the imaginary does not divide forms from appearances but rather reflects a testing of rival claimants within the sphere of the appearances themselves, an effort that is, at bottom, not taxonomical but evaluative, as Gilles Deleuze has pointed out.[14] He writes:

> This problem of distinguishing between things and their simulacra . . . is a question of making the difference, thus of operating in the depths of the immediate. . . . It is a dangerous trial without thread and without net, for according to the ancient custom of myth and epic, false claimants must die.[15]

As division that is always already anterior to full presence, the state of difference itself is prior to the determination of the true, prior to the forms which as a post hoc imposition are intended to ground what must remain heterological and refractory to grounding.

That the golden calf is not an image but rather stanches the flow of runaway images and is an attestation of fixity is implied by Aron's words which attribute theonomic properties to it: "These are your gods O Israel who brought you up out of the land of Egypt." This view re-arises in Schoenberg's Aron who mummifies in the form of the calf, the god that lives in all things, "unchange-able [*unwandelbar*], even as a Law" (*MaA*, 90). In addition to the specter of animism, the opera depicts a crucial episode of violence, the suicides of four virgins, who cry out "Arouse us to first and last rapture" and the pandemic orgy of sexuality and death which ensues (*MaA*, 102).[16] Can Aron, after all, and not Moses, become the redresser of historical grievances, liberator and righter of wrongs if, as Derrida shows, "One never inherits without coming to terms with some specter, and therefore with more than one specter" (*SoM*, 21)?

In his study of Moses, Martin Buber is not unaware of certain spectral manifestations in the account of the golden calf in Exodus.[17] After the post-Davidic kingdom is divided into north and south, Buber suggests, Jeroboam the northern king revives the cultic centers of Dan and Bethel thereby hoping to circumvent the necessity of making pilgrimages to Jerusalem, which would reinforce loyalty to the Davidic kingship rather than to himself (I Kings 12: 26ff). In order to clinch the supremacy of these shrines, Jeroboam makes two golden calves and, in a remarkable act of doubling, repeats Aron's words: "Behold your gods O Israel who brought you up out of the land of Egypt." While some scholars hold that the Jeroboam narrative reflects an older tradi-tion, Buber refuses to credit this view, arguing instead that Jeroboam's calves replicate a common motif in Semitic cultures and are intended merely to serve as markers of God's throne. Not Jeroboam, Buber argues, but the people could not distinguish between the bearer of the God and God, a perspective that is then foisted by an editorial hand upon Jeroboam himself. Thus the specter of an "originary" idolatry is revealed and concealed as a proscription against idolatry in "the malediction inscribed in the law itself" (*SoM*, 21).

It has been argued that rivalry exists not only between Israel's God and the idol as is attested in the prohibition against idols, but also among the idols themselves. A minority view upheld by some contemporary biblical scholars suggests that a positive tradition once provided the basis for the subsequently negative account of the calf. Without entering into the scholarly pros and cons of this interpretation, its claims may be worth noting. It is argued that the pejorative term for golden calf as idol (*egel*) is used in Exodus 32 whereas the term for a bovine animal is denoted by the word *re'em* in the Balaam oracles and in Psalms 22:22. In the latter, the Hebrew version of the text reads "Save me from the horns of the wild ox," but the Greek Syrian version reads "Answer me from the horns of the wild ox (*re'em*)," implying that God himself responds to the lament of the psalmist from out of the horns of the *re'em*.[18]

## Reason, Magic, and the Magic of Reason

In the theosonics of Schoenberg's *Moses and Aron*, the issue of idol and image can be seen to disclose a Platonic pattern that, in Derridean terms, "associates in a strict fashion image with specter and idol with phantasm, with the phantasma in its phantomatic or errant dimension as living-dead" (*SoM*,

147). In the crucial fifth scene of Act II, the golden calf is interpreted by Aron as belonging to a panoply of living theophanic images invoked not by him but by Moses himself, images that include the pillar of fire, the burning bush. Moses, however, falls victim to a category mistake when he fails to perceive the difference between phantomatic idol as stancher of images and the ongoing stream of theophanic conjurations. The golden calf is inert, at once an artifact that lies somewhere between artwork and implement, and a commodity having the value of the gold from which it has been fashioned. By contrast, Moses' own works are dynamic but dangerous conjurations: His rod is changed into a serpent, the Red Sea is split, and the like. The competing claimants in this context are not the idol and the stream of theophanic conjurations but the multiple conjured events themselves.

It is possible for a product of conjuration to appear to replicate the function of the calf. Consider the episode of the Israelites' complaints about the lack of food and water as they trekked through the desert and the Lord's response, the sending of venomous snakes (Numbers 21: 5–9). After Moses intercedes on behalf of the people, the Lord directs him to make a bronze serpent so that anyone looking at the effigy will recover. But Moses' fashioning of the bronze serpent remains an act of conjuration undertaken in the interest of healing. To be sure, the bronze serpent is later interpreted by the Israelites as a cultic effigy before which burnt offerings are made and is smashed by King Hezekiah (II Kings 18:4), an act which might be construed as mimetic of the destruction of the golden calf by Moses. However it is not unreasonable to infer that the bronze serpent, like the staff of Asclepius in Greek mythology, is revered principally for its ongoing thaumaturgical properties. By contrast, the golden calf is, as it were, proto-scriptic, the stancher of images, the one who is identified by the Israelites as the historical god of Israel who brought them out of the land of Egypt (Exodus 32:7–8).[19]

Derrida has described conjuration as a certain efficacity of voice: "[T]he magical incantation destined to *evoke*, to bring forth with the voice, to *convoke* a charm or a spirit. Conjuration . . . makes come by definition, what is not there at the present moment of the appeal. . . . [I]ts words cause something to happen" (*SoM*, 41). In the ancient world, Moses' name was frequently linked to thaumaturgical practices and tributes to Moses' powers as a magician were described by Pliny and Eusebius, among others. Origen, in his negative depiction of Jews as sorcerers, writes in *Contra Celsus* that Jews derived their power from Moses their teacher.[20]

Nowhere does distinguishing between theophanic phenomena and conjuration cause greater difficulty than in the rationalist theology of Maimonides. In a discourse whose misogyny is striking even for its day, Maimonides defends the harsh prescriptions intended to guard against conjuration as practiced in biblical times, even justifying putting witches to death. The grounds of his critique of witchcraft are both pragmatic and ethical. "No analogy and no reasoning can discover any relation between these performances . . . and the promised result," he insists.[21] But witchcraft is also seen as a species of idolatry and, as such, promotes false beliefs generally. In support of the latter claim, Maimonides singles out Sabean religious doctrines as intending "criticism and an attack on the evident miracles by which all people learnt that there exists a God who is judge over all people."[22]

The aporias of the rationalist position are obvious. If authentication is based upon the relation of practice and result and if witchcraft succeeds in producing the promised result, what would distinguish it from miracle? Either the question is begged from the start, i.e., negative outcomes mean that witchcraft is at work, or the line between witchcraft and miracle cannot be drawn on the proposed grounds.

Earlier it was noted that Schoenberg is able to link the golden calf phenomenologically to Moses' acts of thaumaturgy in that each endeavors to capture divine power in sensuous images. Their connectedness does not preclude Schoenberg's observing that there may be rival claimants to sacred power within the sphere of Israelite conjuration itself. In the single completed scene of a contemplated third act written shortly before Schoenberg's death, Moses attributes acts of conjuration to Aron, e.g., forcing water from the rock. Moses remonstrates, "You [Aron] expose them to strange gods. . . . [Y]ou do as the people do" (*MaA*, 126). In the failure to serve the divine idea (*Gottes-danken*) and instead to engage in thaumaturgical practices, there is an inevitable miscegenation of the sensuous images of conjuration. No principle is offered by means of which the genuine and spurious claimants can be distinguished because no principle applicable to sensual images could possibly determine which acts embody God's power.

## Eating One's Words

Perhaps the most astonishing act of conjuration in the golden calf narrative of Exodus is strangely absent from Schoenberg's opera: the ingestion of the ashes of the calf after it is demolished and the pieces burned. Consider the text: "And he [Moses] took the calf which they had made, and burnt it with fire, and ground it to powder, and scattered it upon the water, and made the people of Israel drink it" (Exodus 32:20). Traditional interpretation treats this material as depicting an act of negative conjuration and as a certain archivization of the forbidden idol. Before turning to these interpretations, consider first Derrida's claim that "(repression is an archivization), that is to say, to archive *otherwise*, to repress the archive while archiving the repression; *otherwise* of course . . . than according to the current conscious patent modes of archivization."[23] Israelite consciousness will both repress and remember that which is most feared, idolatry. By ingesting the ash, the people simultaneously conceal and inwardize what has been proscribed but will nevertheless return spectrally. It might be asked, when that which has been ingested is ash, how can ash be transformed into language, into the words of proscription? The material residue must first, to use contemporary terms, be turned into bytes that will, in

e transformed into words, into a system of meaning-bearing signs. Thus
lical narrative can be interpreted as leading from material residue to
_ation, from virtualization to linguistic expression.

This trajectory may appear to be foisted anachronistically upon the biblical narrative out of postmodern considerations, but it can be shown as already
intrinsic to traditional interpretation. Consider the gloss of twelfth-century
commentator Rashi (Solomon, son of Isaac) of Exodus 32:15 in which he links
the ingesting of the ash of the incinerated calf with the testing of the *Sotah*, a
wife suspected of infidelity (Numbers 5: 12–31). The wife appears before a
priest who prepares a mixture of holy water and dust taken from the floor of
the tabernacle, forces the woman to take an oath swearing that she will be
cursed if found guilty, and transcribes the curses into a book. The script is then
washed off in the waters of bitterness to which is added the ash of the woman's
burnt cereal offering. If, after drinking this brew, the woman experiences bitter
pain and her body swells, she is deemed guilty and becomes an execration, one
who is separated from her people; if these corporeal changes do not occur, she
is free. It might be asked whether Moses in forcing the Israelites to ingest the
ash is providing a test comparable to the trial of the *Sotah* and, if so, why this
is necessary when their guilt is clear. Has not the worship of the golden calf
been witnessed by all? Neither Midrash nor Mishnah comment on this point
although it could be surmised that, if tested, the innocence of those Israelites
who were not idolators in their hearts could be demonstrated.

What is crucial from the present perspective is that the characters written
by the priest fall into the water, that the tangible ash must be transformed into
text, archived, to re-emerge corporeally in the manner of a Freudian symptom.
Rashi's linking of the destruction of the golden calf with the rites connected
with the trial of the *Sotah* binds what must be repressed to what must also be
archived, what is to be remembered to what must be forgotten. No physical
remainder of the calf but only that which is written, the graphematic incarnation of lexical and semiotic elements, can be exhumed. The errancy of the
word that demands interpretation will supplant the worship of the idol but the
idol will remain spectrally within the word. No trace of what the priest has
written may remain in the world outside the *Sotah* herself: The outside is now
inside, the non-space where the "true," the "authentic," archive abides. The
Mishnah goes so far as to note that a priest may not use an instrument that
leaves a lasting trace, but must write "only with ink," with what can be blotted
out (Sotah 2:4). Buber remarks without considering the aporias suggested by
his statement: "[By] means of writing one can embody in the stone what has
been revealed . . . so that it is no longer simply an event, but also word by word,
it continues to serve as evidence of a revelation. . . . What Moses says may be
clumsy but not what he writes."[24]

Moses' demolition of the golden calf is hardly surprising; it is more
difficult to account for the smashing of the tablets of the law that precedes this
act. Were they not the tables of the testimony "written on both sides" whose

writing "was the writing of God, graven upon the tables?" Yet
[Moses] came near the camp and saw the calf and the dancin
burned hot, and he threw the tablets out of his hands and b
foot of the mountain." (Exodus 32:19) The traditional exp
Rashi is that an apostate is forbidden to eat the Paschal lamb, .
*one* of the commandments; a fortiori those who violated all the co...
ments cannot possibly receive the tablets from God. What is bestowed upon
the Israelites is a second set of tablets upon which are written the identical
characters as the first. Moreover, although God had promised to inscribe the
text, it is Moses who now writes these words at God's dictation (Exodus 34:27).
Does not the second set unleash the specter of the first? Are the tablets not
haunted by a more originary language, language now indistinguishable save
for a temporal difference? But earlier and later events themselves cannot be
discriminated, for as Derrida claims:

> Repetition *and* first time: this is perhaps the question of the event as
> question of the ghost. *What is* a ghost? What is the *effectivity* of the pres-
> ence of a specter that is of what seems to remain as ineffective, virtual,
> insubstantial as a simulacrum? Is there *there*, between the thing itself and
> its simulacrum, an opposition that holds up? Repetition *and* first time, but
> also repetition and last time, since the singularity of any first time makes of
> it also a last time. (*SoM*, 10)

Are we not with the second set of tablets in the presence of a Derridean
hauntology, a ghostly revanescence that "produces an automatism of repetition, no less than it finds its principle of reason there" (*SoM*, 173)? Not only
would the breaking of the first set prevent the undeserving idolators from
receiving the law, as the tradition states, but it would serve the unstated purpose of preventing the idolatrous worship of the physical tablets. It is the writing itself that can be replicated, that has perlocutionary force, and that soli-
cits interpretation.

The act of ingesting the word is not unique to Exodus. Just as the letters of
words are swallowed by the worshippers of the calf and by the *Sotah*, so too
there are other references to eating God's words. Reversing the negative connotations of ingestion, Jeremiah proclaims: "Thy words were found and I ate
them, And thy words became to me a joy and the delight of my heart" (Jeremiah 15:16). In a more elaborate account of ingestion, Ezekiel is instructed
by a heavenly voice "'Open your mouth and eat what I give you.' And when I
looked behold a hand was stretched out to me, and lo, a written scroll was in
it." Although the scroll contained words of lamentation, yet when eaten,
Ezekiel declares: "It was in my mouth as sweet as honey" (Ezekiel 2:8–3:3).

The intimate connection between sacred food and the written scroll is
attested in a rabbinic account of the classification called "defiling the hands."
Yet far from perceiving sacred defilement as a step toward inwardization,
rabbinic thought is fearful of the reciprocal contamination of scroll and food.

Thus Michael Broyde writes:

> Defiling the hands is a status of ritual purity (or impurity) . . . enacted by the Talmudic sages not to promote ritual purity, but to protect holy works from destruction or desecration. . . . People would store holy food in the ark with holy scrolls, saying both are holy. To prevent this conduct which led to rats, mice, and weasels eating the scrolls as well as the sacred food, the Sages enacted a series of rabbinic decrees to deter this conduct.[25]

Broyde goes on to recount that, despite the sacrality which is common to both food and writing, the latter must be protected against dangers that normally befall the former. The touching of either sacred food or holy scrolls—a holy scroll is defined as one whose rescue from a fire would be permitted on the Sabbath when such labors are normally forbidden—confers uncleanness so that touching one when the other has been touched requires purification. We have seen that the text as sacred food has no place in Schoenberg's theosonics. The ideality of the word precludes confusion with the materiality of what can be ingested. Thus Schoenberg's Moses might have endorsed the rabbinic proscriptions that protect the text, sacred writing, from defilement through tactile miscegenation in what can be seen as a ghostly re-appearance in Schoenberg of this rabbinic separation of kinds.

## Some Faces of Moses

In Augustine's account of Moses, one whose complexity cannot be engaged here, the etiolation or aetherialization of a physical substance that is inwardized is no longer in evidence. It is now the ideality of voice which is identified with truth. The backdrop for Augustine's discussion of Moses is the creation narrative as transmitted by Moses. Longing to see Moses, Augustine laments with characteristic fervor that he can no longer encounter Moses face-to-face so that he might beseech him to explain God's word. "If he spoke in Hebrew, his words would strike my ears in vain and none of their meaning would reach my mind. If he spoke in Latin, I should know what he said. But how should I know whether what he said was true?" Augustine asks.[26] Yet, it would seem, not Moses' words constitute the ultimate court of appeal but rather "truths [that] are deep inside [him], in [his] most intimate thoughts."[27] Not only do foreign languages act as screens but even one's own language is, as it were, a foreign language with regard to inner truth. The univocity of truth is assured only because God is *fons et origo* of all truth. It is God who filled Moses with himself, who attests the goodness of truth, or rather truth as goodness. As Derrida (speaking of Husserl) has shown: "The determination of being as ideality is properly a valuation, an ethico-theoretical act that revives the decision that founded philosophy in its Platonic form" (*SoM*, 53). Intended to ensure the sameness of the object each time it is repeated, this ideality is contingent upon repetition. Does not the specter of a Platonic Augustine haunt Schoenberg's Moses when he insists that his thoughts repeat the "great thoughts" of the patriarchs?

Yet the aporias of voice are not absent from Augustine's discourse about Moses in which image, thing, and phonic element are inseparably intertwined with the notion of a simple source or origin of truth. Moses' account of creation as passed on to us is likened by Augustine to a spring whose waters "are carried by a maze of channels over a wider area than could be reached by any single stream drawing its water from the same source and flowing through many different places."[28] Similarly, Augustine avers, from Moses' words "uttered in all brevity . . . there gush clear streams of truth from which each derives her or his own interpretation."[29] How, it must be asked, do the waters of a flowing stream represent their source? "There are things like reflecting pools and images, an infinite reference from one to the other but no longer a source or a spring," Derrida maintains.[30] What is more, Derrida goes on to say, that without a simple origin, "what is reflected is split in itself and not only as an addition to itself of its image. The reflection, the image, the double, splits what it doubles. The origin of the speculation becomes a difference."[31] Had not Augustine abandoned truth's univocity when he conceded that numerous meanings could be drawn from Moses' text, that semiotic difference was in fact intrinsic to scripture? Were there not myriad meanings and had Moses not seen them all? If he were Moses, Augustine speculates, he would prefer to envision multiple significations rather than "impose a single true meaning so explicitly that it would exclude all others."[32]

Are we to imagine then that Augustine allows for an increment of textual novelty as a text is interpreted over time? Or are we, to use Augustine's spectral evocation of biblical ingestion, to think that truth resides in the great belly of memory, as if Moses had eaten God's words? Does the text not function so that we may have access to some part of the truth which was seen as a whole by Moses? Thus Augustine writes: "Moses was conscious of every truth we can deduce from [Scripture] and others besides that we cannot or cannot yet find in them but are nevertheless to be found."[33] Moses' inmost self is the repository of the entire truth as a collection of theonomic semes, as it were.

Without entering into the complexities of the context in which Derrida's anlaysis occurs, his warning against a certain reading of polysemy is crucial here:

> Polysemy always puts out its multiplicities and variations within the horizon, at least of some integral reading which contains no absolute rift, no senseless deviation—the horizon of the final parousia of a meaning at last deciphered, revealed, made present in the rich collection of its determinations.[34]

Derrida points to a critical difference between "discursive polysemy" and "textual dissemination," a difference that is "precisely 'difference itself,' an implacable difference."[35]

Without difference there can be no meaning, yet when meaning manifests itself in its self-presence it erases difference. It is thus not the polysemic potential of texts that Augustine fears, for he has conceded that Moses can entertain numerous meanings so long as all are true, but rather the uncontrolled outflow of a textual stream whose interpretations cannot be brought to closure.

It is not surprising that the polysemy of texts also fails to alarm Maimonides and even serves a pedagogic purpose so that several meanings may be attributed to key words without theological jeopardy. Thus, Maimonides says, Moses teaches that belief in God's existence can be brought about by exhibiting the meaning of the phrase *Ehyeh asher Ehyeh*, the name *Eyeh* deriving from *hayah*, in the sense of existing.[36] The sentence is not a tautology in that the first *Eyeh* and the second are not identical. Critical issues might be raised by a post-Heideggerian analysis of the sense in which existence is meant, of the semiotic potential of *Eyeh*, but such considerations would divert us from noting the toleration within the tradition of a certain polysemy. For Maimonides the first *Eyeh* is taken as a noun, *asher* as an incomplete noun that must be completed by the second *Eyeh*, the second being the attribute by which the first is to be described. God is the Being (*Eyeh*) whose existence is posited as absolute (*Eyeh*). It is the second *Eyeh* posited as a property of the first and without which the first is meaningless that strives both to maintain unrepresentability and to describe the unrepresentable.[37]

Adorno realizes that the obverse of this process, a striving after a submersion of the concrete in the unrepresentable, is a quest for a spurious and harmful unity. Speaking of the artwork, he contends, "[Its] unity cannot be what it must, i.e., unity of a manifold. By synthesizing the many, unity inflicts damage on them, hence also on itself."[38] If this remark can be taken as a plea for an art of dissemination rather than for multiple meanings that can ultimately be unifed, can Schoenberg's *Moses and Aron* be construed as such a work, a theosonics of fissures and gaps?

In commenting on the disarticulation of artworks, Adorno points to the refusal of certain contemporary works to come to closure once the technical and aesthetic conventions involved in their production have been set aside. "Art of the highest caliber pushes beyond totality towards a state of fragmentation," he declares.[39] Hegel's bad infinite has been chosen, as it were, as an aesthetic technique by modernists such as Beckett. What is more, Adorno continues, such a work of art, one that defies convention, cannot die, "no more than can the hunter Gracchus."[40] Does Schoenberg not proclaim the same fragmentation, repetition, and deathlessness when in the opera version of the single scene in the third act of *Moses and Aron*, Aron falls dead only after Moses utters the words condemning him to eternal repetition: "You were and ever shall be hurled back into the wasteland" (*MaA*, 130)?

Adorno, like Schoenberg, is obsessed with the question of transforming the abstract possibility of art into a concrete possibility. By virtue of a process

Adorno calls *metier,* the artist challenges the forces the artwork embodies so that the work is always already putting itself into question, destroying and resurrecting itself, bringing what is outside itself into itself. Adorno calls this disseminative power "talking back," a radical questioning that, in the case of *Moses and Aron,* can be seen to break into the claims of the Absolute's unrepresentability. Is it not Aron then who talks back, who attacks the inviolability of God's word that Moses believes embodies the Absolute? In Schoenberg's version of Exodus 32:19, Moses proclaims that the tablets of the law set forth his idea, are one with it, but Aron replies scornfully, "They're images also, just part of the whole idea" (*MaA,* 116). It is only at this point when the word of God is reduced to the sensuous image that Moses despairs, proclaiming, "Then I smash to pieces both these tables, / And I shall ask him [God] to withdraw the task given to me" (116).

Is it Aron alone who talks back, whose specter re-arises to haunt presumptions of the Absolute's unity with the word? Is it Aron who contests the ghosts of Maimonides and of Augustine, who re-appear in the Schopenhauerian idealism of Moses? Or is there a double revanescence, Moses and Aron talking back to the God of both calf and tablet, reminding God of his promises? Consider the oratorio version of the third scene of the third act in which Moses appoints Eleazer as his successor and consecrates the people into the service of the Eternal. At that moment Moses addresses these words to Aron: "You know why you will not see the Promised Land/ Because you did not really need to see it—/You beheld it as you took on God's voice through me and grasped God's way/... So you lost God's land but had been already in it."[41] The promised land is not any land, not an original space or time but a there which is not there, a past which has already passed by and cannot be made present, cannot be awaited as such, and yet, impossibly, must be awaited. This is Moses' promise of what cannot arrive, in Derrida's terms, "the impossible itself. . . . [T]his condition of the possibility of the event is also the condition of its impossibility ... the messianic without messianism that guides us like the blind" (*SoM,* 65). Is this impossibility of messianism itself not Schoenberg's Moses talking back?

## NOTES

1. Jacques Derrida, *Specters of Marx: The State of the Debt, the Work of Mourning, and the New International,* trans. Peggy Kamuf (New York: Routledge, 1994), 18. Hereafter cited in the text as *SoM.*

2. David Schiff in "Exodus, 'Moses' and a Lot of Gaps," *New York Times,* Sunday, May 25, p. 25 recounts that Schoenberg superstitiously avoids a thirteen-letter title for his opera by spelling Aron with a single "a." For the sake of consistency, I shall follow this practice except for citations which use the standard spelling.

3. Theodor Adorno, *Aesthetic Theory,* trans. C. Lenhardt (London: Routledge & Kegan Paul, 1984), 33.

4. Ibid., 70 ff.

5. See Alan Philip Lessem, *Music and Text in the Works of Arnold Schoenberg*

(Ann Arbor, Michigan: UMI Press 1979), 181. For an excellent account of the influence of these esoteric traditions upon modernist painters, see Mark C. Taylor, *Disfiguring* (Chicago: University of Chicago Press, 1992), esp. 52–73.

6. For an illuminating account of the transformation from oratorio to opera and of Schoenberg's use of text generally, see Pamela C. White, *Schoenberg and the God Idea* (Ann Arbor, Mich.: UMI Press, 1985), 93–112.

7. Alexander L. Ringer, *Schoenberg: The Composer as Jew* (Oxford: Clarendon Press, 1990), 36.

8. Ibid., 206.

9. Translation by Allen Forte, reprinted with permission of Mrs. Gertrud Schoenberg and B. Schott's Sohne, Mainz, 120. Translations cited are from the libretto accompanying the Pierre Boulez and BBC singers and orchestra version of *Moses and Aron*, SONY, 1975/1982. Hereafter cited in the text as *MaA*.

10. Moses Maimonides, *The Guide for the Perplexed*, trans. M. Friedlander (New York: Dover, 1956; reprint of second revised edition, 1904), 51–52.

11. Adorno, *Aesthetic Theory*, 219.

12. Maimonides, *Guide for the Perplexed*, 228.

13. Ibid., 245.

14. Gilles Deleuze, *Difference and Repetition*, trans. Paul Patton (New York: Columbia University Press, 1994), 60.

15. Ibid.

16. I am indebted to Dominic Crossan for his remarks at the Villanova conference concerning this episode.

17. Buber's account is from *Moses: The Revelation and the Covenant* (New York: Harper and Row, 1958), 147–61.

18. This account can be found in George W. Coats, *The Moses Tradition* (Sheffield: Sheffield Academic Press, 1993), 125–34.

19. I am indebted to a member of the audience at the Villanova conference who asked how the bronze serpent might be interpreted in relation to the golden calf.

20. Louis H. Feldman, *Jew and Gentile in the Ancient World* (Princeton: Princeton University Press, 1993), 285–86.

21. Maimonides, *Guide for the Perplexed*, 332.

22. Ibid., 318.

23. Jacques Derrida, *Archive Fever: A Freudian Impression*, trans. by Eric Prenowitz (Chicago: University of Chicago Press, 1996), 64.

24. Buber, *Moses*, 139–40.

25. Michael Broyde, "Defilement of the Hands, Canonization of the Bible, and the Special Status of Esther, Ecclesiastes, and Song of Songs," *Judaism* 173, no. 44 (Winter 1995): 66.

26. Saint Augustine, *Confessions*, trans. R. S. Pine-Coffin (London: Penguin Books, 1961) XI:3, 256.

27. Ibid.

28. Ibid., XII: 27, 303.

29. Ibid.

30. Jacques Derrida, *Of Grammatology*, trans. Gayatri Chakravorti Spivak (Baltimore: Johns Hopkins University Press, 1976), 36.

31. Ibid.

32. Augustine, *Confessions*, XII, 31, 308.

33. Ibid.

34. Jacques Derrida, *Dissemination*, trans. Barbara Johnson (Chicago: University of Chicago Press, 1972), 350.

35. Ibid., 351.

36. Maimonides, *Guide for the Perplexed*, 94.

37. In rejecting existence as a real predicate, Kant might have warned that because the second *Eyeh* adds nothing to the first any claim to polysemy is undermined.

38. Adorno, *Aesthetic Theory*, 212.

39. Ibid.

40. Ibid.

41. White, *Schoenberg and the God Idea*, 304–305.

# eleven

# Re-embodying

## Virginity Secularized

Françoise Meltzer

I want to frame my essay with three subtexts, which run like various threads through it. The first is Jacques Derrida's "The Double Session" from *La Dissémination*—a text that treats, among other issues, the hymen (Mallarmé, Hegel, Plato). The second is Jean-Luc Marion's notion of "donation" from his new book, *Etant donné*, and the third is the following initial remarks of my own.

Hippocrates, it will be recalled, classified under sacred maladies those that are specific to young girls.[1] They experience hallucinations, delirium, anxiety, and so on because, he says, the blood is blocked from flowing through the orifice by the membrane (I do not say hymen because it is not clear that the Greeks believed in it). This obstruction causes the blood to put pressure on the internal organs, thus causing the symptoms described. Such a hydraulic economy, I would suggest, is no different from that of Freud's notion of feminine hysteria. For both, the pleasure principle strives for a lack of pressure, the opening of canal locks which obstruct the flow—whether it be of unconscious drives or of menstrual blood. For both Hippocrates and Freud, hysteria or sacred malady is sexual in aetiology and can be cured by a puncture, by a man, to the hymen—that dam which holds back access to normal femininity.

This view leaves the virgin, then, not only in a state of abnormality, but of clotted pre-existence: always in *potentia* hovering on the threshold (hymen) of complete womanhood. In this sense, female virginity is like a metaphor of female subjectivity. Paradoxically enough, she will be rendered "complete" by being punctured, when the repression barrier is penetrated. The virgin is, in Edward Leach's sense, a third term marking the place of danger and the sacred. Not yet woman, she also mirrors what complete womanhood is itself: a subject which does not exist as such, and thus a monstrosity (to use Richard Kearney's term in a different context); a foreigner to male subject agency; a ghost of subjectivity. For woman herself is a subject always to come.

Virginity is a *mise en abyme* of the uncanny, of doubled contradictions. The virgin is respected, even revered, from Plato through Freud and beyond because she echoes the notion of not quite being. As woman, she will continue to escape being and so (unsurprisingly perhaps) female virginity is consistently tied to the holy (in its literal notion of set apart) in the West: the *Nicht Ich*, in Fichte's sense, which helps to imagine *das absolute Ich*.

Which brings me to the issue of the voice: The probing hands of the midwife to ascertain Joan of Arc's virginity are echoed by the probing interrogation of Church authority. The Church forced a written confession (or signature to one)—a representation of the spoken "Truth"—in order to force Joan into a heresy they had already determined. Thus the paradox, or ecclesiastical (fatal) double bind: If she died at the stake unrepentant, she was from Satan. If she died looking at the crucifix and calling for God or Jesus (both of which she did), she was a saint wrongly, and too tardily, revealed. What remains unquestioned is the necessity of the fire. As Simone Weil noted, those who declaim about Joan of Arc today would nearly all have condemned her.

We return, inexorably, to psychoanalysis, which Kristeva, for example, sees as a natural link to love in the theological sense.[2] Freud's Dora came to him with the symptom of aphonia. She too, was interrogated by the probing eye (and voice) of psychoanalytic practice (which Freud himself likened to the job of a prosecuting trial lawyer, with the patient standing in place of the criminal). Freud, like Joan's Church, had already established the answers. Thus Dora's voice was not heard, as if her aphonia was the symptom of her absence of agency.

If Dora's is an internalized lack of voice, Joan's is externalized. This is an unsurprising shift given the move since Descartes, for example, from external to internal experience. Joan's voice by itself would be as unheeded as was Dora's, and this by definition. So whereas Dora internalized her absence as subject, and acquired hysterical symptoms (sore throat, aphonia, and so on), Joan projected or ventriloquized her voice onto three saintly sources of command.[3] These three external voices which told her what to do gave her own discourse authority in the eyes of the Church. Indeed, they gave her a voice to be heard, even if it was merely as a medium speaking for invisible deities. Double ventriloquism: Joan projected, or heard, her desire in the celestial personages of Catherine, Margaret, and Michael, to whom she gave voice. They in turn spoke through her mouth. She gave lip service, in other words, to her own desire. Or at least, that is how she presented herself, since nothing can "prove" that there were, in fact, no voices.

Is the female subject perpetually before the horizon of being? Does the female virgin iconize this state in a saturated way? Whose voice do we hear through the transcripts of Joan's trial? Whose voice does Freud give us when he quotes Dora?

Let me finish the frame for this essay with comments on a passage by Kristeva. It is taken from *Au commencement était l'amour*, the work mentioned earlier which partially elides psychoanalysis with love. "Let us admit," writes Kristeva on the analytic situation, "that it is legitimate to speak of a *subject* when language gathers an identity in an instance of enunciation and at the same time confers to it an interlocutor and a referent."[4] What is the "we" here? If the analysand is female, let me say it now: I do not admit it. The French is better for such an expression: *Je ne l'admets pas*. The textual voice here, because it is in the language of the academy, is heard (to some extent) like that of a foster child nicely aping its temporary family. Were the "je" of such a subject real in the sense—experiential, political, etc.—that Kristeva means it, Joan of Arc would have had a very different trajectory.

In the midst of his autobiographical text *L'Avenir dure longtemps*, Louis Althusser opens a chapter on his relationship to marxism with a comment on the eye: "L'oeil est passif," he writes,

> à distance de son objet, il en reçoit l'image, sans avoir à travailler, sans engager le corps dans aucun proces d'approche, de contact, de manipulation. . . . L'oeil est ainsi l'organe speculatif par excellence, de Platon et Aristote à saint Thomas et au-delà.[5]

As is so often the case in late European capitalism and even modernism (in its broadest sense—that is, since the seventeenth century), the polarity between intellectual and manual labor is foregrounded. What is significant here is that Althusser corporealizes this polarity between speculation (philosophy and theology) and the body's labor into a contrast between the eyes and the hands; the body parts, in other words, already prepare for the privileging of embodiment. The eye is passive and does not "work"; while contact and manipulation are the purview of the hands (the word "manipulation" in this passage is followed by a parenthetical remark about why Althusser has always enjoyed having dirty hands). Althusser writes that as a child, he was captured in the realm of the eye "without any contact, or body, for all contact clearly must occur through the body." These comments are followed by a curious state-ment. Althusser "is told," as he puts it, that in 1975, he pronounced a "terrible sentence": "And then there are bodies, and they have sexes" (206).

That such a sentence should need to be stated, and that it could be uttered as a discovery rather than as a fact too obvious to mention, says as much about "postmodern" (which I am using here as a signpost) thought as it does, ulti-mately, about Louis Althusser. Indeed, it has been frequently noted that post-modernism is characterized, in part, as a return to materialism. The anthro-pologist Thomas Csordas has written that "the body is not an object to be studied in relation to culture, but is to be considered as the *subject* of culture, or in other words as the existential ground of culture."[6] For Althusser himself, such a move entails the "discovery" of his body, which began when, as a boy, he lived with his grandfather. Walking in the forest, running, riding his bicycle, digging for potatoes—all of this "replaced forever the simple speculative distance of the futile gaze." He adds:

> Je n'avais rien à voir avec le saint Thomas de la théologie qui pense encore sous la figure de l'oeil speculatif, mais beaucoup plus avec le saint Thomas des Évangiles qui veut toucher pour croire. Mieux, je ne me contentais pas du simple contact de la main pour croire à la réalité, il me fallait la travailler, la transformer pour croire, bien au delà de la simple et seule réalité, à ma propre existence, enfin conquise. (207)

Aquinas's conviction of the comparability of reason and faith, his scholastic moves to "think" Christianity, are discarded by Althusser in favor of the doubting apostle Thomas who needs tactile proof. For Althusser, however, even contact is insufficient to alleviate doubt concerning one's own existence. What is needed is the transforming work of the hand in order to believe, in turn, in the body, and thus in existence. It is necessary, says Althusser, to "think" with the body in order to apprehend reality; not to speculate with the eye.

The speculating doubt of Descartes (which, it will be recalled, is laced with immense scientific discussions on the eye and its anatomical parts) is here rejected for the outstretched hand of the apostle Thomas's need for proof. If the first is satisfied to establish existence by means of the scopic deductions of an inner, philosophical eye, the second will believe only by the sensory eyes and by the touch of the hand. Descartes' famous move away from Plato's Ideas includes being as non-material, and materiality itself as something from which to free oneself. Touch is specifically excluded, for example, as grounds for knowledge:

> Nous ne concevons le corps que par la faculté d'entendre qui est en nous, et non point par l'imagination ny par les sens, et que nous ne les con-noissons pas de ce que nous les voyons, ou que nous les touchons, mais seulement de ce que nous les concevons par la pensée.[7]

For Descartes, the way to avoid confusion between materiality and soul is to free oneself from the body. The founder of modern subjectivity, then, proceeds on grounds of what Charles Taylor has called "disengaged reason."[8]

But Althusser wants, as we have seen, to *re*engage the body, and marxism for him offers the opportunity for embodied thought. Through labor and contact Althusser claims to experience the physicality of thinking, and the capacity to recognize the materiality of existence and ideology. It is Spinoza who leads Althusser in this rejection of the cogito, principally because Spinoza's substantial monism refutes Descartes' division of the human being into thinking soul and extended body. For Spinoza, the human mind is the idea of the body; they are the same thing with different attributes. There is a parallelism between mind and body such that thought cannot be separated from its embodiment. Spinoza, writes Althusser, "is an author who refused all theories of knowledge (of Cartesian or later Kantian type); an author who refused the founding role of the *cogito* in Cartesian subjectivity, and who was content to write 'man thinks,' without drawing any transcendental conclusions." It is clear that Spinoza is important for Althusser because he reappropriates thought as part of extension after its Cartesian exile as mind.

Althusser notes that for Spinoza, the body possesses *mens* (which Althusser translates as "idea," not spirit or soul), and this "idea" is a *potentia* for Spinoza. It is both a *fortitudeo* (surge, character) and an opening onto the world, *generositas*, which Althusser calls a *don gratuit* (an unmotivated gift). The notion of a gift which is unmotivated will help lead us from Althusser to Marx.[9] *Generositas*, which Althusser will later see as a prefiguration of Freud's libido, becomes the door to hope. Far from being the Cartesian divide of mind/body, *generositas* is in itself the gift of thought to the body; it is the "Desire by which each one strives to aid other men and join them to him in friendship." Such a Desire will lead to joining others in the forming of a political state; and so we arrive at Marx. Equally significant, however, is the sense that Althusser has somehow gone full circle by way of a nostalgia for the pre-Cartesian mind, the one that sees, not with instruments and internal scopic deductions, but with the eyes of the body.

Althusser's text articulates the postmodern anxiety, not only concerning Cartesian subjectivity, but also of its transcendental implications. Here "man thinks" has an automatic corresponding mode in thought; and subjectivity is the fragile and fragmentary result of privileged moments when the body is not in doubt because its manual labor permits a fleeting acknowledgment of being. So too, Simone Weil, following the teachings of Alain, has claimed that thought itself must be manual labor if it is to be productive. The resulting syllogism—the body can be felt working, therefore man can think, therefore there is (material) existence—is more than the Marxist dictum that work gives meaning to life. For even though Weil and Althusser, both Marxists of varying sorts and both activists, foreground labor as a necessary aspect of materialism, far more than the centrality of labor to human life is at stake. "I was finally happy in my desire," writes Althusser, "that of being a body, of existing above all in my body, in the irrefutable material proof which it gave me that I existed really and at last" (207).

Doubt of Being is allayed (but not erased) by bodily activity, not philosophy (or indeed, theology). Thus the subject becomes embedded in the body; its sovereignty is not only in question (as in, over and over again, so many of the postmodernist texts)—the very possibility of its existence is captured only in those moments when the body speaks. "And then there are bodies, and they have sexes" is a "terrible sentence" in the sense that what is most obvious, intellectually, to existence—the body—has been lost in our era to such a point that its "rediscovery" is a source of near incredulity. The old Sartrean cliché, then, "existence precedes essence," can in this light be read as more than a refutation of pre-determinism; Sartre, too, is making the body (materiality) the foundation of thought. As Judith Butler has pointed out, in the chapter on the body in *Being and Nothingness* Sartre makes "efforts to expel the Cartesian ghost," but his efforts at "surpassing the body" in themselves presuppose the mind/body dualism. Nevertheless, in Butler's words, "As a condition of access to the world, the body is a being comported beyond itself, referring to the world and thereby revealing its own ontological status as a referential reality. For Sartre, the body is lived and experienced as the context and medium for all human strivings."[10] Although Sartre, unlike Althusser, is concerned with "self-transcendence," nevertheless *Being and Nothingness* betrays an ambivalence toward Cartesianism and the embodiment (or not) of consciousness which can be read as an earlier, less radical version of Althusser's concerns. Sartre cannot decide whether or not consciousness has an ontological status apart from the body; Althusser decides that it does not.

Obvious as this point may seem, Althusser's is a move to ontologize thought in a manner which not only materializes it, but also substitutes the fragmentary for the progressive, syllogistic genealogy of Being proposed by Descartes. In one of the famous passages on "shock," Walter Benjamin articulates this fragmentary aspect of thinking and elides it into the historical materialism Althusser will espouse:

> Thinking involves not only the flow of thoughts, but their arrest as well. Where thinking suddenly stops in a configuration pregnant with tensions, it gives that configuration a shock, by which it crystallizes into a monad. A historical materialist approaches a historical subject only where he encounters it as a monad. In this structure he recognizes the sign of a Messianic cessation of happening, or, put differently, a revolutionary chance in the fight for the oppressed past. He takes cognizance of it in order to blast a specific era out of the homogeneous course of history—blasting a specific life out of the era or a specific work out of the lifework.[11]

It is significant that in this passage, as in that of Althusser, the paradigm of religion serves as metaphor to express a secular conviction. The messianic "cessation of happening" overcomes the homogeneous course of linear history. Further, the monad, that figure of unity within fragmentation, amplifies a peculiar longing for totality. We will return to this longing.

The quiltlike (or aleatoric and quotational) productions of "postmodernism" are founded, not only upon a dismantling of the cogito and the speculative empiricism it engages. They also idealize the body as a totality; a kind of otherness within the self not unlike Freud's topographical unconscious, or the mirrored imago in Lacan's Imaginary. Such a totality is suggested even as the body is continually metonymized: "The body, its exuberant exercise," wrote Althusser, "all of this life at last found and become mine had replaced forever the simple speculative distance of the futile gaze" (207). In Althusser's reading, epiphany itself yields awareness, not of *noumena* (as in Kant, for example), but of the material basis for being. *Cogito ergo sum* becomes *le corps pût penser*. Both the inflected "I" of the *cogito* and its substantiation, *sum*, are modified clauses of the body. The body must be in parallel mode *with* the mind if there is to be any source of knowledge.

This insistence on the materiality of existence is hardly new. It was, after all, Aristotle who noted that for an entity to exist as an individual there must be matter. What one senses in postmodernism however is a nostalgia for a *mens* before the Enlightenment, before the Cartesian subject, and before modernism. As such, this passage by Althusser, which ostensibly explains his attraction to marxism, is more a demonstration of the force underlying the present obsession with critiquing subjectivity. But it is the notion of unity that is at issue, and an imagined time before the Cartesian divide, and its doubts, that is longed for.

It is no surprise then, that Althusser is drawn to Spinoza. As Harry Wolfson has argued, Spinoza "introduces no novelty." For Wolfson, what Spinoza did was to "reinstate, with some modification, the old principles of classical Greek philosophy."[12] If modernism is defined as a repression of the discoveries of the seventeenth century;[13] perhaps postmodernism, with its ability to celebrate the technology which modernism frequently disdains, has its own agenda of repression, even as it seeks to reconsider seventeenth-century thought. That agenda might be articulated as the attempt to repress the fragmentary nature of its own project, and its ensuing uncertainty, through a different turn. Wolfson sees "the great question in the history of religious philosophy" as having only two alternatives: the Hebrew Scriptures or the Greek philosophers. Postmodernism finds a third: early Christianity.

Theological figures from the pre-modern period haunt Althusser's texts (the two Thomases, for example). It is worth noting here that Aquinas, who, one critic claims, "first recognized and defined the principle of subjectivity,"[14] is obsessed with the divide which was the legacy of the Fall. The Fall can be said to have created a wandering of the self not unlike that described by Althusser before he discovered the body. For postmodernism has its own prelapsarian era: before the Enlightenment. If knowledge is distance, as interpreters of the Fall have frequently noted, the modern Cartesian subject imposes a fall and a distance of its own: mind from body; thought from being; speculation from materiality. Small wonder, therefore, that in the contemporary agenda to shed the legacy of the Enlightenment, there is a move to critique the Cartesian subject through a "return" to the body. Althusser has to rediscover, almost re-enter the body; and in this, he is not alone.[15]

I would argue that our interest today in this nostalgia for the thinking body before the Enlightenment constitutes an attempt to participate in what Jean-Luc Marion calls a "saturated phenomenon." Such a phenomenon, for Marion, is one which "an excess of intuition shields from objective constitution."[16] The second type of saturated phenomenon, for Marion, is that of revelation: "an appearance that is purely of itself and starting from itself, which does not subject its possibility to any preliminary determination" (121). There is in secular thought today a nostalgia for religious (theological, hagiographic) texts of the middle ages and before, as any glance at a current bibliography in critical theory will attest. I will be arguing that this is an attempt to witness the witnessing of revelation—to try to *see* how such a totality (as it is imagined to be) was experienced. Indeed, we already find the attempt to depict such a time when the body was totality in the writings of the eighteenth-century historian Vico: "It is . . . beyond our power to enter into the vast imagination of the first men whose minds were not in the least abstract, refined or spiritualised, because they were entirely immersed in the senses, buffeted by the passions, buried in the body."[17]

Marx himself, it will be recalled, used religion as an analogy for explaining the fetishization of objects in capitalism:

> We are concerned only with a definite social relation between human beings, which, in their eyes, has here assumed the semblance of a relation between things. To find an analogy, we must enter the nebulous world of religion. In that world, the products of the human mind become independent shapes, endowed with lives of their own, and able to enter into relations with men and women. The products of the human hand do the same thing in the world of commodities. I speak of this as the *fetishistic character* which attaches to the products of labour, as soon as they are produced in the form of commodities. It is inseparable from commodity production.[18]

We might say that Althusser fetishizes the body (we are back to the "human hand") which is itself curiously objectified as a product of labor. The echoes of Freud are clear (and have been amply noted in recent critical theory). A society which turns the penis into a commodity, for example, and (as in Lacan) "transcendentalizes" it into phallus (his protestations to the contrary notwithstanding) is in an object relations economy with the other and with itself.

The life of almost any early saint in such an economy is particularly evocative.[19] As Edith Wyschogrod and others have shown, the question of saintly corporeality offers a unique example of the problem of the body as both the exemplum and literalization of thought; and as a totality whose valence, but not wholeness, shifts. I would put it this way: Postmodernism's longing for its prelapsarian world finds a strange comfort and fascination in the frequent paradox of the saint's body both as a prison obstructing grace and as a possible gift to God through the Christian notion of *caritas*.[20] The body of the saint is fetishized and becomes itself, through what Marx calls the "nebulous world of religion," an object of postmodern cathexis.

A note of clarification: My use of the term "postmodernism" here is almost exclusively meant to include texts that see themselves as outside religion and theological concerns, from the point of view of *faith*, in general. Clearly, the kind of nostalgia which I am attempting to articulate has a completely different valence, and telos, in a strictly theological or religious context (questions of faith from the perspective of faith). Secular nostalgia for the time of early saints is to be understood as a move to recuperate the metaphysics and (even) experience of what I have argued is seen as a seamlessness between body and idea. As such, therefore, secular postmodernism sees *caritas* (for example) as a philosophical and cultural concept; not as doctrinal or as an issue within the institutionalized faith of Christianity.

While all of this may be seen in itself as a nostalgia for religion, or at least the idea of (the memory of) unity provided by religiosity, the fascination with approaching sacred issues comes in part, and paradoxically, from the fact that secular postmodernism sees itself as rigorously outside religion, outside questions of faith, and unconcerned with issues of divinity except as a cultural, historical aspect.[21] It is then the otherness of faith and of the idea of divinity which, from this contemporary view, motivates the fetishization.

It is perhaps Heidegger, one of the ur-texts of postmodernism, who formulates the chasm between theology and philosophy the most succinctly. "Being and God," he says, "are not identical and I would never attempt to think the essence of God by means of Being. . . . Faith does not need the thought of Being. When faith has recourse to this thought, it is no longer faith." For the early Heidegger, the Christian experience is "so completely different that it has no need to enter into competition with philosophy." Theology must hold fast to the view that "philosophy is foolishness," or it will itself become foolish in the eyes of philosophy.[22]

The otherness of faith from a postmodern perspective, then, lies precisely in the fact that postmodern texts are committed to the problem of being, with its concomitant problematics of thinking the subject (as in the example I have been using, Althusser). Theology, on the other hand, addresses issues of revelation. In Heidegger's words, "The thinker speaks of the 'manifestness' [*Offenbarkeit*] of Being; but 'Being' is an untheological word. Because revelation itself determines the manner of manifestness" (Marion, 62). For faith, philosophy is a *Totfeind*, a mortal enemy, says Heidegger.

In Hegel's master/slave confrontation, as in Freud's double ("the harbinger of death," notes Freud), the mortal enemy is of danger precisely because he or she mirrors, in some way, the sovereignty of consciousness. Perhaps these metaphors will help to articulate the predicament of secular contemporary thought with, for example, early Christianity and theology: Revelation and being constitute a chasm which, as Heidegger notes, cannot and should not be bridged. And yet we see in many texts today the attempt to do so—in its usual démarche of putting together apparently inappropriate moments (from architecture to texts), postmodernism of the kind we have been considering seems to want to have it both ways: revelation *with* being.

The idea of *caritas* in this context cannot fail, it seems to me, to intrigue us by virtue of its spontaneous totalization—a move which, I have been arguing, in itself constitutes an intriguing alterity for postmodernism. Totalization belongs to revelation; being to division. Even Heidegger falls prey to the nostalgia: "Some of you know," he says, "that I come from theology, that I still guard an old love for it and that I am not without a certain understanding of it. If I were yet to write a theology—to which I sometimes feel inclined—then the word Being would not occur in it."[23] Postmodernism, too, comes from theology in a certain manner, as we shall see; and it, too, is not without a certain understanding of it. Faith is as if the last taboo; and therefore, all the more desirable for a culture that fetishizes the body and, even as it interrogates it, Being.

At its most concrete (e.g., the martyrdom of a saint), *caritas* (as any sacrifice) entails not only self-overcoming, or the erasure of self-love in the face of the divine; it also entails the erasure or at least the denial of the concept of otherness. What I mean by this is that difference is willfully unrecognized in anticipation of the transparency to be achieved between the soul and divinity through the gift of the body.[24] It is this transparency, as Starobinsky has so compellingly shown, that haunts Rousseau, that figure whose paranoia positions him outside the ordered categories of the Enlightenment.[25]

In the Christian notion of *caritas* lies the promise of *generositas, le don gratuit*, in Spinoza's sense. Only it is the *don gratuit* of the body, in the service of faith, with little if any consideration for "mind." It is this ability to give the body, that, I am arguing, fascinates much of contemporary thought.[26] From that perspective, which is clearly one of back-formation, such a gift enacts an agency whose definition falls outside the parameters of the cogito. In other words: We may wish to discard the cogito, but it has come to be the mental apparatus by which we also attempt to judge it. What Freud said of the unconscious we can also say of the cogito: we are both the seeker and the unexplored terrain whose limits are being mapped.

The gift of the body is the most material, concrete form of *generositas* of both mind and body; the divide of mind/body is not only overcome, it is not imagined. What early saints often do is persuade with reason, which they then enact through the body.[27] Consider Saint Catherine of Alexandria, one of the few female saints, as Marina Warner points out, renowned for her intellect.[28] To the pagan king who wanted to kill her if she did not renounce Christianity,

Catherine replied, "Whatever the tortures you may imagine for me . . . hurry, for I desire to offer my flesh and my blood to Christ as he did himself for me."[29] She also told the same king, "If spirit govern you, you will be king; if it is the body, you will be slave" (388). Here the body is a temple if devoted to God; but it is a husk of defilement if in the service of other human bodies. At once obstacle and vehicle to grace, the body presents this constant paradox in early hagiographic texts (martyr acts). The mind expresses and unfolds from this paradox; it is not divided from it. In this sense, then, the martyrs whose stories are told in Voragine's *Légende dorée* (including that of Thomas the doubting apostle) are profoundly not subjects in the modern sense. Division and difference play themselves out in the polarized metaphors of body as temple and body as shell of filth in the longing for grace. A successful saint does not overcome the body; he or she uses it as a pure vehicle for expressing *caritas*, if it means self-sacrifice, through what Voragine continually refers to as "the crown": martyrdom.

Contemporary moves to deconstruct sovereign subjectivity, and to refute therefore any transcendental impulse, is, in a strange way, already achieved through faith in the stories of the writers of the Gospels and Voragine. This may seem like an odd claim. And yet the willed scandal of martyrdom contradicts any possibility of rational subjectivity as we understand it. These stories literalize, or concretize, the realm of the divine, such that what even Kant was willing to grant as "intellectual ideas" (*numena*) are indistinguishable (by the saint, and by the narrative) from *phenomena*, or the material realm. The nostalgia which lurks in Althusser's passage is, I am arguing, motivated by a longing for such a seamlessness, such a radical insistence on the materiality of thought. Or, as Althusser puts it, after a long comment on how prophets neither hear nor understand the word of God,

> This filled me with admiration, as did Spinoza's concept of the connection between the religious ideology of the Jewish people and its material existence in the temple, the priests, the sacrifices, observances, rituals, etc. In following him on this last point, as I also did Pascal whom I greatly admired, I was later to insist vigorously on the material existence of ideology, not only on the material *conditions* of existence, but on the *materiality* of its very existence. (210)

Agency flows through, and is realized by, the body.

One of the most striking examples for such a claim again engages the saint from the time of the martyrs: the miracle. The miracle of early Christianity is "religious ideology" become "material existence," to use Althusser's terms. The doubting Thomas of the gospels himself becomes the producer of miracles in the apocryphal book *The Acts of Thomas*. Again, postmodernism reveals its nostalgia for a time before modernity: Althusser, in siding with this Thomas, is himself longing to touch in order to believe in the miracle of the body speaking as one with itself. A similar impulse can be seen in Roland Barthes's notion of *punctum:* "I am looking at the eyes that looked at the eyes of the Emperor," he muses while contemplating a photograph of Napoleon's nephew. *Punctum* is the moment that pierces the modern subject with an imagined memory of full presence.[30] In this metaphor of piercing the body there is something akin to Althusser's awareness of embodiment through physical toil, as if only a wound (to return to Thomas the apostle) could produce the knowledge of being. And of course, this returns us to the virgin.

Through miracles, the gift of the body, and what we might call a relation to the material realm, the saint appears to achieve a transparency which elides the polarity between external and internal. Alterity, or difference, cannot be *personally* acknowledged in *caritas.*[31] What this translates into is that after the saint has achieved the rupture from family in order to follow an apostle, e.g.,[32] the body and mind position themselves as indistinguishable in their surge toward God. Parousia of divinity radically transforms logos. And while such is the case, clearly, in the Hebrew Scriptures as well, early Christianity adds a twist which seems to hold particular fascination for postmodernist malaise: the call for chastity. It is a call which engages the body in such a radical manner, given the historico-cultural context from which it springs, and which places alterity in such an economy of denial, that secular postmodernists overwhelmed with issues of otherness cannot avoid being obsessed by it.

In the first place, those who answer the call to chastity in the texts of early Christianity demonstrate a kind of certainty which in itself must attract our age (for want of a better term). The predicament of modern moral culture, writes Charles Taylor, stems in part from its multiple sources. "The fact that the directions are multiple," adds Taylor, "contributes to our sense of uncertainty. This is part of the reason why almost everyone is tentative today, why virtually no one can have the rooted confidence in their outlook" (317). In an era of uncertainty replete with multiple directions, the single-minded and totalizing ecstasy of the early saint does indeed carry some "icy overtones," as Peter Brown puts it. Not only, I would argue, because of celibacy itself (which is, after all, only one of the several symptoms of the pious life in early Christianity) but because of the attraction, and anxiety, generated by an *engagement* (in the Sartrean sense) so encompassing, particularly from the perspective of the secular, that it dissolves the burdensome ubiquity of the very notion we labor relentlessly to undermine: subjectivity. The cult of the individual in the age of late capitalism may be at issue in every text generated by the Frankfurt School to Foucault, Derrida, Benjamin, Certeau, etc. Nevertheless, individuality is so engrained in our perspective on the world that we scarcely question, on what Andreas Huyssen calls an *experiential level,* Kierkegaard's remark that "subjectivity is the only truth."

There is a significant aspect to Peter Brown's conclusion to his work *The Body and Society: Men, Women, and Ritual Renunciation in Early Christianity* (1988): The Christian world with its "forbidding presences" replaced the Roman Empire and became the foundation of modern Europe and America.

Thus to look back to the early saints is to contemplate our cultural ancestors and to try to glimpse something of ourselves in what seems utterly foreign. Like Freud's definition of the uncanny (taken from Schelling), the vision of the saint seems to be something long familiar and yet repressed at the foundations of our own cultural constructs. To "look back," in Maurice Blanchot's sense, at early saints, is to undertake a perilous and simultaneously obsessive journey in which an attempt is made to recapture beings who, like Eurydice, no longer belong here but are nevertheless somehow a part of us. Certainly the plethora of recent books on the subject of the early Christian notion of virginity attests to such an Orphic obsession.

In any case, a return to the "founders" of modern European and American culture, early Christianity, also engages of necessity issues of nascent nationalism, patriotism, and community. But things are not that simple, as Peter Brown notes along with Foucault, who echoes him. Even though we claim that the call to chastity was specifically Christian, destabilizing the ground of pagan culture and identity, it is at best difficult to draw a clear line between a Judeo-Christian sexual morality and antiquity. Foucault adds:

> The advent of Christianity, in general, as the imperious principle of another sexual morality, in massive rupture with those which preceded it, is barely perceptible. As P. Brown notes, with respect to Christianity in the texts of global Antiquity, the cartography of the parting of the waters is difficult to establish.[33]

It may be difficult, but we seem intent upon establishing boundaries of where, for example, Rome begins to ebb and Europe starts to appear. Such a massive change is a large part of the drama in the acts of the martyrs. Brown puts it succinctly: "We can chart the rise to prominence of the Christian church most faithfully by listening to the pagan reactions to the cult of the martyrs." By insisting upon their new faith, they not only rocked, and ultimately destroyed, the old order; they also, by virtue of their very belief in transparency, paved the way for a Cartesian subject, the divide of which (body and mind) is founded upon an a priori, historical conviction in unity despite the *appearance* of separation from the divine.

Division, in other words, is posited upon a preliminary faith in a totality which defies the material realm; a faith which is no doubt unavoidable with the individualism the cogito posits (e.g., Paul Tillich). A critique of the Cartesian subject, founded as it is in postmodernity upon rejecting that sovereignty, seems with notable frequency to entail a paradoxical examination of what is perceived as the time of unity. Ironically enough, Augustine and other early Christian writers are obsessed with restoring unity to postlapsarian man. Contemporary thought, caught in its own prelapsarian myth, echoes such an attempt at restoration on secular grounds. Here too may lie the motivation for the interest in the life of chastity in early Christianity.

Foucault's reading of chastity as a combat, for example, relies upon the writings of John Cassian who disagreed with Augustine on the role of sexual desire in the nocturnal life of an otherwise chaste monk. In contrast to Augustine (who condemned all concupiscence), Cassian argued that nocturnal emissions were useful reminders to the hapless monk that the danger of egotism and anger were constant. Only when these passions were stilled, writes Brown, "would the monk come to sense a delicious freedom from sexual fantasy, associated with the state of total *purity of heart*" (421). It is this concept of total purity, which we can read as transparency, that fascinates Foucault in Cassian.

Cassian's last stage in the fight for chastity is experienced by the saint, notes Foucault; it is grace. "That is why non-pollution is the mark of sanctity, of the highest chastity possible; a blessing to be hoped for, not acquired"(22). Grace entails a process of "subjectivization": the subject is erased in its abandonment to grace.[34] In this model, then, the state of grace will be attained only if (but not necessarily because) chastity of mind and body has been achieved. In the words of Kenneth Woodward, "Just as the martyrs were made pure by their suffering and death, so, it was thought, were the ascetics purified by the rigor of their spiritual discipline" (61).[35]

Psychoanalysis, with its articulation of an inaccessible and atemporal unconscious, has many affinities with notions of divinity.[36] It is no coincidence, in this sense, that many contemporary studies on early Christianity and on saints in general have recourse to psychoanalytic theory. The idea that the mystics and saints were capable of what I have been calling a transparency, for example, can readily be translated into contemporary psychoanalytic terms: primary narcissism, that stage at which the self feels no boundaries, and makes no distinction between itself and the other, or internal and external.[37] Postmodern reflections on the ascetics betray a nostalgia for this totalizing stage as well. Indeed, primary narcissism is a prelapsarian time of its own: before the Fall from the mother or, in Lacan's terms, before the recognition of lack as constituting the subject. As Kristeva puts it, "the most intense revelation of God, which occurs in mysticism, is given only to a person who assumes himself as maternal." The monks who led lives of pure chastity, in other words, "played the part of the Father's virgin spouses." She continues:

> Freedom with respect to the maternal territory then becomes the pedestal upon which the love of God is erected. As a consequence, mystics, those 'happy Schrebers' (Sollers) throw a bizarre light on the psychotic sore of modernity: it appears as the incapability of contemporary codes to tame the maternal, that is, primary narcissism.[38]

"Stabat Mater," from which this passage is taken, is a postmodern reverie on early asceticism; one of the many which conflate the discourses of psychoanalysis and mysticism. While Kristeva is specifically concerned with the cult of the Virgin Mary, she directly addresses in psychoanalytic terms the modern fascination with mystics. She does so through what she calls "maternality":

ity is doubtless the most refined symbolic construct in which femi-
the extent that it transpires through it—and it does so incessantly—
d on Maternality" (161). Thus the "psychotic sore of modernity" is
y the early mystics who (psychotic as well, but happy) are able, unlike
temporaries, to "tame the maternal."

Gender consciousness (or self-consciousness), another postlapsarian division, seems to disappear into the transparency achieved when one is the "Bride
of Christ." But if femininity "incessantly" transpires through Christianity,
there is more than one catch. On the one hand, the Virgin Mary is as close to
a goddess as Christianity has to offer: Virginal and mother of a god, she is a
model to all Christians, especially those of her sex, in her chastity and unques-
tioning piety. But there are major difficulties here. To begin with, Mary is not
a woman in any of the ways in which the feminine is defined and, indeed,
essentialized. She is rather a being divested of nearly all human female attributes: She becomes pregnant without intercourse; gives birth without pain;
remains a virgin before, during, and after the birth of Jesus; does not menstru-
ate; and does not die, but is lifted into heaven. She is also born without sin,
unlike the rest of humanity. As Marina Warner, whose remarkable book on
Mary directly inspired Kristeva, notes, "The Virgin Mary is not the innate
archetype of female nature, the dream incarnate; she is the instrument of a
dynamic argument from the Catholic Church about the structure of society;
presented as a God-given code.[39] Warner ends her book with the conviction
that the Virgin's days are over; she will not be viable in "the new circumstances
of sexual equality" (339). She adds: "[T]the reality her myth describes is over;
the moral code she affirms has been exhausted." The moral code is the innate
inferiority of women, which Mary both reinforces and gives succor for. Warner's optimism is heartening but not entirely convincing.

If the revelation of God, to return to Kristeva, allows monks to play the role
of the young virgin girl, the Desert Fathers make clear that the chosen are
ultimately male, even if they are born women. This is not contradiction in
early Christianity. Gregory of Nyssa, for example, argues that the distinction
between male and female is absent in God's nature; gender is not an issue in
his ontology. Nevertheless, Gregory uses gendered attributes as symbols for the
progression of the soul.[40] Consider as well (again) the Gospel of Thomas,
where Jesus says, "Every woman who makes herself male will enter the Kingdom of Heaven." The full text, which has been much cited of late, concerns an
argument between Jesus and the disciple Simon Peter about Mary's adherence
to the group. Simon Peter begins the argument by saying, "Let Mary leave us,
because women are not worthy of life." Jesus answers,

> Behold, I myself shall lead her so as to make her male, that she too may
> become a living spirit like you males. For every woman who makes herself
> male will enter the kingdom of heaven. (114)

Fourth-century communities of Christian ascetics consisted of both genders, the argument being, as one critic has noted, "if there is neither male nor female in Jesus Christ, then the symbiosis of male and female ascetics represents the highest form of ascetic perfection."[41] But what would such a symbiosis entail? Elizabeth Castelli has commented on the same text:

> The double insistence attributed to Jesus in the *Gospel of Thomas* saying—
> that Mary should remain among the disciples at the same time as she
> must be made male—points to the paradoxical ideological conditions that
> helped to shape the lives of early Christian women. At once they are to have
> access to holiness, while they also can do so only through the manipulation
> of conventional gender categories.[42]

The martyr acts are full of stories of women dressing as men to follow an apostle, the most famous one being the story of Saint Paul and Thecla.[43] Thecla hears Paul preach and is entranced. She subsequently refuses all sexual relations with her husband, cuts her hair, dresses like a man, and follows Paul throughout his travels. In The Acts of Andrew, the apostle insists that Maximilla leave the marriage bed in order to preserve her mind: "I beg you then, O wise man, that your noble mind continue steadfast; I beg you, O invisible mind, that you may be preserved yourself."

Voragine tells the story of Saint Margaret of Antioch (one of the three saints to appear through Joan of Arc), who on her wedding night cut her hair as well and, disguised as the monk Brother Pelagius, lived in a monastery and then became the head of a convent of virgins. She was accused of impregnating a nun and exiled to the desert without a trial. There she lived until she died. At her death, she wrote a letter saying that her body would be proof of her innocence, and that the women attending to her body would "know" that she was a virgin. Thus virginity, again, becomes proof of purity and virtue, and the body itself evidence of piety. To the prefect who tries to save her from execution, Margaret retorts, "this torment of the flesh is the salvation of the soul" (vol.1, 453). There are many such stories and, while it is true that early Christian men emulated women as well, it is clear in either case that gender categories neither dissolved into androgyny nor in any way were erased from early Christian society. Moreover, as these stories attest, a woman who wishes to lead the true life of chastity and to follow an apostle must do so as a man. The body of a woman, in other words, *shows* chastity through the anatomical proof of virginity. Saint Margaret can leave her body as "proof" of her virginity; the same cannot be said of a male ascetic.

But the Gospel of Thomas also contains a passage in which, rather than the hierarchy of male over female, the Platonic idea of oneness, or union, is espoused. "When you make the two into one," says Jesus,

> and when you make the inner like the outer and the outer like the inner,
> and the upper like the lower and when you make male and female into a
> single one, so that the male will not be male and female will not be female,
> when you make eyes replacing an eye, a hand replacing a hand, a foot

> replacing a foot, and an image replacing an image, then you will enter the
> kingdom. (22)

Here gender distinction is to be obliterated in the perfection of unity. Thus even this apocryphal gospel, for example, problematizes gender in the context of faith, since there are two possible models: Either the woman becomes a man to attain salvation, or woman and man dissolve into one in preparation for the genderless afterlife. Indeed, the famous passage from Galatians on this matter demonstrates in its varying translations the ambivalence of the gendered role of salvation. The Oxford Annotated Bible reads: "There is neither Jew nor Greek, there is neither slave nor free, there is neither male nor female; for you are all one in Jesus Christ" (3:28). But the translation used by Mary Douglas reads, at the end of this citation, "for you are all one man in Christ Jesus" (Douglas, 186). The first translation can be used to argue for the unity model; the genderless oneness into which the soul enters with faith. The second version supports the notion that true salvation must come in the form of man.

Douglas cites the passage from Galations to argue that virginity was important to "the primitive church of the Acts" because Christianity was "setting a standard of freedom and equality which was against the traditional Jewish custom." Virginity was a notion which substituted the Old Eve of the serpent, together with sex pollution, with a "Second Eve, a virgin source of redemption crushing evil underfoot" as a potent new symbol (187). We have seen, however, that the Virgin Mary, potent a new symbol as she was, could only be problematic as a feminine gender exemplum: Precisely because she falls outside any notion of pollution, Mary helps very little in the image of the feminine, or indeed of gender imaging in general. Pollution, in other words, as Douglas argued over thirty-five years ago, not only structures our social codes, but actually gives meaning to existence (Douglas's terms). If Mary were recognized as a goddess, her lack of human gender qualities would be less significant. As it is, however, she is precisely *not* a goddess by doctrine (although mother of a god) and so, the great cults devoted to her notwithstanding, confusing as a model for women.

Even when gender is to be elided into oneness, the specific characterizations of each sex remain clear in the here and now. As Castelli notes, the first-century Jewish philosopher Philo Judaeus catalogues them in his larger attempt to combine Platonism and Judaism. For Philo, spiritual progress

> is indeed nothing else than the giving up of the female gender by changing into the male, since the female gender is material, passive, corporeal, and sense perceptible, while the male is active, rational, incorporeal, and more akin to mind and thought.[44]

Except for the fact that this passage is meant to describe the progress of the soul, it could come straight out of Freud. Contemporary culture is still laboring under the same gender stereotypes at the base of its social constructs,

Warner's optimism notwithstanding. More to the point, however, is the fact that already for Philo (and he is hardly alone), the body is feminine and the mind masculine. "I am a woman by nature, but not by reason," says Amma Sara, who led the pious life.[45] This cleavage, which will have its echoes in Descartes, demonstrates the extent to which gender is implicated *especially* in what regards the soul, which ostensibly transcends the male/female distinction in the face of divinity. "And then there are bodies, and they have sexes."

The greatest of early Christian female martyrs are virgins: Agnes, Agatha, and Cecilia, for example. There are notable examples of married women who are martyred for the Christian faith, such as the mother mentioned in the second Book of Maccabees who witnesses the deaths of her seven sons before being martyred herself.[46] For now, however, I wish to stress that the martyred Christian woman and the feminine virgin who devotes her life to Christ are, according to the Church Fathers, the holiest state to be attained by a woman. The combination of these two is even more glorious. In both cases, and especially in their combination, the specificity of femininity is erased in the socio-cultural (and political) context. Neither male nor female, nor even androgynous, these are Brides of Christ for the Apocalypse, but without clearly gendered attribution in the meantime.

Despite the praise of the Church fathers, female virgins by virtue of their social unconventionality (their refusal to be wives and mothers, or dutiful daughters) disrupt the social sphere. Their exalted state is double-edged. On the one hand, as Mary Beard has noted of Vestal Virgins in Rome, on an official, ceremonial (religious) level, their virginity gives them special status.[47] On the other hand, because they blur traditional gender roles, they are also seen as dangerous to the social code. Ambiguity, as Douglas notes, is always a menace to the social structure.

Female virginity is then both the most sacred vocation for a Christian woman, and the most fragile, even aberrational, state. This double valence persists, and over one thousand years after the great treatises on virginity, this twinned valence underlies the drama of Joan of Arc.[48] In looking at the female virgin in early Christianity, we need to listen again to what Brown calls "the strange tongue of a long-lost Christianity."

## NOTES

1. Hippocrates, "Des maladies des jeunes filles," in *Oeuvres complètes d'Hippocrate*, ed. E. Littré, vol. 8, (Paris: Chez J. B. Bailliere, 1853), 466–71.

2. Julia Kristeva, *Au commencement était l'amour: Psychoanalyse et foi* (Paris: Hachette, 1985).

3. It should be noted that Joan's voices were named and identified by her only at the trial and at the insistence of the prosecutors who refused to believe that for her they were voices of divine but unspecified origin. In this sense too, Joan pitched her voice to a timbre the judges agreed to understand.

Françoise Meltzer

4. Kristeva, 18.

5. Louis Althusser, *L'Avenir dure longtemps, suivi de Les faits: Autobiographies* (Paris: Stock/IMEC), 205. All English translations are my own.

6. Thomas J. Csordas, "Embodiment as a Paradigm for Anthropology," *Ethos* 18 (1990): 5.

7. Charles Adam and Paul Tannery, eds., *Oeuvres de Descartes* (Paris: L. Cerf, 1973), ix–I.26.

8. Charles Taylor, *Sources of the Self: The Making of the Modern Identity* (Cambridge, Mass.: Harvard University Press, 1989), 143–58.

9. See Jacques Derrida, *Donner le temps*, and Jean-Luc Marion, *Etant donné*, on the gift.

10. Judith Butler, "Variations on Sex and Gender: Beauvoir, Wittig and Foucault," in *Feminism as Critique: On the Politics of Gender*, ed. Seyla Benhabib and Drucilla Cornell (Minneapolis: University of Minnesota Press, 1987), 130.

11. Walter Benjamin, "Thesis on the Philosophy of History," in *Illuminations*, ed. Hannah Arendt, trans. Harry Zohn (New York: Harcourt, Brace & World, 1968), 262–63.

12. Harry Austryn Wolfson, *From Philo to Spinoza: Two Studies in Religious Philosophy* (New York: Behrman House, 1977), 64.

13. Wolfson, for example, sees modernism as "a variety of atavism or regression or archaization" (13).

14. Mark Taylor, *Erring: A Postmodern A/theology* (Chicago: University of Chicago Press, 1984), 38.

15. See, for example, Jane Beizer, *Ventriloquized Bodies: Narratives of Hysteria in Nineteenth-Century France* (Ithaca: Cornell University Press, 1994); Judith Butler, *Bodies That Matter: On the Discursive Limits of "Sex"* (New York: Routledge, 1993); Peter Brooks, *Body Work: Objects of Desire in Modern Narrative* (Cambridge, Mass.: Harvard University Press, 1993); Michel Foucault, *The History of Sexuality*, vol. 1, trans. Robert Hurley (New York: Vintage, 1980); Jane Gallop, *Thinking through the Body* (New York: Columbia University Press, 1988); Luce Irigaray, *This Sex Which Is Not One*, trans. Catherine Porter with Carolyn Burke (Ithaca: Cornell University Press, 1985); Thomas Laquerur, *Making Sex: Body and Gender from the Greeks to Freud* (Cambridge, Mass.: Harvard University Press, 1990); Elaine Scarry, *The Body in Pain: The Making and Unmaking of the World* (Oxford: Oxford University Press, 1985); Susan Sontag, *Illness as Metaphor* (New York: Farrar, Strauss & Giroux, 1988); Susan Rubin Suleiman, ed. *The Female Body in Western Culture: Contemporary Perspectives* (Cambridge, Mass.: Harvard University Press, 1986).

16. Jean-Luc Marion, "The Saturated Phenomenon," trans. Thomas A. Carlson *Philosophy Today* 40 (Spring 1996): 103–124.

17. Giambattista Vico, *The New Science*, trans. Thomas Goddard Bergin and Max Harold Fisch (Ithaca, 1948), para. 378.

18. Karl Marx, *Capital*, trans. Eden Paul and Cedar Paul, vol. 1 (London: Dent, 1930), 45–46.

19. By "early" I will be meaning here the second through fourth centuries in the Common Era: the time of the *Apocryphal Acts of the Apostles*, which tells of the conversion to Christianity by upper-class women; the third-century *Acts of the Christian Martyrs*; and Jacques de Voragine's *La légende dorée* (written around 1264 but concerning the early martyrs).

278

20. My definition of *caritas* relies on David Tracy's "The Catholic Model of Caritas: Self-Transcendence and Transformation," in *On Naming the Present: Reflections on God, Hermeneutics, and Church* (Maryknoll, N. Y.: Orbis Books, 1994), 94–106. A measure of the centrality of *caritas* to Christian thought is demonstrated by the fact that the *Dictionnaire de Spiritualité: Ascétique et Mystique, Doctrine et Histoire* (Paris: G. Beauchesne, 1953) devotes 185 pages to the concept of "charity."

I am aware that there are several definitions of *caritas* in Christian thought. For my purposes here, *caritas* is understood as the synthesis of *eros* (human longing, striving of the self for happiness) and *agape* (the pure gift of God's love, grace).

The meaning of *agape* is also still debated; for example, Eugene Outka's *Agape: An Ethical Analysis* (New Haven: Yale University Press, 1975) gives three meanings of love: 1) equal regard, 2) mutuality (desire, but not demand, with an erotic component), 3) self-sacrifice. I am using *agape* in the third sense—for the woman it is necessarily the third because the first and second are impossible for her. Where, one might ask, is the self of self-sacrifice for woman?

21. In *Passage to Modernity*, Louis Dupré describes a nostalgia for lost unity.

22. In *Aussprache mit Martin Heidegger an 06/XI/l 95 1*, privately issued (Zurich, 1952) and now in *Seminare, G. A.*, 15 (Frankfurt, 1986), 436–37. The English translation used here is by Thomas A. Carlson, pp. 61–62 in Jean-Luc Marion's *God without Being: Hors-texte* (Chicago: University of Chicago Press, 1991).

23. Cited in Marion, *God without Being*, 61.

24. Here I am diverging from Edith Wyschogrod's reading of Merleau-Ponty on the body. "Because the body," writes Wyschogrod, "integral to the manner in which perception occurs, can itself be seen, it is in that respect no different from the house or the cube or any other visible object that can be inserted into a world of objects. But as Merleau-Ponty argues, the body is not an object like others because one cannot distance oneself from one's own body so that it can give itself as a totality" (*Saints and Postmodernism: Revisioning Moral Philosophy* [Chicago: University of Chicago Press, 1990], 17). I am not convinced that this is what Merleau-Ponty meant. Indeed, the quotation Wyschogrod gives from his work to prove her point is, it seems to me, open to a different interpretation in light of the nostalgia we have been discussing here: "Movement is not thought about movement and bodily space is not space thought of or represented. . . . A movement has been learned when the body has understood it. . . . We must avoid saying that our body is in space or in time. It inhabits space and time." *The Phenomenology of Perception*, trans. Colin Smith (London: Routledge and Kegan Paul, 1962), 139. In postmortem discussions on the body, it is already experienced as distanced from the self, as we have seen in Althusser. It is precisely the desire to *inhabit* space and time (one thinks here of Heidegger's use of the verb to "dwell" [*wohnen*]) which helps to motivate the fascination in saints who do give the body "as a totality." Certainly, one does not distance oneself from the body in unconscious moments of movement. But the point is that the body has been rendered self-conscious for postmodernism in a manner which others it even from its possessor.

25. Jean Starobinski, *Jean-Jacques Rousseau, La Transparence et l'obstacle* (Paris: Gallimard, 1971).

26. In Voragine's stories, early Christians are constantly being told to sacrifice animals to the pagan gods in order to cleanse themselves of monotheistic tendencies and to demonstrate, through animal sacrifice, that they have returned to a "normal" (and reasonable) religion. Of course the Christians (most of whom are saints in

Voragine) hotly refuse, rejecting animal sacrifice as barbaric and sacrilegious. It is a curious fact, however, that in Voragine these same Christians almost inevitably end up sacrificing their own bodies to God, as if Christianity had not quite thought itself outside of pagan paradigms (notwithstanding the obvious influence of the crucifixion of Jesus). The point is also that a body cannot be sacrificed in the martyr tradition unless it is assimilated to thought. For a view of the gendered aspect of sacrifice for the purpose of maintaining patrilineal ties and as a remedy for having been born of woman, see Nancy Jay's *Throughout Your Generations Forever: Sacrifice, Religion, and Paternity* (Chicago: University of Chicago Press, 1992).

27. The cult of relics (which demands a separate study) deals with, of course, fragments of bodies.

28. Marina Warner, *Joan of Arc: The Image of Female Heroism* (New York: Knopf, 1981), 134.

29. As Kate Cooper notes, taking her point from Bernard Shaw, the enthusiasm of many female Christian martyrs for torture at the hands of a male executioner is almost identical to that of heroines in early Greek romances. The status of the body is not only Christian in this tradition. See *The Virgin and the Bride: Idealized Womanhood in Late Antiquity* (Cambridge, Mass.: Harvard University Press, 1996), 30. See also Page Dubois, *Torture and Truth* (New York: Routledge, 1991).

30. Roland Barthes, *Camera Lucida: Reflections on Photography*, trans. Richard Howard (New York: Hill and Wang, 1981). Punctum is in fact very close to one of the three aspects of the second type of saturated phenomenon Marion delineates: the idol ("the picture as a spectacle that, due to excess intuition, cannot be constituted but still can be looked at" [121]). There is, however, no real "piercing" here, only contemplation.

31. Kenneth L. Woodward, *Making Saints: How the Catholic Church Determines Who Becomes a Saint, Who Doesn't, and Why* (New York: Simon and Schuster, 1990), 62.

I am aware that Christianity has been criticized for precisely this reason; for example, by Barth, Luther, and Nygren. Kierkegaard, in his work on love, insisted that faith is above love because you can't acknowledge the otherness of the loved one. Outka's first and second definitions would be problematic in such a formulation. Also see F. W. Nietzsche's *The Anti-Christ* in *The Portable Nietzsche*, trans. Walter Kaufman (New York: Viking, 1954). See also Lorraine Daston's *Classical Probability in the Englightenment* (Princeton: Princeton University Press, 1988) chap. 6ff.

32. A topus which has been frequently noted. See, for example, Virginia Burrus, *Chastity as Autonomy: Women in the Stories of the Apocryphal Acts* (Lewiston, New York: E. Mellen Press, 1987), 34–35ff. Burrus does a Proppian analysis of the apocryphal narratives.

33. Michel Foucault, "Le combat de la chasteté," in *Communications: Sexualitiés occidentales* 35 (Paris: Seuil, 1982), 24. My translation.

34. It has been noted of late that Foucault's history of Western sexuality relies too heavily upon Plutarch. See, e.g., Simon Goldhill's *Foucault's Virginity: Ancient Erotic Fiction and the History of Sexuality* (New York: Cambridge University Press, 1995), 156–61 ff.

35. The most celebrated example of the ascetic life was *The Life of Antony*, attributed to Athanasius (355 C.E.). Antony's combat for faith is described as a form of daily martyrdom.

36. See Charles R. Elder, "Psychoanalysis, Grammar, and the Limits of Critique" (Ph.D. dissertation, University of Chicago, 1991).

37. See Julia Kristeva, "A Pure Silence: The Perfection of Jeanne Guyon," in *Tales of Love*, trans. Leon S. Roudiez (New York: Columbia University Press, 1987).

38. Julia Kristeva, "Stabat Mater" in *The Kristeva Reader*, ed. Toril Moi (New York: Columbia University Press, 1986).

39. Marina Warner, *Alone of All Her Sex: The Myth and the Cult of the Virgin Mary* (New York: Vintage Books, 1983), 338.

40. See Verna E. F. Harrison, "A Gender Reversal in Gregory of Nyssa's *First Homily on the Song of Songs*," *Studia Patristica* (1992): 35–38.

41. Susanna Elm, *"Virgins of God": The Making of Asceticism in Late Antiquity* (Oxford: Oxford University Press, 1994), ix.

42. Elizabeth A. Castelli, "'I Will Make Mary Male': Pieties of the Body and Gender Transformation of Christian Women in Late Antiquity," in *Body Guards: The Cultural Politics of Gender Ambiguity*, ed. Julia Epstein and Kristina Straub (New York: Routledge, 1991), 33.

43. Cf. Elizabeth Schusser Firenza's *In Memory of Her*, which argues that the post–New Testament tradition ignores the role of women in the New Testament, marking the fact that the hierarchical church took over.

44. Philo, *Quaesteniones et Solutiones in Exodum* I:8; cited in Castelli, "'I Will Make Mary Male,'" 32. It is a curious fact that Philo, a Jew, was more influential to the Christian than to the Jewish tradition.

45. *Apophthegmata Patrum/Sayings of the Fathers*, PG 65, 420D.

46. The story is in 2 Maccabees, VI, 18–31; VII, 1–41. See also Butler's *Lives of Saints*, ed. Herbert Thurston, S.J. and Donald Attwater (New York: Kenedy, 1956), iii, 237–38.

47. Mary Beard, "The Sexual Status of Vestal Virgins," *Journal of Roman Studies* 70 (1980): 2–27.

48. Joan of Arc is a martyr for the faith and not a martyr for France. What kind of martyr was she for the Church? She died, after all, for her faith, which is one of the definitions for martyr the Church has itself established.

# Our Own Faces in Deep Wells

## A Future for Historical Jesus Research

John Dominic Crossan

> *Others taunt me with having knelt at well-curbs*
> *Always wrong to the light, so never seeing*
> *Deeper down in the well than where the water*
> *Gives me back in a shining surface picture*
> *Me myself in the summer heaven, godlike,*
> *Looking out of a wreath of fern and cloud puffs.*
> *Once, when trying with chin against a well-curb,*
> *I discerned, as I thought, beyond the picture,*
> *Through the picture, a something white, uncertain,*
> *Something more of the depths—and then I lost it.*
>
> —Robert Frost, "For Once, Then, Something"

Our subject is Religion and Postmodernism. First, the religion I focus on is Christianity or, to be more precise, the distinction between Catholic Christianity and Gnostic Christianity. I understand that distinction as described by Kurt Rudolph. Gnosticism, he wrote, is a

> "religion of knowledge" or of "insight", as the Greek word *gnosis* may be translated . . . a dualistic religion, consisting of several schools and movements, which took up a definitely negative attitude towards the world and the society of the time, and proclaimed a deliverance ("redemption") of man precisely from the constraints of earthly existence through "insight" into his essential relationship, whether as "soul" or "spirit",—a relationship temporarily obscured—with a supramundane realm of freedom and of rest. It spread through time and space, from the beginning of our era onwards, from the western part of the Near East (Syria, Palestine, Egypt,

Asia Minor) to central and eastern Asia and Mediaeval Europe (14th cent.). . . . One can almost say that Gnosis followed the Church like a shadow; the Church could never overcome it, its influence had gone too deep. By reason of their common history they remain two—hostile—sisters. (Rudolph 1983, 2, 368)

For Gnosis and Church, I read Gnostic Christianity and Catholic Christianity. They each represent a wide spectrum, of course, and the right wing of Gnostic Christianity (John's Gospel?) approaches very close to the left wing of Catholic Christianity (John's Gospel?) but there is basically a profound difference between those two theological world-views.

Second, I do not know whether my own postmodern sensibility derives from James Joyce, critical theory, gospel practice, or all of the above. I do know that *one* Jesus with *four* canonically approved gospels is a very fundamental problem and it gets worse rather than better if one insists that there is simply *one* gospel according to *four* different authors.

Third, when I wrote *The Historical Jesus* in 1991 I did not think it necessary to defend the validity of that enterprise. I considered historical Jesus research an established part of the scholarly landscape. I concentrated there on the *how* of methods and the *what* of results. Granted the scholarly consensus that Jesus materials are original, traditional, and evangelical, all together in glorious undifferentiation, *how* do you distinguish those strata with some academic integrity? And, granted that methodological how, *what* do you get as the end result? I never asked the *why* question. I ask it now. *Is historical Jesus research necessary for Christian faith?* I do not ask: Is the historical Jesus necessary to Christian faith? That could mean the "real" Jesus known only to God or the "gospel" Jesus known only to faith. I ask: Is the Jesus reconstructed by scholarly integrity necessary for Christian faith? My answer will be: *For Catholic Christianity yes, for Gnostic Christianity no.*

## History and Story

> A young woman named Ann described how she recovered in therapy
> memories of terrible satanic ritual abuse at the hands of her parents, and
> also discovered that she harbored multiple personalities. Family
> videotapes and photos showed Ann, prior to therapy, as a vibrant young
> woman and a budding young singer. . . . "I don't care if it's true,"
> asserted Ann's therapist, Douglas Sawin. "What's important to me is
> that I hear the child's truth, the patient's truth. That's what's important.
> What actually happened is irrelevant to me." Asked about the possibility
> that a client's report is a delusion, Sawin did not flinch: "We all live in a
> delusion, just more or less delusionary."
>
> —Daniel L. Schacter, Searching for Memory, 262–63

Forget for a moment about religion, postmodernism, or the historical Jesus. Think instead of that preceding epigraph. It is a particularly horrible example, to be sure. It is bad enough if such abuse happened to Ann; it is worse if it happened and no redress was possible. But it is surely worst of all, for herself, for her family, for her society, if her therapist finds the distinction between fact and fiction, fantasy and history, of no importance whatsoever. In telling that incident from the recent "memory wars" in the United States, Schacter footnoted that "objective or 'historical truth' . . . becomes important when, as in Ann's case, a multimillion dollar law suit is filed against the alleged perpetrators" (343 n.28). But surely, even for therapy or especially for therapy, and apart from potential or actual lawsuits, there is a supreme difference between actual and delusional stories. And it is necessary to decide which is which. History matters. And history is possible because its absence is impossible.

History is not the same as story. Even if all history is presented as story, not all story is presented as history. Imagine this *purely* hypothetical case. In the courtroom, with a man accused of double murder, the defense and the prosecution weave very different stories. In one he is a murderer who must be condemned. In the other he is an innocent who has been framed. They are both highly competent and very entertaining weavers but only one of those two stories is history. The other is lie, mistake, fiction, invention. At the end, when the man walks out of the courtroom, he is either a freed murderer or a framed innocent. He cannot be both. Maybe we will never know for sure *which* version is history-story and which just story-story. But we know that only one version *is* correct. And our decency, morality, and humanity demand that we never say it is all relative, perspective, hype, and spin, or that, since we cannot know for sure, it does not matter at all.

This, then, is my working definition of history. *History is the past reconstructed interactively by the present through argued evidence in public discourse.* There are times we can only get alternative perspectives on the same event. And there are always alternative perspectives even when we do not hear them. But history as argued public reconstruction is possible because it is necessary. We reconstruct our past to project our future. And it is, unfortunately, *not* possible *not* to do it.

I return now, but against that background, to the historical Jesus. Here the objection is more pointed. We have, leaving aside other materials, four accounts of the historical Jesus from Matthew, Mark, Luke, and John. And all of them tell us about continuation from before to after crucifixion at least for the first few days. Four accounts of the peasant Jesus is as good as we have for Tiberius, the imperial ruler under whom he was crucified. We have for him accounts by Velleius Paterculus, Tacitus, Suetonius, and Dio Cassius. The canonical stories are all by anonymous authors, none of whom knew Jesus personally but all of whom wrote before the end of the first century. The imperial accounts are by one first-century historian who slogged with Tiberius through his German and Pannonian campaigns but the others all wrote in the second or third centuries. If one emphasizes how different Jesus appears in

Mark and John, it could be countered that Tiberius is equally different in Paterculus, who worshipped the ground he walked on, and in Tacitus, who hated the air he breathed. Furthermore, for Christian origins we have the Acts of the Apostles which describes earliest Christianity from the 30s to the 60s. There, surely, is the history I seek and all I have to do is read it carefully and thoughtfully.

The problem is that slowly but surely across the past two hundred years of scholarly research we have learned that *gospels* are exactly what they openly and honestly said they were. They are not history though they contain history. They are not biography though they contain biography. They are gospel, that is, good news. *Good* indicates that the news is seen from somebody's point of view, from, for example, the Christian rather than the imperial interpretation. *News* indicates that a regular update is involved. It indicates that Jesus is constantly being actualized for new times and places, situations and problems, authors and communities. They are written for faith, to faith, and from faith. We have also learned that Matthew and Luke used Mark as a source. So we can now see the sovereign freedom with which evangelists adopted and adapted, added and omitted, changed and created the very words or deeds of Jesus himself. And, if, as many scholars now think, John is dependent on those three synoptic authors, that creative freedom is almost as great as we could possibly imagine. That term synoptic, by the way, indicates how easily Matthew, Mark, and Luke can be placed in parallel columns and seen synoptically, that is, at a single glance. It is *our* problem if we wanted journalism. We received gospel instead. But it is all that hard-won understanding of the nature of gospel in general and the relations between gospels in particular that raises the historical problem. What do we know about Jesus and earliest Christianity through historical reconstruction, that is, through evidence arguable as public discourse? But, once again, there is now a prior question. Why not settle for the gospel as *story* and ignore questions about the gospel as *history*? There are, for me, three reasons that compel such reconstruction; one historical, one ethical, and one theological.

## The Historical Reason

> It indeed seems that the recent wave of attempts to recover the historical person of Jesus of Nazareth unwittingly mirrored a movement that reached its apex in Newt Gingrich's "Contract with America." There is a considerable movement from the very guarded steps, taken by German scholars in the first two decades after World War II, to the confidence of the last fifteen years, especially in the United States, the victorious leader of the capitalist world. It is perhaps no accident that almost all the major recent works on the historical Jesus have been produced by American scholars.
>
> —Helmut Koester, "The Historical Jesus and the Cult of the *Kyrios Christos*," 14

The first reason is historical and I propose it in debate with recent articles by Dieter Georgi and especially Helmut Koester. It is the Mallory Principle but applied to historical figures rather than high mountains. People climb Everest because it is there. People study Jesus because he is there. Jesus and his first companions are historical figures and can be studied historically by anyone with the appropriate competence. That says no more or less about them than could be said about Socrates and his opponents or about Julius Caesar and his assassins.

There is always, of course, a general difficulty when contemporary present looks at distant past. It is not that *we* are that different from *them*, as if all of *us* were a single unified *we* and all of *them* a single unified *they*. There is probably as much divergence among modern-us as there ever was among ancient-them. Two individuals from different locations in our present contemporary world may be far more distant from one another than two individuals from different times in ancient and modern worlds. That is not the problem. The problem is that *we* know what happened, *we* know how it all turned out, at least from then to now. We know the future of *their* past. How, for example, do you reconstruct the crucifixion of Jesus as if you did not know gospel descriptions, artistic visualizations, musical celebrations, and two thousand years of Christian worship? What makes it all even, of course, is that we do not know the future of our own present. Only that awareness can make us internalize both their ignorance of past to present and our own of present to future. But that is only the general problem and general gift of any ancient history.

There is also a special problem when religious belief or disbelief, commitment or distaste, love or hate is involved. Writing almost a century ago when the search for the historical Jesus was already in midcourse, Albert Schweitzer divided researchers into *haters* and *lovers*, "for hate as well as love can write a Life of Jesus." He first described the Jesus-haters. "The greatest of them [the Lives of Jesus] are written with hate. . . . It was not so much hate of the Person of Jesus as of the supernatural nimbus with which it was so easy to surround Him, and with which He had in fact been surrounded. They were eager to picture Him as truly and purely human, to strip from Him the robes of splendour with which He had been apparelled, and clothe Him once more with the coarse garments in which He had walked in Galilee. And their hate sharpened their historical insight. They advanced the study of the subject more than all the others put together." He is speaking especially of Hermann Samuel Reimarus, who lived from 1694 to 1768, but was published anonymously only after his death. He is also speaking of David Friedrich Strauss, who lived from 1808 to 1874, but was published at the start of his university career, an achievement which immediately ended it. Schweitzer next described the Jesus-lovers. "But the others, those who tried to bring Jesus to life at the call of love, found it a cruel task to be honest. The critical study of the life of Jesus has been for theology a school of honesty. . . . It was fortunate for these men that their sympathies sometimes obscured their critical vision, so that, without becoming insincere, they were able to take white clouds for distant mountains" (Schweitzer 1969, 4–5). Are hate and love, polemics and apologetics, the inevitable alternatives for historical Jesus research and, if so, does not each option prejudice the evidence in equal but opposite directions? Jesus was received by both belief and disbelief, by both acceptance and indifference, by both worship and crucifixion. Is it not possible to bracket either response today and reconstruct what it would have been like to bracket it two thousand years ago? What did he say and do that begot such divergent responses?

Those twin difficulties do not make reconstructions invalid. They only make them hard. But strange things happen to historians when the subject is Jesus. One example will suffice. I cite it to emphasize that, if historical reconstruction is often a minefield, historical Jesus reconstruction is all mine, no field.

In an article from the early 1990s Dieter Georgi applied to biblical exegetes the same sort of historical criticism that we ourselves apply regularly to our ancient texts. He argues that Hermann Samuel Reimarus's eighteenth-century concerns, for example, were not just personal or emotional idiosyncrasies but were driven by social and historical forces beyond not only his control but even his knowledge. That all began, however, long before Reimarus "in the southern and western Europe of the eleventh and twelfth centuries." From those inaugural moments, "Life of Jesus theology developed further in close interplay with the socioeconomic and ideological evolution of the European bourgeoisie, as one of its motors as well as its conscience. The formation of conscientious and responsible burghers called for an ideal that was able to inspire and direct individuals who would represent and shape the new societal vision. The evolving life of Jesus theology would provide that germinal stimulation" (Georgi 1992, 56). And that social impetus continued right into the middle and into the late twentieth century.

> The origin of the so-called New Quest [for the historical Jesus] in the early 1950s, its rather explosive spread, not only in Germany but also worldwide, and its continuing life were and still are a complete surprise for the historian at least on the surface. There were no new methods or truly new methodological insights, no new texts or any other new historical evidence that had direct bearing on the problems of historical authenticity of the Jesus tradition. . . . For the New Quest the kingdom of God remains central — the theme that since the Middle Ages had remained so fertile for the development of bourgeois consciousness. . . . I observe the main cause in the continuous social and historical situation of the whole quest for the historical Jesus, that is, its location within the evolution of bourgeois consciousness, not just as an ideal but as an expression of a socioeconomic and political momentum. The contemporaneity of the New Quest with the end of the New Deal and the restoration of the bourgeoisie in the

United States and Germany after World War II and within the confines of
a burgeoning market-oriented Atlantic community is not accidental." (80,
82, 83)

Two immediate comments. First, I do not know how such a sweeping
thesis could be verified or falsified. It has the advantage of being beyond
disproof, the disadvantage of being beyond proof. But, in any case, even if it
were absolutely true, it simply shows that socioeconomic factors and religious
emphases interpenetrate one another. And that is surely correct. Second,
Georgi's analysis remains descriptive rather than prescriptive. Whatever he
himself thinks about the rise of the Euro-American bourgeoisie or the development of scholarly research on the historical Jesus, his review is neutral in tone
and impartial in depiction. I presume that, even if his analysis was totally
correct, description is not indictment.

Helmut Koester has accepted Georgi's argument and extended it beyond
description toward indictment. First, he cites Georgi's conclusion and concurs
with it: "The return of interest in the life of Jesus after World War II can
therefore be seen as the consequence of the restoration of the bourgeois
establishment, in which the life of an important individual provides the role
model for either its moral justification or its, albeit revolutionary, criticism"
(Koester 1995, 14; compare 1994b, 539). By the way, if historical Jesus research furnishes a life which can *both* morally justify *and* radically criticize
bourgeois or any other establishment, it is surely well worth investigating how
such a contradiction is possible. To pursue that question would probably tell us
a lot about the historical Jesus and earliest Christianity, about ourselves as
historians or Christians, and about everything else in between. Next, the text
I put in epigraph to this section expands Georgi's review of historical Jesus
research up to its contemporary North American context. I am not sure I
understand that application but it does not seem a compliment. Finally,
Koester concludes another recent article like this:

> Political, social, and environmental problems of our age will not be cured
> through the ever renewed search for the exemplary personality of Jesus and
> his wisdom, in order to legitimize the individual's search for perfection and
> success. A new paradigm that defines the perimeters of a new world that is
> not exploitatitve and that also includes the voices of people outside of the
> Western world may eventually liberate us from the quest for the historical
> Jesus. It may appear then that the comparison of Paul's proclamation of
> God's failure in the world of human affairs as the turning point of the ages
> in comparison with the success of Augustus's eschatological imperialism is
> a more worthwhile topic than the quest for the historical Jesus. (Koester
> 1994b, 544–55)

That is clear enough and quite correct about Paul's proclamation. Rome
had officially crucified Jesus under a governor's legally mandated and imperi-

ally approved right to execute. But the Jewish God of cosmic justice was on the side of Jesus and therefore against Rome despite all its utopian propaganda about Augustus's divine descent, his paternal and personal divinization, and his establishment of Roman fertility, prosperity, and peace. Divergent eschatological visions were at war with one another; Christian gospel was at war with Roman gospel. Koester is perfectly right about that. But why set the historical Paul against the historical Jesus? What if historical Jesus research is not about the "individual's search for perfection and success" or about Jesus' own "exemplary personality" but is about the "new world" of the Jewish God incarnated as human justice opposing the Imperial God incarnated as Roman imperialism? Why set the historical Jesus, because we have to reconstruct him, against the historical Paul, as if we did not have to reconstruct him?

In making those comments, however, I am deeply aware of divergent sensibilities between somebody like Koester and myself. I am Irish and Roman Catholic, he is German and Lutheran. Furthermore, we lived in very different worlds in the 1940s and I was in the far safer but not necessarily the more honorable location, the protected lee of a rejected empire. That does not make one of us right and the other wrong but it gives us different religious, political, and autobiographical sensitivities. I do not undertake historical Jesus research as a quest for "the great human or even superhuman personality" (Koester 1992, 13) or for the "'uniqueness' of Jesus' words and ministry" (Koester 1994b, 541). I do not see the specter of Hitler as inevitably haunting such study. Koester, for example, rejects the term "Jesus movement" (I prefer Kingdom movement, by the way) with this explicit comparison. "The word 'church' seems to have very negative connotations; 'movement' seems to be preferable today. I cannot help but remember that Hitler and the National Socialists called their endeavor a 'movement' (*Die national-sozialistische Bewegung*)" (Koester 1992, 6 n.14). And again later, but even more pointedly: "The term 'movement' has problematic political overtones—one may recall the 'National-Sozialistiche Bewegung' [Nazi movement]. . . . E. Schüssler Fiorenza . . . uses the designation 'Jesus movement' throughout her book [*In Memory of Her*] and characterizes it as 'an inner-Jewish renewal movement'" (Koester 1994a, 544 and n.19). I ask for others less involved to answer, is that association a fair or even decent comment?

I admit, finally, to suspecting those who insist that Jesus cannot be reconstructed historically. I am equally suspicious whether that assertion is made openly and initially or is the implicit conclusion to listing all the difficulties involved. Why is he, alone of all the past, so covered by a cloud of unknowing and a cloak of protective invisibility? That assertion of historical agnosticism seems but a negative way of asserting unique status and transcendental dignity. If Jesus is but a figure like Zeus, historical reconstruction is quite obviously absurd. If Jesus is but a figure like Hamlet, historical reconstruction is equally absurd. The former lives only in myth, the latter only in literature. Jesus may

John Dominic Crossan

also live in both those realms but he also lived in history. Or that, at least, is the first historical question to be asked about him.

## The Ethical Reason

> *What the historian or exegete cannot hope to do by historical research is to resolve what are really philosophical questions (e.g., whether miracles do take place) or theological questions (e.g., whether God has indeed acted in this particular "miracle," thus calling people to faith). Such questions, while important, simply go beyond the realm of history proper.*
>
> —*John P. Meier*, A Marginal Jew: Rethinking the Historical Jesus, *vol. 2, p. 220*

The second reason is ethical and I propose it in debate with the ongoing and multi-volume work of John Meier on the historical Jesus. This ethical reason actually operates on two different but connected levels. One level concerns how we reconstruct, as historians, and it focuses on the present. The other concerns how we believe, as Christians, and it focuses on the past. Together they concern the ethics of public interpretation of the past.

If gospel were story or parable with Jesus challenging our faith as does the Good Samaritan, this reason would not hold. If gospel were theology with Jesus speaking as divine wisdom from the throne of God, this reason would not hold. But Christianity has always claimed an historical basis, so this reason presses. When, in our gospels, are *they* making and *we* reading historical statements and when are *they* making and *we* reading theological ones? Those two italicized words underline the twin aspects of my ethical reason for historical Jesus research.

I give one example, concerning the divine conception of Jesus, as a case study to raise the general problem. John Meier concluded concerning the historicity of that account that, "By itself, historical-critical research simply does not have the sources and tools available to reach a final decision on the historicity of the virginal conception as narrated by Matthew and Luke. One's acceptance or rejection of the doctrine will be largely influenced by one's own philosophical and theological presuppositions, as well as the weight one gives Church teaching. Once again, we are reminded of the built-in limitations of historical criticism. It is a useful tool, provided we do not expect too much of it" (Meier 1991, 222). I am more uneasy than I can specify with that serene disjunction. To say that Jesus is divine or Son of God is theologically beyond historical proof or disproof. That seems to me absolutely correct. It is a matter of faith, that is, of the theologically based interpretation of history's meaning. But to say that he had no earthly father and that Mary conceived him virginally are historical statements open, in principle, to proof or disproof. Those are matters of fact and open to historical discussion.

The conception of Jesus is told by the evangelist Luke writing in the 80s of the first century. It is a miracle of divine and human conjunction, a child conceived from a divine father and a human mother. It occurs without the participation of any human father.

> Luke 1:26–35. In the sixth month the angel Gabriel was sent by God to a town in Galilee called Nazareth, to a virgin engaged to a man whose name was Joseph, of the house of David. The virgin's name was Mary. And he came to her and said, "Greetings, favored one! The Lord is with you." But she was much perplexed by his words and pondered what sort of greeting this might be. The angel said to her, "Do not be afraid, Mary, for you have found favor with God. And now, you will conceive in your womb and bear a son, and you will name him Jesus. He will be great, and will be called the Son of the Most High, and the Lord God will give to him the throne of his ancestor David. He will reign over the house of Jacob forever, and of his kingdom there will be no end." Mary said to the angel, "How can this be, since I am a virgin?" The angel said to her, "The Holy Spirit will come upon you, and the power of the Most High will overshadow you; therefore the child to be born will be holy; he will be called Son of God.

That text makes claims that are historical, that are empirically verifiable, at least in part and in principle. It does not just speak of God but of a Mary who belongs to this earth and to its history. How does the historian respond? One reaction is to insist that any negation is just as theological as affirmation and that neither is historically acceptable. Historical reconstruction must stand mute before such transcendental claims. They are beyond historical verification or falsification and the proper reaction is to bracket them historically without either affirming or denying them. The other reaction is that there has never been adequate empirical proof for such claims throughout past or present history and that the story, or others like it, should not be taken literally. It asserts certain physical consistencies for which exceptions would have to be publicly proved rather than privately asserted. Hold any decision between those two positions and read this second story.

The conception of Octavian, later Augustus Caesar, is recorded by the Roman historian Suetonius in his *Lives of the Caesars*, written during the first quarter of the second century. This divine conception took place over half a century before that of Jesus. As he prepares to narrate the emperor's death, Suetonius pauses to record the omens which indicated his great destiny in birth, life, as well as death. This is how his mother Atia conceived him (Rolfe 1979, vol. 2, 264–67):

> *The Deified Augustus* 94.4. When Atia had come in the middle of the night to the solemn service of Apollo, she had her litter set down in the temple and fell asleep, while the rest of the matrons also slept. On a sudden a serpent glided up to her and shortly went away. When she awoke, she purified herself, as if after the embraces of her husband, and at once there appeared on her body a mark in colors like a serpent, and she could never get rid of it; so that presently she ceased ever to go to the public baths. In the

tenth month after that Augustus was born and was therefore regarded as the son of Apollo.

Augustus came from a miraculous conception by the divine and human conjunction of Apollo and Atia. How does the historian respond to that story? Are there any who take it literally or even bracket its transcendental claims as beyond historical judgment or empirical test? Classical historians, no matter how religious, do not usually do so. That divergence raises an ethical problem for me. Either all such divine conceptions, from Alexander to Augustus and from the Christ to the Buddha, should be accepted literally and miraculously or all of them should be accepted metaphorically and theologically. It is not morally acceptable to say directly and openly that our story is truth but yours is myth, ours is history but yours is lie. It is even less morally acceptable to say that indirectly and covertly by manufacturing defensive or protective strategies that apply only to one's own story.

This, then, is my problem and I repeat that it is an ethical one. Anti-Christian or straight rationalism says that certain things cannot or, more wisely, do not happen. They are so far beyond the publicly verifiable or objectively provable consistencies of our world that, whatever their value as myth or parable, fable or story, they are not to be taken as fact, event, or history. It is easy, of course, to mock that attack but we all live by it every day especially where others are involved. (Where are you on aliens or Elvis?) Pro-Christian or reversed rationalism admits that those same type of events usually do not occur but insists that in one absolutely unique instance they did. A divine conception or a bodily resurrection, for example, has happened literally only once in the whole history of the world. To Jesus. When Christians *as historians* bracket from discussion or quarantine from debate those specific events but not all other such claims, past and present, they do something I consider unethical. But that raises the second aspect of my ethical problem.

We know from the above examples, and dozens others like them, that the earliest Christians lived in a world not yet bedeviled by either straight or reversed rationalism but in a world where divine conceptions were quite acceptable, where, in fact, divine and human, eternal and temporal, Heaven, Earth, and Hades were marvelously porous and open to one another. *They* could never have argued that Jesus was uniquely unique because that conception had happened to him alone in all the world. They could not and they did not. That is the second and more fundamental aspect of the ethical problem. When *we* read *them* as saying that the historical Jesus is uniquely unique and that such events happened only to him, *we* are misreading *them*. But, let me be very clear, they *were* making claims for their Jesus and those claims were comparative over against all other such claims. That was precisely their point. Where, they asked, do *you* find the divine especially, particularly, or even uniquely present? Is it, for example, in Augustus, a Roman emperor backed by fabulous colonial wealth and massive military power, or in Jesus, a Jewish peasant child poor enough to be born in somebody else's stable? Where do *you* find your God? Choose.

## The Theological Reason

> *If it can be demonstrated that Jesus did two different things, it is not therefore legitimate to understand those things in light of each other, as though they were mutually interpretive. The reason for this is clear: we lack knowledge of all the other things Jesus said and did that provide the only real context for the interpretation of specific deeds and sayings.*
>
> —Luke Timothy Johnson, The Real Jesus, 130

The third reason is theological and I propose it in debate with Luke Timothy Johnson's 1996 book, *The Real Jesus*. But, precisely to respond to that book, I offer it as a Christian to a fellow Christian and within the specific model of the New Testament gospels themselves. This dispute, however, is also of interest to anyone who has absorbed enough individual dualism to think of spirit-soul residing in body-flesh as in a lovely distracting house, a run-down motel room, or a ghastly prison cell. This is for me the most important reason why historical Jesus research is necessary. I offer it as a challenge within Christian faith, within the Christian canon, and within Christian theology. It is based quite deliberately and conservatively on the nature of the *canonical* gospels.

*The Real Jesus* argued, as its subtitle said, that the "quest for the historical Jesus" was "misguided" and that it denied the "truth of the traditional gospels." Johnson claimed, first, that the "real" extended far beyond the "historical" and could never be fully or properly grasped by history's limited strategies. That is absolutely true but, being true of everyone in general, is irrelevant for anyone in particular. At a televised debate from New York's Trinity Institute on May 1, 1996, for example, Johnson said that his own wife exceeded as real what he could know about her as history. Of course, even about ourselves to ourselves for ourselves. But the term *real* comes from advertising, not scholarship (Coke is the real thing), and is calculated to make debate impossible. So, with the stipulation that the reality of *any* human being far exceeds what can be known publicly or argued historically, I prefer to retire the phrase *real* Jesus and revert to what scholarship has always discussed: the *historical* Jesus, that is, *the past Jesus reconstructed interactively by the present through argued evidence in public discourse.*

Johnson claimed, next, that "good historical method" could establish "that Jesus existed as something more than a fictional character—the sheer production of ancient literature interpreting him and referring to him suffices to show that—but we can have confidence about such fundamental issues as the time and place of his activity and the manner of his death, as well as some clues as to the character of his activity" (117, 126). But Johnson then denies the validity of "pushing past the framework" he has just advocated and, in the process, negates the possibility not only of historical Jesus reconstruction but, in effect, of all past and even present history. Take, for example, that quite representative sentence cited in epigraph to this section. Once again, the response can only be: Of course. But, in historical reconstruction, you present your best public argument that certain words, deeds, events, or happenings *are* crucially connected for understanding the situation under consideration. That is true for scholars reconstructing an ancient emperor's life and for jurors deciding a modern criminal's fate. And no amount of epistemological uncertainty can preclude the ethical necessity of such judgments. We never know it all, not of the past and not of the present, not of others and not even of ourselves. But we have no choice, even or especially amidst such uncertainty and insecurity, to reconstruct the past that will serve as basis for our preconstructed future.

Since, however, Johnson argues as a Christian and a Roman Catholic, I respond to him ultimately not just with those preceding generalities, but with a three-step theological and canonical counterproposal.

## A Fourfold Typology of Gospels

I ask you, first, to consider four different *types* of gospels, four different ways of telling the Jesus story within early Christianity. It is not just a case of four different gospels, like Matthew, Mark, Luke, and John within the present New Testament canon. It is a case of four different *types*, with those four canonical gospels as but one single type. Three preliminaries. I deliberately use a rather vague term, *types*, rather than a more precise term, *genres*, because there may be several different genres involved in a given type. Also, there is an emphasis not just on content but even more especially on form, and, indeed, on the point where form becomes content, where the medium becomes the message. Finally, it is not significant for my present concern whether or not a given text explicitly calls itself a gospel. What is important is what type of text is used to tell the story of Jesus as good news.

### Sayings Gospels

The first type, *sayings gospels*, includes collections primarily of the words of Jesus. These include aphorisms, parables, and short dialogues. Incidents, insofar as they are present, emphasize the word rather than the deed. There are, for example, few miracle stories, no passion narratives, and no risen apparitions. The classic examples from the middle of the first century are the Q Gospel and the Gospel of Thomas. The former is a *hypothetical written source* discovered during the nineteenth century in the gospels of Matthew and Luke. The latter is an *actual written document* discovered during the twentieth century in the sands of Egypt.

### Biography Gospels

The second type, *biography gospels*, is represented by the four canonical gospels. I emphasize not only that there are four but that all belong to the same single type. In this set Jesus is located back in the late 20s in his first-century Jewish homeland but he is also updated to speak or act directly and immediately to new situations and communities in the 70s, 80s, and 90s. There is an absolute lamination of Jesus-then and Jesus-now without any distinction of Jesus-said-then but Jesus-means-now. In Mark, for example, Jesus confesses and is condemned while Peter denies and is forgiven but those specific events, although dated, say to the year 30, speak directly and were created precisely for a persecuted community in the year 70. You should have behaved like Jesus but even if you have behaved like Peter there is still mercy and forgiveness from Jesus himself. That is why those four gospels could be so different, even when they are copying from one another. Indeed, one might well wonder why they kept all four so that anyone could see those quite obvious differences. The reason becomes clearer, however, when we consider the next type.

### Discourse Gospels

The third type, *discourse gospels*, begins where that preceding type ends. While biography gospels detailed the life of Jesus and ended with his resurrection, discourse gospels began after the resurrection and went on from there. Jesus appears to the disciples and the narrative continues in a mix of monologue and dialogue, of questions and answers between them and him. Two examples will suffice.

The first example is the late first- or early second-century *Apocryphon of James* from a codex discovered at Nag Hammadi (I,2) in 1945 (*Nag Hammadi Library in English:* 30–37 [hereafter *NHLE*]).

> *Ap. Jas.* 2:9–29. The twelve disciples [were] all sitting together and recalling what the Savior had said to each one of them, whether in secret or openly, and [putting it] in books—[But I] was writing that which was in [my book]—lo, the Savior appeared, [after] departing from [us while we] gazed after him. And five hundred and fifty days since he had risen from the dead, we said to him. . . . But Jesus said. . . . They all answered. . . . He said. . . ." etc., etc.

In discourse gospels it is the risen Jesus who speaks and the disciples, especially Peter and James in this case, who ask questions. But the striking feature is not just that dialogue or discourse phenomenon but the fact that it all takes place after the resurrection.

The second example is similarly set after the resurrection but now the questioners are Bartholomew, Mary, Matthew, Philip, and Thomas. It is *The Sophia of Jesus Christ*, also from Nag Hammadi (III,4) and dated to the latter half of the first century (*NHLE*: 222–223):

> *Soph. Jes. Ch.* 90:14–92:6. After he rose from the dead, his twelve disciples and seven women continued to be his followers and went to Galilee onto the mountain. . . . [T]he Savior appeared, not in his previous form, but in the invisible spirit. And his likeness resembles a great angel of light. . . . And he said: "Peace be to you! My peace I give to you!" And they all marveled and were afraid. The Savior laughed and said. . . . Philip said. . . . The Savior said. . . ." etc., etc.

If biography gospels give us twenty chapters before the resurrection, discourse gospels give us twenty chapters afterward.

### Biography–Discourse Gospels

There is one final hybrid type of gospels which I call, to emphasize that aspect, *biography-discourse gospels.* Once again two examples will suffice. But the content of those two examples is very different. The first example is the *Epistle of the Apostles* or *Epistula Apostolorum.* Its content is within Catholic Christianity, its discourse part is far longer than its biography part, but it tries, as it were, to subsume discourse within biography. The second example is *John's Preaching of the Gospel.* Its content is within Gnostic Christianity, its biography part is slightly longer than its discourse part, but it tries, as it were, to subsume biography within discourse.

The first example is a mid– to late–second-century Greek text, the *Epistula Apostolorum* or *Letter of the Apostles*, extant now only in fairly early Coptic and very late Ethiopic translations (*New Testament Apocrypha* [hereafter NTA] 1:252–78). It actually combines biography and discourse gospel models although with far more space for the latter than the former. Of its fifty-one present units, only *Ep. Apost.* 3–12a summarize in swift outline the canonical gospel accounts of Jesus' words and deeds, life and death, burial and resurrection. This outline is actually a catalog of miracles. It begins with the virginal conception and Bethlehem birth, mentions Jesus learning letters but knowing them already, and then goes on to recount the stories of the wedding at Cana, the women with a hemorrhage, the exorcism of Legion into the swine, the walking on the waters, and the multiplication of loaves and fishes. It concludes with the crucifixion under Pontius Pilate and Archelaus (Antipas?), the burial, the women at the tomb and Jesus' appearances to them, the disbelief of the disciples, and, finally, Jesus' appearance to them, despite the doubts of Peter, Thomas, and Andrew.

But all the rest, *Ep. Apost.* 13–51, is a post-resurrectional dialogue with repeated interchanges between the risen Jesus ("he said") and the apostles ("we said"). Here, in 12a, is the point where biography gospel converts smoothly into discourse gospel (NTA 1:256):

> *Ep. Apos.* 12. But we [touched] him that we might truly know whether he [had risen] in the flesh, and we fell on our [faces] confessing our sin, that we had been [un]believing. Then the Lord our redeemer said, "Rise up,

> and I will reveal to you what is above heaven and what is in heaven, and
> your rest that is in the kingdom of heaven. For my [Father] has given me the
> power to take up you and those who believe in me. . . . We answered. . .
> Then he answered. . . . We said. . . . " etc. etc.

Jesus even foretells, in *Ep Apost.* 31–33, that Paul would persecute the church
and be converted to become apostle to the pagans. The entire discourse
section is between Jesus and the disciples as a choral "we" without any individuals singled out as questioners.

The second example of this hyprid type is an early second-century source
usually called "John's Preaching of the Gospel" now embedded in the *Acts of
John* 87–105 (NTA 2:179–86). It is an extraordinarily beautiful text but it
merges those twin types in an equally extraordinary way.

In the first part, *Acts of John* 88b–96, the earthly life of Jesus is summarized but emphasizes the unreality of his body. This is shown by four points,
each of which is mentioned twice in 88b–93 (NTA 2:180–81). First, Jesus'
body is polymorphous and ever changing. The sons of Zebedee see Jesus on
the shore but, at first, James sees "a child" and John sees a "man . . . handsome,
fair, and cheerful-looking." Later as they beach their boat, John sees Jesus as
"rather bald-(headed) but with a thick flowing beard" while James now sees "a
young man whose beard was just beginning." Next, John "never saw Jesus' eyes
closing, but always open." One night, in fact, while John was faking sleep he
saw "another like him coming down" to Jesus. Furthermore, Jesus' body was
both small and huge. "He sometimes appeared to me as a small man with no
good looks, and then again as looking up to heaven." Thus, for example, on the
Mount of Transfiguration, Jesus' "head stretched up to heaven" but when he
turned about he "appeared as small man." Finally, Jesus' body "had another
strange (property); when I reclined at table he would take me to his own breast,
and I held him (fast); and sometimes his breast felt to me smooth and soft, but
sometimes hard like rock." And again, a second time, "I will tell you another
glory, brethren; sometimes when I meant to touch him I encountered a
material, solid body; but at other times again when I felt him, his substance was
immaterial and incorporeal, and as if it did not exist at all."

The second part, *Acts of John* 97–101, takes place at the crucifixion itself.
And in this gospel, consequent on that bodily unreality, Jesus does not suffer
and die except, as John insists, in symbol (NTA 2:184–85):

> *Acts of John* 97. And so I saw him suffer, and did not wait by his suffering,
> but fled to the Mount of Olives and wept at what had come to pass. And
> when he was hung (upon the Cross) on Friday, at the sixth hour of the day
> there came a darkness over the whole earth. And my Lord stood in the
> middle of the cave and gave light to it and said, "John, for the people below
> in Jerusalem I am being crucified and pierced with lances and reeds, and
> given vinegar and gall to drink. But to you I am speaking, and listen to what
> I speak. I put into your mind to come up to this mountain so that you may
> hear what a disciple should learn from his teacher and a man from God."

That sounds like the post-resurrectional Jesus beginning a standard discourse-type gospel but, in this instance, pre-Easter and post-Easter have no meaning since there is only one Jesus who both *is* and *is not* ever embodied. In Jesus' explanation he insists on this paradox (NTA 2:186):

> *Acts of John* 101. You hear that I suffered, yet I suffered not; and that I suffered not, yet I did suffer; and that I was pierced, yet I was not wounded; that I was hanged, yet I was not hanged; that blood flowed from me, yet it did not flow; and, in a word, that what they say of me, I did not endure, but what they do not say, those things I did suffer.

There are, Jesus explains, two crosses, the Cross of Wood on which his unreality suffered and the Cross of Light, on which his reality continues to suffer. The former is the transient passion of body. The latter is the permanent passion of God. God has been, as it were, dismembered and his parts, like fragments of light, scattered within bodies here on earth. Until all those members return home, God is in passion, impaled, as it were, on a Cross of Light.

The third part, *Acts of John* 102–104, begins with the ascension of Jesus: "[H]e was taken up, without any of the multitude seeing him." John then concludes with a commentary of his own. His basic interpretive principle is this: "I held this one thing fast in my (mind), that the Lord had performed everything as a symbol and a dispensation for the conversion and salvation of man." Hence those stunning paradoxes above: Jesus did not really suffer on the Cross (of Wood) but he always suffers on the Cross (of Light). And the former is the symbol of the latter. Similarly, says John, the present persecution of our bodies is important as symbol for the persecution of our spirits; the former may place us on a Cross of Wood but we are always, with God, on a Cross of Light. We are always part of the passion of God. Hence this profoundly beautiful and terribly poignant conclusion (NTA 2:186):

> *Acts of John* 103. (Let us worship) him who was made man (apart from) this body. And let us watch, since he is at hand even now in prisons for our sakes, and in tombs, in bonds and dungeons, in reproaches and insults, by sea and on dry land, in torments, sentences, conspiracies, plots and punishments; in a word, he is with all of us, and with the sufferers he suffers himself, (my) brethren . . . being the God of those who are imprisoned, bringing us help through his own compassion.

That preceding gospel version might strike a contemporary reader as exceedingly strange, but that very strangeness reveals most clearly what is at stake in the fourfold typology.

## A War of Gospel Types

That fourfold typology is not a placid inventory of gospel possibilities but actually a war of gospel types. The center of the war is the clash between biography gospels and discourse gospels but understanding that battle requires some background knowledge of an even more basic and ancient debate.

First, there was a profound fault line in much of ancient thought between, on the one hand, body, flesh, or the material world, and, on the other, soul, spirit, or the immaterial world. But there is an immediate problem with establishing proper *terms* for that disjunction, for the views of those who accepted it and for the views of those who rejected it. In what follows, therefore, I insist on the primary importance of *concepts* rather than just *terms*.

The anti-body viewpoint, or body-against-spirit disjunction, involved a spectrum from the flesh as irrelevant, through the flesh as impediment, to the flesh as inimical for the spirit. At one end of that spectrum was an earlier Platonic dualism, a philosophical anthropology negating flesh as the clinging distraction or degrading downfall of spirit. At the other end of the spectrum was a later Gnostic dualism, a mythical cosmology negating flesh as the stultifying narcosis or evil opponent of spirit. The pro-body viewpoint, or body-and-spirit conjunction, opposed that spectrum at whatever point was appropriate for debate.

That dichotomy between a monism of necessarily enfleshed spirit and a dualism of accidentally enfleshed spirit needs some precise descriptive terminology. If we are talking only about Christ, it is the distinction between incarnational and docetic Christology. The former gives Jesus a full, normal, human body; the latter gives him only a "seeming" or apparent body. It is, as it were, a body for the day, like those assumed by the Greco-Roman gods and goddesses for business purposes on earth. If we are talking only within Christianity, it is the distinction between Catholic Christianity and Gnostic Christianity mentioned at the start of this paper. The former insists on the intrinsic goodness of fleshly body, physical world, and material universe. The latter considers them children of a lesser god, products that have entrapped the goodness of spirit in the evil of matter. But those options are far older and wider than Christianity. They were options between traditional and hellenistic Judaism before Christianity ever existed. And they are options today as flesh is separated from spirit, flesh is then sensationalized, spirit is then sentimentalized, and both are then dehumanized. I call that monism of enfleshed spirit *sarcophilia*, and that dualism of flesh against spirit *sarcophobia* (on the analogy of *sarcophagus*).

Here is a rather stunning example of Platonic dualism, of the spirit's transcendence over the body, and of the body's irrelevance to the spirit. It is a speech placed by Josephus on the lips of Eleazar, leader of the besieged rebels atop Masada at the end of the First Roman War in 74 C.E. The Romans under Flavius Silva had built up a huge ramp against the isolated mesa-like rock fortress and the end was now in sight. The defenders decided to kill their families and then themselves. Eleazer encouraged them to prefer death to slavery (Thackeray, vol. 3, 600–603):

> *Jewish War* 7:344,346. For it is death which gives liberty to the soul and permits it to depart to its own pure abode, there to be free from all calamity; but so long as it is imprisoned in a mortal body and tainted with all its miseries, it is, in sober truth, dead, for association with what is mortal ill

> befits that which is divine. . . . But it is not until, freed from the weight that
> drags it down to earth and clings about it, the soul is restored to its proper
> sphere, that it enjoys a blessed energy and a power untrammelled on every
> side, remaining, like God Himself, invisible to human eyes.

That speech, of course, is not Eleazar speaking to his fellow rebels but Josephus speaking to his fellow Romans. But it is hard to find a more precise formulation of the superiority of soul over body, of spirit over flesh, and of sarcophobia at its most sarcophobic.

Second, there was another presupposition built upon that preceding one. Some moderns may live in a world where immortal and mortal, heavenly and earthly, divine and human are rather transcendentally separated from one another. Not so, in general, for the ancients. Their world was filled with gods, goddesses, and spirits who assumed divergent shapes and figures, who assumed and changed bodies as we assume clothes and change styles. Gods and goddesses, for example, could appear in any material, animal, or human form appropriate for the occasion. But all such bodies were not *really* real. They were only *apparently* real. They were like the interchangeable puppets of a single puppeteer. Could and did gods or goddesses become incarnate? Of course. They did so regularly, differently, and realistically, so that mortals could not recognize the unreality of those apparitional, illusional bodies. But did they really become incarnate? Of course not!

The irrelevance of human flesh, on the one hand, and the unreality of divine flesh, on the other, presented earliest Christianity with a serious and profound problem concerning Jesus. Those believers was poised on that giant fault line in the ancient world, a fault line that involved the whole material world and all humans in it but which was now focused on Jesus. We might think to ourselves: Of course Jesus was human; the question is, was he divine? They had the opposite problem. If you believed Jesus was divine, the question became: How could he be human? How could his body be real rather than apparitional and illusional? Was it not just a seem-to-be body?

There was no point in responding that people saw, heard, or even touched his body. For all those things could be, as it were, arranged by resident divinity. One obvious answer has been brilliantly explored by Gregory Riley. Jesus could be explained not as *god* or *spirit* but as *hero*, as the offspring of a divine and human conjunction, himself therefore half human and half divine but really and truly each half. He could, as such, ascend after a real and true death to take his place among the heavenly immortals. But, if one ever wished to move beyond Jesus as hero to Jesus as spirit or Jesus as god, the unreality of his flesh and the apparitional illusion of his body would have seemed inevitable concomitants in the ancient world.

If Jesus was divine, was his body real and *incarnational* in the sense of fully and validly enfleshed, or was his body unreal and apparitional, only seemingly or docetically enfleshed? One way of describing that clash of interpretation, therefore, is to speak of incarnational as against docetic Christianity. That clash would eventually become a clash of Catholic as distinct from Gnostic Christianity; still, of course, a feud between two major options within the same overarching Christianity. Each wing of Christianity considered the other unacceptable, but it was Catholic Christianity which eventually obtained sufficient power to define Gnostic Christianity as heresy, itself as orthodoxy. And it is, I propose, those disjunctive options about the reality and importance of Jesus' body, that is, about the importance of the historical Jesus, that best explains the clash of gospel types.

It explains how biography gospels, the programmatic gospels of incarnational and/or Catholic Christianity, and discourse gospels, the programmatic gospels of docetic and/or Gnostic Christianity, opposed one another. It also explains how sayings gospels, which were earlier and could have moved in either direction, were doomed by that very ambiguity. They would end up incorporated into either of those opposing types, with the Q Gospel in Catholic Christianity and the Gospel of Thomas in Gnostic Christianity. It explains, finally, those hybrid biography-discourse gospels. On the one hand, the *Epistula Apostolorum* "mimics a form of revelation literature which was popular among many gnostics attempting to combat its opponents with their own theological weapons" (Cameron 1982, 132). If, in other words, Gnostic Christians used *discourse gospels*, Catholic Christians could respond with biography-discourse gospels. On the other hand, the *Acts of John* 87–105 had the earthly Jesus as unreal and docetic, albeit as symbolically significant, as one could imagine.

When, therefore, the canon has four examples of the biography gospel type, it makes normative not only those four but that very type. Biography gospels insist on the utter embodied historicity of Jesus while discourse gospels find that emphasis radically misplaced. By the way, in case you still find this all very strange, let me ask you a question. If you were guaranteed five minutes with Jesus but had to choose between five from history long ago or five from heaven right now, which would you choose?

## The Canonical Gospels as Normative Type

Before proceeding, a short time-out for confession is required. I admit immediately that my own religious sensibilities are irrevocably within incarnational, Catholic, sarcophiliac Christianity rather than within docetic, Gnostic, sarcophobic Christianity. I prefer, in other words, biography gospels over against either discourse gospels or biography-discourse gospels. But I can make that admission without denying Christian status to docetic or Gnostic Christians, without describing them unfairly or unjustly, and without thinking that persecution is the best form of persuasion.

My challenge, however, is a theological one from within canonical normativity. How exactly are those *four gospels as a single type* normative for Christians who invoke their authority and seek to live within that heritage? It is not just their *content* that is normative but especially their very *form*. They are not simply four discourses by the risen Jesus, each giving absolutely orthodox and officially approved doctrines. Such texts, no matter how unimpeachable their content, were not canonically acceptable and that decision was a fateful one for Christianity's future and my present concern with the historical Jesus. Each of those canonical gospels goes back to the historical Jesus of the late 20s in his Jewish homeland but each of them has that Jesus speak directly to its own immediate situations and communities. In every case there is a dialectic of then and now, of then as now, that is, of the historical-Jesus-then as the risen-Jesus-now. It is not the historical Jesus alone-then and not the risen Jesus alone-now, but the two as one within a contemporary faith. It is always that same process but always with slightly or massively divergent products. Think, for example, of how differently the Agony in the Garden appears in Mark 14, which has no garden, and in John 18, which has no agony. But still that dialectic of then and now continues to hold. My proposal is that *the canonical gospel type is normative primarily as that dialectical process.* Those gospels always created an interaction of historical Jesus and risen Jesus and that interaction must be repeated again and again throughout Christian history.

The Easter issues of *Newsweek, Time,* and *U.S. News & World Report* on April 8, 1996, all had cover stories on the historical Jesus. *Newsweek* had the caption "Rethinking the Resurrection: A New Debate about the Risen Christ." It was written across a picture of Jesus rising heavenwards, arms uplifted, hands facing outwards. What struck me immediately as strange was the complete absence of any wounds on those clearly visible hands and feet. I failed to realize that they had mistakenly taken Jesus from a transfiguration instead of a resurrection painting. There were, of course, no wounds on that Vatican work by Raphael because it depicted an event before the death of Jesus. *U.S. News & World Report,* on the other hand (no pun intended), had a correct picture. Its cover had the caption "In Search of Jesus: Who was he? New appraisals of his life and meaning?" written across Jesus from a Bellini painting of the resurrection with the wound in Jesus' right hand clearly visible.

There is, ever and always, only one Jesus. For Christians that is the historical Jesus *as* risen Jesus. And the test is this: Does the risen Jesus still carry the wounds of crucifixion? In Christian gospel, art, and mysticism, the answer is clearly yes. But those wounds are the marks of history and to understand them you would have to know about his death. But to understand the death, you would have to know about his life, for otherwise he might have been a criminal meeting appropriate sentence or his executioners might have been savages operating from sheer random brutality. With those canonical gospels as inaugural models and primordial examples, each Christian generation must write its gospels anew, must first reconstruct its historical Jesus with fullest integrity and then say and live what that reconstruction means for present life in this world. History and faith are always a dialectic for incarnational Christianity. Put otherwise, its insistence on the resurrection of Jesus' body is my insistence on the permanence of Jesus' history. But then, now, and always it is a history seen by faith.

## Face and Well

> What mystery pervades a well! . . .
> But nature is a stranger yet;
> The ones that cite her most
> Have never passed her haunted house,
> Nor simplified her ghost.

—Emily Dickinson, *Poems*, Vol. 3, Page 970 (#1400)

There is an oft-repeated and rather cheap gibe that historical Jesus researchers are simply looking down a deep well and seeing their own reflections from below. I call it cheap for three reasons. First, those who use it against others seldom apply it to themselves. Second, it is almost impossible to imagine a reconstruction that could not be dismissed by its assertion. Your Jesus is an apocalyptic: you are bemused by the approaching millennium. Your Jesus is a healer: you have been hearing Bill Moyers. Your Jesus is an ecstatic: you are interested in brain chemistry. What could anyone *ever* say, that would not fall under that ban? Third, those who repeat it so easily must never have looked down a deep well and pondered what Emily Dickinson calls its pervasive mystery. From now on, therefore, I intend to take that assertion not as cheap gibe but as profound truth.

I accepted that deep-well analogy as destiny rather than taunt during the "Jesus at 2000" symposium at Oregon State University in 1996. That meeting, created and chaired by Marcus Borg, was down-linked through satellite across the country by New York's Trinity Institute so that we had a live audience of over a thousand and a television audience with call-ins from about 800 sites. I was reminded by Tom Hall, calling in from Rhode Island, that the poet Robert Frost had already used the well image in the poem that is the epigraph at the beginning of this essay. So, admonished by those like Dickinson and Frost who had at least looked down some literal wells, I think once more about that taunt of seeing but our own faces in reconstructing the past. And, in the light of what follows, I restate my earlier definition of history: *History is the past reconstructed interactively by the present through argued evidence in public discourse.*

Imagine two alternative and opposite modes of historical reconstruction, one an impossible delusion, the other a possible illusion. The possible illusion is *narcissism*. You think you are seeing the past or the other when all you see is your own reflected present. You see only what was there before you began. You imprint your own present on the past and call it history. *Narcissism* sees its own face and, ignoring the water that shows it up, falls in love with itself. It is the first of the twin images in Frost's poem. It is when the water

Gives me back in a shining surface picture
Me myself in the summer heaven, godlike,
Looking out of a wreath of fern and cloud puffs.

The impossible delusion is *positivism*. It imagines that you can know the past without any interference from your own personal and social situation as knower. You can see, as it were, without your own eye being involved. You can discern the past once and for all forever and see it pure and uncontaminated by that discernment. Positivism is the delusion that we can see the water without our own face being mirrored in it. It thinks we can see the surface without simultaneously seeing our own eyes. It is the second of the twin images in Frost's poem. It is when, even if only once, uncertainly, possibly, and vaguely,

I discerned, as I thought, beyond the picture,
Through the picture, a something white, uncertain,
Something more of the depths — and then I lost it.

But, I would ask, *if the poet's face is white*, how did it see "through the picture" of itself "a something white" that was also "beyond the picture"? *Maybe what it saw was its own face so strangely different that it did not recognize it.* That introduces a third image not given but provoked by Frost's second one.

There is, therefore, a third alternative, and I'll call it *interactivism*, which is, incidentally, the way I understand postmodernism. The past and present must interact with one another, each changing and challenging the other, and the ideal is an absolutely fair and equal reaction between one another. Back to the well. You cannot see the surface without simultaneously seeing, disturbing, and distorting your own face. You cannot see your own face without simultaneously seeing, disturbing, and distorting the surface. It is the third image begging to be recognized behind the two overt ones in Frost's poem. What the poet saw was his own face so strangely different that he did not recognize it as such. It was, indeed, "something white" and "something more of the depths." But it was not "beyond the picture" or even "through the picture." It was the picture itself changed utterly. That is the dialectic of interactivism and, as distinct from either narcissism or positivism, it is both possible and necessary. Two examples, both reviewing classical scholarship, may help as illustrations and warnings.

The first example concerns the historical reconstruction of the Roman emperor Augustus. Richard Mellor frames his book on Tacitus with these comments about four great interpretations of Rome's transition from republican to imperial rule:

> The greatest Roman historians of the last two centuries — Gibbon, Mommsen, Rostovzteff, and Syme — wrote with passion as they saw connections between Rome and their own times. . . . Edward Gibbon, a child of the French Enlightenment which affected his views of religion, was issued in

"Bowdlerized" editions in Victorian England; Theodor Mommsen, the only professional historian to win the Nobel Prize for Literature, wrote a passionate, multi-volume *History of Rome* in which Caesar became the inevitable solution to republican Rome's dilemma as Mommsen himself yearned for a strongman to resolve the chaos of nineteenth-century Germany; Michael Rostovzteff brought his flight from revolutionary St. Petersburg to bear on his *Social and Economic History of the Roman Empire* (1926)—a glorification of the Roman municipal bourgeoisie; and Sir Ronald Syme's *The Roman Revolution* (1939) looked at the rise of Augustus through the spectacles of a liberal who saw on his visits to Italy the names and trappings of Augustan Rome used by a new *dux*, Benito Mussolini, and wished to expose in a very Tacitean way the thuggish similarities between the two regimes. (Mellor 1993, 45, 164)

In all those cases powerful socio-personal interactions between past and present resulted in towering achievements, works we call classical in both senses of that term. And, of course, their multiplicity serves as a corrective each on the other.

The second example concerns the historical reconstruction of earliest Christian art. Thomas Mathews discusses "how the Emperor Mystique came to be the controlling theory for explaining the development of Christian imagery" and he asserts that

the need to interpret Christ as an emperor tells more about the historians involved than it does about Early Christian art. The formulation of the theory can be traced to three very bold and original European scholars in the period between the wars; the medievalist Ernst Kantorowicz, a German Jew of a well-to-do merchant family; the Hungarian archaeologist Andreas Alföldi, son of a country doctor; and art historian André Grabar, a Russian emigré, whose senatorial family held important posts under the last Czars. . . . If there is a single common thread uniting the life and work of these three great scholars, it is nostalgia for lost empire. The three imperial states in which they were raised, and which they fought valiantly to defend, they saw crumble ignominiously in the horrible chaos of the First World War and its consequences. The glory of the czars, the might of the Prussian and Austro-Hungarian emperors, could never be restored. (Mathews 1993, 16,19)

Mathews judges that interaction of present and past to have misinterpreted early Christian art and then draws an explicit analogy between his own corrective reconstruction and the

quest for the "historical" Jesus, an enterprise that verged on reducing him to the product of wishful thinking on the part of his first disciples. Since Christ wrote nothing himself, the historian is necessarily limited to sifting through the distorted impressions of a circle of people who were very deeply affected by their experience of him. The Christ of Early Christian art is quite as elusive as the "historical" Jesus. As in the written sources, so in the visual monuments Christ has many guises, depending on who is

> visualizing him. We are faced, then, with the difficult task of understand-
> ing as far as possible the impression Christ made on people when they, for
> the first time, were seeking to represent him. Hitherto he had existed only
> in the hearts of believers, in the visions of mystics, in the words of preach-
> ers; now he has to have a life in stone and paint. (Mathews 1993, 21–22)

In historical reconstruction the present and past always interact. Even our *best* theories and methods are still *our* best ones. They are all dated and doomed not just when they are wrong but especially when they are right. They need, when anything important is involved, to be done over and over again. That does not make history worthless. We ourselves are also dated and doomed but that does not make life worthless. It just makes death inevitable. I have two corollaries from that understanding of interactivism.

A first corollary concerns the term *search* or *quest*. You may have noticed that I do not speak of the *search* for the historical Jesus nor of the *quest* for Christian origins. Those terms seem to indicate a positivistic process in which we are going to attain an answer once and for all forever. That is not how I now imagine the process. I speak instead of reconstruction, and that is something that must be done over and over again in different times and different places, by different groups and different communities, and by every generation again and again and again. In order to emphasize that viewpoint, I talk hereafter only of reconstructing the historical Jesus as best one can at any given place and time.

Recently, Tom Wright spent very many pages distinguishing three quests for the historical Jesus. The First Quest lasted from Reimarus to Schweitzer, in round numbers from 1700 to 1900. The Second or New Quest was proposed by Ernst Käsemann in 1953 as a reaction to the bracketing of the historical Jesus in the work of his teacher, Rudolf Bultmann. But I think it fair to say that no New Quest ever took place, no Second Search ever followed that mani-festo. Wright proposes, however, that many contemporary scholars, including myself, are simply on a "renewed 'New Quest.'" We are, therefore, past of the discarded past. The Third Quest is actually composed of about twenty schol-ars, including Wright himself. He invented that title just for that group be-cause that "is where the real leading edge of contemporary Jesus-scholarship is to be found" (Wright 1996, 84). Unable to decide whether that cartography is amusing impertinence or annoying arrogance, I limit myself to two brief comments. Positivist delusions haunt such terms as *search* or *quest*. The his-torical Jesus, like the Holy Grail, is to be found once and for all forever. That is not how I see it. Furthermore, I wonder why Wright does not simply put people like myself in a Third Quest and his group into a Fourth Quest. Or, put another way, does Wright imagine a Fourth Quest for the future, and then a Fifth, and a Sixth, etc.? Positivist delusion also haunts the term *third*. In Indo-European folklore, the third time is closure, finish, completion. The hero may fail twice but will succeed the third time. That happens, unfortunately, only in folklore and fairy story.

A second corollary concerns method. I insist that Jesus reconstruction, like all such reconstruction, is always a creative interaction between past and present. But what keeps that dialectic of us and them as even and honest as possible? Method, method, and, once again, method. It will not guarantee us the truth because nothing can do that. But method, as self-conscious and self-critical as we can make it, is our only discipline. It cannot ever take us out of our present skins and bodies, minds and hearts, societies and cultures. But it is our one best hope for honesty. It is the due process of history. And that brings me back once again to Tom Wright. I think we are in agreement on what he calls "critical realism" and I call "interactivism." But the next question is How does it actually work in practice? My answer is by developing a method that protects your subject not from conversation but from violation, not from discussion but from disfigurement. That was why, for example, I gave *my* complete inventory of the Jesus tradition broken down in terms of independent attestation and stratigraphic location as appendix to *The Historical Jesus.* Wright, however, finds, that "despite the postmodern tone which predominates in the book, the massive inventory of material is bound to look like a thoroughly modernist piece of work, appearing to lay firm, almost positivist, foundations for the main argument of the book" (Wright 1996, 50). A postmodern sensibility, that is, an equal awareness of your own and your subject's historicity, does not preclude but demands attention to method. As due process keeps the legal interaction of defense and prosecution fair, so due method keeps the historical interaction of past and present honest. But there is not in my work any presumption that the historical Jesus or earliest Christianity are something you get once and for all forever. And that is not because they are special or unique. No past of continuing importance can ever avoid repeated reconstruction.

This, then, is my challenge. Catholic, as distinct from Gnostic, Christianity is a dialectic between history and faith. That dialectic has its normative model in the canonical gospel *type* and its paradigmatic instances in those four gospel *texts*. They show, across the 70s, 80s, and 90s of that first century, how Jesus-then becomes Jesus-now, how the historical Jesus become the risen Jesus, and how, while you can have history without faith, you cannot have faith without history. In every generation, the historical Jesus must be reconstructed anew and that reconstruction must become by faith the face of God for here and now. If that seems too strange, consider this parallel situation.

Within Catholic Christianity the Bible, the New Testament, and especially the gospels are the Word of God made text, just as Jesus is the Word of God made flesh. It would have been quite possible for Christian tradition to have declared some one, single, given manuscript of the Bible to be official and canonical. Imagine that had happened, for example, to the Codex Vaticanus, a fourth-century vellum copy of 759 leaves, three columns per page, forty-two lines to the column. Imagine that had been declared to be the immutable and inspired word of God with its three-column page manifesting forever the mystery of the Trinity. There might have been discussion on what to do about the indignant scribe who added in the left-hand margin of Hebrews 1:3 this succinct comment on an earlier colleague's work: "Fool and knave, can't you leave the old reading alone, and not alter it" (as shown in Metzger 1981, 74). It would make no difference what tattered fragments or total texts survived from earlier times in the Egyptian sands. It would make no difference what academic scholars or textual critics thought was historically a more accurate original text. The Codex Vaticanus would be it, once and for all forever. The Word of God made text would be safe from the vagaries of history, the excavations of archeologists, and the surprise discoveries of peasant or shepherds.

Instead of that option, I have on my desk the Fourth Revised Edition of *The Greek New Testament* from the United Bible Societies, published in 1993. It gives the closest a committee can come to the original text with the alternative readings in footnote apparatus. It grades any disputed reading from A to D as "an indication of the relative degree of certainty for each variant adopted as the text" (Metzger 1971, viii). Bruce Metzger explains the committee's grading as follows:

> The letter {A} signifies that the text is virtually certain, while {B} indicates that there is some degree of doubt concerning the reading selected for the text. The letter {C} means that there is a considerable degree of doubt whether the text or the apparatus contains the superior reading, while {D} shows that there is a very high degree of doubt concerning the reading selected for the text. In fact, among the {D} decisions sometimes none of the variant readings commended itself as original, and therefore the only recourse was to print the least unsatisfactory reading. (Metzger 1971, xxviii)

I believe, as a Christian, in the Word of God, not in the words of specific papyri or the votes of specific committees. But fact and faith, history and theology intertwine together in that process and cannot ever be totally separated.

As with the Word of God made text, so also with the Word of God made flesh. Historical reconstruction interweaves with Christian faith and neither can substitute for the other. I insist, however, that it did not have to be that way. It is Catholic, as distinct from Gnostic, Christianity that gave itself as hostage to history. (What, for example, if we found a copy of Matthew dated definitely to 100 C.E. and clearly a rather different first draft of what we now have in our New Testament?) It is now too late for it to repent and I, for one, would not want it to do so. But I wonder about this: Is the history of Christianity and especially of Christian theology the long, slow victory of Gnostic over Catholic Christianity?

## WORKS CITED

Borg, Marcus J., ed. 1997. *Jesus at 2000*. Boulder, Colo.: Westview Press.

Cameron, Ron, ed. 1982. *The Other Gospels: Non-Canonical Gospel Texts*. Philadelphia: Westminster.

Crossan, John Dominic. 1991. *The Historical Jesus: The Life of a Mediterranean Jewish Peasant*. San Francisco: HarperSanFrancisco.

Dickinson, Emily. 1955. *Poems: Including Variant Readings Critically Compared with All Known Manuscripts*. 3 vols. Edited by Thomas Herbert Johnson. Cambridge, Mass.: Belknap Press of Harvard University Press.

Frost, Robert. 1979. *The Poetry of Robert Frost: The Collected Poems, Complete and Unabridged*. Ed. Edward Connery Lathem. New York: Holt.

Georgi, Dieter. 1992. "The Interest in Life of Jesus Theology as a Paradigm for the Social History of Biblical Criticism." *Harvard Theological Review* 85:51–83.

Johnson, Luke Timothy. 1996. *The Real Jesus: The Misguided Quest for the Historical Jesus and the Truth of the Traditional Gospels*. San Francisco: HarperSanFrancisco.

Koester, Helmut. 1992. "Jesus the Victim." *Journal of Biblical Literature* 111:3–15.

———. 1994a. "Jesus' Presence in the Early Church." *Cristianesimo nella Storia* 15:541–557.

———. 1994b. "The Historical Jesus and the Historical Situation of the Quest: An Epilogue." In *Studying the Historical Jesus: Evaluations of the State of Current Research*. Vol. 19 of *New Testament Tools and Studies*, edited by Bruce D. Chilton and Craig A. Evans. Leiden: Brill.

———. 1995. "The Historical Jesus and the Cult of the *Kyrios Christos*." *Harvard Divinity Bulletin* 24:13–18.

Mathews, Thomas F. 1993. *The Clash of Gods: A Reinterpretation of Early Christian Art*. Princeton, N.J.: Princeton University Press.

Meier, John P. 1991. *The Roots of the Problem and the Person*. Vol. 1 of *A Marginal Jew: Rethinking the Historical Jesus*. New York: Doubleday.

———. 1994. *Mentor, Message, and Miracles*. Vol. 2 of *A Marginal Jew: Rethinking the Historical Jesus*. New York: Doubleday.

Mellor, Ronald. 1993. *Tacitus*. New York: Routledge, Chapman & Hall.

Metzger, Bruce M. 1971. *A Textual Commentary on the Greek New Testament*. New York: United Bible Societies.

———. 1981. *Manuscripts of the Greek Bible: An Introduction to Greek Palaeography*. New York: Oxford University Press.

NHLE. See Robinson below.

NTA. See Schneemelcher, et al. below.

Riley, Gregory John. 1995. *Resurrection Reconsidered: Thomas and John in Controversy*. Minneapolis: Fortress.

Robinson, James M., ed. 1988. *The Nag Hammadi Library in English*. 3rd ed. Leiden: Brill.

Rolfe, John C., trans. 1979. *Suetonius*. 2 vols. Cambridge, Mass.: Harvard University Press.

Rudolph, Kurt. 1983a [1977]. *Gnosis*. Translated by R. McL. Wilson, P. W. Coxon, and K. H. Kuhn. Edited by R. McL. Wilson. San Francisco: Harper & Row.

Schacter, Daniel L. 1996. *Searching for Memory: The Brain, the Mind, and the Past*. New York: HarperCollins Basic Books.

Schneemelcher, Wilhelm, and R. McL. Wilson, eds. 1991–92. *New Testament Apocrypha*. 2 vols. Rev. ed. Philadelphia: Westminster/John Knox Press.

Schweitzer, Albert. 1969 [1906]. *The Quest of the Historical Jesus: A Critical Study of Its Progress from Reimarus to Wrede*. Translated by William Montgomery. Introduction by James M. Robinson. New York: Macmillan.

John Dominic Crossan

Thackeray, Henry St. John, et al., trans. 1926–65. *Josephus*. 10 vols. Cambridge, Mass.: Harvard University Press.

Wright, Nicholas Thomas. 1992. *The New Testament and the People of God*. Vol 1 of *Christian Origins and the Question of God*. Minneapolis: Fortress Press.

——. 1996. *Jesus and the Victory of God*. Vol. 2 of *Christian Origins and the Question of God*. Minneapolis: Fortress Press.

# CONTRIBUTORS

JOHN D. CAPUTO holds the David R. Cook Chair of Philosophy at Villanova University. His most recent publications include *The Prayers and Tears of Jacques Derrida: Religion without Religion* (1997), *Deconstruction in a Nutshell: A Conversation with Jacques Derrida* (1997), *Against Ethics* (1993), and *Demythologizing Heidegger* (1993). He has served as Executive Co-Director of the Society for Phenomenology and Existential Philosophy, is a past president of the American Catholic Philosophical Association, and was a member of the National Board of Officers of the American Philosophical Association.

JOHN DOMINIC CROSSAN, Professor Emeritus, Religious Studies, DePaul University, was Co-Chair of the Jesus Seminar from 1985 to 1996, editor of *Semeia: An Experimental Journal for Biblical Criticism*, and former Chair of the Historical Jesus Section in the Society of Biblical Literature. He has written eighteen books on the historical Jesus, most recently *The Historical Jesus: The Life of a Mediterranean Jewish Peasant* (1991), *Jesus: A Revolutionary Biography* (1994), *Who Killed Jesus: Exposing the Roots of Anti-Semitism in the Gospel Story of the Death of Jesus* (1995), and *The Birth of Christianity* (1998). He has appeared on segments of the BBC's *Lives of Jesus*, PBS's *From Jesus to Christ: The First Christians*, and A&E's *Mysteries of the Bible* series.

JACQUES DERRIDA, École des Hautes Études en Sciences Sociales (Paris) and the University of California-Irvine, is one of this century's most important philosophers. Among his more recent works are *Cosmopolite de tous les pays, encore un effort!* (1997), *De l'hospitalité* (with Anne Dufour-mantelle) (1997), and *Marx en jeu* (with Marc Guillaume and Jean-Pierre Dumont) (1997). His most recent work to be translated into English is *Resistances to Psychoanalysis* (1998). He has recently been lecturing on hospitality, witnessing, and forgiveness.

ROBERT DODARO, O.S.A., Professor of Patristics and Vice-President at the Patristic Institute in Rome, is co-editor of *Augustine: Select Letters and Sermons* (forthcoming) and *Augustine and His Critics* (forthcoming), and has published articles in *Augustinianum*, the *Journal of Ecclesiastical History*, and *Augustinian Studies*. He is preparing a book, *Language and Justice: Political Anthropology in Augustine's City of God*, based on his Oxford dissertation (1993); co-authoring *Theology through the Looking Glass*, an Augustinian critique of mass media and theology (forthcoming); and preparing a major study of Augustine's use of decorum theory in his theology.

RICHARD KEARNEY is Professor of Philosophy at University College Dublin and Boston College. In addition to his well-known *The Wake of Imagination* (1988), his most recent books include *Poetics of Imagining* (1991), *Postnationalist Ireland* (1997), and *Poetics of Modernity* (1995). He is editor of *Continental Philosophy in the Twentieth Century* and co-editor of *Questioning Ethics: Contemporary Debates in Philosophy* and *The Continental Philosophy Reader*. Kearney is also a novelist (*Sam's Fall* [1994] and *Walking at Sea Level* [1997]), a poet (*Angel of Patrick's Hill* [1991]), and a cultural critic.

JEAN-LUC MARION, Université Paris/Sorbonne and the University of Chicago, is the author of many works in French on Descartes and the phenomenology of religion. He has made a major impact in the English-speaking world through the stream of translations that began with the appearance of *God without Being: Hors-Texte* (1991) and recently *Reduction and Givenness: Investigations on Husserl and Heidegger* (1998). Forthcoming in the near future are *Idol and Distance; Given Being; The Metaphysical Prism of Descartes*; and *Prolegomena to Charity*.

FRANÇOISE MELTZER is Professor and Chair of the Department of Comparative Literature at the University of Chicago, where she is also in the Divinity School and in the Department of Romance Literatures. She has been a co-editor of *Critical Inquiry* since 1982, in which she co-edited with David Tracy a symposium on "God" (Summer 1994). Her most recent book is *Hot Property: The Stakes and Claims of Literary Originality* (1994). She is presently working on a new book, *Joan of Arc: Feminine Subjectivity and the Discourse of Virginity* (forthcoming). The present essay is partially taken from this project.

MICHAEL J. SCANLON, O.S.A., holds the Josephine C. Connelly Chair in Christian Theology at Villanova University. A Past President of the Catholic Theological Society of America, he has taught and written in several areas of systematic theology and has published numerous studies in such journals as *The Thomist, Theological Studies, Augustinian Studies*, the *Proceedings of the CTSA*, the *American Ecclesiastical Review, Proceedings of the Theology Institute* (Villanova University), and several chapters in various collections and encyclopedias.

MARK C. TAYLOR is the Cluett Professor of Humanities and Director of the Center for Technology in the Arts and Humanities at Williams College. His *Erring: A Postmodern A/theology* (1984) is a landmark statement in the dialogue between religion and postmodernism. His latest works include *Hiding* (1997), *Critical Terms for Religious Studies* (editor, 1998), *The Picture in Question: Mark Tansey and the End(s) of Representation* (1999), *About Religion: Economies of Faith in Virtual Culture* (1999), and *The Real: Las Vegas, Nevada* (CD-ROM, 1998). He also edits the series "Religion and Postmodernism" for the University of Chicago Press.

DAVID TRACY is Distinguished Service Professor in the Divinity School of the University of Chicago and a member of the Committee on Social Thought. He is the author of *On Naming the Present: God, Hermeneutics, and Church* (1994), *Plurality and Ambiguity: Hermeneutics, Religion, Hope* (1987), *The Analogical Imagination* (1981), and *Blessed Rage for Order* (1975). Professor Tracy is a member of the American Academy of Arts and Sciences.

MEROLD WESTPHAL is Distinguished Professor of Philosophy at Fordham University. He has written two books on Hegel, two on Kierkegaard, and two in the phenomenology of religion: *God, Guilt, and Death* (1984) and *Suspicion and Faith* (1993). His recent research has been on Levinas and on the relation of postmodern philosophy and Christian faith. He has been President of the Hegel Society of America and the Kierkegaard Society and, most recently, Executive Co-Director of the Society for Phenomenology and Existential Philosophy.

EDITH WYSCHOGROD is J. Newton Razor Professor of Philosophy and Religion, Rice University. Her most recent works are *Saints and Postmodernism: Revisioning Moral Philosophy* (1990) and *An Ethics of Remembering: History, Heterology and the Nameless Others* (1998). She also authored *Spirit in Ashes: Hegel, Heidegger and Man-Made Mass Death* (1985) and her first book, and the first book in English on Levinas, *Emmanuel Levinas: The Problem of Ethical Metaphysics*, will soon appear in a new edition from Fordham University Press. Professor Wyschogrod is a past President of the American Academy of Religion.

# INDEX

# Index

# Index

# Index